# THE PSYCHOANALYTIC STUDY OF SOCIETY

## Volume 16

*A. Irving Hallowell*
*(summer 1946)*

# THE PSYCHOANALYTIC STUDY OF SOCIETY

## Volume 16

## Essays in Honor of A. Irving Hallowell

*Edited by*
L. BRYCE BOYER
RUTH M. BOYER

 THE ANALYTIC PRESS

1991    Hillsdale, NJ    Hove and London

The Analytic Press
365 Broadway
Hillsdale, NJ 07642

ISBN 0-88163-140-X
ISSN 0079-7294


Printed in the United States of America
1  2  3  4  5  6  7  8  9  10

1. Anthropology - Research
2. Sociology
I. Boyer, L. Bryce  II. Boyer, Ruth U.

*The Editors and Editorial Board*

*acknowledge with thanks*

*the generous support of*

*Boyer House Foundation*

# Editors

Paul Parin, M.D., Zurich, Switzerland
Robert A. Paul, Ph.D., Atlanta, GA
Fitz John Porter Poole, Ph.D., La Jolla, CA
Gilbert J. Rose, M.D., Rowayton, CT
Richard Sennett, Ph.D., New York, NY
Bennett Simon, M.D., Cambridge, MA
Melford E. Spiro, Ph.D., La Jolla, CA
Howard F. Stein, Ph.D., Oklahoma City, OK
H. U. E. Thoden van Velsen, Ph.D., Utrecht, Netherlands
Donald F. Tuzin, Ph.D., La Jolla, CA
Piers Vitebsky, Ph.D., Cambridge, England
Vamık D. Volkan, M.D., Charlottesville, VA
Aaron Wildavsky, Ph.D., Berkeley, CA

# Contributors

**Erika Bourguinon, Ph.D.,** Professor Emeritus, Department of Anthropology, Ohio State University.

**L. Bryce Boyer, M.D.** (coeditor), Director, Boyer Research Institute, Berkeley, CA.

**Ruth M. Boyer, Ph.D.** (coeditor), Professor Emeritus, Departments of Humanities and Science, California College of Arts and Crafts, Oakland.

**Jean A. Briggs, Ph.D.,** Professor, Department of Anthropology, Memorial University, St. John's, Newfoundland, Canada.

**Katherine P. Ewing, Ph.D.,** Professor, Department of Cultural Anthropology and Social Studies, Duke University, Durham, NC.

**Raymond D. Fogelson, Ph.D.,** Professor, Department of Anthropology, The University of Chicago.

**Benjamin Kilborne, Ph.D.,** Visiting Lecturer, Department of Psychiatry, University of California at Los Angeles.

**Waud Kracke, Ph.D.,** Professor, Department of Anthropology, The University of Illinois at Chicago.

**Melvin R. Lansky, M.D.,** Adjunct Professor of Psychiatry, University of California at Los Angeles Medical School.

**Robert A. LeVine, Ph.D.,** Chair, Human Development and Psychology, Harvard Graduate School of Education.

**Sarah E. LeVine, Ph.D.,** Research Associate, Harvard Graduate School of Education.

**W. W. Meissner, S.J., M.D.,** University Professor of Psychoanalysis, Boston College.

**Fitz John Porter Poole, Ph.D.,** Professor, Department of Anthropology, University of California at San Diego.

**Theodore Schwartz, Ph.D.,** Professor, Department of Anthropology, University of California at San Diego.

**George D. Spindler, Ph.D.,** Professor Emeritus of Anthropology and Education, Stanford University, Stanford, CA.

**Louise S. Spindler, Ph.D.,** Lecturer in Anthropology and Education, Stanford University, Stanford, CA.

**Melford E. Spiro, Ph.D.,** Professor, Department of Anthropology, University of California at San Diego.

# Contents

# A Tribute
# to Simon A. Grolnick, M.D.

As this volume of the *Study* goes to press, it is our sad duty to announce the passing of Simon A. Grolnick at the far-too-young age of 60, following a valiant and prolonged battle against malignant melanoma, leaving a bereaved wife, four daughters, two grandchildren, and numberless grieving friends, colleagues, and students.

Sy was Associate Editor of Volumes 9 and 10 of the *Study,* which appeared in 1981 and 1984, and, since the resignation of Werner Muensterberger as Senior Coeditor, Sy served as its invaluable, wise coeditor for Volumes 11 through 15, during the years 1985 through 1990. He shared the responsibility for changing one of the editorial policies of the *Study* to the honoring of pioneers in the application of psychoanalysis to other social sciences.

Sy received his doctorate in medicine from the State University of New York Downstate Medical Center in 1955 and graduated from the Downstate Psychoanalytic Institute in 1970. He served as a psychiatrist in the U.S. Naval Reserve at the Naval Hospital in Yokosuko, Japan, from 1957–1959. He served on the Attending Staff of Kings County Hospital in Brooklyn from 1962 until his death, was Medical Director of the Brooklyn Community Counseling Center from 1962–1979, and practiced privately from 1962–1983 in Brooklyn and Great Neck, New York. From 1976 he served continuously on the Attending Staff at the North Shore University Hospital at Manhasset, New York, where he was Director of Training and Education since 1979. He was Associate Director of the Department of Psychiatry between 1986 and 1988 and subsequently served as its Acting Director. His faculty appointments were Clinical Assistant Professor at the State University of New York, Downstate, from 1968 to 1979 and, from 1979 to 1983, Cornell University Medical College, where he subsequently held the post of Associate Professor of Clinical Psychiatry. Beginning in 1975 he served on the faculty of the Psychoanalytic Institute at New York University and, from 1982, on the faculty of the Columbia Center for Psychoanalysis.

Sy's published articles are far too numerous and cover too wide a range of subjects to mention except at random: cerebral spinal fluid cation levels in delirium tremens, psychoanalytic philosophy and symbolic disorders, dreams and dreaming as transitional objects, Etruscan burial symbols, play, myth, theater and psychoanalysis, fairy tales and psychotherapy, reflections on psychoanalytic subjectivity and objectivity as applied to anthropology, and Emily Dickinson. In 1990 he published *The Work and Play of Winnicott,* and in 1978 he coedited, with Leonard Barkin in collaboration with Werner Muensterberger, *Between Reality and Fantasy: Transitional Objects and Phenomena.* His score of book reviews similarly cover too wide a range of subjects to permit enumeration.

Our dear friend and esteemed colleague Simon A. Grolnick will be sorely missed. *Vale.*

L. Bryce Boyer

# Preface

In 1947 Géza Róheim introduced *Psychoanalysis and the Social Sciences.*
He edited five volumes, the last published in 1958. Before his death,
Róheim designated Werner Muensterberger as administrator of his
papers and unpublished manuscripts and requested that he continue the
series. Thus was born *The Psychoanalytic Study of Society,* initially
coedited by Muensterberger and Sidney Axelrad, who published four
volumes, between 1960 and 1967. Following Axelrad's untimely death,
Muensterberger and Aaron H. Esman coedited three volumes between
1972 and 1976; L. Bryce Boyer was Associate Editor of Volume 7.
Muensterberger and Boyer then coedited the *Study* through the publication of Volume 10 in 1984; Gilbert J. Rose served as Associate Editor for
Volume 9 (1981) and Simon A. Grolnick for Volume 10. Muensterberger
then retired from his coeditorship, in order to have more time to devote
to his own writings and practice and to complete the translation of
Róheim's remaining manuscripts. Subsequently, Boyer and Grolnick
have served as coeditors, publishing yearly volumes.[1]

One of the editorial policies Boyer and Grolnick adopted was to use
the *Study* to honor outstanding living pioneers in the application of
psychoanalysis to other social sciences. Prior to the present volume,
books honored Werner Muensterberger, George Devereux,[2] Weston

---

[1]Dr. Grolnick's terminal illness prevented his contributing to the preparation of the current
volume, which is coedited by Ruth M. Boyer, who served as Associate Editor for
Volume 15.

[2]Unfortunately Devereux died just before the volume in his honor was issued.

LaBarre, Paul Parin, and Melford E. Spiro. A second policy was to include a preface with each volume.

Our editorial practice to honor only the living has been altered in the present volume, which is devoted to the late Alfred Irving Hallowell, whose great contributions to the field of culture and personality have been largely overlooked by psychoanalysts. This volume departs in another way from the previous pattern of including papers that had been submitted without their authors' having been informed that the volume in which they would appear was to honor someone. In the present book, the majority of the chapters were written by Hallowell's students and others heavily influenced by them. The chapters either are written specifically as tributes to him, or they apply some of his famous and highly influential contributions to present-day psychoanalytic anthropology. The coeditors are indebted especially to Melford E. Spiro[3] for the selection of authors, although the contributions of Lansky and Kilborne[4] and Meissner[5] had been included in Volume 16 prior to the decision to devote it to Hallowell. Most of the invited contributors ascribe to Hallowell's influence their having come to accept psychoanalytic perspectives as being the most fertile for understanding the mutual influences of social organization, socialization processes, and personality structure. They agree, overtly or covertly, with Devereux and La Barre (1961) that man's amazingly variant expressive culture provides perhaps the richest source of information for anthropological and psychoanalytical understanding of his functioning in nature. However, the development of Hallowell's and the contributors' own thinking pertaining to the fertility of the reciprocal interactions between psychoanalytic and anthropological formulations differs greatly. The authors variously illustrate the evolution of Hallowell's influence on their own thinking and demonstrate also the development of their own positions, with their dominant points of agreement and, at times, their minor but fascinating areas of disagreement. Among the virtues of this volume is its exposition of the way in which all the honoring contributors have incorporated parts of Hallowell's ever-expanding and deepening views and his manifold experimental approaches into their individual avenues of interest and expertise.

---

[3]Spiro was awarded the L. Bryce Boyer Prize by the Society for Psychological Anthropology for outstanding contributions to psychoanalytic anthropology for 1989. He has contributed previously to the *Study* (Spiro, 1990a, b).

[4]Kilborne has been a frequent contributor to the *Study* (1981, 1988a, b, 1990).

[5]Meissner has contributed previous articles pertaining to the application of psychoanalysis to religion and religious history (1984, 1988a, b, 1989, 1990), and others have been accepted to appear later.

The volume proper opens with Hallowell's extensive bibliography. In previous volumes of the *Study,* reviews have been omitted from the cited references. In this case, however, they have been included to illustrate yet further the breadth of the honoree's scholarship and accorded respect.

The coeditors wish to express but a single regret pertaining to anthropologists' and others' use of Hallowell's many stimulating pioneering leads into the study of psychological anthropology, namely, their having failed to exploit to its maximal potential effect the use of projective psychological tests. Fogelson notes accurately in Chapter 2 that "Hallowell was an innovator in the cross-cultural use of the Rorschach Test, a field technique that is now generally considered passé in anthropology."

A glance at Hallowell's bibliography will illustrate the intense interest he had in the cross-cultural use of the Rorschach, and perusal of his various contributions would convince the most skeptical of the value he placed on the results of such studies. Previously, the Boyers have noted that "Hallowell's (1945) discussion of the Rorschach technique in the study of personality and culture remains among the most sophisticated." (R. M. Boyer et al., 1990, p. 272*n*) In the present volume, only the Spindlers' contribution directly reflects ongoing interest in this field and demonstrates its utility.

In our judgment, the main reason for the neglect of this broad and potentially highly useful avenue of research has to do not only with anthropologists' having been inadequately trained in their administration techniques, but also with the confusion that still exists among psychologists themselves regarding optimal means of procuring and interpreting the protocols, particularly those obtained from cross-cultural informants. A main problem lies in determining convincing methods of quantifying affectual as well as structural responses to the ink blots (Elizur, 1949; Schafer, 1954; Piotrowski, 1957; Zubin, Eron, and Schumer, 1965; Potkay, 1971; Aronow and Reznikoff, 1976; De Vos and Boyer, 1989). Following the lead of De Vos (1952), who sought to quantify affectual responses, members of the Boyer Research Institute have spent the last eight years seeking to improve and expand his effort, which they deem the most promising developed thus far (Boyer, Boyer, and De Vos, 1982, 1987; Boyer, De Vos and Boyer, 1983, 1985; Boyer, Miller, and De Vos, 1984; L. Boyer et al., 1987, 1988a, b; Stone and Boyer, 1987; L. Boyer et al., 1989; R. Boyer et al., 1990).

To attempt adequate recapitulations of the contents of the contributions to this volume in a preface would be not only impossible but presumptuous, inasmuch as each, in its own fashion, delineates different and detailed aspects of the development of Hallowell's ideas and the clarification of his expanding thinking. The editors have attempted to resolve the resultant dilemma by giving some brief resumes and quotations, in the hope that by so doing they will convey both flavor and tantalizing content.

# CHAPTER 1

*Melford E. Spiro. "A. Irving Hallowell: An Appreciation."*

In Chapter 1, Spiro tells us,

> Anthropology, for Hallowell, was truly "the study of man." Although much of his scholarly career was devoted to the study of the Northern Ojibwa, a people whose society, culture, and thought he recorded and analyzed with the meticulous detail of a master craftsman, in almost all his ethnographic accounts he was concerned with discovering and displaying the general through the particular. This explains in part why he has had a marked influence on a large group of scholars who know or care little about the Berens River Salteaux. When, in addition, one considers the wide array of subjects to which he made original and pioneering contributions — social organization, psychological anthropology, acculturation, behavioral evolution, world view, cultural ecology, history of anthropology — it is all the more understandable that his influence has been felt in psychology and history, literature and sociology, psychoanalysis and biology, as well as in anthropology.

During the period when psychoanalysts were still attempting to distinguish between the ego and the self and thus clarify some of the confusion inherent in Freud's failure to do so, Hallowell made meaningful contributions to this field. To continue with Spiro:

> Although he was importantly influenced by stimulus-response psychology (especially by learning theory), Hallowell [took] as his point of departure the gestaltists' concept of the "behavioral environment," [and] demonstrated in masterful fashion that (a) Ojibwa (and therefore human) perceptions are mediated not through receptors alone, but through cognitive orientations that

organize and confer meaning upon them, and that (b) these latter organizations are acquired in large measure from the actor's cultural symbol systems. The general conclusion is obvious. Because human cognitive orientations are derived to a considerable extent from cultural symbol systems, and since perceptions are shaped by these orientations, then the human behavioral environment — the environment that they perceive, and therefore to which they respond — is culturally constituted. Hallowell, who had a profound knowledge of psychoanalysis, not only recognized the problem, but in attempting to cope with it, elaborated his seminal concept of the "self." This was a central concept in Hallowell's thought, as important as, and correlative to, the concept of the behavioral environment.

While Hallowell's interest in the clarification and conceptualization of the self proceeded with his knowledge of psychoanalysts' similar struggle, the "clinical" data with which he worked differed greatly from Freud's, Hartmann's and others' and perhaps made the development of his concepts somewhat similar, if less complete, than theirs.

# CHAPTER 2

*Ray D. Fogelson. "A. Irving Hallowell and the Study of Cultural Dynamics."*

Fogelson's chapter deals with numerous other aspects of Hallowell's interests and scholarships; we have chosen to call specific attention to his comments regarding Hallowell's uses of the Rorschach technique:

In retrospect, his original impulse to use the Rorschach with Ojibwa Indians seems less in the service of his growing interest in psychoanalysis and more as a means to study world view, to get at perceptual and apperceptual aspects of the Ojibwa self and its behavioral environment. Early on he employed the Rorschach as a clinical tool to help understand individual cases of mental disorder (see, e.g., Hallowell 1938). Later he used the Rorschach as a multidimensional test to assess collective aspects of personality across different communities. The aggregate results of his Ojibwa research were not entirely dependent upon the conventional meanings of Rorschach responses in Western society; rather they suggested different parameters of Ojibwa personality that could be reasonably inferred to reflect cultural differences. . . . Hallowell consistently emphasized the ontological necessity for separating cultural and psychological levels of explanation, while still appreciating the dynamic interaction of psychological and cultural factors.

It is interesting that Fogelson saw fit to ignore Kardiner's work, which, in part, had obvious similar aims (Manson, 1988).

# CHAPTER 3

*Erika Bourguinon. "A.I. Hallowell, the Foundations of Psychological Anthropology and Altered States of Consciousness."*

Bourguinon's rich contribution can be but briefly reviewed. She notes that Hallowell's

range was immense: from mental health to perception and cognition, from projective techniques to behavioral evolution, from the concept of the self to acculturation. In spite of this apparent diversity Hallowell's contribution forms an integrated whole, a theory of human nature firmly grounded in his vast reading in psychology and philosophy, and facilitated by his strong historical orientation.

Nevertheless, she notes that Hallowell was unconcerned with what many anthropologists considered the central concerns of the personality-culture movement of the 1930s and 1940s, nor did he conduct child-rearing studies. She credits his "The Self and Its Behavioral Environment" (1955) as "being a stepping stone in [his] interest in behavioral evolution where he drew on his understanding of the self and its culturally constituted environment." In "On Being an Anthropologist," Hallowell (1972), states that "dreams, fantasies, myths, art and world views of man as articulated in cultural traditions, may be interpreted as making positive uses of psychological resources in cultural adaptation and personal adjustment" (p. ). To this list, Bourguinon suggests adding altered states of consciousness (ASC) and suggests that we consider them from an evolutionary perspective and to enquire concerning their relevance to our understanding of the reciprocal relationship between imagination and experience in a cultural context.

The remainder of her chapter is devoted largely to the subject of ASC and ranges over a diversity of examples and perspectives too broad to allow brief summarization.

Bourguignon states that her attempt to follow Hallowell's study of dreams led her to consider ASC in the same way "as behavior emerged in human evolutionary history, with roots in mammalian biology and transformed into significant features of human life through the emergence of such features as the symbolic transformation of experience and the capacity to share intra-psychic, subjective states." Unlike dreams, however, these ritualized phenomena are often built on models that derive from psychological states. Depending on the cultures, different models are chosen. They act as coping mechanisms in the context of a certain world view and value systems. Bourguignon concludes, "In Hallowell's evolutionary terms . . . what is individual, internal, private in other animals, in the presence of external shared symbolization, is turned into raw material for culture building."

The Senior Coeditor, reading Bourguinon's contribution, eerily recognized his own experiences working clinically with patients who were undergoing psychotic or near-psychotic regressions in the inevitable transference–countertransference relationship that accompanied their treatment experiences, experiences ascribed by some to projective identification and by others to intuition or empathy.

# CHAPTER 4

*Waud Kracke. "The Self and Kagwahiv Dream Beliefs."*

Kracke[6] presents a concept of self as perceived through the single aspect of "dreams" in the thinking of the Kagwahiv (whom he has studied at length and with great thoroughness): "how the self participates in dreams" in a non-Western culture.

---

[6]Kracke has contributed other articles pertaining to the Kagwahiv to the *Study* (1979, 1990). He received the 2nd annual L. Bryce Boyer Prize by the Society for Psychological Anthropology for outstanding contributions to psychoanalytic anthropology for his "Encounter with other cultures: Psychological and epistemological aspects," *Ethos*, 15:58–81.

Acknowledging the elusiveness of the concept, Kracke does not seek to answer the question of self in full for the Kagwahiv. Instead, he states, "I will explore what Kagwahiv beliefs about dreaming reflect of their beliefs about how the self participates in dreams, and the relation of their selves to other selves in the 'behavioral environment' of dreaming." To a Kagwahiv, the dream experience is on a par with other kinds of experiencing, a kind of perception with a special importance that surpasses that of daytime perception. Most interesting is that dreamed experience is "grammatically coded as a kind of tense: experiences that occur in dreams are marked, when recounted, by tense differences."

Kagwahiv dreams can be interpreted personally in a variety of ways. One basic belief is that they are a nocturnal form of thinking, the continuation into sleep of a train of thought pursued as one goes to sleep. This obviously places dreams as a psychic byproduct of the self, dreams being formed by day residues. At the same time, dreams serve other purposes. They may involve a kind of direct perception of future events and entail a degree of responsibility for the causation of those events. Certain determinate kinds of dreams are regarded as involving direct mental contact with others; nightmares indicate the immediate proximity of an evil spirit or ghost. In contrast to Westerners' ideas pertaining to dreams, for the majority of Kagwahiv, the primary interest of dreams is as symbolic or encoded messages about future potentials.

# CHAPTER 5

*Fitz John Porter Poole. "Cultural Schemas and Experiences of the Self among the Bimin-Kuskusmin of Papua New Guinea."*

In Chapter 5, Poole continues adumbrating his monumental work with the Bimin-Kuskusmin.[7] His focus is on matters of the individual, individuality, and individuation in terms of "experiential shape in [their] conceptions of selfhood and in the contacts in which such concepts are implicated. . . ." He suggests a dichotomy between individualism "as a historical peculiarity of the West" and a "socially constituted . . . self as characteristic of the non-Western world." These facets are usually treated as mutually exclusive, thus inhibiting cross-cultural comparisons. His concern is to understand how local concepts of identity give force and shape to beliefs—learned through processes of socialization and encul-

---

[7]Poole has contributed previously to the Study (1990).

turation, so that they come to have "emotional and directive force, more or less shared." Frequently referring to Hallowell's thinking, Poole examines closely the latter's attention to the "self" as compared with the thinking and various problems faced by both psychoanalytic and anthropological realms. Nearly half the presentation is devoted to various schemata. He finds Bimin-Kuskusmin ideas about the self, despite their considerable elaboration and seeming coherence, to be marked by notable ambiguity in many respects.

Space permits but a few further fragmentary notes taken from Poole's customary detailed attention to multiple aspects of each discussed phenomenon. As an example, focusing only on adult, fully initiated men, he presents attention to the terms, concepts, metaphors, and other modes connected to the complex association of the self. Poole gives the reader a most complex concept of the Bimin-Kuskusmin sense of self

> that is often difficult to articulate in speech. It is ambiguous in many respects and one cannot gain a clear, coherent impression of it either in oneself (except fleetingly in trances) or in others. Speculations on the nature of others' selves are fraught not only with uncertainty, but also with anxiety, for insult can readily be taken at intrusive assessments of others' personal characteristics. It may be presented in "dreams" . . . but one easily "forgets" . . . what he nonetheless somehow "stored in memory" . . .

Divinations of dreams are only partly helpful.

In this essay, Poole argues that the individual, as a reality in some fashion in perhaps any society, is of essential interest to a psychoanalytic anthropology.

# CHAPTER 6

*Robert LeVine and Sarah E. LeVine. "House Design and the Self in an African Culture."*

Following a brief theoretical discussion of culture interpreted as fantasy in the Freudian sense, the authors present Hallowell's divergent view that "focused on the individual's conscious experience and its culturally constituted environment, *both* of which combined adaptive and defensive strategies."

That domestic architecture is a reflection of cultural meaning is, of course, not a new idea, but this study of the institutionalized housing arrangements of the Gusii of southwestern Kenya adds psychological aspects that were neglected previously. The authors support well their belief that those housing arrangements can be understood only

as cultural symbols with psychodynamic meaning and function, notwithstanding their use in food production, social organization and the provision of shelter and warmth. . . . their domestic architecture, furniture and residential arrangement are physical embodiments of the deepest meanings Gusii experience in life: their goals and fears, preferences and aversions, sources of pride and shame and of safety and danger, represented in spatial terms.

The Gusii are an exceptional case, inasmuch as they had no religious shrines or buildings set apart from the residences.

To the Gusii, their domestic arrangement is one in which each spatial arrangement and utensil is a metaphor, freighted with moral and spiritual significance, that defines the course of a person's life and plays an essential part in the social and ritual dramas that maintain personal and familial well-being.

The Levines pose the question: "Can we then claim that the conventional design of the Gusii house is a product of culturally mediated psychodynamics rather than socially mediated economics?" Historical "traditions" are examined and changes in residential pattern noted. Many changes have been influenced by utilitarian considerations, so that the house design cannot be treated just as cultural fantasy exclusive of environmental factors. Nonetheless, traditional culture meanings have not lost their psychodynamic significance. Domestic construction has become more varied over the passage of time, but many of the cultural taboos and practices persist. The house remains a symbol of

maternal protection and nurturance, continues to provide emotional security in the face of life crisis, even for those converted to Christianity. . . . we conclude that Gusii house design is, through its place in culturally constituted defenses, an emotionally charged guide to social action interpretable as fantasy in the Freudian sense.

## CHAPTER 7

*Jean L. Briggs. "Mazes of Meaning: The Exploration of Individuality in Culture and of Culture Through Individual Contacts."*

In Chapter 7, Briggs[8] cogently answers a question frequently asked of her when she discusses her fieldwork with Inuit: "What can a study of the individual contribute to the anthropological enterprise?" She responds by describing and analyzing in depth an experiment she has been conducting for many years in her review of certain "emotionally charged dramas" that she has witnessed and that are universally important in the socialization of Inuit children. She follows the "mindsteps" of one three-year-old girl living in a year-round hunting camp on Baffin Island.

The Inuit initiate small potent dramas "spontaneously" in order to raise to consciousness "issues that the child perceives to be of consequence" at a particular stage of life. The questions are indeed powerful, such as, "Why don't you kill your baby brother?" Commonly, such questions are asked of slightly older siblings by adults, who deem their queries as innocuous. They are teaching devices that assist the growing child in his mastery of the tormenting emotions incited by the questions. "The questions are part play, part teaching device, part test, part challenge and part tease." They are often a means through which adults relive and "perhaps relieve" their own concerns, such as unresolved, but probably largely unconscious, sibling rivalry issues. When the questions no longer frustrate the child and the interplay is taken for granted, the question-dramas cease. As implied above, Briggs analyzes her massive data in terms of hypotheses derived from "psychoanalytically informed introspection." She champions the natural-history mode of analysis that may be viewed at different levels and distances of experience. In this presentation, Briggs analyzed only the plots concerning belonging, attachment, and possession. The plots took the forms of dilemmas. Briggs states:

Working in the non-contextual mode, I began to distinguish the social, cognitive and emotional *processes* involved in the acquisition, the management, and the *experience* of culture from the *substance* of culture, that is, the values, attitudes and behaviors

---

[8]Briggs has contributed previously to the *Study* (1975).

that are created and manipulated in these processes. I also learned to distinguish the *overt substance* of values, attitudes and behaviors—"Inuit are generous," "Inuit value autonomy"—from their psychodynamic functions and meanings.

Although not directly germane to this paper, it would have been interesting to note that the monsters Briggs described in evil-spirit play strongly resemble the tupilaks of Greenland. This is particularly to the point inasmuch as she spoke of the many angles in which Inuit sculpture may be viewed.

While Briggs's is an immensely valuable contribution to the literature, it is unfortunate that in her most accommodating effort to comply with time pressures imposed by the Senior Coeditor she could develop no further the theoretical aspects and to critically review much literature known well to her, including data that unmistakably reveal that the repression of hostility that is effected by Inuit educational games such as these are at best but partially successful (Boyer et al., 1978). Additionally, Briggs did not mention that she had discussed these data in much more detail with psychoanalysts for many years.

# CHAPTER 8

*George D. and Louise S. Spindler. "Rorschaching in North America in the Shadow of Hallowell"*

This historically important chapter is of a highly personal nature. The remarks made here essentially constitute the authors' introduction and are intended to whet the reader's nostalgic appetite.

Most of the assumptions that flourished in the personality and culture movement of the 1940s and early 1950s have since been challenged. Among them was that the projective techniques, and particularly the Rorschach ink blots, could be used to define personality cross-culturally, since they were thought to be "culture-free."

The Spindlers' Rorschach research with the Menominee was inspired by that of Hallowell with the closely related Chippewa and Ojibwa and by Hallowell's personal encouragement, despite the criticism of George Spindler's senior professor. The conjunction between the research programs "is one of the few examples in the behavioral sciences of inter-related, comprehensive, long-term, field-based research that has produced accumulative results." The results of the combined research appear to justify further use of the Rorschach as a research tool in cross-cultural or culture-change studies, as do those of De Vos and the Boyers and Suarez-Orosco (1989).

Few who were part of that culture and personality movement have remained in psychological anthropology

> to 1) establish a sociocultural continuum of adaptations; 2) confirm an areal 'personality' type; 3) establish a 'systematic deviation' for the peyotists; 4) establish that there was a personality reformulation at the 'elite' acculturated adaptive level; and 5) establish specific differences between males and females as they struggled with the exigencies of sociocultural change. We also did a thorough ethnography of the Menominee reservation community and applied an 'expressive autobiographical interview' technique developed by Louise Spindler to selected cases among the women and the men, thus giving us a person-centered view of the acculturative process that we would otherwise have missed.

The chapter is devoted to a summary discussion of each of the five major moves developed in the Spindlers' research with the Menominee and their relation with Hallowell's work.

# CHAPTER 9

*Theodore Schwartz. "Behavioral Evolution Beyond the Advent of Culture."*

In Chapter 9, Schwartz provides an excellent review and critique of Hallowell's ideas concerning, and analyses of, various evolutionary theories pertaining to culture and the individual as expounded by anthropologists. Schwartz indicates that we should objectively restudy Hallowell's early analyses of such evolutionary theories, rather than discard them out-of-hand, simply because errors have been made in judging them. He says:

> Cultural evolution can be studied; individual cultures as well as emergent world culture can be evaluated in evolutionary terms without sacrificing the "cause" or the "message" to which anthro-

pological relativism and anti-evolutionism were well intended. Perhaps reconciliation is possible through a kind of evolutionary relativism in which culture, embodied in human artifacts that are substantial, mental, relational, moral, and aesthetic, are evaluated relative to their evolutionary status and history.

# CHAPTER 10

*Katherine P. Ewing. "Idiosyncrasy and the Problem of Shared Understandings: The Case of a Pakistani Orphan."*

Ewing,[9] noting that the primary thrust of Hallowell's research was to develop concepts that would enable him to capture and accurately convey in immediate terms the interpretive world of the culturally "other," states that her own earliest efforts at articulating Pakistani Muslim concepts of self were directly guided by his papers on the cultural shaping of the Ojibwa self. At the same time, her argument in the present essay draws on recently developed conceptual tools that were unavailable to, but nevertheless sensitively anticipated by, him.

Here she notes that while individuals participate in a social world of shared understandings and activities, they nevertheless organize their experience idiosyncratically. Culture and personality studies of the past limited themselves to those aspects of personality that they regarded as culturally shaped and shared.

> The result was an analytic chasm between the cultural and the psychological. Paradoxically, the psychological has become even more impenetrable for those ethnographers so concerned with being true to the interpretive worlds of individual informants that they can assert only the essential untranslatability of the other's experience.

Nonetheless, the "common sense" of the anthropologist who becomes a participant in the culture he observes tells him that he does understand the feelings, reactions, and experiences of his informants, even though he may unable to articulate how or why he knows.

---

[9]Ewing was awarded the L. Bryce Boyer Prize for 1990 by the Society for Psychological Anthropology for her paper "The Illusion of Wholeness: Culture, Self and the Experience of Inconsistency," published in the September issue of *Ethos.*

Ewing holds that "the primary task facing us today" is to develop more sophisticated tools for identifying how we move through our own experience of another's expressions. She offers suggestions, which include careful observation and tabulation of the speech and action portrayed by the informant, alongside those verbal and nonverbal communications that are culturally shared, and simultaneous recording one's own emotional and physical responses as well as one's fantasies and those dreams that one suspects may be relevant to one's interactions with the informant. Clearly, Ewing is using here clues employed by the psychoanalyst, who seeks to study thoroughly his reactions to his analysand—in common parlance, the countertransference responses that many analysts seek to use to understand better the individual natures of their patients, whether such responses be labeled as resulting from intuition, empathy, or introjection of the analysand's projections.

The present essay depicts Ewing's admirable, complex attempt to clarify the means by which she came to understand as well as she did the personality of an orphaned Pakistani woman named Nilam. As part of her conclusion, she writes:

> In Nilam's case, markers of idiosyncrasy point to the organization of psychological defenses, intrapsychic conflict, and immaturities that impair her adult functioning—in other words, psychopathology. I have chosen to discuss a person with evident psychopathology because in her case idiosyncratic usages stand out sharply and can be easily articulated and interpreted in terms of features associated with western diagnostic categories.

# CHAPTER 11

*Melvin R. Lansky and Benjamin Kilborne. "Circumcision and Biblical Narrative."*

The widely practiced neonatal procedure of circumcision among Jews and non-Jews is explored from a psychoanalytic point of view: "A ritual mutilative attack on the genitals rationalized by hygienic and medical mythology, ritual circumcision not only remains widespread even outside religious custom but is also experienced as a healthful or celebratory event."

Clinical and anthropological studies alike link the act to the castration complex, but neither provide adequate psychoanalytic understanding. This paper views circumcision as "both ritual and compromise formation." The authors supplement former studies with a review of the "six major passages concerning circumcision in the Hebrew Bible and the narrative sequences that provide the context of these texts." The narrative contributes to and "points to the latent meaning of the act." The passages examined and presented in the context of narrative sequences are as follows: two from Genesis and one each from Exodus, Leviticus, Joshua, and I Samuel.

The authors find that "the most striking overall features of these narratives considered as a whole are the number of allusions to murders of sons and the astonishing degree and extent of savageness, both sexual and aggressive." They find that ritual circumcision contains certain structures in common with neurotic symptoms. "This phallocentric ritual, which separates clean, holy and acceptable from dirty, unacceptable, and forbidden, has its mammocentric counterpart in the dietary laws (see Leviticus 12:3)."

The authors do not claim to have exhausted the psychoanalytic possibilities of this subject but hope to have heightened awareness of the Biblical texts and the various conflictual issues that emerge. Obvious aspects involve the castration complex and the theme of displacement of disowned filicidal impulses. The final sentence of the paper reads: "Analysis of Biblical texts in the context of narrative sequences provides a method akin to the associative method that supplements clinical and anthropological investigation."[10]

# CHAPTER 12

*W. W. Meissner. "Cultic Elements in Early Christianity: Rome, Corinth, and the Johannine Community."*

This chapter follows earlier presentations in which cultic aspects of the origins of Christianity were analyzed (Meissner, 1984, 1988a, b, 1989, 1990). The present focus is the variations of the cultic process "within the hellenistic culture of the first century Mediterranean basin and within the political structure of the Roman Empire." Early Christian communities were marked by instability, unrest, and the influence of "various

---

[10]Readers who are interested in further clinical aspects of circumcision are referred to Tractenberg (1977, 1989) and Rascovsky and Liberman (1966).

ideological influences," which led gradually to a common orthodoxy. Pressures of persecution, as well as internal contentions, "set the stage [for] progression from a collection of contending cultic groups toward an organized, structured and universal church." Meissner argues that "even in the face of persecution from a common enemy, the cultic process created splits and divisions within the Christian community that threatened the very existence of the nascent church."

The paper, rich in historical data included with the assumption that psychoanalysts and anthropologists might be unfamiliar with it, is arranged into four sections, the first three concerned with developments in Rome, Corinth, and the Johannine Community, followed by one in which Meissner concentrates on the divisive Cultic Process and the progressive changes it caused in each locality.

# BIBLIOGRAPHY

ARONOW, E. & REZNIKOFF, M. (1976), *Rorschach Content Interpretation*. New York: Grune & Stratton.

BOYER, L.B., BOYER, R.M. & DE VOS, G.A. (1982), An Apache woman's account of her recent acquisition of the shamanistic status. *J. Psychoanal. Anthropol.*, 5:299-331.

_____ _____ _____ (1987), Der Erwerb der Schamanenwürde. Klinische Studie und Rorschach-Untersuchung eines besonderen Falles. *In: Die Wilde Seele. Zur Ethnopsychoanalyse Von George Devereux,* ed. H.P. Duerr. Frankfurt am Main: Surkamp, pp. 220-273.

_____ _____ R.M., DITHRICH, C.W., HARNED, H., HIPPLER, A.E., STONE, J.S. & WALT, A. (1989), The relation between psychological states and acculturation among the Tanaina and Upper Tanana Indians of Alaska: An ethnographic and Rorschach Study. *Ethos,* 17:450-479.

_____ DE VOS, G.A., BORDERS, O. & TANI-BORDERS, A. (1978), The "Burnt Child Reaction" among the Yukon Delta Eskimos. *J. Psycholog. Anthropol.* 1:7-56.

_____ _____ BOYER, R.M. (1983), A longitudinal study of three Apache brothers as reflected in their Rorschach protocols. *J. Psychoanal. Anthropol.* 6:125-161.

_____ _____ _____ (1985), Crisis and continuity in the life of an Apache shaman. *The Psychoanalytic Study of Society,* 11:63-114. Hillsdale, NJ: The Analytic Press.

_____ DITHRICH, C.W., HARNED, H, STONE, J.S. & WALT, A. (1987), *A Rorschach Handbook for the Affective Scoring System-Revised* (Research Ed.) Berkeley, CA: Boyer Research Institute.

_____ _____ _____ _____ (1988a), *A Rorschach Handbook for the Affective Scoring System-Revised.* Berkeley, CA: Boyer Research Institute.

_____ _____ _____ _____ (1988b) *A Rorschach Handbook for the Affective Scoring System-Revised. (Scoring Supple.)* Berkeley, CA: Boyer Research Institute.

_____ MILLER, C.M. & DE VOS, GEORGE A. (1984), A comparison of Rorschach protocols obtained from two groups of Laplanders from northern Finland. *J. Psychoanal. Anthropol.* 7:379-396.

BOYER, R.M., DITHRICH, C.W., HARNED, H., HIPPLER, A.E., STONE, J.S., WALT, A. & BOYER, L.B. (1990), An ethnological and Rorschach study of three groups of Australian Aborigines: The Yolgnu, the Pitjatjatjara, and the "Dark People" of Bourke. The ethnographic and Rorsch. *The Psychoanalytic Study of Society,* 15:271–310. Hillsdale, NJ: The Analytic Press.

BRIGGS, J.L. (1975) The origins of nonviolence: Aggression in two Canadian Eskimo Groups. *The Psychoanalytic Study of Society,* 6:134–203. New York: International Universities Press.

DEVEREUX, G. & LABARRE, W. (1961), Art and mythology. In: *Studying Personality Cross-Culturally,* ed. B. K. Kaplan. Evanston, IL: Row Peterson, pp. 361–404.

DE VOS, G.A. (1952), A quantitative approach to affective symbolism in Rorschach responses. *J. Proj. Tech.,* 16:133–150.

BOYER, L.B. (1989), *Symbolic Analysis Cross-Culturally. The Rorschach Test.* Berkeley: CA: University of California Press.

ELIZUR, A. (1949), Content analysis of the Rorschach with regard to anxiety and hostility. *Rorschach Research Exchange and J. Proj. Tech.,* 13:247–284.

HALLOWELL, A.I. (1938), Shabwan: A Dissocial Indian girl. *Amer. J. Orthopsychiat.,* 8:329–340.

———— (1955), The Rorschach technique in personality and culture studies. In: *Developments in the Rorschach Technique,* Vol. 2, ed. B. Klopfer, M. D. Ainsworth, W. G. Klopfer & R. R. Holt. New York: Harcourt, Brace & World, pp. 458–544.

———— (1972), On being an anthropologist. In: *Contributions to Anthropology: Selected Papers of A. Irving Hallowell,* ed. R. D. Fogelson. Chicago: University of Chicago Press, 1976.

KILBORNE, B. (1981), The handling of dream symbolism: Aspects of dream interpretation in Morocco. *The Psychoanalytic Study of Society,* 9;1–14. New York: Psychohistory Press.

———— (1988a), George Devereux: In memoriam. *The Psychoanalytic Study of Society,* 12:xi-xxiv. Hillsdale, NJ: The Analytic Press.

———— (1988b), Weston LaBarre: Pioneer, gadfly, and scholar. *The Psychoanalytic Study of Society,* 13:1–6. Hillsdale, NJ: The Analytic Press.

———— BOLLE, S. (1990), Mere worldlings; An interview with Melford E. Spiro. *The Psychoanalytic Study of Society,* 15:1–16. Hillsdale, NJ: The Analytic Press.

KRACKE, W. (1979), Dreaming in Kagwahiv: Dream beliefs and their psychic uses in an Amazonian culture. *The Psychoanalytic Study of Society,* 8:119–171. New Haven, CT: Yale University Press.

———— (1990), Don't let the piranha bite your liver: A combined anthropological and psychoanalytical approach to Kagwahiv (Tupi) food taboos. *The Psychoanalytic Study of Society,* 15:205–246. Hillsdale, NJ: The Analytic Press.

MANSON, W.C. (1988), *The Psychodynamics of Culture. Abram Kardiner and Neo-Freudian Anthropology.* New York: Greenwood Press.

MEISSNER, W.W. (1984), The cult phenomenon: Psychoanalytic perspective. *The Psychoanalytic Study of Society,* 10:91–112. Hillsdale, NJ: The Analytic Press.

———— (1988a), The cult phenomenon and the paranoid process. *The Psychoanalytic Study of Society,* 12:69–96. Hillsdale, NJ: The Analytic Press.

———— (1988b), The origins of Christianity. *The Psychoanalytic Study of Society,* 13:29–62. Hillsdale, NJ: The Analytic Press.

———— (1989), Cultic elements in early christianity: Antioch and Jerusalem. *The Psychoanalytic Study of Society,* 14:89–118. Hillsdale, NJ: The Analytic Press.

———— (1990), Jewish messianism and the cultic process. *The Psychoanalytic Study of Society,* 15:349–370. Hillsdale, NJ: The Analytic Press.

PIOTROWSKI, Z. (1957), *Perceptanalysis.* New York: Macmillan.

POOLE, F.J.P. (1990), Images of an unborn sibling: The psychocultural shaping of a child's fantasy among the Bimin-Kuskusmin of Papua New Guinea. *The Psychoanalytic Study of Society,* 15:105-177. Hillsdale, N. J.: The Analytic Press.

POTKAY, C.R. (1971), *The Rorschach Clinician.* New York: Grune & Stratton.

RASCOVSKY, A. & LIBERMAN, D. (ed.) (1966), *Psicoanálisis de la Manía y la Psicopatía.* Buenos Aires: Editorial Paidós.

SCHAFER, R. (1954), *Psychoanalytic Interpretation in Rorschach Testing.* New York: Grune & Stratton.

SPIRO, M.E. (1990a), Culture and human nature. *The Psychoanalytic Study of Society,* 15:17-44. Hillsdale, NJ: The Analytic Press.

───── (1990b), The internalization of a Burmese gender ideology. *The Psychoanalytic Study of Society,* 15:45-67. Hillsdale, NJ: The Analytic Press.

STONE, J.S. & BOYER, L.B. (1987), Projective identification: Despair, suicide and the Rorschach. *Rorschachiana,* Vol. 16, pp. 67-73. Beiheft zur Schweizerischen Zeitschrift für Psychologie und Ihre Anwendungen, No. 63. Eds.: Yazigi, L. and Succar, I. São Paulo: Casa do Psicólogo.

SUAREZ-OROSCO, M.M. 1989 *Central American Refugees and U. S. High Schools: A Psychosocial Study of Motivation and Achievement.* Stanford, CA: Stanford University Press.

TRACTENBERG, M. (ED.) (1977), *Psicanálise da Circuncisão.* Rio de Janeiro: Editorial Civilição Brasileiro.

───── (1989), Circumcision, crucifixion and anti-semitism. *Internat. Rev. Psycho-Anal.,* 16:459-471.

ZUBIN, J., ERON, L. & SCHUMER, F. (1965), *An Experimental Approach to Projective Techniques.* New York: Wiley.

# Publications of A. Irving Hallowell

Compiled and expanded from *Culture and Experience* (1955). Philadelphia: University of Pennsylvania Press; and *Contributions to Anthropology: Selected Papers of A. Irving Hallowell* (1976), Raymond D. Fogelson (ed.). Chicago: University of Chicago Press.

## BOOKS

### 1941

Leslie Spier, A. Irving Hallowell, and Stanley S. Newman (eds.). *Language, Culture and Personality. Essays in Memory of Edward Sapir.* Menasha, WI: Sapir Memorial Publication Fund.

### 1942

*The Role of Conjuring in Salteaux Society.* Philadelphia: University of Pennsylvania Press.

### 1955

*Culture and Experience.* Philadelphia: University of Pennsylvania Press.

### 1967

*Culture and Experience.* 1st Schocken paperback ed. New York: Schocken Books.

### 1971

*The Role of Conjuring in Salteaux Society.* New York: Octagon Books (reprint of the 1942 University of Pennsylvania Press edition).

### 1974

*Culture and Experience.* 1st Pennsylvania paperback ed. Philadelphia: University of Pennsylvania Press (paperback reprint of the 1955 University of Pennsylvania Press edition).

# A. IRVING HALLOWELL

## ARTICLES

### 1920

The problem of fish nets in North America. Master's thesis, University of Pennsylvania.

### 1921

Indian corn hills. *American Anthropologist*, 23:233.

### 1922

Two folk tales from Nyasaland (Bantu texts). *Journal of American Folklore*, 35:216–218.

### 1924

Anthropology and the social worker's perspective. *The Family*, 5:88–92.
Bear ceremonialism in the Northern Hemisphere. Ph.D. dissertation, University of Pennsylvania.

### 1926

Bear ceremonialism in the Northern Hemisphere. *American Anthropologist*, 28:1–175.
Following the footsteps of prehistoric man. *The General Magazine and Historical Chronicle.* University of Pennsylvania, 28:117–122.

### 1928

Recent historical changes in the kinship terminology of the St. Francis Abenaki. *Proceedings, Twenty-second International Congress of Americanists* (Rome):97–145.
Was cross-cousin marriage practiced by the North-Central Algonquin? *Proceedings, Twenty-Third International Congress of Americanists* (New York):519–544.

### 1929

The physical characteristics of the Indians of Labrador. *Journal de la Société des Americanistes de Paris.* Nouvelle Série, 21:337–371.
Anthropology in the university curriculum. *The General Magazine and Historical Chronicle. University of Pennsylvania*, 32:47–54.

### 1930

Editorial comments; The results of the Safe Harbor "Dig," in *Bulletin, Society for Pennsylvania Archeology*, 1.

### 1932

Kinship terms and cross-cousin marriage of the Montagnais-Naskapi and the Cree. *American Anthropologist*, 34:171–199.
Foreward to Henry Lorne Masta, *Abenaki Indian Legends, Grammar and Place Names.* Victoriaville, P. Q., Canada: La Vois des Boisfrancs, pp. 9–12.

### 1934

Some empirical aspects of Northern Salteaux religion. *American Anthropologist*, 36:389–404.
Culture and mental disorder. *Journal of Abnormal and Social Psychology*, 29:1–9.

## 1935

The bulbed enema syringe in North America. *American Anthropologist,* 37:708–10.
Notes on the northern range of Zizania in Manitoba. *Rhodora,* 37:302–304.
Two Indian portraits. *The Beaver,* No. 3, Outfit 266:18–19.

## 1936

Psychic stresses and culture patterns. *American Journal of Psychiatry,* 92:1291–1310.
The passing of the midewiwin in the Lake Winnepeg region. *American Anthropologist,* 38:32–51.
Anthropology—Yesterday and today. *Sigma Xi Quarterly,* 24:161–169.
Two Indian portraits. *The Beaver,* No. 1, Outfit 267:24–25.

## 1937

Temporal orientation in Western civilization and in a preliterate society. *American Anthropologist,* 39:647–70.
Cross-cousin marriage in the Lake Winnepeg area. In: *Twenty-fifth Anniversary Studies,* ed. D. S. Davidson. Philadelphia: Philadelphia Anthropology Society, pp. 95–110.
Introduction. *Handbook of Psychological Leads for Ethnological Field Workers,* prepared for the Committee on Culture and Personality (Edward Sapir, chairman). National Research Council. Mimeographed, 60 pp. Printed in D. G. Haring (ed.) (1948). *Personal Character and Cultural Milieu. A Collection of Readings.* Syracuse: Syracuse University Press, pp. 341–388; and Howard Brand (ed.) (1954). *The Study of Personality. A Book of Readings.* New York: Wiley.

## 1938

Fear and anxiety as cultural and individual variables in a primitive society. *Journal of Social Psychology,* 9:25–47.
Shabwan: A dissocial Indian girl. *American Journal of Orthopsychiatry,* 8:329–340.
The incidence, character and decline of polygamy among the Lake Winnepeg Cree and Salteaux. *American Anthropologist,* 49:235–256.
Notes on the material culture of the Island Lake Salteaux. *Journal de la Société des Americanistes de Paris,* Nouvelle Série, 30:129–140.
Freudian symbolism in the dream of a Salteaux Indian. *Man,* 38:47–48.

## 1939

Sin, sex and sickness in Salteaux belief. *British Journal of Medical Psychology,* 18:191–197.
The child, the savage and the human experience. *Proceedings, Sixth Institute on the Exceptional Child.* Langhorne, PA: The Woods School, pp. 8–34.
Some European folktales of the Berens River Salteaux. *Journal of American Folk Lore,* 52:155–79.
Growing up—savage and civilized. *National Parent-Teacher,* 34(4):32–34.

## 1940

Aggression in Salteaux society. *Psychiatry,* 3:395–407. Reprinted in Clyde Kluckhohn and Henry A. Murray (eds.), (1949). *Personality in Nature, Society and Culture,* New York: Knopf, pp. 260–275.

Spirits of the dead in Salteau life and thought. *Journal of the Royal Anthropological Institute*, 70:29-51.

Magic: The role of conjuring in Salteaux society (Papers presented before the Monday Night Group [1939-1940], Institute of Human Relations, Yale University). Mimeographed.

## 1941

The social function of anxiety in a primitive society. *American Sociological Review*, 7:869-881. Reprinted in D. G. Haring (ed.), (1948). *Personal Character and Cultural Milieu: A Collection of Readings*. Syracuse: University of Syracuse Press, pp. 389-403.

Psychology and anthropology. *Proceedings of the Eighth American Scientific Congress* (Washington, DC), 2:291-297.

The Rorschach method as an aid in the study of personalities in primitive societies. *Character and Personality*, 9:235-245.

The Rorschach Test as a tool for investigating cultural variables and individual differences in the study of personality in primitive societies. *Rorschach Research Exchange*, 5:31-34. (A prospectus written prior to collection of first Rorschach protocols in 1938.)

## 1942

Acculturation processes and personality changes as indicated by the Rorschach technique. *Rorschach Research Exchange*, 6:42-50.

Some psychological aspects of measurement among the Salteaux. *American Anthropologist*, 54:62-77.

Some reflections on the nature of religion. *Crozer Quarterly*, 19:269-277.

(with E. L. Reynolds). Biological factors in family structure. In: Howard Becker and Rueben Hill (eds.), *Marriage and the Family*. Boston: Heath, pp. 25-46.

The nature and functions of property as a social institution. *Journal of Legal and Political Sociology*, 1:115-138. Reprinted in Morris R. Cohen and Felix S. Cohen (eds.), (1951). *Readings in Jurisprudence and Legal Philosophy*. New York: Prentice-Hall.

Araucanian parallels to the Omaha kinship system. *American Anthropologist*, 55:489-491.

Discussion of Ralph Linton, Nativistic movements. *American Anthropologist*, 45:240.

## 1945

Sociopsychological aspects of acculturation. In: Ralph Linton (ed.), *The Science of Man in the World Crisis*, New York: Columbia University Press, pp. 171-200.

The Rorschach technique in study of personality and culture. *American Anthropologist*, 47:195-210.

"Popular" responses and culture differences: An analysis based on frequencies in a group of American Indian subjects. *Rorschach Research Exchange*, 9:153-168.

## 1946

Some psychological characteristics of the Northeastern Indians. In: Frederick Johnson (ed.). *Man in Northeastern North America, Papers of the Robert S. Peabody Foundation for Archeology*, 3:195-225.

Concordance of Ojibwa narratives in the published work of Henry R. Schoolcraft. *Journal of American Folk Lore*, 49:136-153.

1947

Myth, culture, and personality. *American Anthropologist,* 49:544–556.

1949

The size of Algonquin hunting territories, a function of ecological adjustment. *American Anthropologist,* 51:35–45.
Psychosexual adjustment, personality, and the good life in a non-literate culture. In: Paul H. Hoch and Joseph Zubin (eds.), *Psychosexual Adjustment in Health and Disease; The Proceedings of the Thirty-eighth Annual Meeting of the American Psychopathological Association,* New York: Grune and Stratton, pp. 102–123.

1950

Personality structure and the evolution of man. *American Anthropologist,* 52:159–173. (Presidential address, American Anthropological Association, 18 Nov 1949)
Values, acculturation and mental health. *American Journal of Orthopsychiatry,* 20:732–743.

1951

Cultural factors in the structuralization of perception. In: John H. Rohrer and Muzafer Sherif (eds.). *Social Psychology at the Crossroads.* New York: Harper, pp. 164–195.
The use of projective techniques in the study of the sociopsychological aspects of acculturation. *Journal of Projective Techniques,* 15:27–44. (Presidential address, Society for Projective Techniques, 8 Oct 1950)
Frank Goldsmith Speck, 1881–1950. *American Anthropologist,* 53:67–75.

1952

Ojibwa personality and acculturation. In: Sol Tax (ed.), *Acculturation in the Americas* (Proceedings and Selected Papers of the Twenty-ninth International Congress of the Americanists), Chicago: University of Chicago Press, pp. 105–112.
"John the Bear" in the New World. *Journal of American Folk Lore,* 45:418.

1953

Culture, personality and society. In: A. L. Kroeber (chair). *Anthropology Today; An Encyclopedic Inventory.* Chicago: University of Chicago Press, pp. 597–620.
(A. Irving Hallowell, chair, with Alfred Métraux). Problems of process: Methods. In: Sol Tax et al. (eds.), *An Appraisal of Anthropology Today; International Symposium in Anthropology.* Chicago: University of Chicago Press, pp. 85–103.
(A. Irving Hallowell, speaker; Julian H. Steward and D. N. Magunder, chairs). Problems of process: Results. In: Sol Tax et al. (eds.), *An Appraisal of Anthropology Today; International Symposium in Anthropology.* Chicago: University of Chicago Press, pp. 125–41.
(A. Irving Hallowell, speaker; George P. Murdock and Muzafter Senyürek, chairs). Problems of application: Results. In: Sol Tax et al. (eds.), *An Appraisal of Anthropology Today; International Symposium in Anthropology.* Chicago: University of Chicago Press, pp. 160–190.
(A. Irving Hallowell, speaker; Robert Redfield and Eiichiro Ishida, chairs). Values. In: Sol Tax et al. (eds.), *An Appraisal of Anthropology Today; International Symposium in Anthropology.* Chicago: University of Chicago Press, pp. 322–341.

1954

The self and its behavioural environment. *Explorations,* 2 (April).

Psychology and anthropology. In: John P. Gillin and Howard Becker (eds.), *For a Science of Social Man; Convergences in Anthropology, Psychology and Sociology.* New York: Macmillan.

Comments on Clyde Kluckhohn, Southwestern studies of culture and personality. *American Anthropologist,* 56:700–703.

(with Erna Gunther). Daniel Sutherland Davidson, 1900–1952. *American Anthropologist,* 56:336.

1955

Comments on Symposium: Projective testing in ethnography. *American Anthropologist,* 57:262–264.

1956

The structural and functional dimension of a human existence. *Quarterly Review of Biology,* 21:88–101.

The Rorschach technique in personality and culture studies. In: Bruno Klopfer, Mary D. Ainsworth, Walter G. Klopfer and Robert R. Holt (eds.), *Developments in Rorschach Technique,* vol. 2. New York: Harcourt, Brace and World, pp. 458–544.

Preface to Bert Kaplan (ed.), *Microcard Publications of Primary Records in Culture and Personality,* vol. 1. Madison, WI: Microcard Foundation.

1957

The impact of the American Indian on American culture. *American Anthropologist,* 59:201–217.

The backwash of the frontier: The impact of the Indian on American culture. In: Walker D. Wyman and C. B. Kroeber (eds.), *The Frontier in Perspective.* Madison, WI: University of Wisconsin Press, pp. 229–258.

Rorschach protocols of 151 Berens River adults and children and 115 adults from Lac du Flambeau. In: Bert Kaplan (ed.), *Microcard Publications of Primary Records in Culture and Personality,* No. 6. Madison, WI: Microcard Foundation.

1958

Ojibwa metaphysics of being and the perception of persons. In: Renato Tagiuri and Luigi Petrullo (eds.), *Person Perception and Interpersonal Behavior.* Stanford, CA: Stanford University Press.

1959

Behavioral evolution and the emergence of the self. In: Betty J. Meggers (ed.), *Evolution and Anthropology: A Centennial Appraisal.* Washington, DC: Anthropological Society of Washington, pp. 36–60.

The backwash of the frontier: The impact of the Indian on American culture. *Smithsonian Institution, Annual Report for the Year Ended June 30, 1958.* Washington, DC: Smithsonian Institution, pp. 447–472.

1960

Ojibwa ontology, behavior, and world view. In: Stanley Diamond (ed.), *Culture in History: Essays in Honor of Paul Radin.* New York: Columbia University Press.

The beginnings of anthropology in America. In: Frederica de Laguna (ed.), *Selected Papers from the American Anthropologist, 1888–1920.* Evanston, IL: Row, Peterson, pp. 1–90.
Self, society, and culture in phylogenetic perspective. In: Sol Tax (ed.), *Evolution after Darwin. Vol. 2, The Evolution of Man; Man, Culture and Society.* Chicago: University of Chicago Press, pp. 309–371.
(A. Irving Hallowell, panelist; Ralph W. Gerard and Ilza Veith, chairs). The evolution of the mind. In: Sol Tax and Charles Callender (eds.), *Evolution after Darwin. Vol 3, Issues in Evolution.* Chicago: University of Chicago Press, pp. 175–206.

### 1961

The protocultural foundations of human adaptation. In: Sherwood L. Washburn (ed.), *Social Life of Early Man.* Viking Fund Publications in Anthropology, no. 31. New York: Wenner-Gren Foundation for Anthropological Research pp. 236–255.
To Nigeria! *Philadelphia Anthropological Society Bulletin,* 14:7–11.

### 1962

Anthropology and the history of the study of man. Unpublished manuscript prepared for the Social Science Research Council's Conference on the History of Anthropology.

### 1963

Personality, culture, and society in behavioral evolution. In: Sigmund Koch (ed.), *Psychology: A Study of a Science,* Vol. 6. New York: McGraw-Hill.
The Ojibwa world view and disease. In: Iago Galston (ed.), *Man's Image in Medicine and Anthropology.* New York: International Universities Press, pp. 258–315.
American Indians, white and black. The phenomenon of transculturalization. *Current Anthropology,* 4:519–531.

### 1964

Algonkian tribes. *Encyclopaedia Britannica,* 1:628. Chicago: Encyclopedia Brittanica.
Ojibwa. *Encyclopaedia Britannica,* 16:751–752. Chicago: Encyclopedia Britannica.
Frank G. Speck. *Encyclopaedia Britannica,* 21:177. Chicago: Encyclopedia Britannica.

### 1965

The history of anthropology as an anthropological problem. *Journal of the History of the Behavioral Sciences,* 1:24–28.
Hominid evolution, cultural adaptation, and mental dysfunctioning. In: A. V. S. de Reuck and Ruth Porter (eds.), Ciba Foundation Symposium, *Transcultural Psychiatry.* London: J. and A. Churchill.

### 1966

The role of dreams in Ojibwa culture. In: Gustave E. von Grunebaum and Roger R. Caillois (eds.), *The Dream and Human Societies.* Berkeley: University of California Press, pp. 267–292.

### 1967

Anthropology in Philadelphia. In: Jacob W. Gruber (ed.), *The Philadelphia Anthropological Society: Papers Presented on its Golden Anniversary.* Philadelphia: Temple University Press, pp. 1–32.
Preface to the paperback edition of *Culture and Experience.* New York: Schocken Books.

1968

Speck, Frank G. In: David L. Sills (ed.), *International Encyclopedia of the Social Sciences*. New York: Macmillan (Free Press).
Bear ceremonialism in the Northern Hemisphere: Reassessment. Unpublished manuscript in the possession of Frederica de Laguna.

1972

On being an anthropologist. In: Solon T. Kimball and James B. Watson (eds.), *Crossing Cultural Boundaries; The Anthropological Experience*. San Francisco: Chandler Publishing, pp. 51–62.

## BOOK REVIEWS

1925

Ivor H. N. Evans. (1923). *Studies in Religion, Folk Lore, and Custom in British North Borneo and the Malay Peninsula*. Cambridge: The University Press. In: *Journal of the American Oriental Society*, 45:42–43.

1927

Harris H. Wilder. (1926). *The Pedigree of the Human Race*. New York: Holt. In: *Saturday Review of Literature*, April 9.

1935

Forrest E. Clements. (1932). *Primitive Concepts of Disease*. Berkeley: University of California Press. In: *American Anthropologist*, 37:365–368.
John M. Cooper. (1934). *The Northern Algonquin Supreme Being*. Washington, DC: Catholic University Press. In: *American Anthropologist*, 37:673–74.

1936

Robert R. Marett. (1935). *Head, Heart, and Hands in Human Evolution*. London: Hutchison. In: *American Anthropologist*, 38:506–507.
Hilma N. Granqvist. (1931–1935). *Marriage Conditions in a Palestinian Village*. Helsingfors: Akademische buchhandlung Helsingfors. In: *American Sociological Review*, 1:991–993.
Fred Kniffen, Gordon MacGregor, Robert McKennan, Scudder Mekeel and Maurice Mook (A. L. Kroeber, ed.). (1935). *Walapai Ethnography*. Menashe, WI: American Anthropological Association. In: *American Sociological Review*, 1:540–541.

1937

Raymond W. Firth. (1936). *We, the Tikopia. A Sociological Study of Kinship in Primitive Polynesia*. London: Allen and Unwin, Ltd; and W. Lloyd Warner. (1937). *A Black Civilization. A Social Study of an Australian Tribe*. New York: Harper. In: *American Sociological Review*, 2:558–560.
Ralph Linton. (1936). *The Study of Man; An Introduction*. New York: Appleton-Century. In: *Annals* (American Academy of Political and Social Science), 190:249.
Clark Wissler. (1936). *Population Changes among the Northern Plains Indians*. London: Oxford University Press; Peter H. Buck. (1936). *Regional Diversity in the Elaboration of Sorcery in Polynesia*. London: Oxford University Press; Leslie Spier. (1936). *Cultural*

*Relations of the Gila River and Lower Colorado Tribes.* London: Oxford University Press; Ernest Beaglehole. (1936). *Hopi Hunting and Hunting Ritual.* London: Oxford University Press; Willard W. Hill, Navaho warfare. London: Oxford University Press; H. Scudder Mekeel, *The Economy of a Modern Teton Dakota Community.* London: Oxford University Press; Cornelius Osgood, *The Distribution of the Northern Athabascan Indians.* London: Oxford University Press; (Yale University Publications in Anthropology, Nos. 1–7). In: *American Anthropologist,* 39:140–142.

### 1938

Franz Boas. (1938). *The Mind of Primitive Man* (revised edition). New York: Macmillan. In: *American Sociological Review,* 3:580.

Ruth Landes. (1937). *Ojibwa Sociology.* New York: Columbia University Press; and Ruth Landes. (1938) *The Ojibwa Woman.* New York: Columbia University Press. In: *American Sociological Review,* 3:892.

### 1939

Elsie C. Parsons. (1939). *Pueblo Indian Religion.* Chicago: University of Chicago Press; Felix M. Keesing. (1939). *The Menomini Indians of Wisconsin; A Study of Three Centuries of Cultural Contact and Change.* Philadelphia: American Philosophical Society; Viola E. Garfield. (1939). *Tsimshian Clan and Society.* Seattle: University of Washington; W. Z. Park. (1938). *Shamanism in Western North America; A Study in Cultural Relationships.* Evanston and Chicago: Northwestern University; Henri P. Junod, (1938). *Bantu Heritage.* Johannesburg, South Africa: Horfors, for the Transvaal Chamber of Mines; Alfred Guillaume (1938). *Prophesy and Divination among the Hebrews and other Semites.* London: Hodder and Stoughton; Samuel M. Zwemer. (1939). *Studies in Popular Islam; A Collection of Papers Dealing with the Superstitions and Beliefs of the Common People.* London: The Sheldon Press. In: *American Sociological Review,* 4:881–883.

### 1940

Melville J. Herskovits. (1938). *The Study of Culture Contact.* New York: J. J. Augustin. In: *American Anthropologist,* 42:690–692.

Weston La Barre. (1938). *The Peyote Cult.* New Haven: Yale University Press, in *Psychiatry,* 3:150–151.

### 1941

W. Vernon Kinietz. (1940). *The Indians of the Western Great Lakes, 1615–1760.* Ann Arbor: University of Michigan Press. In: *American Anthropologist,* 43:645.

### 1942

Karl N. Llewellyn and E. Adamson Hoebel. (1941). *The Cheyenne Way; Conflict and Case Law in Primitive Jurisprudence.* Norman: University of Oklahoma Press. In: *Annals* (American Academy of Political and Social Change), 220:272–273.

### 1945

Abram Kardiner, Ralph Linton, Cora Du Bois, and James West. (1945). *The Psychological Frontiers of Society.* New York: Columbia University Press. In: *The Scientific Monthly,* 41:394–396.

Leo W. Simmons. (1945). *The Role of the Aged in Primitive Society.* New Haven: Yale University Press. In: *Annals* (American Academy of Political and Social Science), 244:229.

King, Jeff. (1943). *Where the Two Came to their Father. A Navaho War Ceremonial;* text and paintings recorded by Maude Oakes; commentary by Joseph Campbell. New York: Pantheon Books. In: *College Art Journal,* 4:1722–1724.

### 1947

Ruth Underhill. (1946). *Papago Indian Religion.* New York: Columbia University Press. In: *Annals* (American Academy of Political and Social Science), 253:250–251.

### 1950

Paul A. Schilpp (ed.). (1949). *The Philosophy of Ernst Cassirer.* Evanston, IL: Library of Living Philosophy. In: *American Anthropologist,* 52:96–99.

David G. Mandelbaum (ed.), *Selected Writings of Edward Sapir in Language, Culture, and Personality.* Berkeley: University of California Press. In: *Scientific Monthly,* 72:349.

Sister Bernard Coleman. (1947). *Decorative Designs of the Ojibwa of Northern Minnesota.* Washington, DC: Catholic University of America Press. In: *Journal of American Folk Lore,* 43:119–120.

### 1953

Alice Joseph and Veronica F. Murray. (1951). *Chamorros and Carolinians of Saipan; Personality Studies.* Cambridge: Harvard University Press. In: *Journal of Projective Techniques,* 42:106–108.

### 1954

Harold A. Palmer. (1952). *The Philosophy of Psychiatry; Psychiatric Prolegomena.* New York: Philosophical Library. In: *American Anthropologist,* 56:336.

### 1957

Calvin S. Hall and Gardner Lindzey. (1957). *Theories of Personality.* New York: Wiley. In: *American Anthropologist,* 59:936–937.

William N. Fenton. (1957). *American Indian and White Relations to 1830: Needs and Opportunities for Study, An Essay.* Chapel Hill: University of North Carolina Press. In: *American Anthropologist,* 59:1118–1119.

### 1961

Pierre Teilhard de Chardin. (1959). *The Phenomenon of Man.* New York: Harper, In: *Isis,* 52:439–441.

Lewis Hanke. (1959). *Aristotle and the American Indians.* Chicago: H. Regney Co. In: *American Anthropologist,* 11:536–537.

### 1962

H. R. Hays. (1958). *From Ape to Angel; An Informal History of Social Anthropology.* New York: Knopf. In: *American Anthropologist,* 64:174–176.

Sigmund Koch (ed.). (1959–1962). *Psychology: A Study of a Science,* Vols. 1, 2, 3. New York: McGraw-Hill. In: *American Anthropologist,* 64:204–207.

Emanuel F. Hammer. (1958). *The Clinical Application of Projective Drawings*. Springfield, IL: C. C. Thomas. In: *American Anthropologist*, 64:207–208.
Theodora Kroeber. (1961). *Ishi in Two Worlds: A Biography of the Last Wild Indian in North America*. Berkeley: University of California Press. In: *Annals* (American Academy of Political and Social Science), 340:164–165.

### 1963

D. G. Mandelbaum, Gabriel W. Lasker, and Ethel M. Albert (Eds.). (1963). *The Teaching of Anthropology*. Berkeley: University of California Press; and D. G. Mandelbaum, Gabriel W. Lasker, and Ethel M. Albert (Eds.). (1963). *Resources for the Teaching of Anthropology*. Berkeley: University of California Press. In: *Science*, 141:144–145.
Richard Kluckhohn (ed.). (1962). *Culture and Behavior: The Collected Essays of Clyde Kluckhohn*. New York: Free Press of Glencoe. In: *Journal of Higher Education*, 34:237–238.
Elman R. Service. (1962). *Primitive Social Organization: An Evolutionary Perspective*. New York: Random House. In: *American Sociological Review*, 29:314–315.
Edward E. Evans-Pritchard. (1962). *Essays in Social Anthropology*. London: Faber & Faber. In: *American Sociological Review*, 29:424–425.
Margaret Park Redfield (ed.). (1962). *Human Nature and the Study of Society: The Papers of Robert Redfield*, Vol. 1. Chicago: University of Chicago Press. In: *American Sociological Review*, 29:464.

### 1966

Thomas K. Penniman. (1965). *A Hundred Years of Anthropology*, with contributions by Beatrice Blackwood and J. S. Weiner. 3rd ed., revised. London: G. Duckworth. In: *American Anthropologist*, 68:267–268.
Luellen Cole Lowie (ed.). (1966). *Letters from Edward Sapir to Robert H. Lowie*. Berkeley: L. C. Lowie. In: *American Anthropologist*, 68:774.
G. I. Quimby. *Indian Culture and European Trade Goods*. In: *Michigan History 1966* (Sep):225–256.

### 1967

Ramona Morris and Desmond Morris. (1966). *Men and Apes*. London: Hutchison. In: *American Anthropologist*, 69:783.

### 1968

Lee Eldridge Huddleston. (1967). *Origins of the American Indians, European Concepts, 1492–1729*. Austin: University of Texas Press. In: *American Anthropologist*, 70:1185.

### 1969

John O. Brew. (ed.). (1968). *One Hundred Years of Anthropology*. Cambridge, MA: Harvard University Press. In: *American Anthropologist*, 71:725–726.

### 1970

F. M. Barnard (ed. and Trans.). (1969). *J. G. Herder on Social and Political Culture*. London: Cambridge University Press. In: *American Anthropologist*, 72:861–862.

### 1971

Victor E. Hanzeli. (1969). *A Study of 17th and 18th-Century Descriptions of American Indian Languages*. The Hague: Mouton. In: *American Anthropologist*, 73:408–409.

# 1
# Alfred Irving Hallowell:
# An Appreciation

## MELFORD E. SPIRO

With the death of A. Irving Hallowell, anthropology lost one of its most distinguished and influential scholars and teachers. Anthropology, for Hallowell, was truly the "study of man." Although much of his scholarly career was devoted to the study of the Northern Ojibwa, a people whose society, culture, and thought he recorded and analyzed with the meticulous detail of a master craftsman, in almost all of his ethnographic accounts, he was concerned with discovering and displaying the general through the particular. This explains in part why he has had a marked influence on a large group of scholars who know or care little about the Berens River Saulteaux. When, in addition, one considers the wide array of subjects to which he made original and pioneering contributions — social organization, psychological anthropology, acculturation, behavioral evolution, world view, cultural ecology, history of anthropology — it is all the more understandable that his influence has been felt in psychology and history, literature and sociology, psychoanalysis and biology, as well as in anthropology.

As a measure of his wide influence, Hallowell received numerous honors and awards. He was, to mention only some, a Viking Fund Medalist; President of the American Anthropology Association, the American Folklore Society, and the Society for Projective techniques; Chairman of the Division of Psychology and Anthropology of the

This chapter (with some modifications and additions) is reproduced from *American Anthropologist*, 78:3, 1976 by permission of the American Anthropological Association.

National Research Council; a Fellow of the National Academy of Sciences and of the American Philosophical Society. Upon his retirement, the University of Pennsylvania conferred upon him the honorary degree of Doctor of Science.

From his early background, one could hardly have predicted that Hallowell would pursue a life of science and scholarship. He was born in Philadelphia on December 28, 1892. It was assumed by his conservative parents that he would follow a business career; consistent with this assumption, he not only attended a manual-training high school, but upon graduation, he enrolled in the Wharton School of Finance and Commerce of the University of Pennsylvania. Soon, however, ideas of social reform and the social sciences, especially economics and sociology, began to absorb his interests. Lacking the financial resources to pursue graduate studies, he became a social worker for the Family Society after his graduation in 1914, while taking sociology courses in his spare time.

While employed as a social worker, Hallowell took his first course in anthropology with Frank Speck and under Speck's influence, he abandoned his sociological studies and decided to become an anthropologist. With Speck's assistance, he received a graduate fellowship to study anthropology at the University of Pennsylvania and his Ph.D. in 1924. While studying at Pennsylvania, he also traveled to Columbia to participate (together with Melville Herskovits and Ruth Benedict) in Franz Boas's weekly seminar. From Boas and Speck, alike, Hallowell acquired a view of anthropology as a holistic discipline, embracing ethnology, archaeology, physical anthropology, and linguistics, a view that was later to be reflected in the range of his field researches and in the variegated publications that resulted from them. From Speck he also acquired his abiding interest in, and indeed (as he himself said) his identification with American Indians. In fact, all of his fieldwork took place among American Indians: the St. Francis Abenaki of eastern Canada in the 1920s, the Northern Ojibwa of the Lake Winnipeg region over the 1930s, and the Lac du Flambeau (Wisconsin) Ojibwa in 1946. Except for a three-year period at Northwestern University (1944–1947), Hallowell taught continuously at the University of Pennsylvania until his retirement in 1962 at the age of 70. Subsequently, he was a visiting professor at the Universities of Washington, Wisconsin, and Chicago, at Temple University, and at Chatham and Bryn Mawr Colleges.

Hallowell died on October 10, 1974, in Wayne, Pennsylvania.

Hallowell was a rare scholar, not only because he made original and enduring contributions to a wide array of fields, but also because he continued to pioneer in new fields long after his previous achievements had established him as a major figure. Thus, for example, it was only in his later years that his signal achievements in the history of anthropology and in behavioral evolution were accomplished. Since they appeared subsequent to the appearance of *Culture and Experience* (Hallowell, 1955), and since, like many papers that were brought together in that volume, they are scattered across many and diverse publications, it is all the more fortunate that they are included in a second collection of Hallowell's work, *Contributions to Anthropology,* edited by Raymond Fogelson (1976). These collections, together with his highly influential distributional study of bear ceremonialism (Hallowell, 1926) and his definitive historical and ethnographic study of Ojibwa conjuring (Hallowell, 1942), comprise his major publications.

In examining these publications, it is immediately apparent that here a special mind is at work. Although most scholars can be classified as either "foxes" or "hedgehogs" — the fox, according to the Greek poet, Archilochus, "knows many things," whereas the hedgehog "knows one big thing" (Berlin, 1957) — Hallowell was one of the few who transcends such dichotomies. Although his work deals with a great many things, it is almost always concerned with one big thing. Hence it is that in much of his work he attempts to integrate seemingly separate domains. He builds bridges between culture and personality, he discovers continuities between animal and human societies, he uncovers systematic relationships between kin terms and ecology, to mention only a few. This same combination of hedgehog and fox is reflected in his style. In one and the same paper, one discerns the erudition of the historical scholar ("all those footnotes!" as one student put it), as well as the subtlety and lucidity of the theorist.

To assess the importance of Hallowell's work in all of the fields to which he contributed is obviously impossible in this brief review; nor is it necessary, since some of his contributions have have already been evaluated by others in their introductory essays to the papers comprising the Fogelson volume. Hence, my remarks will be confined to his contributions to culture and personality, a field of perduring interest for him; and, because of space limitations, I concentrate on what I believe to have been his signal achievement in this field, his delineation of the relationship between the inner world of social actors and the external social order. For what follows, the reader is referred to the relevant chapters in Hallowell (1955) and Fogelson (1976).

Although he was importantly influenced by stimulus–response psychology (especially by learning theory), Hallowell showed in a series of brilliant papers on the Ojibwa that action is not so much a function of

the objective properties ("stimuli") of the environment, whether physical
or social, as of their *meanings* for the actor. Taking as his point of
departure the gestaltists' concept of the "behavioral environment,"
Hallowell documented in rich detail that the environment to which
Ojibwa actors respond is not *the* environment, but *their* environment,
that is the environment they *perceive*. Going beyond the gestaltists,
however, he demonstrated in masterful fashion that (a) Ojibwa (and
therefore human) perceptions are mediated not through perceptors
alone, but through cognitive orientations that organize and confer
meaning on them; and that (b) these latter orientations are acquired in
large measure from the actors' cultural symbol systems. The general
conclusion is obvious. Because human cognitive orientations are derived
to a considerable extent from cultural symbols systems, and because
perceptions are shaped by these orientations, the human behavioral
environment—the environment that they perceive, and therefore the one
to which they respond—is "culturally constituted." To have established
the existence, and to have explicated the concept, of a "culturally
constituted behavioral environment," was, in its time, a remarkable
achievement, and a singular contribution to psychology and anthropology alike. To remark on its anthropological importance alone, in
demonstrating how different individuals, each initially encapsulated in
the privacy of his own "inner world," nevertheless come to share a
common behavioral environment, Hallowell delineated the process by
which an aggregation of private individuals becomes a group of social
actors. In brief, by elaborating the notion of the culturally constituted
behavioral environment, Hallowell demonstrated, in part, how a human
social order is possible.

Although the cognitive orientations, perceptual sets, and symbolic
meanings of social actors are, in large part, culturally constituted, these
(together with privately constituted cognitions, perceptions, and the like)
comprise only one dimension of their "inner world." And although this
dimension makes a human social order possible, for Hallowell the social
order is always problematic precisely because there are dimensions of the
"inner world" that are not derived from the cultural symbol systems of
the "outer world." The latter dimensions—impulse, affect, imagination,
fantasy, and the like—comprise a set of powerful stimuli that are
potentially disruptive of the social order. Even when they do not lead to
the construction of behavioral environments that differ (as they do in
mental illness) from the culturally constituted environment, they may
lead to action that is inconsistent with the normative requirements of the
social system. For the received anthropological wisdom of the time, this

problem was scarcely recognized, let alone coped with; by drawing rigid disciplinary boundaries, it relegated these dimensions of the inner world to "psychology." Hallowell, who had a profound knowledge of psychoanalysis, not only recognized the problem, but in attempting to cope with it, he elaborated his seminal concept of the "self." This was a central concept in Hallowell's thought, as important as, and correlative to, the concept of the behavioral environment.

Calling once again upon his detailed knowledge of the Ojibwa, Hallowell demonstrated that the self, no less than the behavioral environment, is also culturally constituted. Acquired by means of a set of basic orientations provided by cultural symbol systems, this unique cognitive structure lies at the intersection of the inner and outer worlds and mediates between them. As mediator, the self protects the social order from the potentially disruptive dimensions of the inner world in two ways. (a) To act in accordance with the normative requirements of the social order, social actors must be able in the first instance to distinguish stimuli of the "inner" from those of the "outer" world. In an elegant psychological analysis, Hallowell demonstrated that it is through the development of self-awareness that social actors are able to discern this distinction, and, having discerned it, to adapt their perceptions to culturally constituted cognitions, and to monitor their behavior by reference to cultural norms. (b) But, although monitoring procedures appraise, they don't control behavior. Hence, when the demands of "inner" urges become more powerful than those of "outer" norms, it is the consequent threat to the actors' self-conceptions that assures the persistence of norm-governed behavior.

In sum, many years before "emic" or "phenomenological" approaches became fashionable, Hallowell insisted that the objective constructs of culture and of personality are in themselves inadequate to explain the human social order. An adequate explanation requires, as he saw it, the notion of a phenomenologically conceived psychological field consisting of culturally constituted selves in interaction with a culturally constituted behavioral environment.

Upon Hallowell's retirement, a group of former students, together with some colleagues, presented him with a festschrift volume, *Context and Meaning in Cultural Anthropology* (Spiro, 1965), and following his death, a group of younger students offered two symposia, entitled "The Legacy of A. Irving Hallowell," in his memory at the 74th Annual Meeting of the American Anthropological Association in 1975. Hallowell was one of those few teachers who evoked both intellectual respect and admiration, and personal regard and affection. Although, as a teacher he never persuaded his students to follow his own intellectual interests (as the wide range of topics covered in the festschrift and the memorial symposia testify), his vast erudition, exacting intellectual standards, disdain for disciplinary boundaries, and constantly searching mind served them as a model to be emulated, if not achieved. More important, in his teaching and writing, Hallowell focused his vision on one big thing — the nature of man. Hence, although much of his teaching was concerned with the ethnography of American Indians, his approach to the uniquely Indian was based on and informed by a conception of the generically human; and the latter conception projected a vision of what anthropology could be, a vision that most of his student found exciting and captivating.

That vision, it may now be noted, was importantly informed by psychoanalysis. Influenced in part by Edward Sapir, perhaps the first American anthropologist to have taken psychoanalysis seriously, much of Hallowell's work in culture and personality employs psychoanalytic concepts, more especially repression, the dynamic unconscious, the structural theory, and the mechanisms of defense. Moreover, one (but not the only) reason that Hallowell became interested in the Rorschach test, and pioneered its use in anthropological field work, derived from his concern with uncovering the personality dynamics of individual actors, and with testing psychodynamic interpretation based on ethnographic interviews and observations.

Although influenced by certain aspects of psychoanalytic theory, Hallowell was critical of others; and just as he used certain psychoanalytic concepts to interpret ethnographic data, so also he employed ethnographic data to refute other psychoanalytic concepts. Thus, drawing upon his own field work and that of others, he showed how Freud's recapitulation theory, and the equation of the thought of children and primitive peoples, are egregiously misplaced. (See Hallowell, 1955).

Finally, Hallowell was not only a consumer of some psychoanalytic concepts and a critic of others, but he also anticipated at least one new development in psychoanalysis. I am referring, of course, to his pioneering work on the self.

In 1954, much before the development of self psychology, Hallowell wrote a seminal essay, "The Self and its Behavioral Environment" (Hallowell, 1955) that though not concerned with narcissism, lays the conceptual foundation for the signal relevance of the self, both for psychological and anthropological purposes. Although this essay is as important today as it was when it was first published almost forty years ago, it remains unknown to psychoanalysts, perhaps because, although

Hallowell remained abreast of developments in psychoanalysis, few analysts are acquainted with anthropology.

It is of interest to observe that just as self psychology is often employed as a means for minimizing, if not rejecting, the importance of conflict and oedipal dynamics, so also many psychological and ethnopsychological anthropologists have seized upon the notion of the "culturally-constituted self" as an alternative to attending to the notion of personality and personality dynamics. The difference is that for Kohut (or at least the later Kohut), the turning away from standard psychoanalytic concerns was an *intended* consequence of his innovation; for Hallowell, the turning away from standard culture and personality concerns was an *unintended* consequence of *his* innovation, one which (had he lived to see it) he would have very much regreted.

## BIBLIOGRAPHY

BERLIN, I.(1957), The *Hedgehog and the Fox*. New York: New University Library.

FOGELSON, R. D., ed. (1976), *Contributions to Anthropology: Selected Papers of A. Irving Hallowell*. Chicago: University of Chicago Press.

HALLOWELL, A. I. (1926), *Bear ceremonialism in the Northern Hemisphere*. Amer. Anthropol. 28:1–175.

———— (1942), *The Role of Conjuring in Saulteaux Society*. Philadelphia: University of Pennsylvania Press.

———— (1955), *Culture and Experience*. Philadelphia: University of Pennsylvania Press.

SPIRO, M. E., ed. (1965), *Context and Meaning in Cultural Anthropology*. New York: Free Press.

# 2

# A. Irving Hallowell and the Study of Cultural Dynamics

## RAYMOND D. FOGELSON

Many of the ideas of A. Irving Hallowell now drift unrecognizably in the mainstream currents of anthropological discourse. As as an adjectival compound, "culturally constituted," first used by Hallowell, may once have sounded pompous, awkward, or even lexically constipated, but it now rolls off the tongue unreflectively. Topics whose study he pioneered or invigorated, such as conceptions of self and person, spatial and temporal orientations, native theories of dreams and disease, dimensions of world view, and what he termed "behavioral environment," have become familiar in modern anthropology.

Hallowell is viewed today as an important progenitor of psychological anthropology. He is generally credited with helping push this important subdiscipline in productive psychodynamic and cognitive directions.

Hallowell (1956) was an innovator in the cross-cultural use of the Rorschach Test, a field technique that is now generally considered passé in anthropology. In retrospect, his original impulse to use the Rorschach with Ojibwa Indians seems less in the service of his growing interest in psychoanalysis and more as a means to study world view to get at perceptual and apperceptual aspects of the Ojibwa self and the self's behavioral environment. Early on, he employed the Rorschach as a clinical tool to help understand individual cases of mental disorder (see, example, Hallowell, 1938). Later he used the Rorschach as a multidimensional test to assess collective aspects of personality across different communities. The aggregate results of his Ojibwa research were not entirely dependent upon the conventional meanings of Rorschach responses in Western society; rather they suggested different parameters of Ojibwa personality that could be reasonably inferred to reflect cultural differences.

Far from being a psychological reductionist or a psychological determinist, Hallowell consistently emphasized the ontological necessity for separating cultural and psychological levels of explanation, while still appreciating the dynamic interaction of psychological and cultural factors. He was never really comfortable with the label "Culture and Personality" and deliberately entitled his course in this general area as "Psychology and Culture." For Hallowell, psychology embodied more than the study of personality; he was vitally interested in problems of perception, primate behavior, learning theory, cognitive issues, as well as the study of motivation and psychodynamics.

In addition to his course, "Psychology and Culture," and two-semester sequences on "Social Organization" and on the "History and Development of Anthropology," Hallowell in his later years regularly taught a course on "Cultural Dynamics," which I was privileged to take in 1956 and 1957. The course encompassed processual notions of culture change, including evolution, diffusion, assimilation, history, and the then prevalent concept of acculturation. The explanatory power of the culture concept, both in its generic and specific aspects, was assumed. We were exposed to the ideas of Julian Huxley and George Gaylord Simpson, of Spengler and Danilevski, of Burkhardt and Sorokin. Several lectures were devoted to a detailed dissection of the macrohistorical theories of the then fashionable Arnold Toynbee. We were introduced to the Kroeber–Boas debate on the relations between history and anthropology, to British theories of social change; but most of the course, including student seminar reports, was given over to theoretical and substantive studies of acculturation.

Hallowell frequently commented on the youth of acculturation studies. He was convinced that as more and more particularized studies accumulated, general theoretical principles would emerge. He was critical of the implicit ethnocentric bias in acculturation studies toward inevitable Westernization; he held out hope that acculturation theory might increasingly be applied to contacts between non-Western peoples. Examples were often given in class of unique adjustments made by American Indian cultures to Euro-American influences in which the essential native ethos was preserved. He was also interested in changes wrought in the dominant culture during situations of extended culture contact, as well as in individual efforts to embrace an alien culture—a phenomenon that he labeled transculturization (see Hallowell, 1963, pp. 498–529).

Hallowell's conception of cultural dynamics can, perhaps, best be discerned through a retrospective consideration of his primary research agenda. *Bear Ceremonialism* (1926), his published doctoral dissertation, is a seedbed work. Not only does the monograph anticipate later work in ethnoecology, the concept of persons, and the magico-religious basis of hunting in northern boreal societies, but the cultural embeddedness of psychological processes is clearly asserted. To quote him directly:

> Therefore, the explanation of customs and beliefs by some simple psychological formula, couched in terms of "individual psychology," whether applied to origins or later developments, is putting the cart before the horse. That is to say, a specific practice or belief, whether found in one tribe or many, never represents a direct psychological response of individuals to some aspect of the outer world. The cultural *milieu* too early conditions the subjective attitudes, as well as the overt behavior of individuals, for this to be possible. The source of their beliefs and practices is, therefore, the historic tradition (culture), and the history of particular customs and beliefs must be pursued at the cultural, not the psychological level [Hallowell, 1962, p. 19].

Darnell (1977) rightly demonstrates that Hallowell's monograph on *Bear Ceremonialism* reflected a transition in the Boasian program away from simple trait diffusion and toward greater concern for cultural integration—a shift that later eventuated in the cultural and personality movement. Nevertheless, despite these theoretical currents, Hallowell's comprehensive survey of the available literature on bear ceremonialism was categorically organized, and some pervasive traits were seen to reflect a deep and ancient stratum extending from Lappland to Labrador. Breaks in this continuum were thought to result from secondary historical modification, differentiation, and assimilation (Hallowell, 1926, p. 162).

Hallowell's interests in historical changes in social structure dates from 1928 when he published two articles: one that documents historical changes in Abnaki kinship terminology and a second (1930) that hypothesized the former existence of cross-cousin marriage in the Northern Algonkian area. The latter question, first posed by Rivers, was persued through several articles, culminating in a decisive 1937 statement on "Cross-cousin Marriage in the Lake Winnipeg Area." The solving of this problem required a good deal of careful detective work. The first clues came from lexical terms and suggestive notes buried in early documents. The continued existence of cross-cousin marriage among remote Naskapi bands and Western Cree groups was independently reported by William Duncan Strong and by Edward Curtis and subsequently confirmed by observations of Frank Speck, Father John Cooper, and others. However, Hallowell's focused research in the Lake Winnipeg area, where he collected solid genealogical material along with critical demographic and ethnographic data, clinched the case. Modern anomalies in kinship terminology were seen as systematic variations from, or what we might today call transformations of, a basic pattern of cross-cousin marriage. These changes could be accounted for in light of Western acculturative influence, particularly in religious and economic spheres. It is worth noting that Hallowell was interested in the ethnographic and cognitive reality of cross-cousin marriage for his informants, rather than treating the institution only as an abstracted analytic category removed from native understanding. As he comments,

> cross-cousin marriage among the Lake Winnipeg Cree and Saulteaux is certainly something different from cross-cousin marriage among the Miwok and other California groups, or from that occurring on the Northwest coast, or elsewhere. To discuss it as a "culture trait" divorced from the social context of which it is a part and in terms of which it is integrated with other traits in different ways among different peoples, can only lead to superficial and inept comparison, if it does not involve an actual distortion of fact [Hallowell, 1937, p. 327].

Considerations of context and meaning were rarely made so explicitly in the American anthropology of the 1930s.

Probably the work for which Hallowell is most known is his large-scale investigation of personality changes among the Northern Ojibwa as measured by the Rorschach Test (Hallowell, 1955, pp. 307–366). Here, following a quasiexperimental approach, he compared composite Rorschach profiles of three Ojibwa communities representing different degrees of acculturation in terms of their proximity to, and the accessibility of, Euro-Canadian culture. He found statistically significant differences in mean scores of important Rorschach variables between the groups. The least acculturated group showed the most psychologically integrated personality profiles (by Rorschach standards), whereas the more acculturated communities manifested progressively more signs of pathology and symptoms of personality disintegration. Essentially, Hallowell was positing longer-term diachronic changes through a synchronic comparison of differently situated, contemporaneous groups. The critical variable was differential exposure to, and penetration by, Euro-Canadian culture. He attempted to support the implications of his thesis by demonstrating that a reconstruction of late 18th- and early 19th-century Ojibwa typical personality, as derived from early documentary descriptions, more closely coincided with that of his least acculturated modern community than with the more acculturated groups. The assumptions, methods, and conclusions of this bold study were duly questioned, and later investigators benefited from this criticism.

In retrospect, it seems clear that the focus of contention centered on the reliability and validity of the Rorschach Test as an adequate cross-cultural measure of personality. Nevertheless, many of the differences discovered were statistically significant, and other results were in predicted directions. Whatever the a priori deficiencies of the Rorschach Test, it evidently was picking up nonrandom responses. Personality here, as elsewhere for Hallowell, was taken as a dependent variable, whereas culture and social structure were the independent variables. The consequences of acculturation operated indirectly on personality structure by undermining the normative expectations implicit in the traditional value system and world view.

Cultural dynamics continued to be a central concern in Hallowell's later writings, mostly produced after the appearance of his first collection of essays, *Culture and Experience,* in 1955. For the sake of convenience, these later papers can be discussed under four headings: 1) Ojibwa world view; 2) behavioral evolution; 3) the reciprocal effects of acculturation; and 4) the history of anthropology.

First, Hallowell continued to draw upon his data bank of field and archival materials to produce profound, phenomenological interpretations of Ojibwa culture (Hallowell, 1963, pp. 357–476). He vividly delineates the culturally constituted Ojibwa world through critical informant testimony, by means of cogent behavioral observation, often couched in memorable anecdotal form, and by controlled use of linguistically derived, native systems of classification. These insights are tempered and welded together by Hallowell's remarkable grasp of the mainsprings of Ojibwa culture and social structure.

Almost in direct counterpoint to these brilliant interpretations of the specifics of traditional Ojibwa culture, Hallowell, in a second set of broad-ranging, yet interlocking papers, addressed the generic study of culture by investigating issues in human behavioral evolution. In this endeavor, he was primarily concerned with the necessary and sufficient conditions for defining a human level of existence. He contended that accounts of human behavioral evolution solely in terms of morphological criteria were incomplete without considering the influence of psychosocial factors and ultimately, cultural determinants, in shaping this process. Crucial for the emergence of human culture was the development of extrinsic modes of symbolic communication and self-awareness derived through a capacity for self-objectification. Our knowledge of primate behavior, of processes of symbolization, and of the fossil record of human evolution increased greatly in recent years. However, Hallowell remains one of the first sociocultural anthropologists to recognize the philosophic significance of behavior evolution for establishing general theories of culture. Many of the issues he voiced continue to be vital and await new phrasings (see Hallowell, 1976, pp. 230–312 for a summary statement).

A third cluster of late Hallowell papers dealt directly with the problem of decentering acculturation studies by examining the native side of the contact situation. In articles on the frontier situation in America, he stressed the bidirectional flow of cultural influence and the now, more widely appreciated fact that the American Indian had a significant impact on the shaping of American culture (Hallowell, 1963, pp. 481–530). Thus, the discovery of America is of central importance to Wallerstein's world systems theory (1974), as it was for historical geographers such as Crosby (1972) who analyze the ecological consequences of the Columbian exchange. American historians generally have become more sensitive to the active role that native peoples played, and continue to play, in the continuing drama of New World culture history.

In class, Professor Hallowell often remarked that cultures do not come into contact, but individuals do. This observation is elaborated in his article on transculturization, the process by which an individual, through varying circumstances, takes up residence among an alien group and accommodates to that alien culture. Societies can differ in the degree to which they tolerate transculturites, but, as Hallowell demonstrates, and as colonial historians subsequently confirmed, transculturites frequently served as important agents of cultural change and as salient symbols of the virtues and vices of "otherness."

A final set of papers brought to the fore Hallowell's long-standing interest in the history of anthropology (Hallowell, 1976, pp. 21–158, 163–229). These were not narrowly conceived essays on disciplinary history; they concerned the intellectual roots, or protoculture, to recycle one of his terms, of anthropology, with situated social and cultural forces that gave rise to the specialized discipline of anthropology. To borrow from the title of one of Hallowell's influential essays in this area, the history of anthropology could be seen as an anthropological problem. His contributions not only gave new impetus for studying the history of anthropology, but can be regarded as an important early prefiguration of current interests in critical, reflexive, or postmodern anthropology that view professional anthropology as an historical product of Western industrial capitalism.

To conclude, a major unifying theme in Hallowell's approach to anthropology was his abiding interest in cultural dynamics. Cultural dynamics, for Hallowell, was an encompassing rubric that included not only different forms of cultural change, but also considered the crucial role of culture in mediating and monitoring human mental processes and behavior. In behavioral evolution, a capacity for self-objectification and its sequelae represented a critical stage in the continuous development of culture. Self-objectification would also entail the emergence of collective and individual consciousness.

In this connection, I think Hallowell might have been fascinated by Jaynes's (1976) book, *The Origin of Consciousness in the Breakdown of the Bicameral Mind.* In the fifteen years since its publication, Jaynes's thesis has been all but ignored, and probably rightfully so, by anthropologists. The book does seem to be located beyond the fringe, and certainly beyond the filmy screen that William James felt separated consciousness from other systems of reality. Stripped to its essentials, Jaynes's thesis argues that modern consciousness is a late development in Western civilization, that the peoples of the Bible and the ancient Greeks, as their texts tell us, *did* hear voices, and *did* live in a world of auditory hallucinations. The voices of the dead fathers and elders, originating from the right hemisphere of the brain, were imbued with the moral authority of tradition, served as a means of social control, and functioned to maintain cultural continuity. Such a situation is not unlike Hallowell's description of the Ojibwa behavioral environment, an area populated by culturally constituted persons, both human and other-than-human. These other-than-human persons, the personages of myth, or "our grandfathers," as the Ojibwa gloss the term *at so kanak* (Hallowell, 1963, p. 365), kept in regular communication with members of the local community. For Hallowell, initial fascination with Jaynes's thesis would probably have rapidly given way to left-brain, rational rejection, since considering consciousness, itself, as culturally constituted would verge on the tautological, and viewing consciousness as merely an altered state of REM time would border on the oxymoronic!

## BIBLIOGRAPHY

CROSBY, A. W. (1972), *The Columbian Exchange: Biological and Cultural Consequences of 1492*. Westport, Ct: Greenwood Press.

DARNELL, R. (1977), Hallowell's "bear ceremonialism" and the emergence of Boasian anthropology. *Ethos*, 5:13–30.

HALLOWELL, A. I.(1926), Bear ceremonialism in the northern hemisphere. *Amer. Anthropol.* 28:1–175.

_____ (1928), Recent historical changes in the kinship terminology of the St. Francis Abnaki. *Procs. 22nd Int. Cong. Americanists*, pp. 97–145.

_____ (1930), Was cross-cousin Marriage Practiced by the North-central Algonkian? *Procs. 23rd Int. Cong. Americanists*, pp. 519–44.

_____ (1937), Cross-cousin Marriage in the Lake Winnipeg area. In: *Contributions to Anthropology: Selected Papers of A. Irving Hallowell*, ed. R. D. Fogelson. Chicago: University of Chicago Press, 1976, pp. 317–332.

_____ (1938), Shabwan: A dissocial Indian girl. *Amer. J. Orthopsychiat.*, 8:329–340.

_____ (1955), *Culture and Experience*. Philadelphia: University of Pennsylvania Press.

_____ (1956), The Rorschach technique in personality and culture study. In: *Developments in the Rorschach Technique*, Vol. 2, ed. B. Klopfer. Yonkers, NY: World, pp. 485–544.

_____ (1963), American Indians, white and black: The phenomenon of transculturization. In: *Contributions to Anthropology: Selected Papers of A. Irving Hallowell*, ed. R. D. Fogelson. Chicago: University of Chicago Press, 1976, pp. 498–529.

_____ (1976), *Contributions to Anthropology: Selected Papers of A. Irving Hallowell*, ed. R. D. Fogelson. Chicago: University of Chicago Press.

JAYNES, J. (1976), *The Origin of Consciousness in the Breakdown of the Bicameral Mind*. Boston: Houghton Mifflin Company.

WALLERSTEIN, E.(1974), *The Modern World-System*. New York: Academic Press.

# 3

# A. Irving Hallowell, the Foundations of Psychological Anthropology, and Altered States of Consciousness

## ERIKA BOURGUIGNON

## INTRODUCTION

A. Irving Hallowell contributed to virtually all areas of psychological anthropology as it exists today. His range was immense: from mental health to perception and cognition, from projective techniques to behavioral evolution, from the concept of the self to acculturation. In spite of this apparent diversity, Hallowell's contribution forms an integrated whole, a theory of human nature firmly grounded in his vast reading in psychology and philosophy, and facilitated by his strong historical orientation.

A striking feature of Hallowell's work is that, notwithstanding the breadth of his interests in the area of overlap between anthropology and psychology, the area of overlap remained, throughout his career, only a portion of his contributions to anthropology. From his first publication in psychological anthropology in 1934, this field was never his only concern, so that he always carried this work forward simultaneously with his many other anthropological interests. It is also noteworthy that Hallowell never concentrated his efforts on what have appeared to many to be the central concerns of Personality and Culture as a movement in American anthropology in the 1930s and 1940s. He conducted no study of child rearing in his years of research among the Saulteaux, nor did he

The first section of this paper was presented as part of a symposium on "A Century of Anthropology at the University of Pennsylvania: The Legacy of A. I. Hallowell" held at the annual meeting of the American Anthropological Association, December 3, 1986.

formally relate child rearing to adult personality, or make broad generalizations about the Saulteaux personality. He did write a series of highly focused, classic papers in the personality and culture field, using ethnographic data to test psychiatric hypotheses. Interestingly, these papers were published in psychiatric and psychological journals, and, in addition to being contributions to anthropology, they served to educate practitioners in the importance of cultural as well as individual variables in the development of individual behavior patterns. In these papers, he set out clearly and forcefully the cultural and social context in which the behavior occurred. In time, he came to think of personality and culture studies, not as ends in themselves, but only as parts of a much larger intellectual edifice. Thus Hallowell wrote in 1955, in *Culture and Experience:* "Personality and Culture studies open up wide vistas of inquiry, once the facts of cultural variability and patterning are linked with our knowledge of the conditions necessary for the development of a personality structure in man, and the determinants relevant to its variability in form and functioning" (p. 32). Reflecting on his contribution to the field as a whole, Hallowell (1972) wrote: "My own conception of psychological anthropology has always been a broad one that transcends the study of personality and culture in the narrow sense. There are many psychological areas that should be dealt with" (p. 57).

Thus, in the 1930s Hallowell also explored, a much rarer phenomenon in those days, aspects of perceptual orientation among the Ojibwa with regard to space, time, and measurement. The Rorschach experiments, which he began in 1937, related as much to his interests in perception and the possibility of culture free tests as to studies of personality. As he noted in "On Being an Anthropologist," he became interested in psychoanalysis and psychiatry, as well as academic psychology, very early on, in the 1920s. In the 1930s, he writes, "I became directly involved in psychological anthropology through Edward Sapir" (1972, p. 58). At the National Research Council, Sapir set up a committee on "Personality in Relation to Culture" to which he invited Hallowell as well as Ruth Benedict, Harry Stack Sullivan, Adolph Meyer, and A. A. Brill. It was during this period that Hallowell began to publish in this area.

"Culture and Mental Disorders," published in the *Journal of Abnormal and Social Psychology* in 1934, was Hallowell's first paper to deal with psychological concerns. From then on, his published writings of psychoanthropological interest appeared regularly until 1965. The last paper in this series was titled "Hominid Evolution, Cultural Adaptation and Mental Dysfunction." It brought together after 30 years three principal strands of Hallowell's life work.

In 1937, only three years after his first psychoanthropological paper,

Hallowell wrote his introduction to an intended Handbook of Psychological Leads for Ethnographic Fieldworkers (Hallowell, 1948). Not published until 1948, the 60 pages of mimeographed text were pored over by generations of students. This important paper shows an aspect of Hallowell's scholarship that was revealed increasingly in the following years, namely his erudition. It showed his very thorough grounding in a vast literature of several different disciplines and his ability to produce a significant synthesis of these materials of relevance to the problem at hand; and the problem was human nature. At this early stage of what were later to become dominant interests for him, Hallowell draws attention to the significance of comparative psychology for anthropology, and to human distinctiveness as revealed in the enormous human intraspecific variation. He draws attention to psychoanalysis as it helps us to understand the large measure of acquired behavior in the satisfaction of human needs through delayed and indirect means. He draws on child psychology, studies of perception, mental illness, and so forth — the whole range is covered. Strongly opposing single factor explanations, he stresses the need for a "delicate weighing of each" of a multitude of determinants, (Hallowell, 1956, p. 345). Although he cites a number of ethnographic examples, the emphasis, throughout, is on the broader issues. All of this, clearly, foreshadows his later work in behavioral evolution.

This broad topic, however, is approached only gradually. In the meantime Hallowell began, in 1937, his Rorschach experiments with the Saulteaux, and in 1939 he published an extensive critical and historical review of the recapitulation theory. Originally titled "The Child, the Savage, and Human Experience," it shows the significance of 19th century evolutionary thought in the work of Freud and his contemporaries, and the havoc it wrought in everything from educational theories to notions of "the primitive mind" in anthropology. This thorough review and critical analysis surely helped to put that series of myths to rest. Perhaps it also helped to exorcise the errors of the old evolutionary anthropology and to provide room for the new evolutionary thinking that was to loom so large in what followed.

Although Hallowell's first public utterance on behavioral evolution came in 1949 (1950a) in his presidential address to the American Anthropological Association, some of its underlying thoughts were foreshadowed in 1942 in a paper co-authored with the physical anthropologist E. L. Reynolds on the "Biological Factors in Family Structure."

Many of the theoretical formulations and much of the literature review that appeared in a series of his important papers during the 1950s and 1960s were already present in his teaching in the mid-1940s. I should like to cite two (approximate) quotations from his 1946 lectures at Northwestern. He began his course by noting that "[w]e of the 20th century have a unique perspective in relation to the study of human nature." This means that we have some very sound knowledge as a base to build on, as compared to the speculations of other or earlier cultures. Our perspective includes a Copernican view of the universe, a substantial knowledge of physics and chemistry, and a Darwinian view of evolution and knowledge of biology and heredity. Anthropology provides a distinctive perspective on mankind as a whole, spatially and temporally, in contrast to the other social sciences. In the same vein he said, "Regardless of the specificity of any given task, the anthropologist never loses sight of the total of humanity." In his course, as in his writings, he insisted on four orders of determinants, phylogeny, ontogeny, physical environment, and sociocultural environment, in any attempt to understand human behavior, shunning cultural determinism along with other single factor explanations.

Much of the course was devoted to the necessary and sufficient conditions for the development of culture. It was all there; the symbolic transformation of experience, the behavioral environment, the development of the self. It is striking to see how many of the ideas Hallowell developed so much later in writing were complete at that time, how carefully he expanded the supporting evidence before launching what constituted a systematic revision of thinking about the relationship between biology and culture, evolution and human nature. Indeed, to talk of human nature in the heyday of relativism was a remarkable undertaking.

Hallowell brought this perspective on human nature to all his work. Using the Rorschach in his study of the psychological consequences of acculturation among the Ojibwa led him to raise questions striking directly at the heart of relativism. In "Values, Acculturation, and Mental Health" (1950) he wrote of "studying systems of values in different societies from the standpoint of total personality integration and functioning viewed in the perspective of our knowledge of mental health" (p. 759).

He concluded that acculturation had produced a "psychological impasse" for the Ojibwa. Values need to be consistent with the structure of the culturally constituted behavioral environment and the ecological adaptation of a particular society. Yet different value systems could allow for total personality integration and functioning. That is, a single standard of values need not be imposed to produce mental health.

Hallowell's work in psychological anthropology is informed by a profound sense of history, and this in several different ways: He is concerned with the ethnohistorical record of the American Indian and the light it sheds on contemporary psychoethnographic information; he is concerned with the history of anthropology, particularly in its formative period and with its contacts with psychology over the past century; he is concerned with the history of science as a cumulative process, as it gave rise to and influenced the development of anthropology, the youngest of the sciences, and with the historical moment. He asked, what has science, all of science, led up to and what does it allow us to understand on the basis of accumulated sound scientific knowledge that no other period and no other culture was able to understand? How does our own accumulation of historical and scientific knowledge make us different, as students of human nature, from others, who formulated their theories on the basis of belief and speculation?

Hallowell saw anthropology as science, thinking in terms of research design and hypothesis testing. He laid the foundations for our major interests. At a time when it was unpopular, he developed a concept of human nature as a species specific, generically and uniquely human set of capacities and attributes. He studied a single society and culture intensively and often used materials from it to illustrate points with broader application. But he kept his eye on humanity at large, conceiving of anthropology as a whole and as a comparative science. He took his starting point in philosophy with Cassirer, and Langer, and Grace De Laguna, in evolutionary biology, in comparative psychology, and in primatology. He valued the work of scholars in numerous fields and drew on their contributions, often illuminating obscure aspects of the development of anthropology.

The full impact of his work and influence is still to be felt. Like most anthropologists of his generation, with notable exceptions such as Melville J. Herskovits and Margaret Mead, Hallowell was a student of the American Indian. Yet his observation about cultural anthropology in general might be applied, first and foremost, to his own work. "It has become increasingly clear," he wrote (Hallowell, 1960, p. 19), "that the potential significance of the data collected by cultural anthropologists far transcends in interest the level of simple, objective, ethnographic description of the peoples they have studied." Just how far it can transcend this level, and how broad and profound the resulting exploration can be in the mind of a scholar of Hallowell's stature and erudition, is seen in the scope of his life's work. In his autobiographical piece, "On Being an Anthropologist," he showed the development of his interests from the specific to the general. Starting with the investigation of one group of Canadian Indians to recover as much as possible of their traditional culture, he moved on to a study of acculturation. It was this that led him, he tells us, "to attempt and expound the world view of the most conservative Ojibwa" (1972 p. 58), whose culture and world was so different from that of their acculturated kin in Wisconsin. From this attempt grew the concept of the behavioral environment, "an environment culturally constituted in such a way that it structures the major psychological field in which individuals act, forming their basic cognitive orientation" (Hallowell 1972, p. 59).

Interest in the implications of the concept of a culturally constituted behavioral environment, in its turn, led Hallowell to questions about human evolution, developing a perspective that goes beyond physical anthropology and archaeology. This inclusive perspective, in turn, led him "to bring together the organic, psychological, social and cultural dimensions of the evolutionary process, a process that creates the conditions for human existence" (p. 59). Thus, to describe the traditional Ojibwa behavioral environment was a necessary step in the definition of a "human existence," and implying answers to questions about its origins. How has man "so fully assimilated subjective and unconscious experiences and integrated them with the acquisition and accumulation of pragmatic knowledge of the world, in a manner difficult to disentangle" (p. 59)? And so we get the definition of man as an "animal that has been able to survive by making cultural adaptations in which his own imaginative interpretations of the world have been fed back into his personal adjustment to it" (p. 59). That is to say, imagination, in this sense, is necessary to the construction of reality. The movement of Hallowell's exploration then is not only from the specific and local to the broad and general. It is also a movement from surface to depth, and from present to past. It is a movement in which the study of the transformations of the behavioral environment of one cultural group stimulated considerations about how the construction of human behavioral environments were made possible in the course of human evolution, behavioral as well as organic evolution.

## ALTERED STATES OF CONSCIOUSNESS AND BEHAVIORAL EVOLUTION

Spiro (1976, p. 363) credited Hallowell's important 1954 paper, "The Self and Its Behavioral Environment" with "laying the foundation of the 'phenomenological approach' to the anthropological study of both culture and personality." In the context of this paper, it is also to be seen as a stepping stone in the development of Hallowell's interest in behavioral evolution, where he drew on his understanding of the self and its culturally constituted behavioral environment. How did such a self arise? How could a behavioral environment be constructed with cultural as well as biological materials? He tells us (Hallowell, 1972) that "dreams, fantasies, myths, art and world views of man as articulated in cultural traditions, may be interpreted as making positive use of psychological resources in cultural adaptation and personal adjustment" (p. 59).

I should like to add altered states of consciousness (ASC) to Hallowell's list, to consider them from an evolutionary perspective, and to explore their relevance to our understanding of the reciprocal relationship between imagination and experience in a cultural context. To do so, I begin by noting what leads we find in Hallowell's writings with regard to this subject. Thus, I want to ask once more, to what extent it is possible to draw on what Hallowell taught us through his intensive study of one group of North American Indians to expand our understanding of other, often very different cultures, and, indeed, to shed light on the relationship between culture and human experience broadly viewed.

Hallowell's longest and fullest statement concerning an important institution in Saulteaux life was his 1942 monograph on the *Role of Conjuring in Saulteaux Society*. Here he brought together his materials on performances that dramatized the relationship between humans and the spirit world. In his later evolutionary writings, Hallowell is interested in the relationship between experience and imagination and vice versa. In his conjuring book, he appears, as yet, to be far removed from such considerations. A closer look, however, may give us some insights into his views about such matters at that stage of the development of his thinking. This, in turn, may lead us to some considerations regarding altered states of consciousness and both their role in the structuring of a behavioral environment as well as their evolutionary sources or roots.

For the Saulteaux, the Northern Ojibwa he studied intensively, Hallowell (1942) tells us, "conjuring . . . is an institutionalized means for obtaining the help of different classes of spiritual beings by invoking their presence and communicating their desires to them" (p. 9). And, he continues, "the conjurer is a specialist in invocation." As to who the conjurers are, he finds that only rarely have women conjurers appeared, and then only older women, past menopause. This, then, is a male specialty, tied in many respects to hunting and the world of animals, for many of the spirits are indeed the "bosses" of animal species. By invoking the spirits, "a Salteaux conjurer brings into the midst of a group of human beings . . . a large selection of spirit beings" (Hallowell, 1942, p. 12). He does so by entering a specially built lodge, into which he invites the spirit beings to come. There they manifest themselves to the audience assembled outside it by the shaking movements of the structure and by the voices heard to issue from within. Ventriloquism may be used in this connection. Hallowell says "the Saulteaux conjurer belongs to the 'non-inspired' type of [shaman] in which the spirits speak *to* or *in the presence of* the shaman rather than enter his body and speak *through him*" (p. 12). It is only in the context of this classification that Hallowell refers to the Saulteaux conjurer as *shaman*. Almost 50 years later, that term is still under some dispute. The Saulteaux conjurer exhibits none of the characteristics of the prototypical Siberian shaman: the spirit journey, initiatory illness involving experiences of death and rebirth, the capacity to fly or to be transformed into animals, ecstatic experience, the position of charismatic leader in a hunting and gathering society, and so on. (see Eliade, 1964; Húltkrantz, 1966, Winkelman, 1989; Wright 1989). On the other hand, the Saulteaux conjurer is a healer who deals with spirits on behalf of his community, the economy of which is based on hunting, fishing and gathering; all characteristics of role incumbents referred to as "shaman" elsewhere. Also, the conjurer does not seek his position, but rather it is the spirits who select him — in dreams, or at earlier times — in a solicited dream in the course of a vision quest.

What does the Saulteaux conjurer experience? How does Hallowell account for his performance? In this connection, Hallowell (1942) notes that "Shirokogoroff [1935] says that the Tungus shaman 'falls into ecstasy.' So far as I know, nothing of the sort is believed to happen to Saulteaux conjurers, nor do I think that trance actually takes place" (p. 13).

The problem of ascertaining the presence or absence of trance is of course compounded by the fact that the conjurer is shielded from the audience's view by being concealed in the lodge. The only evidence of trance would have to come from his own report and, perhaps, from the qualities and characteristics of the voices heard. In some sense, by hiding the conjurer, the lodge acts in a manner analogous to masks in other cultures. There, too, the face and often the body of the masker cannot be seen and his experience (and maskers are almost always males) must be inferred from the individual's statements (for example, Prince, 1964).

Hallowell (1942) also notes that "the belief that a spirit may enter the body of a human being and control his behavior is as foreign to most New World cultures as it is conspicuous in many Old World ones" (1942, p. 14*n*). In support of this assertion he refers to Boas (1925) and to Oesterreich's (1930) monumental study of possession. This contrast between the new world and the old has since been confirmed statistically

(Bourguignon and Evascu, 1976) on the basis of a large sample of world cultures. In a comparison of six major world areas, the greatest, statistically significant contrast appeared between North America, where possession trance is rare, and sub-Saharan Africa, where it is very widespread.

By contrast, visionary trance (not linked to a belief in possession) is virtually universal in North America and rare in Africa. In his writings, as we have just seen, Hallowell clearly distinguishes between "trance" as something that "takes place" (that is, behavior, or experience), and spirit possession as a belief. Moreover, it is a belief that accounts for changes in behavior, not in health status or power. That is, he is talking about "possession trance," which combines a belief with a change in behavior, in contrast to trance, which occurs in the absence of such belief. Whereas evidence of trance, such as among the Tungus, is open to observation by the shaman's audience, including the ethnographer, evidence of the existence of a belief in spirit possession can come only from statements of informants. The Northern Algonkin, including the Saulteaux, had no such belief to account for the conjurer's dealings with the spirits.

The special case of the *windigo* needs to be mentioned here. Hallowell (1938) said that the Saulteaux "believe that human beings can be *transformed* into cannibals [*windigo*] by sorcerers" (p. 31, italics added). However, Teicher (1960), in his broad survey, also found possession of humans by a windigo regarded as an explanation for the existence of windigo (cannibalistic) behavior. He quotes, among others, Thompson, who says with reference to a case reported to him that the father of a young man at Lake of the Woods "called the men to a Council . . . their decision was that an Evil Spirit had entered into him [the young man] and was in full possession of him to make him become a man eater (a Weeteego)." Thompson further comments on this case by saying: "The word Weeteego is one of the names of the Evil Spirit and when he gets possession of any man (women are wholly exempt from it) he becomes a man eater" (quoted in Teicher 1960, pp. 46–47). Note the shift in this report from "an Evil Spirit" to "the Evil Spirit" — whereas the first may be any wicked spirit, the second seems to refer to the Devil. Also, there is a difference between "gets possession of" and "enters into." Much of the reporting of native beliefs, when rendered only in English, may be tainted both by the language and the beliefs of writers. Because belief in demonic possession is a prominent feature of the Judeo-Christian tradition, the possibility of such a distortion in reports of this type should not be overlooked (cf. Bourguignon and Pettay, 1965). On the basis of reports such as Thompson's, Teicher, (1960) is led to the conclusion that "windigo is comparable to demoniacal possession" (p. 111), and that "the windigo concept appears to be a unique example of this phenomenon [i.e., belief in spirit possession] in the Americas" (p. 112). However, other examples do in fact occur in the ethnographic literature of North America.

How, then, does Hallowell account for the conjurers' performance? He does not believe them to be charlatans or impostors. Nor does he himself believe in the reality of the spirits heard from the conjuring lodge. He denies neither the honesty of the men nor the possibility of an actual validating experience. However, as we have seen, he does not believe that trance occurs. His answer is subtle and complex. With hindsight, we can see how Hallowell's later thinking about the self and its behavioral environment is rooted in his field observations and in his conversations with his informants. The conjurers, first of all, were men who had experienced a culturally appropriate call. In earlier times, this took the form of a dream blessing during the puberty fast. (The line between dream and vision in this setting is difficult to define in the retrospective reports of informants. However, Hallowell speaks of this experience as a dream.) In more recent times, the call came in a series of four dreams – unsolicited, nighttime dreams that provided the validation and the instructions for the act of conjuring. In some reports, this included foreseeing the case a conjurer would encounter and the reasons for the illness in question. Hallowell (1942, p. 73) notes that "a conjuring performance provides perceptual evidence for the reality of spiritual beings." It does so both for the performer and the witnesses. All present see the tent, or lodge, shake, putatively by winds that enter it, hear the voices of the spirits and can, in fact, engage them in conversation.

Conjurers themselves had witnessed such performances by others, which probably constitutes at least part of their preparation for this role. The conjurers or former conjurers to whom Hallowell spoke were themselves not skeptics. Quite to the contrary, he tells us, and the passage is well worth citing in full:

As individuals these conjurers had played a role that had been set up by their culture. And they had played it successfully . . . They unconsciously invested the act of conjuring with an emotional aura which was experienced as if some objective forces were involved. Such an emotional vortex is not an unfamiliar psychological phenomenon, and while it may verge on the abnormal in certain types of personalities, individuals with certain creative gifts are well acquainted with it. . . . To play a role successfully that is thoroughly validated by the ideology and values of any human society is only to act a part in the sense that we all act a part. The successful conjurer thoroughly identifies himself with his role. The approved means are part of the total situation and inseparable from it. When as outsiders we raise questions about insincerity and fraud, therefore, it simply indicates that we find it impossible to penetrate and understand the behavioral world in which these Indians live [Hallowell, 1942, pp. 75–76].

The "approved means" seem to refer to sleight-of-hand, ventriloquism, or whatever "tricks" are required by the situation. One is reminded of the story of the Kwakiutl sorcerer Quesalid, published by Boas (1930) and retold by Lévi-Strauss (1949) in his famous article "The Sorcerer and His Magic." Unlike Quesalid, who originally was a skeptic, the Saulteaux conjurers believe in their magic—the reality of the spirits and of their interaction with them. One conjurer told Hallowell that he had indeed shaken the lodge himself and produced the voices that the people outside heard. But while admitting this, the conjurer also said that though it was night time and dark outside, inside the lodge was brightly lit, that he saw *wisakedjak,* who told him the cause of the patient's illness, and what to do. Of these visions Hallowell says that they were real from the standpoint of the man's behavioral world. "Yet," Hallowell (1942) remarks, "we know that psychologically speaking, these were in the nature of projections" (p. 78). And, with a slight change in tone and meaning, he adds: "On that occasion he was truly inspired!" We appear to be dealing here with altered visual and auditory perceptions and with a heightened emotional state that brings together the conjurer's cultural knowledge of how conjuring works, what the experience of the performance is, and his awareness of the community expectations concerning illness. Might this not be what is principally involved in many types of shamanism and what others have called "trance"? Winkelman (1989) notes that the trance of the North American shaman is typically "light." Perhaps this might be better described, as Price-Williams (1987) suggest, following French psychiatry, as a "waking dream" (rêve éveillé)?[1]

Sleight-of-hand and trance (or possession trance) are, of course, not mutually exclusive. And sleight-of-hand as part of ritual and as an adjuvant to religious belief has very wide distribution,[2] and is by no means limited to shamanism. In the case of the Saulteaux conjurer, the

---

[1]The term appears also in Breuer and Freud (1895) in reference to the case of Anna O.
[2]See Oz (1989) for a description of the miracle of the Greek fire at Easter in Jerusalem.

hidden nature of the performance is relevant to this issue. A shaman who acts in full view of his audience, as is the case among the Tungus, is likely to be called upon to give more dramatic evidence of his contact with spirits in his person. Among the Saulteaux, the lodge itself gives this evidence by shaking, and does so, it is tempting to say, in lieu of the conjurer, tremors of either a fine or a gross nature being one of the most typical bodily manifestations of trance (see Simons, Erwin, & Prince, 1988, and Ervin, Palmour, Pearson Murphy, Prince, & Simons, 1988 for a discussion).

Noll (1985) has suggested that visions in shamanism may be the result of "mental imagery cultivation," that is, training in visualization. There is, however, no evidence of such practices among the Saulteaux. What appears to be more to the point is Hallowell's reference to the imaginative and symbolic transformation of experience, which translates aspects of the environment inhabited by the Saulteaux into other-than-human persons, with whom communication in human language is possible, and who may be addressed by kinship terms. The beings the conjurer sees in the lodge are not strangers but persons with whom there exists previous acquaintance, if not familiarity.

In a later paper, when he had developed his ideas concerning the self, the culturally constituted behavioral environment, and the behavioral dimensions of human evolution, Hallowell (1966) wrote on the subject of dreams in an evolutionary framework and about dreams among the Ojibwa from the perspective of their social and cultural use within their behavioral environment, including their relations with other-than-human persons. For the Ojibwa, as in many traditional cultures, dreams are actual experiences of the self. He notes that in their "mode of cultural adaptation . . . man's capacity for dreaming has been made an integral part of [their] life adjustment" (p. 261). It is part of their cognitive adaptation. Dreams are one of several situations of contact between humans and spirits. They included, in earlier times, dreams (or visions) induced during the puberty fast that granted power to young men. Other contacts with spirits occurred during conjuring, as we have seen, and in myths. These, Hallowell tells us, are not perceived by the people as fiction. Rather, myths, like the spirits that appear in them, are referred to as "our grandfathers" (p. 268). The spirits appearing in myths and dreams are culturally defined as crucial to practical survival in activities such as in hunting or curing; they reaffirmed traditional knowledge and strengthened confidence. Under traditional conditions, spirits might also be perceived in ordinary waking life, where some experiences, as reported anecdotally, might be interpreted as spirit encounters. Among the highly acculturated Ojibwa (Chippewa) of Wisconsin, I was told in 1946 by a young woman of encounters with her dead father's spirit after he had been burnt to death in his house:

> If I was walking some place alone, I used to hear him whistle. He had lots of pet names for me. It got so I could understand his whistle. I used to go out in the woods all the time. Just sit in a tree. Two times my mother lost me. They found me in a swamp some place. It was in the winter time. I never knew what I was doing. . . . It seems like I was the only one he was around after he died. He bothered me. I could hardly breathe, my ears were ringing . . . just couldn't move [Bourguignon, 1956, pp. 3–4].

To this young woman, and to her grandfather, a member of the Medicine Society, these were real experiences, not auditory hallucinations. Though idiosyncratic, they fit into the larger picture Hallowell has given us, where, as in the conjuring lodge, many of the contacts with spirits are auditory in nature.

When Hallowell (1966) turned to the study of dreams, substantial systematic research on dreams and sleep had been made possible by technological innovations, and the subject had taken strong empirical and biophysical shape. He therefore wondered "whether systematic observations on living infrahuman primates would yield any of the objective indicators of dreaming which have been observed in man" (p. 258), noting the important anthropological implications of "a consideration of dreams in an evolutionary frame of reference" (p. 258). In this connection, he goes on to say that the "new behavioral plateau, characterized by language and fully developed forms of cultural adaptation was also that which enabled dreams, visions and products of imaginative processes to be articulated and thus assume the social significance we find in *Homo sapiens*" (p. 259). It is not only the capacities for, and experience of, intrapsychic phenomena that is of importance here (dreams, visions, imaginative processes) but the ability to share these with others. In doing so, common sets of meanings, relating both to the self and to the culturally constituted behavioral environment, are developed over time. More recently, Tedlock (1987) and contributors to a volume on dreams and dreaming have termed emphasis on dream sharing, and communication through dream sharing a "new direction" in the anthropology of dreams. In Hallowell's (1966) words:

[o]nce in possession of psychological capacities, which made symbolic modes of personal expression and communication possible, the inner life of individuals could take on new personal significance and be communicated to others through verbal and graphic means. The inner world of private experience and the outer world of publicly shared experience, now became intricately meshed through symbolic representation. Unconscious psychological forces, hitherto latent in hominid evolution, but now mediated through dreams, visions and other imaginative processes, intruded themselves upon man . . . [p. 269].

When we study contemporary cultures, we find long established, ongoing systems of interpretations of experience, including dreams. These are modified over time by new experiences of individuals and groups. For the Saulteaux, dreams of the puberty fast and private dreams as well as conjurer's experiences in the lodge were both culturally stylized and individually modified. In time, the vision quest disappeared and so did conjuring. The public function of dreams and dreaming as established in the traditional culture was lost.

The question Hallowell raises with regard to the study of dreams in an evolutionary framework can be considered with equal justification with regard to altered (or alternate) states of consciousness (ASC), a broad, all-encompassing concept that came into use in the 1960s. We know from holocultural research that upward of 90% of preindustrial societies institutionalized one or more types of ASC within a religious context (Bourguignon, 1973; Bourguignon and Evascu, 1976). Paraphrasing Hallowell's comment on dreams cited earlier, we may then say that in their "mode of cultural adaptation . . . man's capacity for *ASCs* has been made an integral part of [their] life adjustment" (Hallowell, 1966, p. 271). The expressions of alterations of consciousness are structured in human societies within their culturally constituted behavioral environments: The manner in which ASC are induced and terminated, the content of the experience, the manifestation of the experience, the uses to which the experiential and behavioral changes are put, and the types of ASCs themselves all show a broad range of variations. Yet, like dreams, which themselves may be considered manifestations of certain types of ASC, namely particular forms of sleep, ASCs, however culturally structured, are limited by psychobiological parameters. Belief systems, as expressed in language and shared through verbal and other symbolic means, encourage and structure ASC experiences and their culturally patterned expressions. Goodenough (1990) explored at some length the evolution of the human capacity for beliefs and this capacity's linkage to the evolution of language, arguing that important aspects of both beliefs and of language were present prior to the emergence of *Homo sapiens.* Earlier, Hockett (1960) and Hockett and Ascher (1964) explored the evolution of language, analyzing it into a series of "design features," most of which are found in the communication systems of other species.

As with Hallowell's statement regarding dreams, we can similarly note concerning ASC that whatever private experiences existed on a prehuman level, with language and the symbolic transformation of experience, these could be shared, communicated, culturally patterned, and integrated into a culturally structured, public symbolic system. Ultimately, they could be made use of for social ends.

What evidence is there that the roots of ASCs we observe in human cultures go back to a precultural past? There is, to my knowledge, no systematic study of this subject. Yet a number of leads exist that we may explore. In humans, ASCs are induced in a variety of ways in ritual contexts and occur in ordinary life situations as well as in contexts of pathology. The most exhaustive classification of ASCs is that of Ludwig (1972, 1968), which has been widely cited. Ludwig (1972) defines ASCs as "any mental state(s) induced by various physiological, psychological or pharmacological maneuvers or agents" recognized subjectively or by an observer as a "sufficient deviation in subjective experience of psychological functioning . . . from [that of] alert, waking consciousness" (p. 10). If we limit ourselves to objective norms established by observers and for the moment forgo evidence of subjective experience, we can locate animal evidence. Ludwig lists five broad categories of methods of induction of ASCs: (1) Reduction of exteroceptive stimulation and/or motor activity (here he includes among many other types of ASC also sleep and related phenomena such as dreaming); (2) increase of exteroceptive stimulation and/or motor activity and/or emotion; (3) increased alertness or mental activity; (4) decreased alertness or relaxation of critical faculties; and finally (5) presence of somatopsychological factors. These include a vast array of factors ranging from fevers and states resulting from various types of physiological malfunction to changes produced by the administration of diverse sorts of drugs. Given such a broad definition of ASC and such diverse, and contradictory methods of induction, a great array of states is covered. We may therefore look for sources of ASCs as exhibited by humans in religious contexts in a number of different types of animal behavior. Drug research, like other biomedical research, has been carried on with various mammalian species (mice, rats, guinea pigs, monkeys), providing information on physiological, as well as behavioral, changes produced by psychoactive substances (for example, Jacobs, 1984). To the extent that animals in the wild eat fermented fruit, or hallucinogenic plants, or suffer from fever, hyper- or hypoglycemia, and so on, the physiological bases of ASCs are present. They also exist in the phenomena of sleep. Moreover, the fact that fermented fruit is attractive to various species of birds and monkeys, for example, suggests that these are pleasurable experiences that these animals learn to seek out.

Lewis-Williams and Dawson (1988), state flatly:

> The strong evidence that chimpanzees, baboons, monkeys, cats, dogs and other animals hallucinate suggests that altered states of consciousness are a function of the mammalian, not just the human nervous system and that "non-real" visual percepts were experienced long before the Upper Paleolithic. Indeed, australopithecenes probably hallucinated [p. 202].

They then go on to state that "the nervous system is a human universal" and that they accept that "by the Upper Paleolithic it was much the same as it is now" (p. 202). They are, however, cautious to note that, because "cultural expectations inform the imagery to a considerable extent," the content of early human imagery remains problematic (see also Lewis-Williams and Dawson, 1989). In other words, whereas we can be fairly sure of the existence of mental imagery not only in early *Homo sapiens* but in other mammals as well, in humans, culture is relevant to the way in which this imagery is perceived. In this connection, Lewis-Williams and Dawson distinguish between entoptic phenomena and iconic hallucinations. The latter, according to Lewis-Williams and Dawson (1988), "have no foundation in the actual structure of the optic system" and include "iconic visions of culturally controlled items" (p. 202). Entoptic phenomena, however, first studied by Klüver (1926), are luminous percepts generated by the visual system independent of external light sources. Lewis-Williams and Dawson (1988) note that "in altered states the nervous system itself . . . produces a variety of images including entoptic phenomena" (p. 203). Thus, for these authors, the presence of entoptics, without regard to other aspects of an individual's psychological or physiological condition, establishes the existence of an altered state of consciousness. Scintillating and other types of scotomata, for example, are often associated with migraine. Sacks (1985) presents extensive descriptions and illustrations, as provided by patients, of the patterns seen. He recognizes some specific types of frequently reported features of migrainous scotomata: shimmering lights, wavy lines, zigzag patterns ("fortifications"), and so on. He refers to these as hallucinations and notes that some patients interpret the forms they see. He discusses the medieval mystic, Hildegard von Bingen, who left drawings of her visions. These, Sacks (1985) says "were indisputably migrainous" (p. 106). Interestingly, these were drawn, described, and presumably experienced by her in interpreted form, invested with allegorical and mystical meanings. In Sacks's words: "They provide a unique example in which a physiological event, banal, hateful, or meaningless in the vast majority of people, can become, in a privileged consciousness, the substrate of a supreme, ecstatic inspiration" (p. 108).

Both Sacks and Lewis-Williams and Dawson are speaking of the graphic representation of entoptic phenomena. In the case of Hildegard von Bingen, the mythic and symbolic elaboration is clear and explicit. Her paintings are part of her theological expositions.[3] In the case of Upper Paleolithic nonfigurative art, we only have the authors' speculation that it is, in fact, entoptics that we are dealing with, and if indeed this is what we have, we still don't know anything about the meaning and cultural content associated with them. In this connection it is interesting to note that, among American Op artists of the 1960s, optical phenomena were at times used and on occasion, it would appear, intentionally provoked. Here no cultural meanings, other than those of an aesthetic type, were intended. Lewis-Williams and Dawson are interested in the possibility of a connection between entoptics as evidence of an ASC in the context of shamanism and shamanistic art. Hildegard von Bingen (Sacks, 1985) describes her experience in the following terms:

The visions which I saw I beheld neither in sleep, nor in dreams, nor with my carnal eyes, nor with the ears of the flesh, nor in hidden places; but wakeful, alert, and with the eyes of the spirit and the inward ears. I perceived them in open view and according to the will of God [p. 106].

Summarizing the literature on the subject, Lewis-Williams and Dawson (1988) defined three stages in the development of mental

---

[3]Sacks bases his descriptions of Hildegard von Bingen's migraine visions on previous work by Singer (1958). Their analyses have not gone unchallenged. Critics fail to note that the migraine explanation of the visions does not address the theological meanings Hildegard von Bingen, and others, drew from them, nor does it devalue them. One who accepts Singer's and Sacks's analysis is Flanagan (1989), in her important, recent biography of Hildegard von Bingen.

imagery during ASC, moving from entoptics to an elaboration of the percepts, into iconic forms by which subjects attempt to make sense of what they see, and finally, in experimental settings, using LSD or mescaline, entoptics are replaced altogether by iconic hallucinations. Experimental research, as well as reports of subjects undergoing spontaneous experiences, show that hallucinations of this type may be produced by various stimuli, ranging from hallucinogenic drugs to sensory deprivation. In the latter case, they are produced, in terms of Ludwig's 1972 classification, through "reduced exteroceptive stimulation and/or motor activity" (p. 13). As LaBarre (1970) and Henney (1973) have shown, sensory deprivation experiments of the 1950s, which produced hallucinations, exhibited much similarity to the practices of the North American puberty fast and other methods for obtaining visions and supernatural contacts (as practiced in many cultures). In so far as entoptic phenomena imply altered states of consciousness and form a potential basis for iconic hallucinations, a continuity between humans and other mammals is implied.

Another perspective on the evolutionary dimension of ASC may be found in the study of play. Susan Parman (1977) suggested that dreams and play are based on a common neurophysiological process. The biologically adaptive significance of both lies not in their symbolic dimension, which is unique to *Homo sapiens*. Dreams in sleep and play in waking life, she argues, are similar in that both meet the need for neurophysiological arousal, the disruption, or discontinuity of, synchrony. Parmen (1977) notes the "correlation between evolutionary advancement ([that is] . . . the development of a complex nervous system) and the elaboration and frequency of play" (p. 25). For Roger Caillois (1961) the element of *ilinx* (vertigo), with its temporary loss of control and associated thrill, is a key element in play. Consider the popularity of roller-coasters and horror films. Vertigo-creating and thrill-seeking behavior are frequently found in the induction of altered states as well as in play. These may range from light-headedness produced by sweat baths as part of the preparation for the puberty fast in North American, to whirling and spinning to induce possession trance in Haitian *vodoun* or Brazilian *umbanda,* or in the rituals of so-called whirling dervishes. Euphoria following psychological stress, such as that expressed in thrill-seeking behavior, like that resulting from physical stress (as in the so-called jogger's high), has been related to the production of endorphins (endogenous opiates). These substances have been studied in experimental animals, as has play activity.

Another type of ASC has also been studied from the perspective of animal behavior and animal models. The British psychiatrist William Sargant, in a series of well-known books (1957, 1967, 1974), explored intensively what he referred to as "religious and non-religious possession" (Sargant, 1974, p. xi). He likened "possession" (i.e., possession trance) and religious conversion to both brain washing and abreactive shock treatment, which he himself had used with World War II psychiatric casualties. This work was based on that of Pavlov, whose experiments with dogs had led him to the formulation of the concept of "transmarginal inhibition," resulting from excessive excitation or stress. Sargant (1974) defined it as "state of brain activity which can produce a marked increase in hysterical suggestibility" (p. 13). It first brings about a loss of learned behavior and then, given the heightened suggestibility, an opportunity for rapid new learning. Sargant interprets a broad range of religious activities in these terms. He is particularly interested in the collapse that is frequently seen at the end of a ritual possession trance and is induced by the excitement and stress of the ritual activity. All of these phenomena belong to Ludwig's (1972) category of "increased exteroceptive stimulation, motor activity and/or emotion." On the basis of their induction, these ASCs are quite distinct from those involving visions or hallucinations. Given the work of Pavlov, it appears that, in terms of Sargant's model, there is here also continuity between human and animal behavior.

Focussing on psychophysiological methods of induction and on biological manifestation of ASCs makes considerations of an evolutionary continuity between humans and other mammals reasonable, if not, indeed, obvious. The question, however, arises, how these physiological and neurological events are turned into materials for cultural use, indeed use that, in one form or another, is virtually universal. Unlike food, sex, and the sleep phenomena of dreams, ASCs as defined by their methods of induction, are not universal human experiences, although they appear spontaneously in at least some individuals, in potentially and probably all populations.

These behaviors and experiences, when they do occur spontaneously, represent deviations from normal, ordinary wakefulness, and, as responses to stress, are often frankly pathological. Winkelman (1989) attempted to explain behavior Sargant attributes to "transmarginal inhibition" as due to temporal lobe activity, that is, as epileptoid in nature. This is in contrast to visionary types of trance experiences deliberately induced either by drugs or through techniques of sensory deprivation. Gussler (1973) showed striking parallels between Southern Bantu possession illness (*ukuthwasa*) and symptoms of pellagra. However, Schwartz (1976) criticized the view taken by Wallace (1966) that religious trance behavior is indeed pathological. Schwartz prefers to speak of the behavior as "pathomimetic," (p. 184) arguing that such religious behavior is patterned on pathological models but not itself pathological. Jilek (1971) similarly speaks of "ritualized pathomorphic" (p. 32) rather than pathological states. This is strikingly confirmed by the observation that the disorders for which help is sought in possession trance cults are generally not of the type mimicked by the possession trance performance. For example, reproductive or marital problems of women are likely to play a significant role (see Boddy, 1989 for this in connection with the zar cult in the Northern Sudan).

The question now becomes: Why are pathological states used as models for ritualized states? Pathology of these types is likely to occur in primates outside of experimental conditions. Ritualized pathomimetic or pathomorphic states, on the other hand, clearly represent a human phenomenon.

Ludwig (1972) gives us not only a list of the methods through which ASCs are produced, but also a series of characteristics of ASCs as experienced. These provide us with clues for an understanding of their transformation from painful experiences into valued ones. He offers the following experiences: alterations of thinking, disturbed time sense, loss of control, change in emotional expressions, change in body image, perceptual distortion, change in meaning or significance, sense of the ineffable, feeling of rejuvenation, hypersuggestibility. Some of these can be seen in animal experiments, for example, hypersuggestibility (that is, ease of new learning) in Pavlov's dogs. Others, such as change in meaning or significance, require articulation of meaning or significance in symbolic terms. What in Pavlov's dogs, other experimental animals, or animals in the wild are internal, private experiences, frequently of a pathological nature, in humans, are turned into materials for cultural elaboration. Through language and other symbolic systems, including the evolution of beliefs, interpretations and secondary elaborations of the experience are to be expected and sharing of the experience is made possible. Sharing involves its own rules, requiring a degree of processing, and varying degrees of stylization and transformation; it also requires the choice of a medium of sharing. This, in turn, provides a template for others who may then experience a derived, pathomimetic version of the original spontaneous event. In Hallowell's (1972) terms, noted earlier, the individual's "own imaginative interpretations are fed back" (p. 59) into the personal and cultural adjustment of the individual and the group to a behavioral environment so constructed.

If the experience is private, as in dreams or visions, the medium may be verbal or graphic. In the shaman's performance, a public demonstration is given of the existence of the spirits and of the shaman's interaction with them. In possession trance cults, particularly widespread in sub-Saharan Africa, Afro-America, and Southeast Asia, such performances involve the enactment of complex roles, in which the spirits speak and act *through* their human hosts. If the ASCs used for ritualized communications between humans and the spirit entities that inhabit their behavioral environments are indeed pathomimetic, societies at different levels of complexity, characterized by different trance types (Bourguignon, 1973; Winkelman, 1989), appear to be using different pathological states on which to pattern their ASCs.

A number of features of possession trance performances are notable in the context of the present discussion. We may highlight these by contrasting them to the Ojibwa conjurer's performance. Although the conjurer works alone, for an audience, there are always many participants in possession trance cults. Whereas the Ojibwa conjurer is a man, the majority of possession trancers are almost always reported to be women. And whereas the spirits that inhabit the behavioral world of the Ojibwa and who appear in the conjurer's lodge are, or represent, animals, those of the possession trance cults have decidedly human attributes and represent humans, usually ancestors or foreigners. For example, Boddy (1989) described the zar spirits that are impersonated by women of one village in Northern Sudan. They are generally male or, in some instances, prostitutes, and belong to various types of foreign groups. The Ojibwa need to "deal with" animals as hunters. The behavioral environment of these Sudanese women includes a broad range of foreign human groups, whose identities they attempt to come to terms with by enacting their stereotypical roles.

Thus, the human potential for altered states of consciousness is put to varying uses, depending on the culturally constituted behavioral world a particular group lives in, and on the needs of the society. These needs reflect subsistence economy, social structure, contacts with other inhabitants of the behavioral environment, both human and other-than-human persons. Moreover, the people who will act out the socially and culturally significant models by means of ASCs will also vary: Men (and sometimes old women) among the Saulteaux, women in agricultural villages and their urban derivatives. Boddy (1989 p. 354) argued that through possession trance, enacting spirit roles, these Sudanese "women might step outside their world and gain perspective on their lives." The experience may help them deal with their problems and thus be therapeutic. What is also important in the context of the present discussion is the observation that new spirits appear on the scene from time to time, make new demands, and thus change the picture of the world they dramatize. The women thereby revise and reconstruct their behavioral environment and provide a tool for dealing with it, not only psychologically and perceptually, but often in practical terms. Nor is this flux and transformation of behavior and belief in possession trance cults unique to this one example. It occurs over and over again in the literature.

## CONCLUSIONS

An attempt to follow in Hallowell's footsteps has led us to consider altered states of consciousness as he considered dreams as behavior that emerged in human evolutionary history, with roots in mammalian biology and transformed into significant features of human life through the emergence of such features as the symbolic transformation of experience and the capacity to share intrapsychic, subjective states. In contrast to dreams, however, these widespread ritualized phenomena build frequently on models that derive from pathological states. Moreover, depending on the needs of particular types of cultures, different models are chosen: hallucinations in the case of visionary trance ("shamanism") and dramatic changes in behavior (possession trance), whether due to temporal lobe involvement, transmarginal inhibition, pellagra, or other types of stress-induced states, in societies with larger populations and more complex social organizations. One of the important functions of ritualized altered states we have noted is their contribution to the development and modification of a group's culturally constituted behavioral environment, by feeding back personal experience, imagination and creativity into personal adjustment and cultural adaptation; they act as coping mechanisms, both for the individual and the society. In some instances, as in the well-documented case of Hildegard von Bingen and the contribution of ritualized altered states to her writings and musical compositions, personal creativity, imagination and capacity for artistic and philosophical innovation is seen to be of a very high level indeed. The personal contribution becomes one of cultural and historical significance when it is integrated into an existing body of knowledge and belief, in the context of a certain world view, value system, and artistic style.

Sacks's (1985) comment, cited earlier, narrowly refers to the art and religious experience of one exceptional woman. However, to the extent that bodily experience represents the substrate of, and model for, a great deal of what anthropologists study as culture, it can serve as a broad generalization. Moreover, with regard to ASC, personal physiological events, spontaneous or induced, many of which are indeed "banal, hateful or meaningless" (p. 108) in and of themselves, are much of the stuff that the symbolic dimensions of culture, religion, and art are made of.

In Hallowell's evolutionary terms, here too, what is individual, internal, private in other animals, in the presence of systems of external shared symbolization, is turned into raw material for culture-building.

### BIBLIOGRAPHY

BOAS, F. (1925), America and the old world. *Proceedings, International Congress of Americanists,* pp. 21–28. Goteborg.

\_\_\_\_\_ (1930), *The Religion of the Kwakiutl.* Columbia University Contributions to Anthropology, Vol. 10, Part 2, pp. 1–41.

BODDY, J. (1989), *Wombs and Alien Spirits: Women, Men and the Zar Cult in Northern Sudan.* Madison WI: University of Wisconsin Press.

BOURGUIGNON, E. (1956), A life history of an Ojibwa young woman. In: *Microcard Publications of Primary Records in Culture and Personality, I* ed. B. Kaplan. Madison WI: The Microcard Foundation pp. 1–9.4.

\_\_\_\_\_ (1973), Introduction: A framework for the comparative study of altered states of consciousness. In: *Religion, Altered States of Consciousness and Social Change.* ed. E. Bourguignon. Columbus: Ohio State University Press, pp. 3–35.

\_\_\_\_\_ T.L. EVASCU (1976), Altered states of consciousness within a general evolutionary perspective: A holocultural analysis. *Beh. Sci. Res.* 12:197–216.

\_\_\_\_\_ L. PETTAY (1965), Spirit possession, trance and cross-cultural research. In: *Symposium on New Approaches to Religion.* ed. M.E. Spiro *Proceedings of the 1964 Annual Spring Meeting of the American Ethnological Society.* Seattle, WA: AES, pp. 38–49.

BREUER, J. & FREUD, S., (1895) Studies on hysteria. *Standard Edition,* 2. London: Hogarth Press, 1955.

CAILLOIS, R. (1961), *Man, Play, and Games.* New York: Free Press.

ELIADE, M.(1964), *Shamanism: Archaic Techniques of Ecstasy.* Princeton, NJ: Princeton University Press.

ERVIN, F.R., PALMOUR, R.M., PEARSON MURPHY, B.E., PRINCE, R., & SIMONS, R.C. (1988), The psychobiology of trance / II: Physiological and endocrine correlates. *Transcult. Psychiat. Res. Rev., 25:267–284.*

FLANAGAN, S.(1989), *Hildegard von Bingen, 1098–1179: A Visionary Life.* London: Routledge.

GOODENOUGH, W.H.(1990), Evolution of the human capacity for beliefs. *Amer. Anthropolog.* 92:957–612.

GUSSLER, J.D. (1973), Social change, ecology and spirit possession among the South African Nguni. In: *Religion, Altered States of Consciousness and Social Change.* ed. E. Bourguignon. Columbus, OH: Ohio State University Press, pp. 88–126.

HALLOWELL, A.I. (1934), Culture and Mental Disorder, *J. Abn. Soc. Psychol.*, 29:1-9.
_____ 1938), Fear and anxiety as cultural and individual variables in a primitive society. *J. Soc. Psychol.*, 10:25-47.
_____ (1939), The child, the savage and human experience. In: *Proceedings of the Sixth Institute on the Exceptional Child.* Woods School, Lanhorne, PA, pp. 8-34, 1955. Reprinted as The recapitulation theory and culture. In: *Culture and Experience.* Philadelphia.
_____ (1942), The role of conjuring in Saulteaux society. *Publications of the Philadelphia Anthropological Society, Volume 2.*
_____ (1948), Introduction: Handbook of psychological leads for ethnological fieldworkers. *In: Personal Character and the Cultural Milieu: A Collection of Readings.* ed. D.G. Haring. Syracuse, NY: Syracuse University Press, pp. 341-388, 1956.
_____ (1950a), Personality structure and the evolution of man. *Amer. Anthropol.* 52:159-173.
_____ (1950b), Values acculturation, and mental health. *Amer. J. Orthopsychiat.* 20:732-743.
_____ (1955), *Culture and Experience.* Philadelphia: University of Pennsylvania Press.
_____ (1960), Ojibwa ontology, behavior, and world view. In: *Culture and History: Essays in Honor of Paul Radin,* ed. S. Diamond. New York: Columbia University Press, pp. 19-52.
_____ (1965), Hominid evolution, cultural adaptation and mental dysfunctioning. Ciba Foundation Symposium. *Transcul. Psychiat.,* ed. A.V.S. de Reuch & R. Parker. London: J. & A. Churchill, pp. 26-54.
_____ (1966), The role of dreams in Ojibwa culture. In: *The Dream in Human Societies,* eds. G.E. von Grunebaum & R. Caillois. Berkeley: University of California Press, pp. 267-292.
_____ (1972), On being an anthropologist. In: *Crossing Cultural Boundaries,* eds. S.T. Kimball & J.B. Watson. New York: Chandler, pp. 51-62.
_____ REYNOLDS, E.L. (1942), Biological factors in family structure. In: *Marriage and the Family* eds. H. Becker & R. Hill. Boston: Heath, pp. 25-46.
HENNEY, J.H. (1973), The shakers of St. Vincent: A stable religion. In: *Religion, Altered States of Consciousness and Social Change.* ed. E. Bourguignon. Columbus, OH: Ohio State University Press, pp. 219-263.
HOCKETT, C. (1960), The origins of speech. *Scien. Amer.,* 203:88-96.
_____ R. ASCHER (1964), The human revolution. *Current Anthropol.,* 5:135-147.
HULTKRANTZ, A. (1966), The ecological and phenomenological aspects of shamanism. In: *Shamanism in Siberia* eds. B. Dioszegi and B. Hoppal. Budapest: Akademiai Kiado, pp. 27-58.
JACOBS, B. L., ED.(1984), *Hallucinogens: Neurochemical, Behavioral and Clinical Perspectives.* New York: Raven Press.
JILEK, G. W.(1971), From crazy witchdoctor to auxiliary psychotherapist: The changing image of the medicine man. *Psychiat. Clinica,* 4:220.
KLUVER, H. (1926), Mescal visions and eidetic vision. *Amer. J. Psychol.,* 37:502-515.
LABARRE, W. (1970), *The Ghost Dance: The Origins of Religion.* Garden City, NY: Doubleday.
LEVI-STRAUSS, C. (1939), The sorcerer and his magic. In: *Structural Anthropology* (trans. C. Jacobsen & B. Schoep). New York: Basic Books, pp. 167-185, 1963.
LEWIS-WILLIAMS, J. D. & T. A. DAWSON (1988), The signs of all times: Entoptic phenomena in upper Paleolithic art. *Curr. Anthropol.,* 29:201-246.

_____ (1989). *Images of Power: Understanding Bushman Rock Art.* Johannesburg: Southern Book Publishers.

LUDWIG, A. (1972), Altered states of consciousness. *Arch. Gen. Psychiat.,* 15:225–234. Reprinted in: Altered States of Consciousness, ed. C. T. Tart. New York: Doubleday, pp. 11–24.

_____ (1968), Altered states of consciousness. In: *Trance and Possession* ed. R. Prince. Montreal: R.M. Bucke Memorial Society, pp. 69–96.

NOLL, R. (1985), Mental imagery cultivation as a cultural phenomenon: The role of visions in shamanism. *Curr. Anthropol.,* 64:443–462.

OESTERREICH, T. K. (1930), *Possession, Demonical and Other* (trans. D. Ibberson). New York: University Press, 1966.

OZ, A. (1989), *Jerusalem, City of Mirrors.* Boston: Little, Brown.

PARMAN, S. (1977), An evolutionary theory of dreaming and play. In: *Forms of Play in Native North Americans* eds. E. Norbeck & C. R. Farrer. *Proceedings of the American Ethnological Society.* Seattle WA: West, pp. 17–34.

PRICE-WILLIAMS, D. (1987), The waking dream in ethnographic perspective. In: *Dreaming: Anthropological and Psychological Interpretations* ed. B. Tedlock. Cambridge: Cambridge University Press, pp. 246–262.

PRINCE, R. (1964), Indigenous Yoruba psychiatry. In: *Magic, Faith, and Healing: Studies in Primitive Psychiatry.* ed. A. Kiev. Glencoe, IL: Free Press, pp. 84–120.

SACKS, O. (1985), *Migraine: Understanding a Common Disorder.* Berkeley: University of California Press.

SARGANT, W. (1966), *Battle for the Mind.* London: Heinemann.

_____ (1967), *The Unquiet Mind.* London: Heinemann.

_____ (1974), *The Mind Possessed.* Philadelphia: Lippincott.

SCHWARTZ, T. (1976), The cargo cult: A Melanesian type-response to Change. In: *Responses to Change: Society, Culture, and Personality,* ed. G.A. de Vos. New York: Von Nostrand, pp. 157–206.

SHIROKOGOROFF, S.M. (1935), *The Psychomental Complex of the Tungus.* London: Kegan Paul.

SIMONS, R., ERVIN, F.R., & PRINCE, R. (1988), The psychobiology of trance / I: Training for Thaipusam. *Transcul. Psychiat. Res. Rev.,* 25:249–266.

SINGER, C. (1958), The visions of Hildegard von Bingen. In: *From Magic To Science.* New York: Dover. pp. 199–239.

SPIRO, M.E. (1976), Introduction, Part 4, Ojibwa culture and world view. In: *Contributions to Anthropology.* Chicago: University of Chicago Press, pp. 353–356.

TEDLOCK, B., ed. (1987), *Dreaming: Anthropological and Psychological Interpretations.* Cambridge: Cambridge University Press.

TEICHER, M.I. (1960), Windigo psychosis: A study of a relationship between belief and behavior among the indians of northeastern Canada. *Proceedings of the Annual Spring Meeting of the American Ethnological Society.* Seattle: AES.

WALLACE, A.F.C. (1966), *Religion: An Anthropological View.* New York: Random House.

WINKELMAN, M. (1989), A cross-cultural study of shamanistic healers. *J. Psychoactive Drugs,* 21:17–24.

WRIGHT, P.A. (1989), The nature of shamanistic consciousness: A review. *J. Psychoactive Drugs,* 21:25–34.

# 4

# The Self and Kagwahiv Dreams[1]

## WAUD KRACKE

The self is an elusive concept, yet one that is at the heart of the question of the relationship between psychology and culture. It was a central concept for Hallowell's thought, and his seminal article on it (Hallowell, 1955a) probes many of its complexities, which have become focal in present-day psychoanalytic discussion (Kohut, 1971, 1977; Winnicott 1960). For most of us, the self is at — or is — the center of the experienced world that is the domain of introspective psychology. And when it is not — when the very sense of being a self is problematic — that lack constitutes the most profound kind of psychological pathology, leading to a disruption of the ability to participate in social life. At the same time, sociologists, since George Herbert Mead, have insisted that the self is itself socially patterned, modeled on others' reactions to one and expectations of one.

The basic model of the self in the first view is that of the subjectively experienced bodily self — *"das Ich ist vor allem ein körperliches"* — and develops out of the sense of one's body and the multiple routes of sensory experience one receives about one's own body (simultaneous tactile and visual information about the movement of a limb, for example, whereas one receives only visual information about the movement of an extra-

---

[1]First presented in the symposium "The Body and the Self: The Concrete Philosophy of Person, Self and Psychology in Lowland South America" organized by Anthony Seeger and Waud Kracke at the 79th Annual Meeting of the American Anthropological Association, Washington, DC, December 7, 1980. The present, revised version benefited much from discussions with other participants.

body object). In the second view, the self is more anchored in social relationships, and its development depends more on how one's initiatives and expressions of feeling are mirrored back to one. The first view would stress the universal character of the self as an essential part of human nature, grounded in the infant's earliest experiences of self-discovery: the second stresses the variability of the shape of the self from one family to another and from one culture to another.

A basic methodological issue concerning the self has grown out of attempts to apply the method of psychoanalytic interviewing in widely different cultures. Psychoanalytic interviewing depends entirely on the interviewee's ability and readiness to report introspectively, to observe and verbalize the flow of his feelings and fantasies, including some degree of recognition that the feelings and fantasies are products or inner experiences of the self as differentiated from direct sensory experiences of external reality. Participation in such interviews, therefore, requires some implicit notion, at least, of an experiencing, thinking, and feeling self. Some anthropologists who have tried such interviewing in their fieldwork argue that, in certain cultures, the concept of self is so different from ours that such interviews are impossible. If Lienhardt's (1961) picture of the Dinka self is literally true, for example, and all Dinka emotional experiences are perceived as having their origin in the external world, like sense perceptions, then searching for precursors of a feeling in one's own past emotional life would make no sense at all. If feelings of guilt over a hurt done to a neighbor are conceptualized as a kind of emanation of the fetish Mathiang Gok that the neighbor has put out to entrap anyone who does him harm—a kind of direct sensory experience of its presence—then a Dinka would not be able to identify a feeling of guilt as his own inner response to an act he had performed against someone else. He would not be able to relate the inner response introspectively back to earlier occasions on which he had experienced similar guilt feelings, or back to a childhood experience of learning that such acts against others were wrong. If the Dinka experienced all thoughts and emotions as things outside himself, "happening to him"— his very memories as having a kind of Platonic external existence and acting continually on his life—rather than as products or states *of* the self, then he would not be able to participate actively in the psychoanalytic task of exploring the connections between intrapsychic events, discovering in his perturbations unacknowledged wishes of the self.

What is this "self" that is so important in introspection? As we conceive it, it is an experiencing center of consciousness that has continuity ("cohesion") in space and time, linked to, if not coterminous with, the subjectively experienced body;[2] it is the active subject of thinking, experiencing emotion, attending to outer stimuli, wishing, intending, and initiating activity, as well as a recipient of sense impressions and messages from other selves; and it has more or less distinct boundaries from a region of the subjectively experienced world that is not self, but that contains other (separate) selves, other willful centers of feeling and initiative. Kohut (1977) called it a "delimited, abiding, independent center of initiative" (p. 229).

The term "self" has assumed a central importance in current psychoanalytic discussion, in part through the accident of Strachey's translation of one term of Freud's. Strachey took the very experience-near term "Ich"—*das Ich,* "the 'I' " (perhaps even more experience-near than "self"), which in most usages could most naturally be translated "the self"—and instead turned it into a very experience-distant latinate term, "the ego."[3] It took two generations for psychoanalytic thinkers to work themselves back from the abstractions of ego psychology, via such constructions as "ego-identity," to the concreteness of the concept of "self," now introduced as an "experience-near" concept in counterposition to Freud's *Ich* which is now seen as abstract and "experience-distant" (Kohut, 1971, p. XIV–XV).

The self generally embraces those aspects of experience which can be unmediatedly modified by an exertion of will—such as raising one's arm, suppressing a feeling, concentrating one's thoughts, or perhaps changing one's attitude or belief about something. Also, in our (adult Western) concept of self, we postulate that the self is private—one cannot directly (unmediatedly) gain access to the experiences (perceptions, thoughts, feelings) of any self other than one's own. This, as Hallowell has pointed out, is a conceptualization of self that is not universal. Finally, the organization of experience that we label self is not present from the beginning but is achieved at some struggle at an early age. This is

---

[2]Jacobson (1964) prefers the term "identity" for this aspect of the self.

[3]This translation introduces various problems into the reading of Freud. For example, in "The Ego and the Id," Freud (1923) wrote as if the notion of unconscious Ich posed an inherent self-contradiction. Now, if Freud was posing an abstract entity, which he named the "ego," there appears to be no reason why he should not posit as one of its characteristics that it can be unconscious. Only if you translate it as "self," or "I," does the contradictoriness of "unconscious Ich" become self-evident.

Defenses, too, came to be thought of as abstract entities, "devices" or "mechanisms," rather than as actions of the self to ward off recognition of unacceptable thoughts or wishes. Much of the hypostitization of psychic processes into mental entities to which Shafer's (1976) purism of language is a response may be laid at the door of this distancing and mechanization of Freud's initially experience-near concept.

recognized in many cultures in the explicit division of early childhood into a phase before which the child is not held responsible—has not yet begun to be a person—and an "age of reason" (in Inuit, for example, *ihuma* [Briggs, 1970, pp. 111–113]) after which the child is capable of sufficient self-reflection to begin learning to act according to cultural standards (see also Geertz, 1974, pp. 254–255).

The self is by definition an intrapsychic concept. The term self denotes subjective reflexivity; it is impossible to conceive of "self" without self-awareness. "Self" is in this sense a strictly psychological concept, in contrast to "person," which I see as a sociological term. "Person" implies a view from outside the self; it is the self as presented to others. The person is in interpersonal space; the self is intrapsychic.

This does not mean, though, that culture is irrelevant to the self concept, for language, as Hallowell (1955a) points out, provides the terms for articulating the self and talking about it—beginning early in life with mastery of the first-person pronoun. A whole domain of language and concepts maps out the intrapsychic world of which the self is the center.[4] It is this domain of concepts that I would like to explore for the Kagwahiv.

I cannot in this brief space adequately answer this question for the Kagwahiv. Nor are my data at this point adequate to flesh out all aspects of the Kagwahiv self-experience and of their conception of the self. Indeed, it is doubtful whether anything so intimately personal as one's experience of oneself can be characterized for a group of however many people. I have, however, selected one important domain of experience that I have discussed more fully with many Kagwahiv (Kracke, 1979)— a domain that Hallowell (1955a, 1966) also found interesting with respect to self concepts—that of dreaming. I will explore what Kagwahiv beliefs about dreaming reflect of their beliefs about how the self participates in dreams, and the relationship of their selves to other selves in the "behavioral environment" of dreaming.

The beliefs about dreaming I am talking about here are not, I should make it clear, the same as a Kagwahiv's individual experience of himself in dreaming. Self-experience is as variable among Kagwahiv as among ourselves. Rather I am talking about the language and concepts that form the conceptual framework in terms of which a Kagwahiv individual can *articulate* his sense of self.

---

[4]The very term "self"—the use of the reflexive pronoun to designate the person's subjectivity and his schema of it, usually referred to in other European languages by the nominalized first-person pronoun—is unique to English, as Brazilian colleagues pointed out in the symposium at which this paper was first presented.

Dreams may seem an esoteric and peripheral, indirect way of approaching the topic of the self. But the apparent triviality of the dream experience itself reflects an important difference between our concept of the self and that of many other cultures. We tend to see dreams, if they are self-related at all, as a kind of waste product of the self or, at best, as a world of fantasy that may reveal inner wishes of the self precisely because they are not subject to the constraints of more significant, reality-oriented domains of consciousness. To a Kagwahiv, dream experience is at least on a par with other kinds of experiencing, in fact a kind of perception with a special importance that surpasses that of daytime perception. The degree to which dreaming is integrated with other kinds of experience for Kagwahiv is indicated by the fact that dreamed experience is grammatically coded as a kind of tense: experiences that occur in dreams are marked, when recounted, by the almost obligatory particle *ra'u,* which distributes like a tense marker. (Thus: *oho ra'e,* "he went already," "he went in the recent past"; *oho ra'u,* "I dreamed that he went"). Some use this particle interchangeably with the tense marker *ramenhumi,* "temporarily" (see Kracke 1979: 127).

On the other hand, *ra'u* is more specifically part of the series of past-tense particles that refer to events that one knows *indirectly* rather than through firsthand experience, things that one has heard about rather than actually participated in — suggesting a contrast between dreaming as an indirect, unreliable form of knowing and the direct, reliable knowledge that comes of direct participation in the events. (Etymologically the particle *ra'u* is associated with deceit or prevarication; and dreamers often end their accounts of a dream with the value-laden observation "It seemed as if it was real, but in the end it wasn't.")

One question raised by this term *ra'u* is especially germane to the questions about the self I raised earlier. We regard dreams as a psychic product — perhaps as the most essentially psychic product (reflecting most directly the inner core of self-experience) — since they occur under conditions of the suspension of reality judgment. The Kagwahiv see dreams as on a par with waking experience, even if they are an experience of a specially marked kind. We "dream *that* x happened"; we seldom say "X happened to us in a dream." Dreams to us are a kind of thought process for which we are ultimately responsible. Do Kagwahiv forswear psychic responsibility for the content of dreams by regarding them as "real" events?

An argument could be made from the use of this particle, *ra'u,* for the idea that dreaming is regarded as a real experience of the soul, as Hallowell (1955a, 1966) describes for the Saulteaux Ojibwe. For *ra'u* is evidently derived from the noun *ra'u(va)*,[5] which is often used to designate the dream-representative of a person; this noun is often used in contexts where it might be translated as "soul." (When a shaman is in a trance, for example, his *ra'uva* goes through various levels of the universe talking to different spirits.) Thus the remark "I saw so-and-so's *ra'uva* in a dream" might be interpreted as a kind of direct interaction between souls. While this interpretation might be plausible for Kagwahiv concepts of some particular types of dream, which I will discuss later, I think it is an erroneous interpretation of the general usage of *ra'uva* in dream texts; for the root meaning of the noun, from which I believe its sense as "soul" is derived, is as a *representation* of something. When children use an object in play to represent something else — a leaf for a "fish" a boy has caught, for example — it is referred to as the *ra'uva* of what it stands for. I believe that the simplest interpretation of the meaning of "*ra'uva*" in accounts of dreams is "the image of so-and-so in the dream," emphasizing the *distinction* between the real person and his or her dream-image. In this interpretation, the use of *ra'u* and *ra'uva* actually *emphasizes* the imaginary nature of the dream as a symbolic psychic product.[6]

Other common beliefs about dreams reinforce this impression. A very basic belief is that they are a nocturnal form of thinking. Dreams are said to be the continuation into sleep of a train of thought pursued as one was going to sleep. Informants will explain a dream by saying, "I was thinking about a particular thing. I went to sleep on it and took it along with me into sleep, and it caused/turned into my dream."

This belief incorporates an insightful observation of the process of formation of a dream, which definitely places dreams as a psychic product of the self. It is a way of formulating how dreams are formed from day residues: Catarina, for example, who first formulated this concept for me, explained that after my telling a tale the night before of how my aunt had almost been swept away in a flash flood (which I had just learned of by letter), she had slept on it and carried it into sleep with her, and it had formed her dream of being caught in a flood herself.[7]

---

[5]Kagwahiv nouns generally have two alternating forms in free variation, one ending in a stressed vowel or a consonant, the other adding a consonant and unstressed neutral vowel off-glide.

[6]One elderly man I talked to in 1985, since deceased — João Messias or Kwahãm — did, nevertheless, explain dreams as the experiences of the *ra'uv,* here clearly "soul," traveling outside the body. This illustrates the flexibility of Kagwahiv dream discourse for permitting various personal interpretations, as I shall point out later.

[7]Catarina, Interview 5, p. 5: "*Koa nde imombe'ui oji'i, kirame . . . a'e ji aki hehe . . . Oro ji kiri hehe — oro ji herokiri:*" "You told us that thing the other day, yesterday, I slept on it — so I slept on it, so I took it with me into sleep."

Another belief that conforms to the view of dreams as psychic products is that dreams may express the dreamer's frustrated wishes (Kracke, 1979, p. 136). Often an informant will attribute a dream of, say, feasting on a pig to his hunger for pork. This may be partly what enabled Catarina to understand and readily accept my suggestion that she dreamed of Francisco killing a sick, disgusting deer because she was angry at Francisco for not sharing more of the tapir he had killed, and she dreamed that her own son killed many fine deer because she was envious of Francisco's success. The important point here is not, of course, the correctness or incorrectness of my interpretation of the dream, but that such an explanation could be meaningful to her.

In sum, Kagwahiv do have the conceptual tools to understand dreams as imaginative products that may reflect frustrated or even hidden wishes of the self — quite a psychologically sophisticated view of dreams, and one that takes responsibility for their content as a mental product created by the self.

Some other beliefs, on the other hand, suggest quite different kinds of extension of the self into dreams. Dream predictions imply a kind of direct perception of future events, even if mediated by symbols that must be interpreted; but beyond this, they entail a degree of responsibility for causations of the events predicted in the dreams. A negative form of responsibility is shown in the belief that, if a dream augurs an undesirable event, one may prevent its coming about either by telling the dream by the fire or, more actively, by performing the ritual act of "breaking medicine" (opohãmondok) — shredding a palha-palm leaf bit by bit while repeating a negation of the dream's predicted outcome. Thus, an old man assured me that, although he had dreamed of a fire raging in the part of the settlement where I was sleeping, I was safe from the fever that it predicted because he had broken medicine on awakening. But this sense of responsibility for the outcome also occurs in a more positive form: Catarina was once somewhat annoyed at her son for not going hunting when she had dreamed game for him. In these instances at least, as in descriptions of a shaman's "dreaming game" for someone, ordinary predictive dreams may be regarded as having a causative power. In such instances, one may be perceived as actively influencing reality through one's dreams.

Certain determinate kinds of dreams seem to be regarded as involving direct mental contact with others (people or spirits). These are predominantly dreams with strong affect. Sexual dreams and dreams with warm feelings toward a person mean that the person is thinking about the dreamer or has "spoken" the dreamer's "name." Nightmares are said to indicate the immediate proximity of an evil spirit or ghost, *anhang*. These beliefs, which indicate direct communication with other selves through dreams, are the closest to suggesting that the *ra'uva* of others that populate dreams might be their "souls" rather than simply their "dream images." Yet, even here, the belief is not necessarily that the dream image itself is a direct portrayal of the real person or of his or her thought, but simply that such dreams *indicate* that the dreamed-of person has such feelings about the dreamer, or, in the case of nightmares, *signal* the presence of an *anhang*. The dream itself is not necessarily a direct perception of the person's thought or of the *anhang*.[8]

The set of beliefs I have outlined about dreams allow for various ways for a Kagwahiv dreamer to experience and think about his dreams. While it is possible for a Kagwahiv to interpret his dream as a real perception of some kind — of future events, of others' thoughts, or of the presence of spirits — it is equally possible for him to think about his dreams as self-products and therefore to use them to introspect about his own inner wishes. As I have shown in some of the examples I cited, some of my informants did perceive motives of their own expressed in their dreams and could trace the day residues that entered into their formation. On the other hand, a number of the dream concepts also involve kinds of extension of the self into dreams not consonant with our purely psychological view and may entail self-related kinds of responsibility that we do not associate with dream experiences. A Kagwahiv may feel guilty over a dream not simply because of the wish expressed in it, but also because of harm that may befall another in consequence of an event foreseen in a dream and not prevented by breaking medicine.

Dreaming is, of course, only one area of self-experience. A full account of the Kagwahiv concept of self would also include such areas as their ideas about the subject of thinking and feeling; the initiation of action; distinctions between wishing, intending and doing; and awareness of how people may differ in their ways of experiencing situations. One would need to explore the emotion terms that label states of the self; ideas about the nature of the body, its boundaries and its relationship to subjectivity; the ways in which ideas about initiative and personal responsibility are bound up in verbs of personal activity and receptivity; and notions of the continuity and discontinuity of the self and self-experience. Ideas about the nature of relationships with key others, such as members of the nuclear family, define the boundaries between self and other or, contrariwise, areas in which the self and other blend into one

---

[8]A particular form of the *anhang* dream is the dream of a person who has just died and who thus announces his death to the dreamer.

another (as when the father's or mother's violation of a food taboo by eating a forbidden species directly and immediately causes harm to his or her infant child). Indeed, Hallowell (1955a) devoted a good part of his lengthy article on "the Self in its Behavioral Environment" to cataloging the various domains of culture that are relevant for shaping how one thinks about oneself in that culture.

But dreaming is a particularly interesting and problematic area of self-experience precisely because in dreams the location of self and other are often unclear, even dissolved into one another. I think this may be why Hallowell (1955a, 1966) found in dreams one of the most striking examples of differences in the conception of the self in elation to its behavioral environment. This sketch of Kagwahiv beliefs about dreams shows that beliefs that regard the dream experience as a kind of perception of reality are not altogether incompatible with psychological views of dreaming that make dreams also sources of insight into the wishes of the self.

Personalities and personal styles of thinking vary within any culture, as Hallowell (1955b) pointed out, and this array of beliefs permits various personal versions of individual conceptualization of dreams and diverse ways of thinking about and interpreting one's own dreams. At least one man did, indeed, see his dreams as portraying events external to himself, in the classic "traveling soul" schema as presented by Tylor (1865, p. 7). For this man, João Messias, dreaming was a spiritual adventure taking place in a real space, located outside himself like the space of waking reality. A few others, on the other hand, viewed their dreams as primarily taking place within themselves, constructed of memories. While they acknowledged the possibility of real encounters with spirits in the form of nightmares, they did not see any of their own dreams as being examples of meetings with spirits and were thankful for their freedom from such encounters. For the majority of the dreamers, the primary interest of dreams was as symbolic or encoded messages about the future or, more exactly, about future potentials.

In summary, Kagwahiv theories of dreaming entail four different kinds of relationship between the dreamer, the dream and reality outside the dream.

(1) A basic set of dream beliefs portray dreams as mental processes — either as representations that are transformations of a waking train of thought or as expressions of desire (representations of wish as fulfilled).

(2) Dreams are often seen as indexical predictions of the future, using a traditional code that links certain dream images with specific

events they represent, metaphorically or metonymically. These dreams seem to be seen as a kind of perception of a certain aspect of reality—the incipient future—but insofar as they represent through a complex code, they are perhaps more like a *communication about* the incipient future than a perception of it.

(3) A limited kind of dream—nightmares or night terrors—are interpreted as real perceptions of the presence of dangerous spirits. In these, it is the *affect* of the dream, not its imagery, that constitutes the perception.

(4) Certain other dreams are seen as reception of emotional communications from others, communications of their desires concerning the dreamer: sexual desire or a wish to see the dreamer. Again, the perception in the dream is the *affect* with which the other is invested in the dream, not the whole manifest content of the dream. With the exception of one or two informants who seem to have more ideosyncratic variants of dream belief, most Kagwahiv do not see dreams as *direct* perceptions of either present reality or of the future. More often they are seen as communications received by the dreamer; but when they *are* seen as perceptions, the perception is generally represented by the *affect* in the dream, not its visual content.

These different ways of experiencing dreams entail diverse experiences of self, as diverse as one might find in our own society. The point to be noted is that, in this society at least, the variety of self-experiences includes not only those who see dreaming as an experience of purely external events but also those who see it as a form of thought and are able to trace memories that appear in the dreams from the day's residues and, indeed, to gain insights from them. Perception of dreams as a kind of perception of reality does not necessarily exclude *also* understanding them as psychic products. For the person examining the self in context — interviewing members of a "primitive" culture to understand their personalities and personal concerns—it is important not only to understand *how* they conceptualize various kinds of self-experience, so that one can ask the right questions and understand their communications about themselves; but also to recognize that those concepts may be a vehicle to self-understanding through different routes from our notions of the self.

## BIBLIOGRAPHY

BRIGGS, J. (1970), *Never in Anger.* Cambridge, MA: Harvard University Press.
FREUD, S. (1923), "The ego and the id." *Standard Edition,* 19:12–59, London: Hogarth Press, 1959.

GEERTZ, H. (1974), The vocabulary of emotion: A study of Javanese socialization processes. In: *Culture and Personality: Contemporary Readings,* ed. R. LeVine. Chicago: Aldine, pp. 249–264.

HALLOWELL, A.I. (1955a), The Self and its Behavioral Environment. Ch. 5 in *Culture and Experience.* Philadelphia: The University of Pennsylvania Press. (Reissued by Waveland Press, Prospect Heights, IL, 1988, pp. 75–110.)

———— (1955b), Fear and anxiety as cultural and individual variables in a primitive society. In: *Culture and Experience.* Philadelphia: University of Pennsylvania Press. (Reissued by Waveland Press, Prospect Heights, IL, 1988, pp. 250–265.)

———— (1966), The role of the dream in Ojibwa culture. In: *The Dream and Human Societies,* ed. R. Caillois & G. E. von Grunebaum. Berkeley: University of California Press, pp. 267–292.

JACOBSON, E. (1964), *The Self and the Object World.* New York: International Universities Press.

KOHUT, H. (1971), *Analysis of the Self.* New York: International Universities Press.

———— (1977), *Restoration of the Self.* New York: International Universities Press.

KRACKE, W. (1979), Dreaming in Kagwahiv: Dream beliefs and their psychic uses in an Amazonian Indian culture. *The Psychoanalytic Study of Society,* 8:119–171.

LIENHARDT, G. (1961), *Divinity and Experience.* Oxford: Clarendon Press.

SHAFER, R. (1976), *A New Language for Psychoanalysis.* New Haven, CT: Yale University Press.

TYLOR, E.B., (1865), *Researches into the Early History of Mankind and the Development of Civilization* (3rd ed.). New York: Henry Holt & Co., 1878.

WINNICOTT, D.W. (1960), Ego distortion in terms of true and false self. In: *The Maturational Process and the Facilitating Environment.* London: Hogarth Press, 1965, pp. 140–152.

# 5

# Cultural Schemas and Experiences Of The Self Among The Bimin-Kuskusmin of Papua New Guinea

FITZ JOHN PORTER POOLE

This essay explores certain aspects of the nexus between cultural schemas and personal experiences of the self among the Bimin-Kuskusmin of the West Sepik hinterland of Papua New Guinea.[1] The focus of the exploration is concerned primarily with the senses in which matters of the *individual, individuality,* and *individuation*—that is, personal differences not readily subsumed under status role or other social differences— are both culturally and personally constituted, instantiated, represented, articulated, and given experiential shape and force in Bimin-Kuskusmin conceptions of selfhood and in the contexts in which such concepts are implicated. This focus on the facets of self that mark some sense of individualization and on their role in conceptions of agency brings an ethnopsychological perspective to significant problems concerning not only the predication of the individual in anthropological accounts (compare Emmet, 1960; Evens, 1977), but also the personal configurations of identity that interrelate and give a semblance of coherence and continuity to "personal symbols" (Obeyesekere, 1981) in experience. The intent of the essay is to suggest that a more or less rigid dichotomy

[1]Field research among the Bimin-Kuskusmin (1971–73, 1982) was generously supported by the National Institutes of Health, the Cornell University-Ford Foundation Humanities and Social Sciences Program, and the Center for South Pacific Studies of the University of California, Santa Cruz. The New Guinea Research Unit of the Research School of Pacific Studies, Australian National University, and the Department of Anthropology and Sociology of the University of Papua New Guinea provided valuable assistance. To the Bimin-Kuskusmin people, for revealing something of their resilience and fragility in their experience of themselves, is owed the primary debt of gratitude.

between individualism (often subsuming diverse ideas about the individual, individuation, and individuality) as a historical peculiarity of the West[2] and holism or sociocentrism (connoting a socially constituted and embedded self) as characteristic of the non-Western world, usually framed as mutually exclusive, monothetic categories, unduly inhibits cross-cultural comparison, blunts the subtlety of single-case analysis, and distorts sensitivity in ethnopsychological ethnography (see Geertz 1973, 1984; compare Dumont 1977, 1986; Poole 1982, 1984, 1985, 1986a, b, 1987a, b; Fajans 1985; Kirkpatrick 1985; McHugh 1989; Kondo 1990).[3] Indeed, certain conceptual distinctions among individual, person, and self—here taken to illuminate potentially significant (albeit phenomenologically intertwined) aspects of various mosaics of identity,[4] *mutatis mutandis,* in any culture and society—may facilitate description, analysis, and comparison in important ways (see Harris, 1989). Such analytic discriminations need not be simply an uncritical, undeconstructed artifact of any of the various notions of the individual implicated in Western ideas of individualism, which is itself susceptible to comparative analysis.

The common blurring, conflating, or a priori dismissal of such distinctions, however, may have unfortunate epistemological and theoretical entailments and consequences in a confounding of potentially

---

[2]As Mauss (1938) once demonstrated (see Carrithers 1985; Allen 1985), the Western cultural complex known as "individualism," in its various economic, ethical, philosophical, political, psychological, and other sociocultural senses, is generally recognized to have a complicated historical development, about which there is still considerable controversy. For example, see Swart, 1962; Lukes, 1973; Hanning, 1977; Macfarlane, 1979; Baumeister, 1987; Morris, 1987; and Taylor, 1989.

[3]Perhaps the most influential portrait in anthropology of the Western notion of the individual has been Geertz's (1984) view that

the Western conception of the person as a bounded, unique, more or less integrated motivational and cognitive universe, a dynamic center of awareness, emotion, judgment, and action organized into a distinctive whole and set contrastively both against other such wholes and against its social and natural background is, however incorrigible it may seem to us, a rather peculiar idea within the context of the world's cultures [p. 126].

Yet, the Melanesian studies of Read (1955), Strathern (1988), Herdt (1989), and Battaglia (1990) more delicately probed whether or not and, if so, how individualistic ideas are recognized in or encompassed by relational notions of person and self. Thus, for example, Read (1955) notes that "people are markedly aware of themselves as individuals" (p. 254) among the Gahuku-Gama.

[4]In this essay, the term *identity* is used somewhat atheoretically to encompass the senses of individual, person, and self that are more theoretically elaborated. It should be noted, however, that there are clear affinities between aspects of these concepts and Erikson's (1950, 1968) notion of identity.

illuminating discriminations of "human beings as . . . living entities [with general (in some senses "universal") characteristics] among many such entities in the universe . . . [as personally differentiated entities] . . . [as] centers of being or experience, or . . . [as] members of society" (Harris, 1989: p. 599; compare Geertz 1973, 1984). However such aspects of identity may or may not be constituted, discriminated, emphasized, or valued locally, there may be heuristic utility in analytically partitioning them to provide a framework for conceptually mapping any particular configuration on a comparative landscape and in exploring what differences, if any, such concepts make in the shape and texture of the complexly intertwined dimensions of cultural, psychological, and social organization in any community.

The immediate interest in concepts of individual, person, and self is at once both ethnopsychological (experience-near) and analytic (experience-distant). The concern is to understand how local concepts of identity give shape and force to beliefs — learned through processes of socialization and enculturation, internalized (in some sense) so that they come to have emotional and directive force, and more or less shared — about human nature, personal experience, and institutional forms in a "culturally constituted behavioral environment" (Hallowell, 1955a, p. 87), and also to constitute an analytic framework that permits a comparative assessment of the similarities and differences among such local concepts in order to explore their cultural, psychological, and social concomitants. If ethnopsychological constructs are more than idioms for selected common features of a universal psychic unity and less than the sum of imaginable experiences (conscious, preconscious, and unconscious; interpersonal and intrapsychic) in a local community, and if their interpretation can yield some manner of interpretation or explanation of their salience and significance in terms of cognition, emotion, motivation, and behavior, then the psychological dimensions of the ethnopsychological — and there is no warrant a priori, contra Lutz (1988), for assuming their identity — become an important and still little understood focus of inquiry in psychological anthropology.

In this essay, however, the emphasis is placed on aspects of the individual, individuality, and individuation as manifested in representations of the self. The inspiration for the analysis is drawn from Hallowell's (1955a, b; 1958; 1960; 1976a, b, c, d) remarkable and prescient concern for developing a phenomenological perspective in psychological anthropology, in which significant and principled attention would be focused on personality and the inner world of experience from the perspective of the actor. Hallowell (1976a) imagined that a critical and central problem of any psychological anthropology is an understanding of the nexus of culture and perception or cognition, for he insisted that humans in any sociocultural milieu are invariably confronted by an interplay of internal and external worlds, and comprehend this dual reality through complex and subtle cognitive frames, schemas, lenses, or filters intricately constituted both by personal life experiences and by more or less shared cultural meanings. Hallowell's psychocultural interests lie, therefore, not only in explicating indigenous notions of self as collective representations, but also in exploring what such ideas reveal about the cultural organization of personal experience — of the ways in which people constitute senses of identity, deal with mundane and extraordinary interactive and solitary problems, pursue their senses of purpose in everyday life, and, in so doing, confront some variant of the puzzle of the *individual-in-society*. Such local, culturally constituted ideas not only, as Hallowell (1955a, p. 91) noted, "become psychologically significant" in regard to "motivations, goals and life adjustment," but also are conceptualized in relationship to diverse matters of personal and social concern in the myriad contexts in which experience takes form.

In the spirit of Hallowell's seminal contributions to the study of the nexus of culture and self, it will be argued that, for any individual in any culturally distinctive community, culturally constituted notions of the self are a loose assemblage of often diverse ideas about identity which become, partially and selectively and in particular transformations, articulated with various senses of identity manifested in different contexts, under variable circumstances, and at differing moments in a life. Connected to the construction of "personal symbols" (in Obeyesekere's, 1981, sense), however, these multiple personal representations of self are imagined, structured, contextualized, negotiated, and otherwise constituted in narrative form — whether that of monologue or dialogue, private or public. To the extent that the personal self appears to be a "cohesive self" (Kohut, 1971, 1977) in any given narrative configuration, although it may also be rendered problematically as fragmentary, inconsistent, or contradictory as well, that sense of cohesion may be more apparent in the occasion of its construction than among such occasions despite attendant senses — whether real, illusory, or both — that some facets of the self endure as a core of personal identity. Yet, the notion that any culture provides only a single model of the self which is similarly understood, reconstructed, and used by any individual of that culture to enfold and to inform the full range of personal experience seems both unwarranted and inadequate for approaching the ethnographic or the clinical description of how selves are imagined, experienced, and represented in any society.

In both theoretical formulations (Hallowell, 1955a, 1960, 1976a) and ethnographic studies of the Ojibwa (Hallowell, 1955b, 1958, 1976b, 1976c, 1976d; compare Black, 1977; Hay, 1977), Hallowell (1955a) presents a portrait of the self (or self orientations) in terms of spatio-temporal, object, motivational, and normative orientations that inform and shape the "culturally constituted behavioral environment" (p. 87) of the self. In Hallowell's terms, the self refers to the conceptualization of the character, locus, reflexivity, power, and agency of the perceiving and experiencing "ego" (akin to *das Ich* in Freud's prestructural formulation) as it is known—whether articulately or intuitively—to the actor himself or herself. The self, therefore, implies an understanding or a constitution of the human being as a locus of experience, encompassing the experience of being a more or less distinctive someone beyond one's identity as a person. It is that perceptual object that is the referent of such notions as "I" (as subject and author of experiential states and processes and, thus, of thoughts, feelings, motivations, and behaviors) and "me" (as cognized and recognized object) and that is distinguished from a contrasting set of phenomena experienced and represented as other-than-self. Whether or not the self is perceived as a unique, socially embedded, or natural and universal entity, this sense of personal identity is, in important respects, a product of social interaction and experience and of a cultural repertoire of ideas about the possibilities and proclivities of identity, which it also informs. In turn, more or less shared and public notions of self complexly participate in the shaping of personal experience, providing the cultural repertoire of ideas and idioms in terms of which personal aspects of self can be imagined, articulated, and communicated. The developmental acquisition of a self and of self-awareness, Hallowell argues, is crucial for the operation of a human social order because, to the extent that a social order is also and inevitably a moral order, social actors must assume responsibility and accountability for their own conduct. To have a sense of self is to have an orientation in sociomoral space, a way of finding one's bearings and moorings, a manner of locating oneself as an interlocutor in a sociocultural realm of ontologically basic questions, a means of imagining those horizons within which one more or less knows where one stands and what meanings phenomena have for one (see Taylor, 1989). Indeed, it is perhaps when these horizons, or one's locus within them, become uncertain or come to lack a stable significance that forms of disorientation—and pathology—vis-à-vis the self arise.

This perspective is of crucial importance to a concern with the power of psychoanalytic insights in anthropological analysis, for, it may be argued, modern psychoanalytic theory places a particular and strong emphasis on separation, individuation, and autonomy as essential to normal personality development, and, beyond infancy and early childhood, the impairment of these developmental accomplishments is deemed to have pathological consequences (compare Doi, 1990; Kakar, 1990; LeVine, 1990). Indeed, a complex configuration of separation, individuation, autonomy, and dependency is embedded in most psychoanalytic concepts of self, with significant entailments for normalcy and pathology. On this foundational set of assumptions, the notion of the self, however, has been conceptualized in various ways in psychoanalysis. Thus, Freud (1914, 1930) sometimes used ego (*das Ich*) to mean self (*das Selbst*) or even individual (*das Individuum*), particular before the emergence of his structural hypothesis, and set the self in contrast to objects in certain conceptual formulations. Hartmann (1958) discriminated ego as a set of psychic functions from self and suggested that self-representations are formed by identification with internalized object representations. Jacobson (1954) used self to refer largely to the whole person or individual and conceptualized self-representations to be intrapsychic structures that develop gradually. Schafer (1976, 1989) discriminated the self as agent, the self as locus, and the self as object. Kohut (1971, 1977) imagined the core or nuclear self as an independent center of initiative. Stern (1985, 1989) conceived of the self as a way to refer to experience, either as a sense of the self or as the development of self in a world at once constituted by subjectivity and interrelatedness. Whether regarded as a psychic structure or a subjective point of reference (or both), however, such formulations constitute a concept of self, *mutatis mutandis,* more closely related to experience (and the clinical encounter) than the id, ego, and superego of Freud's structural hypothesis.

Yet, the Hallowellian notion of the self — well attuned to interests in psychoanalytic anthropology — must be mapped onto a conceptual land-scape that includes discriminations of person and individual, although any particular cultural repertoire of notions of identity may differently recognize, contextualize, emphasize, submerge, interlink, and value aspects of these analytic distinctions. Indeed, these distinctions are intended to mark relative emphases of local concepts as they are imagined and instantiated in various contexts and facilitate various interpretations of events in these contexts. They are constituted as analytic points of reference and not as monothetic categories intended to encompass local concepts. The comparative issue is not one of the presence or lack of identity in any of these senses, but is a matter of assessing the possibilities of "family resemblances" (in Wittgenstein's sense) comparatively in how, when, where, and under what circumstances particular local ideas having affinity with analytic notions of person, self, and individual are deployed in particular sociocultural contexts.

Personhood, following Mauss (1938), Fortes (1973), and Harris (1989), refers to those culturally constituted attributes, capacities, and signs that mark a moral career and its jural entitlements in a particular society. An interest in personhood implicates a concern with the cultural forms and social forces that together publicly render the individual present in a culturally constituted *human nature* that is socially encompassed, and in some array of social positions that are the contexts, entitlements, and emblems of the achievement of particular kinds and degrees of personhood. Indeed, social personhood endows the culturally recognized individual with those powers or capacities upon which human agency depends, enables, and constrains his proper actions, casts him as possessed of judgment and thus responsibility, and calls him to account in a legal, moral, political, and social order. Although the capacities of personhood may be anchored to the powers and limitations of the human body and thus seen as natural attributes, they are at once judgmental, social, and mystical capacities; and persons are essentially social beings who develop in different ways and to differing degrees over the course of the social life cycle. Thus, a person is fundamentally a social being with a certain moral status and is a legitimate bearer of rights and obligations. Yet, a person has a sense of self and of individuality, a notion of past and future; he can hold values, perceive goals, recognize resources, acknowledge constraints, make choices, and thus adopt plans that are attributable to him as a being with the conscious, reflective capacity to frame culturally appropriate representations of phenomena and to have purposes, desires, and aversions that require judgment. To be a person, or a moral agent, is to be sensitive to certain standards of the sociomoral order of the community and to suffer a sense of shame when the breach of this order may be attributed to one's personal judgment and responsibility. Personhood, thus, is fundamentally a conceptual adjustment of a culturally constituted sense of *human nature* to a socially constituted jural-moral order.

Analytic notions of the individual, individuality, and individuation inevitably draw, albeit tentatively, on analogies vis-à-vis Western ideas, but it is nonetheless the apparent case that most cultural models of

person and self implicate some attention to the foci and contours, the
entailments and consequences of individuality and to the significance of
individual differences. Indeed, notions of proper personhood often take
account, by exclusion or inclusion vis-à-vis concepts of the person, of
some sense of individuality and its social entailments and consequences.
Thus, it seems essential to examine how the individual is recognized (if at
all), given prominence (or not), and variously valued (or disvalued) in a
sociocultural milieu. Such exploration directs attention to the kinds and
degrees of unity, separateness, exclusiveness, boundedness, privacy,
interiority, autonomy, natural development, power, control, and agency
attributed to the individual, of recognition of the endogenous causal
force of a more or less self-contained, singular human being in the social
order. Although the individual may be endowed with variable significance, shape, force, and expression in different sociocultural milieux,
most societies appear to recognize in some fashion aspects of normalcy
and deviancy, of virtue and vice, that may inhere in the confluence of
ethnobiological, ethnopsychological, and ethnosocial dimensions that
culturally constitute a single, individuated member of the human kind —
however ethnically or socially restricted that reckoning — and the implications of such characteristics in the capacity for language, culture, and
social signification for developing a self and becoming a person and,
thus, an agent. Yet, the attribution of various kinds and degrees of
human agency to the individual in differing social categories, networks,
and groups remains variable and importantly bound up with the loci of
socioculturally significant difference with respect to self and person and
the difference such difference makes in experience within a "culturally
constituted behavioral environment" (Hallowell, 1955a, p. 87).

The self and its more individualized dimensions, although apparently a focus of self-awareness or self-consciousness, is not an object in
the sense that it can be defined in neutral terms and outside of an
essential cultural framework of questions and understandings about
identity that have significance in a particular social milieu — beyond the
concerns that constitute a sense of self and inform an experience of self.
On the one hand, the self is culturally constituted and represented and
socially instantiated through public and personal narratives in which the
cultural terms of subjective experience are recognized, codified, articulated, subjected to scepticism, transformed experientially, and given
personal meaning in the construction of self-interpretations (or, indeed,
in interpretations of the selves of others). On the other hand, the self is
only partly constituted by one's self-interpretations, for the self's interpretations probably cannot ever be made fully explicit, not only because

of their preconscious and unconscious aspects, but also because what is taken as culturally given, what is reckoned with, in using a local discourse of the self is necessarily implicit or beyond awareness. Thus, the self—as a culturally shaped personal sense of identity—is both deeper and more multifaceted than any given articulation or instantiation of it. Indeed, it is not uncommon for anthropological informants or psychoanalytic analysands to acknowledge—verbally or nonverbally—some discomfort, frustration, anger, or despair in the inability to express certain nuances of an experience of the self in cultural terms, in the often inchoate sense of a lack of "fit" between the personally felt and the culturally codified. Yet, to study culturally shaped experiences of the self is to explore aspects of being that largely exist in, or are accessible through, or are partly constituted by, a certain discourse. Such discourse exists and is maintained and used only within a community of speakers. Consequently, a self is a self only or primarily among and in reference to other selves who comprise that community of speakers and cannot be described without reference to those who significantly surround, envelop, and interpret it. Cultural languages of the self initiate, institute, focus, activate, and negotiate common spaces in which the self is most readily imagined to be at issue. Thus, the self is constructed and articulated in relationship to interlocutors—those who are significant others in one's achievement of self-definition and those who become crucial to a continuing grasp of local languages of self-understanding and self-expression. There is no private language in this sense, but there are, perhaps inevitably, partly unexplored and unarticulable, often dark, powerful, inchoate feelings, affinities, fears, anxieties, desires, and so on that are unsaid and unsayable in the public language of the self except obliquely, by means of hedges, analogies, nonverbal accompaniments, and so on. Nonetheless, illuminating access to the culturally constituted self may be gained through attention to the terms, concepts, and schemas that give the self local form and significance.

Following D'Andrade (1981, 1984), shared cultural schemata or folk models are fundamentally involved in perception, recognition, interpretation, problem solving, and other modes of processing information that facilitate representation of, and enable or guide action in, those situations in which particular crystallizations of the schemata are instantiated. A schema usually consists of a number of conceptual elements and their relations to one another as they are linked in semantic networks. The conceptual elements of a schema exhibit a range of values, can be variously interlinked within the schema or among other schemata, and can be variously bound to different aspects of the environment on different instantiations of the schema. The typical constraints on the concepts of the schema — that is, on their values and interrelationships — serve two critical functions: (a) they facilitate the use of the schema as a hypothesis about the identity or conceptual properties of an event or situation; and (b) they permit an interpretation to proceed beyond the information given in guiding inferences about unobserved, tacit, or ambiguous aspects of the situation or event. Yet, each conceptual element of a schema may itself be a complex schema, for schemata encompass subschemata in a hierarchical mode of organization that may be simultaneously activated *both* from the top down (that is, from whole to part) *and* from the bottom up (that is, from part to whole) as the construction of an instantiation and an interpretation proceeds.

As D'Andrade implies, a distinctive attribute of most cultural schemata, as marked simplifications of reality, is that they are not precisely specified or explicit in all respects as they are represented in natural discourse. Indeed, certain aspects of such folk models remain tacit, ambiguous, or even opaque. Tacit dimensions presume other schemata that are implicated by, but are not explicitly embedded in, or otherwise articulated with, the focal folk model, and thus require implicit criteria of relevance and processes of inference to interconnect and to interpret these covert schemata. By virtue of some manner of intersubjective sharing of these cultural schemata in a community, certain aspects of folk models are often perceived as being obvious and natural facts of the world and need not be made explicit. These implicit aspects, however, are commonly the premises of the more explicit features of folk models. Ambiguous features of cultural schemata leave unresolved the problem of which of several potentially linked schemata, each with somewhat different implications for the hierarchical organization of relevant schemata, may be implied. Opaque features are lacunae in the structure of the folk model that are not readily articulated with other available cultural schemata, and mark certain disjunctive aspects of the linkages among those concepts that are articulated by a schema. These several characteristics of cultural schemata suggest that the interwoven networks of concepts that constitute a schema may variously exhibit strong and weak, complex and simple, dense and diffuse, and other variable qualities of connectivity or even gaps of articulation.

Certain cultural schemas, or congeries of schemas, may exhibit a particular centrality among the linkages that interconnect other schemas; that is, they are implicated and instantiated in a large array of events or situations to be interpreted in a "culturally constituted behavioral environment" and come to be intimately and intricately bound up with personal construals and evaluations of diverse dimensions of that sociocultural milieu. Schemas of the self appear to exhibit such centrality insofar as they are probably implicated in some fashion in all social events or situations in which aspects of personal identity intrude upon interpretation. It is perhaps the case that they are more complexly or deeply internalized than other schemas and have more self-orienting functions, for they are learned over the course of a lifetime in myriad contexts and under marked conditions in which one participates and evaluates the personal significance of participating and being evaluated in such contexts. In consequence, cultural models of the self, as they are personally constituted and instantiated with some degree of intersubjective sharing, appear to have orientational, evaluative, affective, and motivational, and other psychological force (see D'Andrade, 1984). Nonetheless, although perhaps contributing to the apparent psychological force of cultural schemas of the self, Bimin-Kuskusmin ideas about the self, despite their considerable elaboration and seeming coherence, are marked by notable ambiguity in many respects (compare White, 1978).

To explore the more individualized dimensions of the Bimin-Kuskusmin cultural schema(s) of the self requires initial attention to the terms, concepts, idioms, metaphors, and other expressive modes in regard to which the self is articulated, for these features of cultural discourse about self and individual are indexical of the underlying cultural schemas that inform the patterns of such discourse and the tacit significance it may have. Although what follows includes many dimensions of the Bimin-Kuskusmin self that would pertain, *mutatis mutandis,* to any Bimin-Kuskusmin, the particular focus of this essay concerns only adult, fully initiated men. Aspects of selfhood with respect to the young, the old, and the female have been partially explored elsewhere (see Poole 1982, 1984, 1985, 1986b, 1987a). Among Bimin-Kuskusmin, concepts analogous to analytic constructs of individual, person, and self are constituted in highly overlapping semantic networks of cultural notions that are largely differentiated with respect to matters of emphasis given shape in particular contexts (see Kirk and Burton, 1977).

Considerations of Bimin-Kuskusmin notions of bearing "family resemblance" to self, person, and individual invariably focus on the animating forces of *kusem* ("spirit or life force"), for the two senses of *kusem*—the *finiik* and the *khaapkhabuurien*—implicate central organizing schemas in their myriad, context-bound instantiations throughout diverse realms of social life and personal experience. Both, but especially the *finiik,* are elaborately marked by gender and age and by ritual status.

The *finiik,* strengthened by male anatomical substance, food, ritual activities, knowledge, experience and social concern and nurturance, is a male procreative contribution to the formation of a fetus of either sex and is transmitted through semen. It emanates from an ancestral clan corpus of spirit substance, which it reenters when it is transformed into an ancestral spirit at death. Thus, the *finiik* is a focal idiom of intergenerational continuity and of the social regeneration of lineage, clan, and ritual moiety. The concept of *finiik* is highly polysemic, is much elaborated metaphorically, and acquires somewhat different significance in different contexts.

In general, however, the *finiik* represents certain critical social dimensions of personhood—the ordered, moral, proper, restrained, reflective aspects of the person that are ideally learned in ordained ways and settings, which are associated with the very foundations of Bimin-Kuskusmin tradition. Ideally and under normal circumstances, the *finiik* is located, is nurtured, and develops in the heart, which is symbolically the focal organ of the "male anatomy" in any person and the complex site of myriad processes of "thinking/feeling".[5] The heart, and the *finiik* embedded in it, are nourished by semen, bone marrow, bone, male *finiik*-bearing foods, and the experiences and substances associated with the male domain (especially the realm of male ritual), and thus the *finiik* is deemed normally stronger and more active in men than in women. It is the *finiik* that absorbs the vital experiences of a decade of male initiation rites and other ritual performances, and that encompasses socially valued capacities of personal "control" (*khaak'kiin*) and "shame" (*fiitom*). It is the foundation and directive force of deliberate learning; it stores socially significant knowledge and experience; and it is the valued intellect, source of legitimate emotion, judgmental capacity, and Durkheimian *conscience* of the person. It is strengthened by all ritual enhancement of masculinity or male parts of the anatomy. It is the substantial link that connects a person to a sociomoral order, and it is the idiom in terms of which rights and obligations in that order are phrased.

The *finiik* encompasses the social capacities of "will" (*faaran*), "desire" (*kaaragaam*), "intention" (*diikhraa*), "motivation" (*tabiin'khraa duur*), "consciousness" (*yuguuraamiin*), "concentration" (*kiim'fuugaar*), "understanding" (*fuugunaamiin*), "wisdom" (*agetnaam*), and "social

---

[5]It should be noted that Bimin-Kuskusmin do not distinguish unambiguously between matters of intellect and emotion, and some 17 different verb forms refer to differing kinds of "thinking/feeling," each with its own, more or less distinctive modes of insight and puzzle-solving capabilities.

competence" (*buurgaang*), all of which have a distinctively social scope and force in this context. One thinks and feels with the *finiik* in ways that have been learned through expected modes of socialization – ritual and nonritual – and, thus, in ways that enhance the capacity of "assessment of social situations" (*kiiinkiin'duuraakhaan*), which is an especially valued aspect of judgmental capacity. Indeed, the state, process, scope, force, and focus of the *finiik* instigate and guide thought, feeling, action, and reflection, especially in the realm of the rights and obligations that are linked to the privileges and demands of status. Thus, the *finiik* involves the capacity to identify, to understand, to evaluate, to plan, and to translate or transform "thinking/feeling" into socially comprehensible, sensible, and responsible action, and the *finiik* is the foundation of recognizing the character of accountability for one's actions. It facilitates perceiving socially regular and, therefore, predictable experience, and the very capacity to learn the predictability of such social patterns is *finiik*. It fuses desire and will with the social propriety of legitimate motivation. It affects bodily growth and dexterity, intellectual acuity, and emotional stability. It gains essential sustenance from interpersonal relations, in which it represents demands of appropriate reciprocity for the person, and, when thwarted, produces "justifiable anger" (*kuurdaam ken*), which ideally elicits shame.

The *finiik* is present in the fetus from the moment of conception, and its source in a clan reservoir of spirit substance shapes, with ancestral guidance, the "fate or destiny" (*kwan werkhaak*) of the person in the social realm in some ambiguous way. These ancestral spirits guide its developments, shapes, forces, directions, movements, and interconnections, bringing illness when "self-centeredness" (*kaar dugaamkhaa*) goes too far or when "social encompassment" (*taak faraak*) becomes too oppressive, for the *finiik* is the fulcrum of proper balance between autonomy and dependency. Although ancestral fate or destiny limits and directs its maturational capacity, it must be "planted" (*duurgaamiin*) in a human community where it is nurtured and socialized, grows, and acquires shape and strength and vitality through proper learning and experience. Tales of isolated, feral beings in ancestral times and at the periphery of human habitation clearly suggest that the *finiik* cannot develop outside of an essential social context. Flagrant parental violations of important jural, moral, and ritual understandings (most notably in the form of incest, rape, or attempted abortion) may produce a fetus in which the necessary endowment of *finiik* is blocked by the combined force of ancestral wrath and community anger. Various forms of witchcraft, sorcery, pollution, illness, spirit attack, violation of taboos, and so on may damage, deflect, or arrest its proper developmental course, as may enduring forms of heightened emotional states, which often dislodge it from its locus in the heart.

The social communities of the living and the dead together give shape and vitality to the *finiik* in its passage through the life-cycle. At death, it departs from the body to enter the clan corpus of ancestral spirits from which it originated, and eventually will return to the living in the form of a new fetus of its own volition, or when summoned by ritual activity to promote conception. The weak *finiik* of the infant, however, does not at all or altogether return to the ancestral underworld at death, but tends to fragment and largely to disappear. Similarly, the irrevocably damaged *finiik* of the witch, sorcerer, killer, defiler of sacred things, and other asocial beings appearing as proper persons have no certain passage of return to the ancestral underworld. In turn, the *finiik* of a warrior, whose battlefield death remains unavenged, becomes an *aiyepnon* spirit until the clansmen of the deceased take the action that will open the mountainous path to the ancestral abode.

Among the living, the *finiik* is a medium or channel of communication with the ancestors, especially when it is condensed and invigorated in the heart during participation in ritual performances. During dreams, certain illnesses, trances, forms of spirit possession, and other genres of mystical experience, the *finiik* may temporarily depart from the body to wander abroad and even to visit the ancestral underworld, and there is always the danger that some misfortune may obstruct its return, bringing derangement or death. But when the *finiik* departs, the critical attributes, capacities, and signs of Bimin-Kuskusmin personhood are no longer present in an embodied sense, for the body is primarily the external symbol and vehicle of personhood. On occasion, the *finiik* of one person may come to resemble that of another when the relationship is one of longterm and special importance, is encompassed by common gender and clan membership, and is regularly strengthened by a sharing of male substance, clan myths, ritual participation and secrecy, and social support. Thus, male "bond friends" (*nakunum'khaaben*), fathers and sons, or brothers may be seen to share each other's social qualities in a way that suggests an affinity between their *finiik*. More generally, all social relationships and interactions have the potential of affecting the growth, strength, and stability of the *finiik* for better or worse, for the *finiik* is intricately linked to and shaped by the states and processes of the social milieu in which the person is embedded as an actor. Indeed, the *finiik* is the socially legitimate basis of the constitution of the agency of persons in diverse social contexts.

Although the *finiik* represents many critical features of the person as agent in a sociomoral order, however, this notion is not synonymous with the "person" (*kunum kwan'minkhaa*) who is also defined in terms of the nexus of a variety of social categories, status-role configurations within these categories, allegiances and alliances that cross-cut such categories, ritual participations (including especially initiatory, purificatory, divinatory, and sacrificial rites), and myriad rights and obligations demanded and honored in social action. Although the images of the *finiik* are associated with the realm of masculine endeavors and substances, it is the focus of ordained social development in both males and females. It contrasts with the more "unruly" (*kutaang*) form of *kusem* spirit, the *khaapkhabuurien,* which gains rigor from female substance and ritual and represents the more idiosyncratic, unmodulated aspects of a human being in society. The dominance of the *finiik* over its antithesis — the *khaapkhabuurien* — ensures the proper development of *la personne morale,* which is said to be most highly developed in senior male ritual elders. In turn, unmodulated behavior, as exemplified in the "man of perpetual anger" (*atuur kunum*), "promiscuous woman" (*waasop waneng*), or "witch" (*tamam*), is held to be a sign that the *finiik* has become weakened and the *khaapkhabuurien* is becoming dominant (see Poole 1984, 1986a). The erratic, unpredictable behavior of the infirm, entranced, insane, or very young, however, may be viewed as a temporary and ideally remediable imbalance of two aspects of *kusem* spirit, an imbalance that sometimes can be remedied by ritual means and wellorchestrated social–psychological support. This notion of relative "balance" (*kuurkuuraak*) between *finiik* and *khaapkhabuurien* is highly elaborated in contexts of divination, purification, and curing rites. Male ideological assertions suggest, however, that women, with the sole exception of female ritual elders who are strengthened through male rites and substances, are forever dominated by the unpredictable forces of the *khaapkhabuurien,* as symbolized in the abdominal scarification of female initiation at menarche. Thus, infants and young children, in the exclusive care of women and nurtured on female substances, are often noted to possess a highly dominant *khaapkhabuurien.* Consequently, preadolescent boys must undergo a decade of intensive, ordeal-ridden male initiation to shift the imbalance of *kusem* toward the dominance of the *finiik.*

The *khaapkhabuurien* is created de novo in each human being at conception. It is formed from "vapors" (*uunaan*) that swirl in the warm womb and is activated by the first heartbeat. From that moment onward, it is entirely the product of individual experience — both socially and idiosyncraticallyshaped.Overstimulationfromthemother'sangrythinking/ feeling, exertions, accidents, improper diet, anxieties, lack of desire to become pregnant, give birth, or tend a child, may produce persisting flaws of character wrought by the excessively active *khaapkhabuurien,* which can never be overcome by the more slowly developing *finiik.* Furthermore, because the *khaapkhabuurien* takes the impress of all of life experience (both socially ordained and not), it has the power to weaken, transform, and subvert those experiential influences that enliven, sustain, and expand the force of the *finiik.*

During life, the *khaapkhabuurien* affects others only through the individual in whose body it remains more or less contained, usually in the vicinity of the gall bladder. It may sometimes become detached from the body in dreams, shadows, reflections, certain kinds of spirit possession, self-induced trances, and particular illnesses, but it rarely causes harm independently as long as the individual lives. However, it is seen to be instrumental in motivating antisocial behavior in the individual, for it fuses will and desire to idiosyncratic impulses (*yaamyaam*) rather than social goals and constraints. In any state or condition, it is indelibly marked by the peculiar characteristics or traits by which the person is recognized as an individual actor sometimes disruptive of social contexts. At death, the *khaapkhabuurien* emerges from the corpse to become a wandering, capricious ghost that lingers near the lifetime haunts of the deceased. It may appear in the form of mist, or smoke, or a bird suddenly taking flight. Sometimes it is recognized as a wizened, red-skinned figure crouching in semidarkness near gardens or settlements. Almost always, it possesses recognizable individual characteristics of the deceased, characteristics associated with his more idiosyncratic, asocial, or antisocial behavior when alive. It may attack passersby at whim, but more often it attacks those who have inherited from, or succeeded, or are known to have injured, angered, or maligned the deceased. It often attacks mourners whom it perceives to be insincere in their grief. Eventually, when it has taken its measure of revenge for real and imagined wrongs, it wanders into the deep forest where it preys on unwary travellers or frightens away the game or pollutes the ground of sacred shrines and groves. On occasion, it may return to garden or settlement areas to wreak havoc of some kind, but there are ritual techniques for driving it away. The *khaapkhabuurien* of the dead infant, having little content or structure from its limited life experiences, is said to attack only the mother and father and perhaps a sibling before soon disappearing forever. After the deaths of older persons, the *khaapkhabuurien* lingers longer, for it preserves itself by retaining a fragment of the *finiik,* which has otherwise descended into the ancestral underworld. Divinations of the burial platform of the deceased and subsequent exorcisms, nonetheless, finally force it to release this remnant of *finiik,* and it then begins to dissolve in nearby streams and flow beyond the boundaries of the community where it no longer has reason to inflict harm.

In life or after death, the behavior of the *khaapkhabuurien* remains the product of the totality of personal experience and lacks the aura of coherence and continuity attributed to the *finiik.* Its impulsive forces are generally contained in the "interior" (*mutuuk'keraan*) of the body, ideally encased by a dominant *finiik.* Unlike the *finiik,* its forces are bound up with both real events in the world and illusions, fantasies, and the like that distort that world. When those illusions or fantasies are denied, thwarted, or otherwise contradicted, it is energized; and its forces invade the heart, displace the *finiik,* and become manifested in public behavior. Yet, its often negatively valued attributes are occasionally recognized to be a source of creativity and innovation in the sociocultural domain, and in this respect it also contrasts with the usually more positively valued *finiik,* which is largely bound up with the regenerative perpetuation of tradition. The behavior attributed to the *khaapkhabuurien* is more or less predictable, only to those who have known the individual intimately for a long time and are privy to many important but highly personal and private experiences. In contrast, the behavior attributed to the *finiik* is believed to be largely predictable from the known social identity of the person, and the more or less recognized behavioral expectations and status-bound experiences that such social identity entails.

Because the *finiik* and the *khaapkhabuurien* always exist in a tensive relationship and in an ever-shifting balance (or imbalance), however, neither aspect of "thinking/feeling", motivation, or behavior is ever entirely comprehensible or predictable. There is always present a dimension of individual proclivity—of "thinking/feeling", motivation, and behavior—that Bimin-Kuskusmin acknowledge to be unfathomable by any person's ordinary knowledge and perception of another or by any divinatory means. Indeed, the actor himself may be surprised by an unexpected insight, change of mood, or disruption of social harmony in which he has unknowingly been instrumental. Indeed, the *khaapkhabuurien* is in some ways more powerful than the *finiik,* for it must be harnessed, contained, suppressed, transformed, dominated, and so on by the *finiik* lest its forces be unleashed. Massive socializing effort, especially in the form of initiation ritual, is designed to keep the *khaapkhabuurien* in place and subdued, although the rhetoric of initiatory oratory is focused almost entirely on the enhancement of the *finiik* and the qualities of personhood that it implies. The *khaapkhabuurien* has an agency of its own that almost inevitably leaves its impress on the actions attributed to the *finiik,* and, thus, the actions of the person, however socially ordained, proper, and predictable, are simultaneously the recognizable actions of a particular individual. Even among senior ritual elders, who are endowed with the most powerful *finiik* of all persons among Bimin-Kuskusmin, prescribed ritual behavior—the most tightly scripted of local behavioral displays—is almost invariably recognized to be shaped by certain individual eccentricities, which are often taken to be signs of the innovative creativity attributed to such ritual adepts.

The "self" (*kaaranarep'baataan*), the most generalized locus of experience and agency, located itself "on the inner and outer surfaces of the skin" (*kaar babgep'khaan magaang khaa sauk'khaan ker*), is both inward facing and outward facing. It is associated primarily with the tensive "gap" (*tem'khraan*) and "nexus" (*kuun'fuugaam*) between the *finiik* and the *khaapkhabuurien,* with the *khaapkhabuurien* as a locus of the sum total of life experiences, and with various aspects of the "skin" (*kaar*). Certain notions concerning the skin are central to conceptualizations of the self, for the skin is the site of "scars" (*guur*), the indelible marks of both initiatory ordeals and personal experience, a visible map of accidents, warfare, hunting, gardening, traveling, and so on, that individuates the human being while incribing him with the emblems of ritual that give him a clearly defined position in the social order of the community. Beyond the scars visible on the exterior of the skin, however, are the scars that adhere to the skin's interior surface, that are "hidden" (*niimteywa*) from public knowledge and scrutiny, that are "interior" (*mutuuk*), that are sometimes intuited by intimates and sometimes unknown to their bearers. Even the unmarred skin is believed to be akin to a partially completed canvas, which subsequently will take the impress of further scars, other experiences. The skin is said to have "skin roots" (*kaar kiimkiim*), sometimes an idiom for the self, which extend both into the public domains of community life in which the individual acts and leaves his characterological mark (itself a sense of scar), and into the inner recesses of the body where "thinking/feeling" takes shape.

This complex concept of the self connotes a sense of "character or personality" (*iraap ku'kaar*—literally, "skin enfolding"), of "personally marked social identity" (*ugaam'kaar uniikhaan*). It implicates a genre of "awareness or consciousness" (*vogogaamin'baakuur*), with personally "distinctive features" (*kaarap*), resulting from one's "inchoate feeling" (*tubiibuuru*) of being "alone" (both *iraa* [in the sense of being "singular"] and *uruu* [in the sense of being "isolated"]), of being "disengaged or turned inward" (*kuupkuur*), of "clinging to" (*ataam diik'saniim*) certain "experiences" (both *utaamiin* ["through the senses"] and *utuurmiin* ["inside the chest cavity"]). It is recognized that such disengagement and inwardness may make one "blind to a situation" (*kiin kuubaabisugiin*) and, thus, "behave inexplicably" (*kuguum biiram'kemiin*), but that such inward reflection allows one to sense what is 'alien' (*fiitaar*—"inconsistent with a sense of self").[6]

The self is constituted, in part, by a set of "images" (*kiin'kadaak*) and is often difficult to articulate in speech (see Poole, 1987b). It is ambiguous in many respects, and one cannot gain a clear, coherent impression of it, either in oneself (except fleetingly in trances) or in others. Speculations on the nature of others' selves are fraught not only with uncertainty, but also with anxiety, for insult can readily be taken at intrusive assessments of others' personal characteristics. It may be represented in "dreams" (*iraam*), but one easily "forgets" (*amuuniin*) what is nonetheless somehow "stored in memory" (*weng uuyo kwaak'a-buumiin*); and divinations of dreams can reveal only those aspects most clearly associated with the forces of the *finiik*.

Certain behaviors, idiosyncratic acts that one is "always doing" (*suun'kwaakhaan*), are seen to be indexical of the self, to be distinctively personal characteristics. Yet, it is distinctive "facial expressions" (*tibii-t'uunaak*) that are most noted as indices of self, although they are invariably reflected in others' descriptions of them. The self is implicated in accountability for happenings that are recognized to "be one's own fault" (*iraasaan dinaan'kaariin*) and not the consequence of others' behaviors. When something is made private, is "kept back for oneself" (*diir tiik'saaniin*) and not disclosed, it is deemed to be bound up with the self. When something is identified as "my individual own" (*ariigaap-'naara*), it is recognized to be identified with one's personal interests and identity. When one recounts an experience that is marked as pertaining to "I only, I alone" (*naara'siin* [*ón*]), the claim marks the experience as personal. When one takes a distinctive position in a conversation or dispute and marks his opinion as emanating from "I (different)" (*naagaraami*), the implication of a personal orientation is clear.

Not only is the self of another generally considered to be largely unfathomable by both possible perception and appropriate etiquette, but also the self is held to be mostly uninterpretable in divinations of dreams,

---

[6]In contrast, another sense of "alien" (*igaar*) connotes what is foreign to the sociocultural order.

reflections, and shadows of the individual. Thus, if some malady is attributable to the self, the only interpretation may be revealed in personal trance. There is diagnostic recognition in serious matters of severe depression and being highly suicide prone that some self-disorder is centrally involved, but it cannot be specified beyond perceptions of external circumstances; and remedy is sought by the provision of carefully orchestrated, but generally unfocused and nondirective, social–psychological support for the suffering individual.

The presence of the self as a force of agency in interaction is most clearly recognized in a set of distinctive signs that mark the individual as such publicly. Among the many names that are formally bestowed upon males in ritual contexts and that denote particular identities in social categories, there is one name—a "personal name (or nickname)" (win doroom'kaar), which is said to adhere to the skin—which marks the individualized self. It is given by one's father during the rite of couvade in early infancy, draws upon some circumstance of birth deemed significant for enduring character, and usually becomes a form of address and reference for a lifetime, but only among intimates. This name is an essential linkage between facets of individual identity and forms of personal interlocution. Being drawn into a conversation as one who can be addressed, referred to, and speak with respect to a personal name is to be recognized as an individual beyond one's social statuses, which are inevitably also recognized. Among Bimin-Kuskusmin, personal names are believed to capture, to reflect, and even to constitute certain essences or powers of the individual as a locus of experience and as an agent, and there are strong taboos on the use of personal names beyond a small circle of intimates and close kin.

Beyond personal names, there are also individualized personal totems, guardian spirits, and body shadows and reflections, all of which are believed to signify a distinctive self. These markers of individuality are often introduced into personal narratives and fantasy constructions—sometimes even taking the form of monologues when one is "working through" a personal problem of a private kind—when reference to the self is made either explicitly or implicitly. Among such narratives are autobiographical vignettes, in which the individual is understood to mark an individuated sense of self when these references are deployed. Beyond such narratives, however, references to personal names, totems, guardian spirits, and body shadows and reflections can be used by the individual as publicly opaque signs of personal interest, investment, concern, puzzle, or problem in various ritual domains in which such references are incorporated in a cultural repertoire of ritual speech, are discursively and experientially connected to more public and collective symbols, and come to acquire some of the characteristics that Obeyesekere (1981) attributes to "personal symbols" as often therapeutic expressions of psychic difficulty in the terms of cultural discourse.

Many narrations implicating the self are simple tales told in the course of ordinary conversations that focus on the dilemmas of sensing oneself to be an individual, to be different, to be alone, not to be readily encompassed in all respects by the otherwise enveloping social order. Most dramatic are the stories of primordial feral beings, wanderers, hermits, ostracized persons, lost hunters, strangers, and the like who find themselves beyond the pale of community and must rely only on themselves for survival. The narrative emphasis on personal resources — on resilience, cleverness, strength, insightfulness, and so on — suggests a positive value of resources of the self, at least under certain circumstances. Other tales portray the creativity emanating from the self under conditions of ritual isolation and deprivation, in which trance somehow activates the unscripted imagination of the self that yields significant innovation for the community, as though the socially unfettered self was itself a social resource. Indeed, more traditional legends of renown ritual elders lay clear emphasis upon their personal resources of insight, talent, and skill in imagining new solutions to old problems before domesticating the innovation and making it consensually acceptable by means of their authority and power of their ritual positions. Some tales directly address tensions between the *finiik* and the *khaapkhabuurien* as a soon apparent idiom for expressing identity struggles of their own; for example, between following the ritual course of highest male prestige and becoming a man invested in familial relationships.

The most poignant stories implicating ideas about the self, however, are tales portraying the fears and anxieties of being alone, isolated, removed from the resources of social support, and reliant only on one's own fragile resources to endure. Kaamneng (31 years old), using the rich lexicon of self terms, tells a tale of his being lost in the far forests beyond human settlement in the course of hunting wild pigs. He knew that there were settlements within a day's trek, but their inhabitants were beyond the pale of the human moral order known to him. They lacked *finiik* and all that it implied. As he climbed down the wall of a cliff, his grip slipped. He tumbled down a great waterfall and plunged deep into the water below. He was submerged for a long time and began to see lights of rainbows and hear sounds of cassowaries. He was in trance. His trance portrayed a young woman in the reeds by the water gathering frogs and tadpoles. She carried a small boy. In his trance, he spoke to her, and then, silently, she followed him. As long as she was following him, he could see the faint track that he had lost and could begin his journey home out of the wilderness. When she paused for rest, however, the track again disappeared. In time, he returned home with the woman and child, and they became his family. Kaamneng had not gone on such a hunt, nor had the other features of the tale actually occurred. He was being pressured by kinsmen to abandon his young wife and child in favor of a politically advantageous marriage and he had been much depressed about "making a choice for himself" (*diiranan saaniinin*). He felt secure and warm with the family he had and distant from the woman he would marry if he succumbed to the political pressures being placed on him. As his story implies, he had decided to forego the prestige of the marriage to be arranged and to remain with his supportive family. Only in imagined isolation and trance, however, had he been able to articulate his decision. And his tale was intricately cast in the idioms of the self.

Kuunan (24 years old) developed a narrative of two leaves that appeared in his dream. One leaf was alive and green and growing on a tall tree in the midst of a thriving garden. The other leaf was black and rotting, floating on an eddy of the nearby river's current. He was ill, and the leaves were known to be medicinal. His elders had told him that only the green leaves had medicinal value. He tried to climb to the green leaf time and time again, but on each attempt he fell and injured himself. His illness worsened until he could no longer climb the tree at all, and he then believed that he would die. There was no one to help him reach the leaf needed for his recovery. As he sat on the ground, however, a *tibiik*—his personal totem marsupial—came to the tree and watched him for a long time. Then, the *tibiik* entered the water and retrieved the dead leaf, mashed it to paste, and fed it to Kuunan. Soon he recovered and journeyed home. Kuunan was engaged in a demanding apprenticeship with a curer that had been arranged by his father, a powerful ritual elder. Kuunan loathed his apprenticeship, which involved much tedious learning of the esoterica of divination and of medicinal plants, and yearned to extricate himself from this subservient relationship, but feared offending his father. Finally, he understood that this potentially valued status was not his aspiration, informed his father, and returned to his passion for exploring and hunting along the rivers of his domain. His *tibiik*—a personalized idiom for his individualized self—had shown him that he could follow the path of his choice without dire consequence, and in time he did. He too sought a solution to a socially imposed dilemma through a narrative that was formulated in terms of the resources of the self.

What follows are brief selections from a long narrative by the man Maakeng, which focuses on his narrative representations of his sense of himself in the loss, grief, and suffering following the death of his five-year-old son, Weniyok, killed in a raid on his hamlet in 1972. The narrative unfolds some five months after Weniyok's death among a group of five local men, all of whom had known him long and well. Although a ritual elder of some renown and publicly distant from his then seven living children by three wives, Maakeng had taken special delight in this delightful, precocious little boy—an unexpected lastborn child of his youngest wife, now beyond her reproductive years, when he was in his mid-40s. It had become increasingly apparent to all who knew him that his relief that all other members of his family had survived was insufficient to blunt his anguish at Weniyok's death. Only three people had perished in the raid, although others had been injured. At first, in his raging anger, Maakeng had to be restrained from going alone among the Enkiakmin to the southwest to avenge his son's death, for all recognized, as he no doubt did too, that he would almost certainly have been killed in such an effort.

> At the end of the first pandanus harvest of this time, the little boy who laughed no longer laughed. . . . His breath fluttered . . . gurgled in his throat. . . . I was not there. . . . I saw no omen . . . my heart was closed. . . . Later, . . . I tried to bring the wind of my heart inside him . . . to make him strong again. . . . The tears inside my eyes were there. . . . The wind of my heart could not go to him. . . . His breath came no more. . . . His eyes had become like a 'falling star' (*suurii*). . . . His breath has entered my heart. . . . I remain Kiindaanam'ar. . . .

Maakeng notes Weniyok's falling ill in the Spring of 1972. There is no mention of the fact that the boy was killed by the blow of a club in a raid on their hamlet, his skull smashed, for Maakeng had not been able to accept his failure to defend his son. Indeed, he had been away when the raid occurred, returning the next day to find the charred remains of his hamlet but all of his family among the survivors except Weniyok. He notes that he saw no omen of the misfortune, that his "heart was closed" (*iboorop irom'kam*)—an expression of the failure of a father's powers of *finiik* to foresee and to forestall the impending misfortune of his child. Although there is no taboo on using the name of a child dying at this age after a few weeks following death, Maakeng, now some five months after the boy's demise, still refuses to utter his name or even to refer to him as his son; for to do so would be to acknowledge his passing as irrevocable. He permits the teknonym Weniyok'ar — father of Weniyok — to be used, however, although such teknonyms are usually abandoned immediately after a death as cruel reminders of misfortune. He does not ever use this teknonym in self-reference, but in this instance refers to himself as Kiindaanam'ar ("father of the bright-eyed one"), alluding to a personal name bestowed upon his son at birth and focusing his individuated sense of his identity now on his paternal bond with Weniyok. He mentions attempting to bring the "wind in the heart" (*iboorop iniim*) — a metaphor for his *finiik* — to encompass, protect, and strengthen the boy, but to no avail. Yet, the "tears inside the eyes" (*tiinak kiin'tem*) — unexpressed grief — make his efforts come to naught. His *finiik*, weakened by grief, could not be ritually detached to enfold his child in a moment of dire need. Weniyok died, the reflective quality of his eyes dulling as he was dying. In noting that the breath of the dying little boy entered his heart, Maakeng again refers — as he has in referring to the wind in his heart — to the affect of his grief on his *finiik*, on his processes of "thinking/feeling", on his stability as a person.

> When I went to my taro garden, I passed the place of his home. . . .
> I stopped there . . . many times. . . . A *kigiir* bird called *'kaawii, kaawii, kaawii'*, but I threw stones at it. . . . In my taro garden, I looked into the stream and saw his face . . . but not my own. . . .
> A small *taaginok* marsupial ran by, . . . up the cliff. . . . I followed. . . . I climbed the cliff there . . . and stood alone . . . I alone. . . . I, Taanok, screamed from the cliff . . . but the wind took my speech back in my throat. . . .

Maakeng tells of visiting the rock crevice where Weniyok's body had been placed. Indeed, he seems to have visited the rock crevice almost daily on his solitary walks to his garden, leaving small trinkets and bits of food at its opening. He refers to the rock crevice as his son's "home" (*am*), and it was rumored that he conducted secret magical rites there to resuscitate his son. The appearance of the *kigiir* bird — a spirit messenger from the ancestral underworld — intones not *"kiikwii, kiikwii, kiikwii,"* which is the usual onomatopoeic representation of the call of this bird, but *"kaawii, kaawii, kaawii,"* which approximates the sound of *kawii* or the term for death compensation. At this reminder of his responsibility and guilt for the protection of the boy, he hurls stones at the bird — refusing not only this ancestral sign of responsibility, but also a sign of ancestral encompassment and support. In this way, he implies a withdrawal from community, from the external anchorage of his *finiik,* from social interaction with dead or living. In the stream, he not only sees an image of the face of his dead son, which is an omen that the *khaakha-buurien* of his son has somehow entered him, but also fails to see a reflection of his own face, which for a living person is an indication that his *finiik* is fragmented or damaged. In turn, he follows the *taaginok* marsupial — one of his personal "totems" and a sign of his individualized self — to the cliff. At the top of the cliff, he stands alone, emphasizing his being alone, and refers to himself by the personal name Taanok, which is a personal name associated with the aftermath of a time when he was near death himself from war wounds and has not been used for him for many years. This name marks another moment of personal crisis. The wind pushing his screams back inside him is another expression of his being alone, by himself, without the effective support of others, in solitary grief. This self-presentation is seen by other men listening to this narration to be ominous — a possible indication that he may be contemplating suicide. The image of his standing alone on the cliff-top reinforces this concern, for leaping from heights to one's death is a well-known style of suicide second only to hanging oneself in the deep forest.

> Then, I wandered into the forest above my taro garden. . . . I walked alone until night. . . . I built no fire there. . . . The *kigiir* bird followed me there . . . calling . . . calling. . . . I saw it calling . . . I could not hear it anymore. . . . I could not hear it before. . . . Then, I saw the *taaginok* marsupial near a rushing stream. . . . It must have fallen from the cliff below, . . . it bled. . . . There was a long wound on its side. . . . Its blood fell on the leaves beneath it. . . . Its breath was heavy. . . . The wind carried the blood-soaked leaves into the stream . . . they floated away. . . . I tried to catch them and . . . grabbed a few. . . . There was no blood left on them then. . . . I could cup no blood in my hands . . . only leaves and water. . . . A feather of the *kigiir* floated with the leaves . . . it never touched them. . . . The moonlight faded behind the clouds. . . . I could see nothing anymore. . . .

Maakeng portrays his wandering into the high forest at night, alone, and without fire — a common narrative image of "depression" (*sakhiik mutuuk*) emanating from inside one. His inability to hear the call of the *kigiir* bird is another sign of his turning inward and also of his incapacity to perceive omens, which are often associated with the behavior of spirit messenger birds. In noting that he could not hear it before, he may well be referring to his failure to perceive omens of his child's impending death. Both allusions connote the disarray of his capacities of *finiik*. In turn, the injury to the *taaginok* marsupial — a personal "totem" — suggests the image of a "scar" (*guur*), which is a common idiom for an experience of indelible significance marking the individuated self. Yet, the wound is both fresh, as marked by the still flowing blood, and agonizing, as indicated by the labored breathing. As he tries to retrieve the blood, it eludes him — just as the meaning of his son's death eludes his understanding. He captures only leaves and water — only the vehicles of the blood, only the obvious 'facts' of the tragedy. The blood — a medium of divination — washes away and reveals nothing. The feather of the *kigiir* bird floats by too, never touching the blood-soaked leaves and also disappearing in the stream. His understanding — his *finiik* — cannot encompass what has happened; his social anchorage — his *finiik* — cannot sustain him and also deserts him. Without his powers of "thinking/ feeling", of *finiik,* which provide his means of orientation in the world, he is left in darkness without the ability to see — to understand — the significance of the signs of his loss which fleetingly appear and then disappear before him. The moon, which is the light of the sacred hearth fires of the ancestral underworld, fades when he needs it most. He seems to sense himself both distanced from the social world which offers him no solace now and beyond being able to understand, accept, or deal with deep feelings of loss and grief. Maakeng is a man, like many Bimin-Kuskusmin men who have sought and won renown in the political-ritual realm, whose obviously deeply felt affection for his little boy was expressed mostly at a distance, for he was little involved in the intimacies of the boy's daily life except on the rarest of occasions. Thus, it is difficult for him now to enfold his anguished feelings with the expression of emotion — either to himself or to others. Indeed, this narrative self-revelation discloses far more of an inchoate sense of profound grief and quiet desperation than is usual for men of his age and prominence under the circumstances of the death of a child.

> When I speak to you, the speech is like water, . . . the blood remains inside. . . . I cannot speak it. . . . There is a 'spirit arrow' (*on kusem*) in my chest. . . . It will always stay there. . . . It cannot be cut out. . . . The gentle boy's *khaapkhabuurien* holds it there. . . . He does not want to go. . . . He wants to live inside me. . . . He pulls the spirit arrow into my heart. . . . I feel its

sharpness. . . . I cannot tell you how it feels inside. . . . When I sit among you, it [the spirit arrow or the boy's *khaapkhabuurien?*] pulls my *finiik* into a dream . . . [in which] I alone am with him. . . . But my *khaapkhabuurien* must struggle to be there. . . . His face is there. . . . Your faces are blurred in smoke, . . . in mist. . . . But sometimes I cannot hear him . . . or you, . . . only the dripping of my blood inside. . . .

Maakeng acknowledges the inadequacy of his words to express what he feels and portrays an interiorized realm of feelings which are his alone to comprehend. In the company of his intimates, he emphasizes that he cannot share with them these internal sensations of grief. He speaks of a spirit arrow in his chest, with the implication that it pierces his heart and, thus, his *finiik*. The spirit arrow seems to be both a sign of his guilt over his failure to foresee his son's danger and to protect him — as marked in the earlier image of the *kigiir* bird — and a sign of his still unacknowledged recognition that his son is forever dead and incorporated into the "ancestral underworld" (*kusem am*) from which spirit arrows are sent as omens. In both senses, the spirit arrow also seems to portray his sense of the "sharpness" (*atuur'naam*) — both the painfulness and the depth — of his feelings of loss and grief, and his sense that such feelings will not recede — that the spirit arrow cannot be removed. The boy's *khaapkhabuurien* — his full experiential self — is lodged within him, pulling the spirit arrow into him, wanting to remain inside his father, not wishing to depart from him. Yet, Maakeng cannot articulate that sensation of the boy's closeness to him in death, for they were not close in life. It is his *finiik* — his social persona — which is pulled into the dream in which he sees the boy's face and is alone with him; but his *khaapkhabuurien* — his more individuated, personal self — must struggle to be present with his son in the dream, for that sense of himself was hardly known to the boy or a part of their relationship. Nonetheless, his sensation of the presence of his son — of his face, the image of his individuality — is vivid while the faces of others blur and recede around it. However, he can hear neither his son nor others, only the sound of his blood, of his fresh wound of loss and grief within himself. Again, he focuses on his being alone, in some interior realm, with his feelings.

These narratives represent the forms in which the terms and concepts of person, self, and individual, and their implied underlying schemas are often cast. Personal knowledge of cultural models or schemas of ideas analytically identifiable through analogy to person, self, and individual is directed both outwardly and inwardly toward arrangements of status-role configurations and what underlies their occupancy, enactment, judgmental expectations, and measures of accountability, and toward not only the shaping and understanding of personal experience in myriad contexts of the Bimin-Kuskusmin "culturally constituted behavioral environment" (Hallowell 1955a, p. 87), but also, albeit more tentatively, fragilely, and circumspectly, the prognosis or retrospective assessment of "other minds" as other selves. To focus on selves is to construct queries and to direct observation with reference to culturally posited intrapsychic and interpersonal structures and processes as they are deemed to shape a sense of being, to inform experience, and to lend significance to being the locus and perhaps, in part, the agent of that experience. Cultural schemas are apprehended by the experiencing self and internalized in some manner; and, thus, cultural formulations of self-interest (however such a notion may be socially and personally defined and realized) may become a source of goals, ideals, problems, ideas, concepts, and beliefs complexly incorporated by selves and in service of defining critical contexts for the self's growth, development, expression, and interpretation (both by the self and by others). To focus on persons as agents in society brings the forms and forces of the sociomoral order to the foreground of attention, for these phenomena become constitutive of human agency as a public fact. Indeed, person and sociomoral system form a set, eliminating the awkward necessity of dealing with communities merely as agglomerations of individuals or only as stages for the dramatic presentations of selves. Betwixt, between, interwoven with, and in some ways beneath person and self, however, are often fundamental notions of the biologistic, psychologistic, sociologistic, and mystical dimensions of human nature that endow the individual with the capacity for culture, for participation in a sociomoral order, and for reflective and reflexive experience, and that establish the grounds for reckoning significant dimensions of intracultural similarity and difference as they are recognized in a sociomoral order through the status-bound character of expressions, enactments, and legitimations of persons and in the personal experiences of selves. Among Bimin-Kuskusmin, analogs of person, self, and individual are complexly represented and interwoven, and yet the individual is a presence on this landscape. The Bimin-Kuskusmin concept of the individual, as it is variously formulated in contrast to, and in interaction with, notions of person and self, is not the individual of Western "individualism," which involves local cultural schemas of its own, but some of its distinguishable features exhibit certain "family resemblances" to an analytically construed image of the individual that, itself, draws comparatively on Western ideas (see La Fontaine, 1985). In this essay, it has been argued that the individual is a reality in some fashion in perhaps any society, is a focus of essential interest to a psychoanalytic anthropology, and is a concept of considerable cultural elaboration and personal significance among the Bimin-Kuskusmin of Papua New Guinea.

## BIBLIOGRAPHY

ALLEN, N.J. (1985), The category of the person: A reading of Mauss's last essay. In: *The Category of the Person,* ed. M. Carrithers, S. Collins & S. Lukes. Cambridge: Cambridge University Press, pp. 26–45.

BATTAGLIA, D. (1990), *On the Bones of the Serpent.* Chicago: University of Chicago Press.

BAUMEISTER, R.F. (1987), How the self became a problem: A psychological review of historical research. *J. Pers. Soc. Psychol.,* 52:163–176.

BLACK, M.B. (1977), Ojibwa taxonomy and percept ambiguity. *Ethos,* 5:90–118.

CARRITHERS, M. (1985), An alternative social history of the self. In: *The Category of the Person,* ed. M. Carrithers, S. Collins & S. Lukes. Cambridge: Cambridge University Press, pp. 234–256.

D'ANDRADE, R.G. (1981), The cultural part of cognition. *Cog. Sci.,* 5:179–195.

_____ (1984), Cultural meaning systems. In: *Culture Theory,* ed. R.A. Shweder & R.A. LeVine. Cambridge: Cambridge University Press, pp. 88–119.

DOI, T. (1990), The cultural assumptions of psychoanalysis. In: *Cultural Psychology,* ed. J.W. Stigler, R.A. Shweder, & G. Herdt. Cambridge: Cambridge University Press, pp. 446–453.

DUMONT, L. (1977), *From Mandeville to Marx.* Chicago: University of Chicago Press.

_____ (1986), *Essays on Individualism.* Chicago: University of Chicago Press.

EMMET, D. (1960), How far can structural studies take account of individuals? *J. Royal Anthropol. Inst.,* 90:191–200.

ERIKSON, E. (1950), *Childhood and Society.* New York: Norton.

_____ (1968), *Identity.* New York: Norton.

EVENS, T.M. (1977), The predication of the individual in anthropological interactionism. *Amer. Anthropol.,* 79:579–597.

FAJANS, J. (1985), The person in social context: The social character of Baining "psychology." In: *Person, Self, and Experience,* ed. G.M. White & J. Kirkpatrick. Berkeley: University of California Press, pp. 367–397.

FORTES, M. (1973), On the concept of the person among the Tallensi. In: *La notion de personne en afrique noire,* ed. G. Dieterlen. Paris: Centre National de la Recherche Scientifique, pp. 283–319.

FREUD, S. (1914), Zur Einführung des Narzissmus. *Gesammelte Werke,* 10:138–170. Frankfurt: Fischer Verlag, 1946.

_____ (1930), Civilization and its discontents. *Standard Edition,* 21:64–145. London: Hogarth Press, 1964.

GEERTZ, C. (1973), Person, time, and conduct in Bali. In: *The Interpretation of Cultures,* ed. C. Geertz. New York: Basic Books, pp. 360–411.

_____ (1984), "From the native's point of view": On the nature of anthropological understanding. In: *Culture Theory,* ed. R.A. Shweder & R.A. LeVine. Cambridge: Cambridge University Press, pp. 123–136.

HALLOWELL, A.I. (1955a), The self and its behavioral environment. In: *Culture and*

Experience, ed. A.I. Hallowell. Philadelphia: University of Pennsylvania Press, pp. 75–110.

_____ (1955b), The Ojibwa self and its behavioral environment. In: *Culture and Experience,* ed. A.I. Hallowell. Philadelphia: University of Pennsylvania Press, pp. 172–182.

_____ (1958), Ojibwa metaphysics of being and the perception of persons. In: *Person Perception and Interpersonal Behavior,* ed. R. Tagiuri & L. Petrullo. Stanford: Stanford University Press, pp. 63–85.

_____ (1960), Self, society and culture in phylogenetic perspective. In: *Evolution after Darwin,* Vol. 2, ed. S. Tax. Chicago: University of Chicago Press, pp. 309–372.

_____ (1976a), Personality, culture, and society in behavioral evolution. In: *Contributions to Anthropology,* ed. A.I. Hallowell. Chicago: University of Chicago Press, pp. 230–310.

_____ (1976b), Ojibwa ontology, behavior, and world view. In: *Contributions to Anthropology,* ed. A.I. Hallowell. Chicago: University of Chicago Press, pp. 357–390.

_____ (1976c), Ojibwa world view and disease. In: *Contributions to Anthropology,* ed. A.I. Hallowell. Chicago: University of Chicago Press, pp. 391–448.

_____ (1976d), The role of dreams in Ojibwa culture. In: *Contributions to Anthropology,* ed. A.I. Hallowell. Chicago: University of Chicago Press, pp. 449–474.

HANNING, R.W. (1977), *The Individual in Twelfth-Century Romance.* New Haven: Yale University Press.

HARRIS, G.G. (1989), Concepts of individual, self and person in description and analysis. *American Anthropologist,* 91:599–612.

HARTMANN, H. (1958), *Ego Psychology and the Problem of Adaptation.* New York: International Universities Press.

HAY, T.H. (1977), The development of some aspects of the Ojibwa self and its behavioral environment. *Ethos,* 5:71–89.

HERDT, G.H. (1989), Self and culture. Contexts of religious experience in Melanesia. In: *The Religious Imagination in New Guinea,* ed. G.H. Herdt & M. Stephen. New Brunswick: Rutgers University Press, pp. 15–40.

JACOBSON, E. (1954), The self and the object world. *The Psychoanalytic Study of the Child,* 9:75–127. New York: International Universities Press.

KAKAR, S. (1990), Stories from Indian psychoanalysis: Context and text. In: *Cultural Psychology,* ed. J.W. Stigler, R.A. Shweder, & G. Herdt. Cambridge: Cambridge University Press, pp. 427–445.

KIRK, L., AND BURTON, M.L. (1977), Meaning and context: A study of contextual shifts in the meaning of Masai personality descriptors. *Amer. Ethnolog.,* 4:734–761.

KIRKPATRICK, J. (1985), How personal differences can make a difference. In: *The Social Construction of the Person,* ed. K.J. Gergen & K.E. Davis. New York: Springer-Verlag, pp. 225–240.

KOHUT, H. (1971), *The Analysis of the Self.* New York: International Universities Press.

_____ (1977), *The Restoration of the Self.* New York: International Universities Press.

KONDO, D.K. (1990), *Crafting Selves.* Chicago: The University of Chicago Press.

LA FONTAINE, J.S. (1985), Person and individual: Some anthropological reflections. In: *The Category of the Person,* ed. M. Carrithers, S. Collins, & S. Lukes. Cambridge: Cambridge University Press, pp. 123–140.

LEVINE, R.A. (1990), Infant environments in psychoanalysis: A cross-cultural view. In: *Cultural Psychology,* ed. J.W. Stigler, R.A. Shweder, & G. Herdt. Cambridge: Cambridge University Press, pp. 454–474.

LUKES, S. (1973), *Individualism.* Oxford: Basil Blackwell.

LUTZ, C. (1988), *Unnatural Emotions.* Chicago: The University of Chicago Press.

MACFARLANE, A. (1979), *The Origins of English Individualism*. Cambridge: Cambridge University Press.

MAUSS, M. (1938), Une catégorie de l'esprit humain: La notion de personne, celle de "moi." *J. Royal Anthropolog. Inst.*, 68:263–282.

MCHUGH, E.L. (1989), Concepts of the person among the Gurungs of Nepal. *Amer. Ethnolog.*, 16:75–86.

MORRIS, C. (1987), *The Discovery of the Individual 1050–1200*. Toronto: University of Toronto Press.

OBEYESEKERE, G. (1981), *Medusa's Hair*. Chicago: The University of Chicago Press.

POOLE, F.J.P. (1982), The ritual forging of identity: Aspects of person and self in Bimin-Kuskusmin male initiation. In: *Rituals of Manhood*, ed. G.H. Herdt. Berkeley: University of California Press, pp. 99–154.

_____ (1984), Symbols of substance: Bimin-Kuskusmin models of procreation, death, and personhood. *Mankind*, 14:191–216.

_____ (1985), Coming into social being: Cultural images of infants in Bimin-Kuskusmin folk psychology. In: *Person, Self, and Experience*, ed. G.M. White & J. Kirkpatrick. Berkeley: University of California Press, pp. 183–242.

_____ (1986a), Personal control, social responsibility, and image of person and self among the Bimin-Kuskusmin of Papua New Guinea. *International Journal of Law and Psychiatry*, 9:295–319.

_____ (1986b), Self and experience in the Bimin-Kuskusmin culturally constituted behavioral environment. Presented at the 85th Annual Meeting of the American Anthropological Association, Philadelphia.

_____ (1987a), Morality, personhood, tricksters, and youths: Some narrative images of ethics among Bimin-Kuskusmin. In: *Anthropology in the High Valleys*, ed. L.L. Langness, & T.E. Hays. Novato: Chandler & Sharp, pp. 283–366.

_____ (1987b), The voice of "thinking/feeling" and the power of speech: Ethnopsychological discourse among Bimin-Kuskusmin. Presented at the 86th Annual Meeting of the American Anthropological Association, Chicago.

READ, K.E. (1955), Morality and the concept of the person among the Gahuku-Gama, Eastern Highlands, New Guinea. *Oceania*, 25:233–282.

SCHAFER, R. (1976), *A New Language for Psychoanalysis*. New Haven: Yale University Press.

_____ (1989), Narratives of the self. In: *Psychoanalysis*, ed. A.M. Cooper, O.F. Kernberg, & E.S. Person. New Haven: Yale University Press, pp. 153–167.

STERN, D.N. (1985), *The Interpersonal World of the Infant*. New York: Basic Books.

_____ (1989), Developmental prerequisites for the sense of a narrated self. In: *Psychoanalysis*, eds. A.M. Cooper, O.F. Kernberg, & E.S. Person. New Haven: Yale University Press, pp. 168–178.

STRATHERN, M. (1988), *The Gender of the Gift*. Berkeley: University of California Press.

SWART, K.W. (1962), "Individualism" in the mid-nineteenth century (1826–1860). *Journal of the History of Ideas*, 23:77–90.

TAYLOR, C. (1989), *Sources of the Self*. Cambridge: Harvard University Press.

WHITE, G.M. (1978), Ambiguity and ambivalence in A'ara personality descriptors. *American Ethnologist*, 5:334–360.

# 6

# House Design and the Self in an African Culture

ROBERT A. LeVINE
SARAH E. LeVINE

The question of how culture may be interpreted as fantasy in the Freudian sense generated a variety of positions, particularly concerning which aspects of culture are amenable to such interpretation. For Roheim (1943) and others who identified themselves with Freud's own position, no aspect of culture was too practical to be excluded from psychoanalytic interpretation. For revisionists like Kardiner (1939, 1945) and Whiting (Whiting and Child, 1953), culture was divisible into two parts, which Kardiner called primary and secondary institutions and Whiting called maintenance systems and projective systems. In each case, the first part included institutions, like subsistence patterns and household structure, that are linked to survival and adaptation and can be interpreted in ecological and socioeconomic terms; the second institutions, like religion and folklore, that provide collective media for the expression of personal fantasy and are amenable to a symbolic interpretation based on psychoanalysis.

Hallowell (1955) initiated a different line of thought focused on the individual's conscious experience and its culturally constituted environment, both of which combined adaptive strategies and defensive fantasies. For Hallowell, the crucial distinction was between the level of

The writing of this article was supported by a grant from the Spencer Foundation. Field work among the Gusii was supported by the Ford Foundation (1955–1957), the Carnegie Corporation of New York (1964) and the National Science Foundation and the National Institute of Mental Health (1974–1976). Our 1988 visit was funded by the Spencer Foundation.

personal experience and that of institutionalized culture, which, though influencing one another, are not identical and therefore require independent assessment. The fantasies of interest from a psychoanalytic point of view might be found in either personal experience or collective representations, and though the latter are constitutive of the former, it is the anthropologist's task to investigate their relationship in a particular cultural context rather than to assume it. That this approach continues to produce illuminating, psychoanalytically informed ethnography is evident in recent works (for example, Herdt, 1981; Obeyesekere, 1981), which demonstrate cross-cultural variability in forms of expressive media and in the relationships of cultural symbolism to the individual's emotional well-being and sense of reality.

It is evident from research conducted in this vein that there is no fixed institutional locus for cultural fantasy, and that it is only by examining how individuals in a particular community use cultural representations that we can discover their place in personal adaptation and defense. In our view, influenced by Hallowell and his students (for example, Spiro, 1987; Wallace, 1956), an institution is a compromise formation offering participants private satisfaction of unconscious motives together with public approval and other rationally calculated benefits (R.A. LeVine, 1973, pp. 137–152). Economic institutions, even when rational in their means, can be directed toward ends that owe their incentive value to the unconscious, symbolic significance they have for participants. Conversely, religious institutions, though propagating myth and ritual, can be sustained by participation motivated more by conventionalism and ambition than by personal attachment to their symbolic content. In this perspective, the institutions studied in anthropological field work and the explanations for them offered by informants are products of the imagination stabilized in the adaptive practice of a community — composites of symbolic fantasy and rational strategy (R.A. LeVine, 1984).

This view is not entirely accepted in anthropology, even among psychological anthropologists. Everyone might agree, following Weber (1947), that religious symbolism must be socially routinized and conventionalized in order to survive more than a few years, but the idea that patterns of technology, economics, household structure, and sociopolitical organization have a symbolic/psychodynamic component is strongly resisted. Yet the widely held "symbolic action" theory (Geertz, 1973) claims all social behavior to be guided by cultural models that organize the perception of reality as well as reflect it; cultural symbols mediate all environmental effects on human behavior. This is quite close to Hallowell's phenomenological perspective and leaves open the possibility that unconscious motives contribute to the design of "utilitarian" aspects of culture closely connected to survival and adaptation.

In this chapter, we will show that the institutionalized housing arrangements of an African people can only be understood as cultural symbols with psychodynamic meaning and function, notwithstanding their use in food production, social organization, and the provision of shelter and warmth. We claim that neither the Gusii habitat in southwestern Kenya nor their means of surviving in it dictated the particular designs of buildings and homesteads that came to be embodied in traditional norms and to which Gusii individuals remained attached after economic conditions changed. On the contrary, their domestic architecture, furniture, and residential arrangement are physical embodiments of the deepest meanings Gusii experience in life: their goals and fears, preferences and aversions, sources of pride and shame, and of safety and danger, represented in spatial terms. Their house design must be interpreted in terms of its place in the symbolic world of Gusii culture and what it does for the emotional stability of Gusii individuals. Conversely, that culture cannot be understood without a knowledge of the "built environment" in which its central narratives of the self, that is, its fantasies, are located.

The claim that domestic architecture reflects cultural meanings in three-dimensional space is not new (see Rapoport, 1969). The symbolism of building design among West African peoples, especially in the Sahel, has long been noted (Fortes, 1949; Griaule, 1965; Blier, 1987). Sieber (1980), in the companion volume to an exhibit of African furniture and household objects, states that "in Africa utilitarian objects may be individually owned and . . . carry intensely personal meanings . . . [Unfortunately] the nature of the powerful psychic bond between owner and object is all but unstudied" (p. 17).

The customary house design and household objects of the Gusii of Kenya may be of particular interest because the Gusii had no religious shrines or other buildings set apart from the residential homestead. Their houses were, and are, largely lacking in what would appear to be decoration from a Western perspective; and their furniture and household objects are similarly unadorned and used in the mundane activities of everyday life. There is nothing that speaks to an outsider of symbolic representation in an aesthetic or religious mode. Yet, to the Gusii, this domestic environment is a design in which each spatial arrangement and utensil is a metaphor, freighted with moral and spiritual significance, that defines the course of a person's life and plays an essential part in the social and ritual dramas that maintain personal and familial well-being. In the following sections, these cultural meanings and their psychic functions are considered from three perspectives: the stages of life, the settings for social drama, and the metaphors of danger and well-being.

## BACKGROUND: THE DOMESTIC ENVIRONMENT IN GUSII SOCIETY

The Gusii are a Bantu-speaking people of about 1 million who live in the southwestern corner of the Kenya highlands south of the equator near Lake Victoria. Inhabiting these fertile and well-watered hills since the 18th century, the Gusii practiced shifting cultivation of millet grains and maintained sizable herds of cattle. They had no centralized leadership; territorial groupings of patrilineal clans were politically autonomous and conducted blood feuds and cattle raids against each other, as well as against surrounding Nilotic-speaking peoples. Military defense was a constant need, and most of the cattle were kept in camps (*ebisaraati*), where they could be protected by resident warriors. Each homestead (*omochie*) was a self-governing unit ruled by its patriarch (*omogaaka*), who lived there with his several wives, their unmarried children, and their married sons (with their wives and children). Patrilocal residence and initiation rites for both sexes were universal; polygyny was an ideal frequently attained.

The British conquered the Gusii in 1908, imposed colonial rule, and disbanded the cattle camps in 1913. Foreign influences on the religion, economy and health care of the Gusii grew over the next 50 years, though at a relatively slow pace due to their isolated location and fertile land. For most Gusii, the major changes in education, economic participation, and family life occurred after Kenya's independence in 1963. The field work reported on here was conducted in 1955–1957, 1964, and 1974–1976.

The traditional Gusii house (*enyomba*) is a round structure made of a framework of saplings, with dried mud walls and a conical, concentrically thatched roof. There are no windows; a stick protrudes as a steeple (*egechuri*) from the peak of the roof. Men perform all the building tasks except applying mud to the walls, which must be done by women. The interior layout shown in Figure 1 is the two-room house of a married woman. Most houses were of this type because every married woman was entitled to one. The only exceptional structures (not found in every homestead) were the smaller, one-room houses built for the circumcision

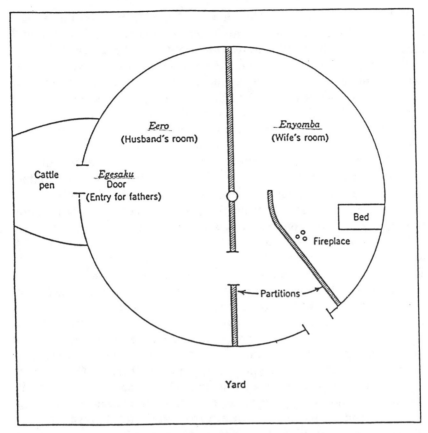

**Figure 1**
Traditional Gusii house.

of boys or for the polygynous patriarch to sleep in occasionally apart from his wives and, were he a political leader, to entertain his male friends and settle disputes. Each house of a married woman was located on the land she cultivated, which her husband (and later, her son) would inherit from his father. Thus, the houses of a homestead were dispersed across the land of its owner, representing the homestead's internal divisions through marriage.

In his admirable monograph on the Gusii lineage, Mayer (1949) showed how domestic imagery supplied the metaphorical vocabulary for Gusii social organization. The word *egesaku,* which literally means the smaller doorway from the cattle pen into the traditional house, is used to refer to a lineage, autonomous group, or political entity at any level, including the nation-state. What is the connection between this apparently minor feature of domestic architecture and the wider social order? Egesaku is the only entry permitted the brothers of the father of the man who owns the house, according to Gusii norms of kin-avoidance. A cardinal rule of kin-avoidance is that the actual father may never enter his married son's house under any circumstances, which is understood as a barrier against the patriarch's possible sexual exploitation of his daughter-in-law. The father's brother, whom the son calls *tatamoke* ("little father") and who as a kin equivalent can assume the paternal role should the father die, is permitted to enter his nephew's house, but only through *egesaku,* coming from the cattle pen and thus avoiding contact with that part of the house identified with the woman. In other words, this restriction on the father's brothers is a weaker version of the total prohibition on entry applying to the actual father.

Taken as a group, the men to whom this prohibition applies, that is, the father's brothers, represent the patrilineage as a center of authority from the viewpoint of an adult man. They are the elders who settle disputes to which he may be a party and who can curse him if he refuses to accept their will. The word egesaku refers to this group, bound together by patrilineal kinship and collective authority, and by extension to the wider Gusii lineages, in which this nuclear group is embedded, and to all other self-governing units, including Kenya and other nations. Thus the word *egesaku* is a multivocal symbol in Turner's (1967) sense, referring to the avoidance of sexuality in the father–son relationship at its sensory pole and to the principle of collective governance at its ideological pole. And the metaphor is drawn from domestic architecture.

The complementary term to egesaku is *enyomba* (plural, *chinyomba*), literally meaning "house." In its domestic context, *enyomba* refers both to the standard (two-room) house as a whole of a married woman and to the room within that house, which is identified with the woman, and in which the hearth and the sleeping place are located (see Figure 1). At a somewhat metaphorical level, the homestead of a patriarch is said to be divided into *chinyomba,* each consisting of the sons of a particular mother, who were, of course, born and raised in her (actual) house and became social units of inheritance and mutual loyalty after they have grown up and built their own houses (near hers). It is expected that these sons will compete with, and even conspire against, their half-brothers in the other *chinyomba* for a larger share of the patrimony and that such tensions, though suppressed by the patriarch, may well be carried down into future generations, with ortho-cousins forming local factions in the neighborhood. Given this kinship situation, it is no surprise that the word *enyomba* also designates a segment of a sociopolitical unit at any level, with the expectation that *chinyomba* will act as divisive factions threatening its unity. If *egesaku,* the patrilineal principle, refers to collective solidarity, then *chinyomba* refers to the fault lines, originating in wives and mothers, along which division tends to occur. Domestic architecture supplies the images for a vocabulary of social relations with an implicit political philosophy.

A third term Mayer (1949) mentions is *riiga,* meaning hearthstone, of which the Gusii house has three, on which pots are supported over the cooking fire. As a category of ethnosociology, *riiga* refers to the localized patrilineage that herds its cattle together, thereby collaborating in productive activity. Here again, domestic imagery is drawn upon to symbolize solidarity in social relationships, a point emphasized by Mayer in his Radcliffe–Brownian analysis of Gusii society.

The use of terms derived from the canonical structure of the Gusii house in their ethnosociology is part of a larger tendency in Gusii discourse to use spatial or locational metaphors for social relationships and identities. Thus, when Gusii meet they ask what place (*aase*) the other comes from rather than what lineage or clan he belongs to, and the answer begins with the locational (*bo-* prefix) version of the clan name, even though the clan may have moved over the course of the speaker's life. In other words, speakers locate themselves in (metaphorical) social space, using terms that refer literally to ostensive, geographical space (Evans-Pritchard, 1940). This social geography of personal identity extends downwards into the homestead, where the identity of persons with houses is central to culturally organized experience.

Mayer (1949) emphasized the normative aspect of the Gusii house as a publicly mandated, domestic structure and as a source of metaphor for social structure in general, which accurately represents one way in which Gusii experience it. But the Gusii house also represents a design deeply desired by the individuals who build and live in accordance with it; and it is their personal motivation that commands our attention in this chapter.

## THE STAGES OF LIFE

For every Gusii person, the progress of life is charted by residence in a succession of houses. A man can look forward to four basic stages of life: (a) childhood, in his mother's house, where he was born; (b) a premarital stage, living in the one-room hut in which he was secluded after circumcision; (c) the marital stage, living with his wife and immature children in a standard two-room house; (e) death and interment in a grave outside his first wife's house. (Before 1913, there would have been another house (*egesa*) in the cattle-camp, in which a man would reside intermittently between his own circumcision and that of his firstborn son.) Each of these stages contains several, described substages, that represent progress toward the next higher stage.

A Gusii woman can look forward to three basic stages of life defined by residence in a house: (a) childhood, in her mother's house, where she was born; (b) marriage, in her own house within the homestead of her husband's father; (c) death and interment in a grave outside her marital house (but on the left side of the house rather than the right side where the husband is buried). A major difference between the male and female patterns is occasioned by the patrilocal residence pattern, that is, all of the male stages are within his father's home or on adjacent land, whereas the female at marriage moves away permanently from her natal residence to that of her husband, in an alien clan possibly far away.

Personal progression through these basic stages can be clarified by a description of the steps that define their substages. The male child actually sleeps in his mother's house only until about 7 or 8 years of age (or up to 10 years of age in the case of widows' sons), after which — in recognition of his growing sexual awareness and the sense that he should not be present where parental coitus might occur — he sleeps with older boys and unmarried men in another house (sometimes a circumcision hut) within the homestead, at least when his father is sleeping in the main house (LeVine and LeVine, 1966, pp. 161, 177). In this second substage of childhood, the boy is still regarded as living at his mother's house; he goes there to be fed by her and is not limited in where he can go within her house during the daytime. It is in the move to the next basic stage, through the circumcision at ten or eleven years of age (and subsequent seclusion in a separate hut) constituting initiation into manhood, that the Gusii male's identity with his mother's house is explicitly and permanently severed. A major part of the instruction received by the initiate from older boys during seclusion concerns avoidance of the mother's house. After his emergence from seclusion as an *omomura* (young man or warrior), he is forbidden to enter his former residence, and after payment of a goat to his mother (reduced by the 1950s to some meat purchased at the market), he is permitted only into the foyer of her house (see Figure 1), avoiding the sleeping area (where parental coitus takes place) for the rest of his life.

An omomura would have spent most of his time in the cattle camp (*egesaraate*) prior to 1913, but later it became normal for him to live in his circumcision hut when at home and to continue living in it with his bride in the earliest period of their marriage. The building of a marital house with two rooms was required for, and symbolic of, a man's passage to the role of husband and (potential) father, but as marriage itself was a gradual process with several phases and became more so in the 1970s when elopement without bridewealth became the norm (Hakansson, 1988), so the building of the full house was often postponed. A man can be a husband while living with his wife in his circumcision hut, but if this temporary state goes on too long, it becomes scandalous and detrimental to the higher status that goes with being a married man. Taking up residence in a real, newly built *enyomba* confirms this status and sets the stage for parenthood.

While this is the last major stage transition before death, there are two substages of great importance to every Gusii man: the building of a house for each additional wife he marries, and the addition of a house for each of his sons as they marry. Success for a man in traditional Gusii terms is equivalent to becoming a polygynist with married sons, which requires wealth, and in earlier times led to more wealth. The proliferation of houses in a man's homestead attests to his becoming wealthy and important; conversely, a man with only a few houses (after his father died and the brothers divided the land [see R.A. LeVine, 1964]) is considered impoverished and insignificant. Thus houses are, in effect, a form of conspicuous consumption enhancing a man's prestige in the community as well as a form of investment in economic and reproductive terms. When a man has two or more wives, he usually rotates his residence among them (spending more time with the youngest), and he might construct a separate hut for himself, where he can retreat from all of them when he wants. This hut, known as *esaiga,* also serves as a sleeping place for children regarded as too old to sleep in the mother's house anymore.

The married son's house represents an important paradox: it marks the establishment of a man as a patriarch with authority over adults of the next generation (when his eldest son marries, a man is entitled to be called *omogaaka,* "patriarch," by everyone in the homestead), but also the limit on that authority, namely the ban on his entering the house. In the Gusii view, this prohibition is what makes the homestead a moral community in which authority is restrained by a sense of righteousness (the avoidance of incest) rather than a despotic patriarchy in which power is unrestrained. Like the code of kin avoidance (*chinsoni*) of which this prohibition was part, the restraint is also a symbolic statement made in an action language that censors evil without verbalization. In any event, the sons' houses, though off limits to the father, are also the greatest sources of the father's pride and power in the community.

When a man dies, he is buried outside his house on its right-hand side, that is, outside of *eero,* where he entertained his guests, and the cattle pen, where he kept the animals that constituted his most cherished property. The Gusii burial is an elaborate symbolic statement about the meaning of a man's life (R.A. LeVine, 1982), but not the final statement, as subsequent sacrifices have to be performed to "let him back in" to the houses of each of his sons and grandsons — a process that can go on for decades and even generations. In Gusii thought, then, a man never completely leaves the homestead he has built.

The stages of a woman's life are different but no less marked by the houses in which she lives. Like a boy but at a younger age (5 to 6 years old), a girl begins sleeping outside her mother's house during childhood (in her grandmother's or mother's co-wife's house), although remaining primarily identified with the house in which she was born and continued to be fed. Girls undergo initiation like boys, but after clitoridectomy they are secluded in their mothers' houses for a period of weeks; there is no female equivalent to the male circumcision hut. After initiation, a girl lives with a postmenopausal woman in the homestead (her grandmother or grandmother's co-wife), though still under the authority of her mother until marriage and the shift to the husband's family. This move at marriage is the major transition in her life, and if a woman has to live for a long time in her husband's circumcision hut, she feels demeaned. Once lodged in a standard marital house of her own, she acquires a certain autonomy, despite working under the direction of her husband and his mother, and she gradually gains authority in the family through the bearing of children and their maturation. The Gusii take pride in the fact that each woman has her own house, and they look down on other peoples who house co-wives together.

A young Gusii wife may be dominated by her mother-in-law and beaten by her husband, but her own house gives her not only a symbolic place in the world but a real sphere of control. As the householder, she is responsible for her unmarried children who eat there and work under her direction in the cultivation and processing of food. Her sons, as they marry and append their new houses to hers in the metaphorical *enyomba* she has founded within her husband's *omochie* (homestead), remain her loyal source of support and increase her status in the world with their reproductive accomplishments.

When she dies, the Gusii woman is, like her husband, buried outside of her house, but on the left side, near the yard in which many of her daytime activities were conducted. Thus, she remains after death in the domestic setting to which she came as a young woman and in which she grew in social status with the expansion of her own descendants (R.A. LeVine, 1982).

This outline of the house markers of life stages for Gusii males and females indicates the close connection between particular domestic units and progress through the life course for all Gusii individuals. It represents a set of cultural ideals that permit a number of variations. As previously mentioned, older children remain socially part of their mothers' houses even when they are sleeping in other dwellings in the homestead, and both men and women may live for periods of time elsewhere without dissolving the connection between themselves and their houses. Furthermore, a man may move the entire homestead to a new location in pursuit of more and better land and replicate the dwellings there.

There is, as this outline indicates, a symbolic identity between a person and a house; the house represents life goals sought and attained, and it is uniquely important in defining a person's status, not only in the domestic hierarchy, but also in the hierarchy of respect within one's local age and gender group. No wonder that Gusii individuals are so intensely concerned with having the right house at what is considered the right time according to Gusii convention. Young men in the 1970s built houses for themselves in their fathers' rural homesteads, even when they had no intention of living there, because they had to have a house to be buried by should they die an untimely death. Indeed, when an old woman died in 1976 without a house of her own still standing, a house was built on the spot "so she could be buried" (R.A. LeVine, 1982, pp. 31–32). Furthermore, a wife and her husband can be humiliated if he does not provide a proper house; for example, if he keeps her in his circumcision hut too long or if he neglects the upkeep of the thatched roof so that it leaks on his wife and children, or permits the structure to become obviously decrepit (S. LeVine, 1979). The community judges a man's performance as husband and father, in part, by observing the condition of the house in which he keeps his wife and children; if it is obviously neglected, he loses respect. He may be deliberately neglectful in order to punish a wife, but he is the one who will be adversely regarded if he fails to maintain minimal standards of housing for his family. Thus domestic housing is the locus of evaluation for a person by his reference group.

# THE SETTINGS FOR SOCIAL DRAMA

The traditional Gusii house design depicted on Figure 1 is regarded by the Gusii as an absolute prerequisite for normal social life and ritual action — or was until the 1960s, and even now represents the ideal standard. It is the essential backdrop to all customary narrative dramas in which the self is presented and represented. Each Gusii family, with some help from neighbors and kin, builds its own house, but until recent decades did not regard itself as having the option to depart from this design. To design one's own house or follow a pattern that deviated substantially from this template would have been considered not merely odd or eccentric but mad and immoral. Thus all families built according to a standard pattern, and the conventions of routine encounters and ritual drama specified action in this spatial setting.

The most fundamental division of the Gusii house is into its two rooms (Figure 1): *enyomba,* the same word that refers to the house as a whole but in this case designates the area in which cooking and sleeping go on, and *eero,* the room on the right hand side of the house, as the Gusii see it, in which the husband entertains his male visitors. *Enyomba* is identified with the wife, although the husband also sleeps there, and *eero* is identified with the husband because male activities occur there and it is next to the cattle pen. In other words, the house is divided into male and female spaces, and routine social encounters involving visitors are segregated accordingly. *Eero* is where a man would normally entertain men of his own generation (those he calls "brother") for beer drinking and eating; women would be entertained by the wife in *enyomba;* and elderly kin, particularly men of the paternal generation, can be entertained with food and drink in the yard outside, which is a neutral space open to all. The purpose of this segregation as described by Gusii informants is to prevent violations of their code governing face-to-face interaction among kin.

Thus men other than the husband (and uncircumcised sons) should be kept out of *enyomba,* not only because it is identified with sexuality as the place where marital coitus occurs, but also because the wife and other women may be squatting indecorously while tending the cooking fire and should not be seen in this condition by other men. Conversely, women should stay out of *eero* when men are drinking there (except when the wife is called to pour more boiling water into the beer pot) because they may be using obscene language or discussing sexual topics. Since such obscenity and sexuality are also forbidden in speech between classificatory sons and fathers, it is also considered safest to keep the beer-drinking group in *eero* to one generation, at least on nonritual occasions. Entertaining those of other generations outside the house, that is, in the yard or even in another house in the homestead, keeps the distance necessary for propriety. The general principle is that men and women and "fathers" and "sons" should be separated so that expressions of sexuality, aggression, and assertiveness across these boundaries will be prevented, hence the house is designed to facilitate this pattern of segregated social interaction.

The consumption of millet beer (*amarwa*) provides a good example of how the Gusii house was used at different times to maintain decorum in social behavior. In the early part of this century, beer drinking was a prerogative of the elders (*abagaaka*) whose sons were some distance away in the cattle camps, and they drank through bamboo tubes in a single pot located in the *eero* of one of them. When the cattle camps were abolished in 1913, the warriors, their military activities proscribed by the British administration, were brought back to the homesteads of their fathers. As these young men began drinking beer, the rule was established that they must drink in a separate house in the homestead by themselves rather than with their fathers, who feared that alcohol would make them disrespectful and even rebellious to their elders. Segregation was the recipe for the maintenance of order and the prevention of threats to paternal authority. For the next half century, however, only men were permitted to drink at all, with the exception of elder women, who were allowed into *eero* to take a few sucks on their husbands' drinking tubes while standing near the doorway. It was feared that alcohol would make younger women sexually unrestrained, thereby threatening the marital bond, and they were, as late as 1957, simply kept out of the places where beer was being drunk. By 1974, this form of segregation no longer worked, as there were bars (at the market place and in nearby homesteads) where any one could purchase a drink, and women as well as men were getting drunk. The domestic boundaries were superseded by a larger world of market relations.

It should be emphasized that the maintenance of the social decorum involved in kin avoidance and other traditional norms of interaction was regarded by Gusii elders as essential to a moral community, and that the erosion of the domestic segregation patterns that kept kin apart by age and sex was, as they would have predicted, accompanied not only by a sharp decline in their authority, but also by an apparent rise in drunkenness, family violence, and unregulated sexual activity between 1957 and 1974. As long as the Gusii world of social interaction was circumscribed by the domestic environments of homesteads related by kinship, the Gusii house could serve as an effective instrument of social control.

The traditional house design, nevertheless, remains central to the culture that all Gusii share, and is a primary source of the symbols invoked in ritual. Its importance in funerals, previously mentioned, is described in detail elsewhere (R.A. LeVine, 1982), where the norms of proper death for a woman (in *enyomba*) and man (in *eero*) and of proper burial are spelled out. When a man dies, the "steeple" (an obvious phallic symbol) is removed from the house, only to be restored when a leviratic relationship has been established for the widow, and in the interim, she must invert her cooking pot and other objects for a period of time until a sacrifice is performed that permits them to be turned right side up and frees her to select a leviratic husband. In these examples, as in many of the details of mortuary rituals, the house and its objects serve as the primary manipulated symbols.

The dominant ritual drama of the Gusii is seclusion, that is, the confinement of an individual to a house, usually his or her own house, for a period of time (usually lasting several weeks) under specified conditions, terminated by a ceremony of emergence (*ekiarokio*). The canonical form of seclusion is the one that takes place after circumcision or clitoridectomy, which involves the community annually in the celebration of personal transition, but ritual seclusion is also required for less frequent events such as anomalous births (twins and breech deliveries), and certain omens, such as seeing light in the sky (*erioba*). When a person is secluded in a circumcision hut or residential house, the fire in the hearth must never go out, and the secluded one (*omware*) must be provided with more than adequate food to build physical strength. When the time comes for emergence, the person is treated as highly vulnerable and in need of last minute protection, which involves the sacrifice of a goat and the pouring of libations of beer (in *eero* if it is a two-room house) as well as the administration of protective medicines (*obosaro*) into incisions made on the body. Many other ritual details are specific to the particular reason for seclusion.

In seclusion, the house and its ordinary contents such as the hearth, cooking fire, beer pots, become "sacramental objects" with spiritual power and significance. For example, it makes no difference if a cooking fire is extinguished under ordinary circumstances, but if this happens during seclusion, the consequences are believed to be dire and long lasting. Thus the furniture and household objects of everyday use are transformed by the occasion into ritual symbols of special potency, and the house itself is endowed with extraordinary protective qualities. In

Gusii tradition, the distinctions of sacred versus profane and utilitarian versus symbolic serve, not to mark off different spaces and physical objects, but to mark off different actions and occasions involving the same domestic environment.

# METAPHORS OF DANGER AND WELL-BEING

A close examination of Gusii cultural narratives reveals that features of the traditional house and its objects operate as symbols of feared and desired conditions, metaphorical representations of the self in states of danger and well-being. For example, the avoidance of the female part of the house by men, and specifically by the son (who was formerly free to be there), after his ritual initiation into manhood, represents a fear of incestuous encounters between son and mother. Male informants in the 1950s reported uneasiness about being in the presence of the bed where their parents had sexual intercourse, and they asked R. LeVine if, in America, he could enter his parents' bedroom when they were not there. (A positive reply elicited shudders.) Similarly, the prohibition on the patriarch's entering his son's (meaning son's wife's) house represents a fear of sexual contact between a man and his daughter-in-law. Much more could be said about the meanings of the kin avoidance code, but the point is that the rooms and household objects most associated with the sexual role of women arouse feelings of emotional ambivalence in Gusii men, and the symbolic resolution, the culturally constituted defense, is to be found not only in avoidance norms but also in the construction of partitions within the house (like the one behind the entrance foyer and the wall between *eero* and *enyomba*) as well as the deliberate separation between the houses of different generations, that create separate social spaces for men and women.

Witchcraft narratives provide another clue to emotional meanings embedded in the design of the Gusii house. High up on the wall of the *enyomba,* there is a small loft called *rirongo,* where a wife keeps possessions of her own that are not visible to someone standing in the room. Female witches are said to keep their witchcraft poisons and other dangerous objects there. In the standard narratives told in the 1970s as well as the 1950s (R.A. LeVine, 1963), Gusii witches are usually groups of married women who run naked at night together to disinter corpses for purposes of cannibalism and magical murder; their motive for murder is jealousy of more fortunate neighbors. Men walking at night claim to have heard witches quarreling over the parts of bodies and report being terrified. It is also said that these body parts are kept in a witch's *rirongo*. A man usually knows whether or not his wife is generally suspected of being a witch, but there is considerable ambiguity about this, and accusations are common. Men have said that they would not examine the articles in their wife's rirongo; they regard it as a source of potential danger. This feature of the Gusii house embodies something fearful about adult women for their husbands, symbolized as a space that is entirely for her personal use and under her own control, and perhaps its concealed location in the dark interior of the house suggests that it represents a dangerous aspect of women's sexuality. By giving this terrifying aspect a circumscribed physical location, the rirongo metaphor encourages a man to believe that keeping away from it will make him safe. This is consistent with the basic assumption of the Gusii avoidance code that safety lies in physical and social distance from dangerous sexuality.

In contrast with the Gusii house as a design for everyday life that controls the dangers of sexuality and aggression among kin, the ritual context of seclusion dramatizes the house as a haven of safety, protection, and nurturance. The person who enters seclusion is considered to be weakened and endangered by the loss of blood in circumcision, or childbirth, or by an omen of ancestral displeasure (or both, in the case of anomalous births). In Gusii belief, such a person is particularly vulnerable to contact, even through visual interaction, with all forms of danger generated by the interpersonal relations of neighbors, namely their malevolent intentions (potentially leading to *oborogi,* witchcraft) and their marital infidelities (transmitted through *amasangia,* a spiritual process that accelerates bleeding and worsens fever), which present an imminent threat to survival. Seclusion in the house provides a protective barrier against interpersonal visibility as well as the warmth of the constant fire and the feeding of good food to "make blood" and rebuild bodily strength. Once strength has been regained, the person may emerge into the dangers of social visibility, but only after performance of the aforementioned *ekiarokio* ceremony with its sacrifice, libations, and protective medicine.

Gusii seclusion appears, in many of its details, to be a ritual reenactment of gestation, a metaphorical return to the womb for healing and strengthening, followed by rebirth into a world full of potential dangers. (An equivalence between life in the womb and the safety of one's house is embedded in the Gusii term for neonate, *mosamba mwaye,* "he who has burnt his own home.") In terms of this metaphor, the house is a protective enclosure, the hearth a source of sustenance. This house contains no hidden dangers. It seems to be a representation of the mother from the viewpoint of a young child who has not yet discovered sexuality, and in this sense stands in stark contrast to the metaphorical house of everyday social life, designed to contain by segregation the ubiquitous danger of sexuality. The contrast is most apparent in the case of the hearth: In the seclusion narrative, it provides the nurturing warmth that never fails, whereas for the son newly initiated into the norms of adult social life, it represents a dangerous place near the parents' marital bed where mother might be encountered squatting in an immodest position. Thus the same domestic spaces and objects can symbolize maternal nurturance or incestuous sexuality according to the narrative contexts in which they appear. As in many other cultures, the mother is unconsciously symbolized as both the ultimate source of emotional well-being and a dangerously sexual and aggressive outsider. In the Gusii case, the house supplies the metaphors for well-being as well as for danger.

In Gusii culture, the kin avoidance rules constitute defensive actions necessary to minimize a sense of anxiety and danger to the self in the interpersonal contexts of routine social life. Ritual seclusion, however, is employed only when extraordinary danger threatens the very survival of the self; in that case, the defensive resolution involves a drama of healing through gestation and rebirth, with the house serving as a womb-like symbol of safety. Our hypothesis is that these cultural narratives, particularly the domestic metaphors embedded in them, function to maintain and restore states of emotional well-being in Gusii individuals. If it holds true, then it might be argued that the Gusii house is designed for that psychodynamic function rather than for economic utility in food production or energy conservation—that the house is a fantasy embodied in physical structure rather than an instrument of environmental adaptation. This argument is examined further.

## CONCLUSIONS: THE GUSII HOUSE AS FANTASY

The Gusii house was, and to a large extent still is, a cultural form with a standard design, a preferred arrangement in relation to other houses in the homestead, and a specific set of normative directions for the organization of people and interaction in its interior and exterior spaces. Each person's social identity as a responsible adult of a certain age, gender, and kin status is defined by spatial location in a particular house

within a domestic context. Houses are psychologically salient to Gusii
men and women as markers of progress in their lives, as formal contexts
for their everyday social interaction and ritual performance, and as
metaphors for their wishes, fears, and moral sensibilities. Furthermore,
as we have seen, the place of the Gusii house and household objects in
cultural narratives indicates their symbolic significance in the experience
of sexuality, male–female and parent–child relations, and the fear of
interpersonal hostility. It is no exaggeration to say that Gusii representations of self and their patterns of emotional experience and intrapsychic defense are inextricably connected with domestic symbolism. Can
we then claim that the conventional design of the Gusii house is a product
of culturally mediated psychodynamics rather than socially mediated
economics?

To answer this question in a definitive way, we need evidence
concerning Gusii house design during the historical period in which they
arrived at the form we now understand as "traditional," in order to assess
the degree to which the operative norms of house design were responsive
to economic and ideological change. In addition, we need to examine
how and to what extent change occurred in more recent times under the
rapidly changing conditions of the 20th century. Our evidence, particularly on the earlier period, is fragmentary but illuminating.

First, it must be stated that the design shown in Figure 1 is taken from
houses of the 1950s that were built with iron nails, specifically in which
nails were used to connect the framework for the roof with the
supporting poles of the outer walls. This apparently permitted the
construction of a larger house than the Gusii had built in precolonial
times, when (in the absence of nails) the trunks of saplings were bent over
to serve as framework for the roof as well as the outer walls. A smaller
house would have meant greater interpersonal density in the interior, and
a greater probability of violating avoidance rules concerning obscene talk
heard by certain kin and accidental male–female and intergenerational
touching, making it more difficult to achieve the desirable decorum in
social gatherings. Decorum was probably achieved by the existence of
more houses, that is, the warrior's house (*egesa*) in the cattle camps and
the *etureti,* a house built by an important man (*omonguru*) specifically to
entertain his male friends and followers in his homestead. There were
probably more huts for children and circumcision (*chisaiga*) in those days
too. In other words, in the precolonial period before they had iron nails,
the Gusii probably built smaller houses but more huts of the one-room
variety in order to maintain the optimal distance in social gatherings and
sleeping arrangements required by the avoidance norms. When nails

became available, they were able to build larger houses of the two-room *enyomba* type, and did so, depending more on interior partitions (and strict adherence to the rules), and less on numerous houses to maintain the desired social distance.

Second, there is other evidence of change in Gusii housing style under the pressure of environmental conditions, even though it did not affect all Gusii. In the 1890s, when the rinderpest epidemic swept westward through Kenya, decimating cattle herds, the Kipsigis people living east and north of the Gusii began raiding border settlements of Gusii. To protect themselves and their cattle, the Gusii near the border built and moved into walled villages called *chindoaki;* some of the ruined walls, made of sun-dried mud bricks, were still standing in 1964 (near Nyamaiya in North Mugirango), when Donald T. Campbell and R. LeVine were interviewing elderly Gusii who had lived in them as children. After the Gusii won a decisive military victory over the Kipsigis (in 1902), these people went back to living in dispersed homesteads, apparently building their houses according to the standard plan considered traditional. But this historical episode shows that the housing arrangements of the Gusii changed adaptively in precolonial times, in response to environmental threats to survival and livelihood. The absorption of warrior sons into their fathers' homesteads after the cattle camps were abolished in 1913 is another example, from early in the colonial period, also indicating that change in housing arrangements in response to environmental conditions was by no means unknown to the Gusii. The standard plan was not an immutable structure.

Changes during the last 35 years are better known and more revealing. Many Gusii deviated from the standard house design between 1957 and 1974 (and even more by 1988) by building rectangular houses with metal roofs in place of the traditional round houses with thatched roofs, as a result of the increasing availability of new building materials and techniques and of the diminished supply of thatching grass in an environment of land scarcity. Furthermore, and more significantly, the diminished supply of firewood combined with the increased availability of warm blankets and heavy clothing (resulting from higher cash incomes), meant that people no longer kept the cooking fire going through the cold highland nights and no longer needed to for warmth. Thus, it became possible to disengage the sleeping and cooking areas of *enyomba,* and families began building a separate cook house, with their main house containing a bedroom (for the parents and young children), and a sitting room, in place of *enyomba* and *eero,* respectively. By 1988, most newly built houses we saw had the kitchen in a separate building.

Furthermore, the gender segregation of visitors to the house also changed with erosion of the prohibition against female drinking previously mentioned, so that by 1974, the segregation of women from men in large social gatherings was less pronounced than in 1957.

These changes demonstrate conclusively, in our opinion, that the design and use of houses by the Gusii is influenced by utilitarian considerations such as the availability of building materials and of ways of keeping warm and by a larger social environment in which, for example, barriers to female beer consumption have collapsed outside the home. It is clear that, between 1957 and 1988, increasing access to nails, metal roofs, and blankets, combined with decreased supplies of thatching grass and firewood, as well as the attraction of imported house styles, altered the design of many Gusii houses. Gusii house design cannot be treated simply as cultural fantasy without taking into account the environmental factors and economic utilities that help shape the house-building decisions of individual Gusii.

The domestic behavior of Gusii adults as we observed them in the mid-1970s is best interpreted as the joint outcome of several factors: (1) personal preferences for the spatial organization of interaction, reflecting traditional Gusii cultural models of kin relationship that retain psychodynamic significance; (2) novel social identities derived from the wider institutional environment of independent Kenya, shaping aspirations toward what are perceived as modern ways that transcend kinship; (3) economic and other ecological factors affecting house construction, domestic energy conservation, and household density. Individual decisions and social consensus about house building and spatial behavior are best seen as compromise formations, synthesizing these three factors in a way compatible with the standards of self of Gusii adults at that time.

This synthesizing process does not mean that traditional cultural meanings have lost their psychodynamic significance, as indicated by the following anecdotes from the field work of 1974–1976 and our visit of 1988:

1. A prosperous and highly educated Gusii who lived in a large house in Nairobi invited his father to visit him. When the father arrived from Gusiiland, his son told him that in a large Western style house, each room was equivalent to a Gusii house; thus it was all right for the father to stay in the son's house so long as he slept in a room of his own and did not enter the son's marital bedroom. The father rejected this argument, refused (on the basis of Gusii kin avoidance norms) to enter the son's house at all, and insisted on staying with kin elsewhere in Nairobi.

2. A married couple with a circumcised son who was living at home (in his own hut) had built a "modern" rectangular house with the parental bedroom separated from the kitchen by an interior wall. Later, they built a separate cook house behind and used the former kitchen as a store room. Their son never entered the parental bedroom or the storeroom, due (apparently) to its location in the kitchen that would have been an avoided location for him in the past. Furthermore, the mother's teen-age brother, who was living there after the parents died, also avoided both of these rooms, although the rules of kinship do not require such avoidance by a brother. (Now as in the past, Gusii individuals often exceed the formal requirements of the kin avoidance rules and generate new rules consistent with the ideals of avoidance when they encounter novel situations. This kind of flexibility suggests that the emotional responses to the house endure, even when some of the practical arrangements change.) The growing separation between kitchen and parental bedroom also revealed that in most families, the bedroom is a stronger focus of avoidance than the kitchen, suggesting the salience of the incest theme in the Gusii experience of domestic order.

3. Despite the innovations and individual variations in house design, we observed during the 1970s that virtually none put married adults who were not each other's spouses together in a single residential house, whether they were parents and children, brothers or co-wives, despite the fact that other arrangements would have been feasible and convenient and were obviously acceptable elsewhere. (The one exception was a notoriously deviant man who housed his non-Gusii wife together with his Gusii wife.) The underlying assumption is that domestic arrangements, including those for temporary sleeping, must not unite in a single house two people who are in legitimate sexual unions with other persons. The sense of identity with a house and the entitlement to have a house separate from others, particularly for a married woman, remain absolute.

4. Seclusion rituals were widespread and frequent during 1974–1976, for the initiations of all boys and girls, for twins and breech-delivered babies, and for the other reasons connected with omens of ancestral displeasure. The use of rituals involving the house and its objects in seclusion and burial rites showed no sign of declining.

Thus, visible changes in house construction were not necessarily accompanied by changes in the cultural meanings of the Gusii house or in its psychodynamic functions for those who built and inhabited it. As domestic construction became somewhat more varied, it became more evident that Gusii kin avoidance is not simply a fixed set of rules but a cultural model of relationship and distance, based heavily on the fear of incest, that can generate new and even idiosyncratic rules in the face of new spatial conditions. In addition, the domestic narratives of seclusion rituals and funerals, based on the house as a symbol of maternal protection and nurturance, continue to provide emotional security in the face of life crisis, even for those converted to Christianity.

This may change among future cohorts of Gusii, as kinship identities are increasingly subordinated to social identities derived from participation in translocal institutions (school, church, occupation, and exposure to mass media). For them, domestic context may be less important as a stage for social drama and less involved in their self-representation and emotional equilibrium than it was in the past. On the basis of our observations to date, however, we conclude that Gusii house design is, through its place in culturally constituted defenses, an emotionally charged guide to social action interpretable as fantasy in the Freudian sense.

BIBLIOGRAPHY

BLIER, S.P. (1987), *The Anatomy of Architecture: Ontology and Metaphor in Batammaliba Architectural Expression.* Cambridge: Cambridge University Press.
EVANS-PRITCHARD, E.E. (1940), *The Nuer.* London: Clarendon Press.
FORTES, M. (1949), *The Web of Kinship Among the Tallensi.* London: Oxford University Press.
GEERTZ, C. (1973), *The Interpretation of Culture.* New York: Basic Books.
GRIAULE, M. (1965), *Conversations with Ogotemmeli: An Introduction to Dogon Religious Ideas.* London: Oxford University Press.
HAKANSSON, T. (1988), *Bridewealth, Women and Land: Social Change Among the Gusii of Kenya.* Uppsala, Sweden: Uppsala Studies in Cultural Anthropology, No. 10.
HALLOWELL, A.I. (1955), *Culture and Experience.* Philadelphia: University of Pennsylvania Press.
HERDT, G. (1981), *Guardians of the Flutes: Idioms of Masculinity.* New York: McGraw-Hill.
KARDINER, A. (1939), *The Individual and His Society.* New York: Columbia University Press.
——— (1945), *Psychological Frontiers of Society.* New York: Columbia Press.
LEVINE, R.A. (1963), Witchcraft and sorcery in a Gusii community. In: *Witchcraft and Sorcery in East Africa,* ed. J. Middleton & E. Winter. London: Routledge and Kegan Paul, pp. 221–255.
——— (1964), The Gusii family. In: *The Family Estate in Africa,* eds. R. Gray & P. Gulliver. Boston, MA: Boston University Press, pp. 63–82.
——— (1973), *Culture, Behavior and Personality.* Chicago: Aldine.
LEVINE, R.A. (1982), Gusii funerals: Meanings of life and death in an African community. *Ethos* 10:26–65.

_____ (1984), Properties of culture. In: *Culture Theory: Essay on Mind, Self and Emotion,* eds. R. Shweder & R. LeVine. Cambridge: Cambridge University Press, pp. 67–87.

_____ LEVINE, B.B. (1966), *Nyansongo: A Gusii Community in Kenya.* New York: Wiley.

LEVINE, S. (1979), *Mothers and Wives: Gusii Women in East Africa.* Chicago: University of Chicago Press.

MAYER, P. (1949), *The Lineage Principle in Gusii Society.* International African Institute, No. 24. London: Oxford University Press.

OBEYESEKERE, G. (1981), *Medusa's Hair: An Essay on Personal Symbols and Religious Experience.* Chicago: University of Chicago Press.

RAPOPORT, A. (1969), *House Form and Culture.* Englewood Cliffs, NJ: Prentice-Hall.

ROHEIM, G. (1943), *The Origin and Function of Culture.* New York: Nervous and Mental Dis. Monogr. 69.

SIEBER, R. (1980), *African Furniture and Household Objects.* Bloomington, IN: Indiana University Press.

SPIRO, M.E. (1987), *Culture and Human Nature: Theoretical Papers of Melford E. Spiro.* Chicago: University of Chicago Press.

TURNER, V.W. (1967), *The Forest of Symbols.* Ithaca, NY: Cornell University Press.

WALLACE, A.F.C. (1956), Revitalization movements. *American Anthropologist* 58:264–281.

WEBER, M. (1947), *Theory of Social and Economic Organization.* Glencoe, IL: The Free Press.

WHITING, J.W.M., & CHILD, I.L. (1953), *Child Training and Personality: A Cross-Cultural Study.* New Haven, CT: Yale University Press.

# 7

# Mazes of Meaning: The Exploration
# of Individuality in Culture
# and of Culture Through
# Individual Constructs[1]

## JEAN L. BRIGGS

At a recent conference on current thinking and research in psychological anthropology,[2] I was asked to address the question: What can a study of the individual contribute to the anthropological enterprise? This essay is my response to that question.

I have noticed that when anthropologists talk about "individual and society," they often insert the definite article before individual, thereby, in one simple three-letter stroke, obliterating all the rich detail of individual lives — the essence of individuality. The expression *the* individual focuses the lens on what individuals have in common and creates a homogeneous individual to set off against society. Why do we do this? Sometimes, I think, *the* anthropologist (there we go again), who has been fascinated — and overwhelmed — in the field by all the variety of detail, fears that all that same detail will overwhelm readers, too, and not fascinate but bore them. More fundamentally, I think we tend to perceive

---

[1]My thanks, and more than thanks, to Robert Paine, valiant colleague and friend, who always helps but this time outdid himself by struggling through the mazes of not one but two versions of this paper, line by line, pointing out obscurities and seasoning the pages with skepticism, leavened with interest and encouragement. This formulation of the paper is, to some extent, a dialogue with him — though my contribution to the conversation has more often taken the form of clarification than capitulation.

[2]The meeting was sponsored by the Society for Psychological Anthropology, a division of the American Anthropological Association, and was held in San Diego in October 1989. The session for which the first version of this paper was written was on "The Collectivity and the Individual."

too much detail (with too much diversity inherent in it) as an impediment to our project of generalizing about human behavior.

At the same time, the Zeitgeist at this moment very much favors the study of "process," and in particular, the processes through which people create meaning. The notion that meaning inheres in culture and that people receive it passively, as dough receives the cookie cutter, is rapidly being replaced by the idea that culture consists of ingredients, which people actively select, interpret, and use in various ways as opportunities, capabilities, and experience allow. But it is not *the* individual that creates meanings, it is individuals who do so. So, how are we to reconcile our interest in these individual activities with our uneasiness about diversity and detail? How are we to go about studying the processes by which meaning is created? Do we risk losing our grip on generalization if we attend to individuals? Or can bringing individuals clearly into focus contribute to our understanding of how culture operates in persons and how persons operate with culture, each creating the other?

In this essay, I want to describe an experiment I am making in the analysis of certain emotionally charged dramas that form an important part of the socialization of Inuit children. The experiment consists in following in the footsteps, the mindsteps, of one three–year–old child, as she tries, by guess and by gorry and with occasional sharp insights, to make sense of her world, to create patterns, meanings, in her life. My aim in telling you about it is to demonstrate how much can be learned, both about individuals and about society, by attending to this process of creating meaning. I am discovering that the more I follow this little girl, the more I see; and paradoxically, the more detailed my analysis of one drama, directed on one occasion to one child, the broader and richer becomes my vision not only of the workings of that one child's psyche but also of the psychodynamic underpinnings of Inuit culture and the potentials for interrelationship among various bits and pieces of that culture. To the extent that the processes of Inuit psychology and culture resemble what we find elsewhere in the world, I am also learning something about psychology and culture in general—how they actively reconstitute themselves and each other in the tangle of experience[3].

---

[3] I will not speculate about these broader issues here; I will only point out how similar the view of culture that I have arrived at by my route is to the views that other anthropologists to right and left of me are arriving at these days by their routes. How a Zeitgeist manages to infiltrate into the world of someone who is so thoroughly immersed in her own data that she rarely reads is a marvel—a rather disconcerting marvel to one who cherishes individuality. I am sure there are interesting explanations, but speculations on that subject are also outside the realm of this paper.

In order to put my experiment and its ethnography into context, I begin by making some general remarks about the world I observed, about Inuit socialization practices, and about the role of dramas therein. I say a little about the more conventional way in which I used to analyze the dramas, in order to point up the contrast with my present mode of analysis, and then I give an extended example of the latter, describing and analyzing one dramatic sequence that I saw enacted on one occasion with Chubby Maata[4]. Finally, I compare in more general terms the harvest garnered from this detailed and individuated kind of observation with the more modest gleanings obtained from my earlier, more conventional, analyses of similar dramas.

## ETHNOGRAPHIC BACKGROUND

The observations that I use here were obtained in Qipisa, a permanent — that is, year-round — hunting camp of about 60 Inuit on the southeastern part of Baffin Island in the eastern Canadian Arctic. Qipisa was the only remaining camp in Cumberland Sound during the years in which I visited it, and the nearest community, the town of Pangnirtung, was on the other side of the Sound, some 100 miles away. Under normal circumstances, small groups of Qipisa men traveled back and forth between camp and community quite frequently to shop, to visit relatives, to seek medical help, and so on, and Pangnirtung men also came to Qipisa to visit and to hunt. So, the people of Qipisa rarely felt themselves really isolated. At the same time, in most respects, life in the camp proceeded quite independently of Pangnirtung. The elements of foreign culture, material and otherwise, that had been incorporated into camp life were of the people's own choosing. A few of the older children of Qipisa had attended school briefly during periods when their families lived in Pangnirtung, but when living in Qipisa, they were under no pressure to go to school and they did not go. As far as I could see, they were brought up entirely by Inuit methods.

Almost all the children of Qipisa were very well loved and tenderly nurtured. Many Inuit love babies and small children very much and give them a great deal of sensitive care and attention, nursing or feeding them when they are hungry, putting them gently to sleep when they are tired, comforting them when they are unhappy, holding and cuddling them a

---

[4]I am using here the same pseudonyms that I use in the book I am currently writing about this child, so that anyone interested in acquiring a fuller picture of her will recognize her when they come across her in that other context.

great deal of the time when they are awake, chanting to them over and over again special affectionate refrains that weave strong dyadic bonds between them and their caretakers, and always including them in the company and activities of others, both children and adults. I heard older women tell young mothers that they should not leave a baby or a small child alone when awake. Parents expressed momentary annoyance, now and then, when a child was obstreperous or disobedient, but rarely anger. To be angry with a child was demeaning; it demonstrated one's own childishness, and one older woman told me that, as an educational device, it was likely to backfire and cause a child to rebel. When anger was expressed toward a child, the community strongly disapproved.

So the children were growing up in a very small and warm world. To an outsider from an immense and complexly structured society, accustomed to strangers, to formal organizations, to the machinations of overwhelming powers whose intricate operations are dimly or not at all perceived, it must seem, from a social point of view, a simple and a safe world. But I think that to adult Inuit it was neither simple nor safe; it was full of hidden dangers. Socialization was in part a matter of becoming sensitive to these dangers, and the dramas that I mentioned were an important mechanism in this process, creating, focusing, and maintaining a sense of danger in social life.

## CHARACTERISTICS OF THE DRAMAS

It is possible to make a number of generalizations about Inuit educational processes and about the dramas in particular. Inuit education is by no means a straightforward process. To be sure, it is multifaceted, as I suppose most educational systems are, and some of its techniques are familiar. Adults frequently instruct children concerning proper social behavior, telling them what they should and should not do, and they may reward a small child's good behavior with an affectionate nod or comment, or, once in a while, create some other pleasant experience in support of an approved value. Older children are not given much praise; they are not thought to need it. Qipisa people, unlike the Utku with whom I lived earlier, sometimes raise their voices at children, too, but scolding is disapproved of. Instead of insisting that children obey instructions and punishing them if they don't, adults have various other options. They may ignore the misbehavior, remind the child of proper behavior, laugh, or make a disapproving sound, a wordless "moo."

But all these simple devices play bit parts on the educational stage. A central idea of Inuit education is to "cause thought" (*isumaqsayuq*) (Stairs, 1989, p. 10). *Isumaqsayuq* is, in fact, a North Baffin word for education. Inuit techniques for causing thought are complicated, indeed, and, as we will see, they also stimulate feelings.

Thought and feeling are inevitably related in any culture, because emotions always provide the motives for thinking; and because, conversely, thought defines emotions and makes it possible for us to experience them. But whereas we downplay the importance of this relationship, and even like to imagine that emotions and "rational" thought are in opposition, Inuit utilize the relationship in powerful ways, creating intense emotions as a means of stimulating thought, including the most pragmatic and "rational" varieties.

They do this by initiating small spontaneous dramas, which are related to the child's personal situation and frequently grow out of the latter's own innocent behavior. These dramas create, or raise to consciousness, issues that the child will perceive to be of great consequence for his or her life, and they are usually built around an emotionally powerful question, which has the potential for being personally dangerous to the child being questioned. "Why don't you kill your baby brother?" "Why don't you die so I can have your nice new shirt?" "Your mother's going to die—look, she's cut her finger—do you want to come live with me?" "Your daddy's no good, shall I stone him to death—like this?" "Look, Juusi is nursing at *your* mother's breast. Do you mind? Shall she be *Juusi's* mother?"

These questions and others equally potent are asked frequently and repetitively in interactions between adults and all small children. The adult questioners quite consistently perceive themselves, and are perceived by other adults, to be good-humored, benign, and playful,[5] but

---

[5] I do not know whether Inuit themselves think in terms of two single opposed categories, "playful" and "serious," and for purposes of this discussion I don't think it is very important whether they do have two overarching verbal categories, or indeed, whether they create conceptual links between the various acts and attitudes that I label "playful." They do have words that label the separate phenomena and that contrast them with the other attitudes and acts for which I have created the overarching gloss of "serious." In other words, the distinction between two styles of interaction is made linguistically by Inuit themselves.

Inuit attitudes toward playfulness and seriousness contrast sharply. Although seriousness has its place, and rational behavior is very highly valued, nonetheless, seriousness and thought are, in many contexts, disapproved of and even feared, whereas a consistently playful style of interaction is characteristic of a happy person, a sign that one is a happy person. Inuit place great importance on happiness, not merely because it is pleasant to be happy, but because a happy person can be trusted. I would even venture to say that playfulness is a sign that one is rational. Hence, the ability to distinguish

the children don't know this, at first. The questioning begins in infancy, long before the baby understands speech, and continues until the child's responses become unremarkable — a point that will be clarified presently. A very large proportion of the interaction between adults and small children consists of this questioning. On the part of the adult questioner, it is part play, part serious, part teaching device and part test, part challenge and part tease. It is also frequently a means through which adults can express, relive, and perhaps relieve, their own concerns and problems. For the uninitiated child, on the other hand, who is not in a position to understand the playful aspect of the questions, the challenge may be severe, and the tease a torment.

The questions have all these qualities in continuously shifting combinations, depending on particular players and particular circumstances, but always they are designed to be thought and emotion provoking for the children who are being played with. Thus, in the Inuit educational process, questioning of this sort is an essential ingredient. The questions are often focused on transitions or crises that a child is known to be going through: weaning; adoption; the birth of a sibling; the transition from being a baby, securely attached to its mother's back or lap to being a child, who comes and goes with his or her peers. And if the child is not aware of such a transition or crisis, the questions may create one or bring it into focus: "Are you a baby?" "Who's your daddy?" "Do you love your baby brother?"

When a child has learned to disentangle the playful from the serious in a particular drama, and when she or he can no longer be drawn into the trap that the adult is setting, adults will stop playing that game with him or her. As one Alaskan Inuk said (in English): "When children begin to respond like adults, it's not fun any more [to question them]."

The dramas that develop around the kernel question grow spontaneously out of, and fade back into, the surrounding, ongoing interaction. They are informal and highly personalized, intimately related to the adult's immediate concerns and those of the child, as well as to the child's reactions to the questions asked. The plot, therefore, may be different on different occasions. At the same time, it is a striking fact that this mode of socialization and the questions themselves are highly uniform across

---

playful from serious behavior is not a trivial matter. These points are most fully elaborated in Briggs, 1979a.

The dramas I am discussing here could not exist at all if they were not enacted in "play" mode, because they violate the rules of moderation and control that govern "serious" behavior. Indeed, questioning itself is a violation of behavioral norms among adults, and when it occurs in serious mode, it is very often perceived as a scolding.

Inuit time and space — from West Alaska to East Greenland, among groups that have not been in contact for generations or centuries. And I have known cases in which Inuit women married to non-Inuit men and bringing up their children in the south have used these techniques to teach various lessons. The durability of this behavior clearly indicates its emotional power and its importance to Inuit ways of being[6].

## MODES OF ANALYSIS

I began my investigation of these dramas in a relatively conventional way by defining, one after another, areas of social behavior that interested me, looking for dramas that seemed to bear on this behavior, and then examining those dramas — removed from most aspects of their immediate contexts — to see what messages they might contain, which might influence behavior in the area in question. In this manner, I looked at the formation of values, the management of conflict, and the development of skills relevant to coping with an environment fraught with dangerous uncertainties (see, for example, Briggs, 1979b, 1982, 1983, 1991).

My focus, of course, was on the common denominators of behavior, that is, behaviors and attitudes that I had found to be frequently repeated and/or widely understood. I identified the messages in the dramas by drawing on my background knowledge of Inuit social relations, knowledge impressionistically distilled from observation of, and participation in, many interactions, in many places, with many Inuit, over a long period of years in Alaska and Canada. Then, again utilizing background knowledge of the same sort, as well as psychodynamic hypotheses derived from psychoanalytically informed introspection, I interrelated these messages across dramas, and in this way created "plots," composite messages, often tangled and contradictory, that I thought would influence action in the domain under study.

An example of such a plot, which draws on several dramas played with many children, is as follows. I have mentioned that in some dramas children are asked whether they love (or wish to kill) their new baby siblings, and ways of killing the baby are demonstrated. In other dramas, children are cross-examined on their own lovability: "Are you lovable? Are you *really?* No, you're not, you're no good; *aaaaq!*" (an expression of disgust). And in still others we have seen it suggested that they might

---

[6]It would be interesting to know whether the ways in which these themes are developed, the plots that are built on them, are also similar across the whole area, or whether they vary in historically and socially different environments.

lose their parents: Mother might die—"Look, she's cut her finger"; or father fail to return from a trip—"And who are you going to live with, then?" It seemed to me highly likely that the first kind of drama would make children aware of any jealousy they might feel toward a newborn sibling—or would help to create it if they did not feel it—and this awareness, combined with the knowledge that they were supposed to love and nurture those babies, would exacerbate any doubts about their lovability that might be engendered by the second kind of drama, whereas the third drama might make them wonder who would rescue an unlovable child in the event of a parent's death or defection.

This analytic procedure, which I shall call the "noncontextual mode," resulted in images of the psychodynamics—the fears, wishes, motives— underlying Inuit social phenomena that were complex and untidy enough to seem realistic to me, and that were recognizable to Inuit who heard or read my ideas. So it seemed to me that my approach taught me a good deal about the psychic motors that drove Inuit behavior in the areas I was investigating, as well as carrying me some distance toward an understanding of what the dramas accomplished in Inuit society and how they worked.

However, the more I wrote, the more I noticed that I was saying the same things all the time, using the same data, making the same arguments, and I began to wonder whether I was in a rut, able to see only one dynamic. Fortunately, I expressed these thoughts to Don Handelman, with whom I was teaching a course at the time, using my material on these dramas. He suggested that it was not I who was in a rut but, in a sense, Inuit culture. In other words, said he, all the domains I was looking at—values, conflict, uncertainty—were connected, so the dramas I was analyzing really did contain messages or lessons that were relevant to all of them. So I began to see potentials for illuminating more of Inuit culture.

At the same time, Handelman pointed me further into the realm of the individual. It happens that these dramas are usually, if not always, sharply focused on one child at a time. It also happens that they often occur in sequences, one spontaneously leading into the next, sometimes five or six in succession, as precipitating circumstances change. An adult asks a question; the child makes a certain response, trying to solve the problem posed; adults respond by dramatizing the consequences of the child's attempted solution or by asking new questions, which make the child think about what such consequences might be. The child responds again, and again the adults counter with new problems, and so on. Or the surrounding situation may change in some way: New actors may enter and old ones leave; somebody changes position or cuts a finger. The slightest occurrence may be picked up and utilized as an ingredient in the drama.

Handelman suggested that I look at these naturally occurring sequences to see if I could find cumulative messages — plots — in them, as I had previously found, or created, plots by drawing individual messages out of the separate dramas that I considered relevant to the subject I was investigating. My very first experiment showed me the fruitfulness of this new line of inquiry, and thus was born the idea of looking in detail at all the dramas that I saw played with one child during the seven–month period of a field trip.

This second procedure I will refer to as the "natural history mode" of analysis. Submersed in data on one individual's experiences, I am now writing more than 70 pages on one instance of one drama focused on one child, where previously I had written five pages on ten "typical" dramas and made the assumption that all Inuit (or at least Qipisa) children experienced the same dramas in the same ways. At the same time, I find opening to me another sort of generalization: a vision broader and, I think, deeper, than the one I had previously had of the ways in which Inuit culture may be psychologically constituted and experienced. Here now is an example of the sort of analysis I am doing in the natural history mode, which I hope will illustrate the value of looking in depth at one small event in the life of one small child.

## THE DRAMA DESCRIBED

One January evening, Maata and I arrived at about the same moment to visit in Liila's house. Liila, a young mother, and her two daughters, Rosi, age four, and Chubby Maata, age three, were at home, and two of Liila's brothers, Juupi, a man of 27, and 10-year-old Juda, were visiting them. Chubby Maata was playing with a little pup, named Puppy, which someone in Pangnirtung had sent to her as a present the last time her father had gone in to trade. Maata, almost as soon as she arrived, began to suggest to Chubby Maata that she and Puppy come to live in their house. Her voice was soft, persuasive, seductive. Chubby Maata consistently wrinkled her nose, "No." After a while, Maata called Puppy to her, petted him, picked him up, and turned toward the door, with Puppy in her arms. Chubby Maata let out a cry, rushed to the puppy, grabbed him around his neck with such force that I feared she would choke him, and pulled him strenuously away from Maata. She was half laughing but the laugh sounded anxious too. I heard an edge of tears in it, and she exerted a great deal of energy.

This drama was repeated several times during the first part of the visit, each time initiated by Maata. Once, Chubby Maata, tugging at Puppy, trying hard to separate him from Maata, protested: "He's all shitty!" Maata ignored this argument; she didn't let go of Puppy—but she didn't take him out of the house either.

The last time Maata asked Chubby Maata if she and Puppy wouldn't like to come and live with them, Chubby Maata said something I didn't hear before she said "No"; then, after refusing, she commented, as if cheerfully surprised at herself: "Oops! I almost agreed!" Maata's ear was quick. She exclaimed: "Oh, you agree!" And this time she picked up Chubby Maata instead of Puppy and started toward the door. Chubby Maata struggled and cried out in protest and, after a few minutes, Maata put her down. Chubby Maata ran first to her mother, who ignored her, and then to Juupi, who picked her up and set her on his lap. From that protected position, she looked over her shoulder, laughing with a triumphant gleam at Maata.

The next thing I noticed was that Chubby Maata had initiated a game with herself, in which she ran, over and over again, from the door to Juupi and back, saying: "One, two, talee [three], GO!" as she started each lap of the "race," and flinging herself across his lap every time she returned to him. Once when she returned, Juupi hit her butt lightly, and when she cried out, protestingly, he said, in a light and innocent tone: "It wasn't me, it was Yiini." I was sitting beside Juupi on the couch, well within reach. It could have been me.

Chubby Maata looked at me, her small face serious, her eyes watchful. Liila asked her: "Do you like Yiini?" Chubby Maata wrinkled her nose, looking at her mother, not at me. Liila, her voice amused, asked: "Why on earth don't you like her?" Chubby Maata put her head down on the seat of the couch and hid her face in both hands. But she was not to escape that way. Maata, her eyes fixed observantly on her, took up the interrogation: "Who, then? Who do you like?" Everyone was watching Chubby Maata. She didn't answer. Maata persisted: "Do you like *me?*" Chubby Maata, with a great burst of energy, resumed her game of "One, two, talee, GO!" but that didn't save her, either. It was Juupi's turn: "Do you like *me?*" This time Chubby Maata raised her brows, "Yes." Would that answer satisfy? No. Juupi inquired further in a soft and confidential voice: "Just me alone, yes?" Chubby Maata responded again with "One, two, talee, GO!" Poor Chubby Maata. Both Maata and

Juupi pressed her for an answer, but all the response they got was "One, two, talee, GO!" and a great deal of energetic running.

At this point, two new visitors came in: Maata's adoptive sister Rota[7] and Rota's son Saali, who was just a few weeks older than Chubby Maata. As the visitors stood by the door, hesitating politely for a moment before coming in and sitting down, Liila exclaimed to Chubby Maata: "Look, your darling little mother's brother is wearing your shirt! He's trying to steal it! Look at him!" Chubby Maata ignored her mother's remarks—as did Rota and Saali—and Liila did not pursue the subject.

Rota came into the room and sat down on the couch, while Saali stood between her legs in the usual position of the visiting three-year-old, leaning against her while he watched the activities in the room. In a few moments he turned around to his mother and demanded a suck. But Rota said: "Go run wildly with Chubby Maata, instead." Saali did run with Chubby Maata for a few minutes, from the couch to the door, back and forth, back and forth: "One, two, talee, GO!" until Rota said to him: "Pretend to be an evil spirit." Saali immediately hunched his shoulders, bowed his arms like an ape, closed his eyes tight, and so transformed into a miniature monster, began to stalk Chubby Maata and Rosi, rolling from leg to leg like the proverbial sailor just come ashore. The two little girls cried, "Iq!"—an expression of alarm, sometimes of delighted alarm—and, watching Saali over their shoulders as they ran, they fled to the far end of the room, where they huddled together, holding each other tightly and laughing. Saali stopped in the middle of the room, and when the girls relaxed, he began again to stalk them, and again they ran, holding onto each other, watching him and laughing from a distance. Rota, her eyes amused, showed Saali how to stick out his tongue as well as screwing his eyes shut: "Do this." He imitated her gesture and the adults laughed.

The evil spirit game was repeated a number of times. I don't remember how it came to an end—perhaps the children just lost interest—but when it did, Saali returned to stand in front of his mother. And as he stood there, facing her this time, Chubby Maata came up behind him, grabbed him in her arms, pulled his hair, and said happily: "I'm attacking

---

[7]Maata and Rota were both adopted children. Maata was adopted in infancy by her mother's father and Rota by her mother's mother, who later married Maata's mother's father and moved to Qipisa. The two girls were therefore brought up together throughout a large part of their childhood. The sibling group also included two boys, who had been adopted by their father's father (Maata's mother's father) in midchildhood, when each lost a parent through death.

[*ugiat*-]!"[8] Saali protested with a wordless cry, and Liila said to Chubby Maata: "Don't do that!" Chubby Maata stopped attacking Saali, but when she had withdrawn, he again asked his mother for a suck, this time in a plaintive voice, and this time she gave him what he asked for. He stood leaning his face against her bared breast, sucking contentedly, his mother's arm lightly around his back.

But suddenly, as he stood there, sucking, Juupi, who was sitting on the couch beside Rota, said to him: "Shall *I* nurse? Shall I kiss it?" And he pushed his head in between Saali and his mother and made as if to snuff the soft skin of the breast. Saali bit the nipple in a mighty effort to hang onto it, and Rota laughed in pain: "A'aaa!" and protested to Juupi: "He bit it! Don't do that!" whereupon Juupi, switching his tactics, asked Saali, "Shall I tickle your mother?" and proceeded to do so. Rota hastily withdrew from the couch to the floor, and Saali, still sucking, went with her.

At this point, one of the other women, Maata or Liila, suggested to Chubby Maata that she turn in circles, and Chubby Maata innocently followed the suggestion, but after she had turned herself around a number of times, the two women, pretending excitement, exclaimed: "Look at that thing up there!" Chubby Maata was easy prey. When she raised her eyes, dizziness came upon her, she fell to the floor, and the adults laughed. But the game appealed to her; she got up and repeated the performance several times, and all the other children present, Rosi, Saali, even 10–year–old Juda, joined in — Saali in spite of his mother's admonition not to. Finally, Chubby Maata fell hard, cried, and came to fetch her bottle from Liila. Standing near her mother, her face still tearful, she sucked comfort. No more dramas were enacted that evening.

## THE DRAMA ANALYZED: INTENTIONS, MOTIVES, UNDERSTANDINGS

It is clear that this is not just one drama but several, and that, usually, each succeeding play arises spontaneously from the preceding. There is no prior planning; it just happens as the spirit moves the players.

---

[8]The word she used, *ugiat*-, means literally "to kill without weapons," as an animal does, but when the actor, the *ugiat*-er, is a person — especially when it is an adult — it usually means "to attack playfully, mindlessly, or in an access of affection." Adults perceive the *ugiat*-ing of children to lie somewhere between that of animals and that of adults: It is neither reliably motivated by affection nor safely contained within socially acceptable limits. Chubby Maata has often been warned not to *ugiat*- people, not to hurt them, but when someone has attacked *her* playfully, she has been told that it happened because she is such a darling little baby that the attacker loves her very much.

The first thing that happens is that Maata, on entering Liila's house to pay an evening visit, notices that Chubby Maata is playing with her puppy and almost immediately inquires whether the two of them wouldn't like to come and live at her house. This is by no means the first time that Chubby Maata has been asked this question; it is a very usual question for people who belong outside the intimate family circle to ask small children. Maata in particular is fond of asking it, both to Chubby Maata and to another little girl, the four-year-old daughter of Rota. Occasionally, she would add: "You'll be my baby," so I wondered whether her liking for this drama was related to the fact that she was newly married and was looking forward to having children of her own. It is also just possible that the drama resonates for her with her own history of adoption.[9] As I have mentioned, adults often do dramatize their own life situations, as well as those of the children they play with, in the dramas they initiate. On this occasion, when she issues her invitation to Chubby Maata, her voice is soft and seductive. It is a voice that goes with the question she asks — as well as with many other questions and suggestions that Chubby Maata has heard; it belongs to a repertoire of voices that adults regularly use with small children to dramatize the emotional content of their words. The "saccharine-persuasive" voice, as I have labeled it, is used, as the name suggests, when an adult wants a child to do something, and Chubby Maata would do well to be suspicious of it, because the activity proposed is not always one that the adult approves of, nor one that is in her own interest.

Maata is a frequent visitor to Chubby Maata's house, and ordinarily, the little girl plays readily with her. She does not withdraw timidly to her mother's side when Maata visits. But she is not easily tempted to give up her own home and go to live with Maata. She consistently refuses her invitation. Maata, however, is not readily discouraged. She switches to a more forceful tactic that may make Chubby Maata change her mind. Instead of affectionately and directly offering a home to Chubby Maata and her beloved Puppy and giving her — it must seem to Chubby Maata — an open choice of whether to accept the offering or not, she cuddles Puppy and pretends to start home with him. Now Chubby Maata has either to give up mother and home in order to follow Puppy, who is being removed against her will, or to exert a force greater than Maata's to keep him, and herself, at home. Does she love Puppy or her mother more? Her mother or Maata? And how strong are those loves? What will she do to protect them? What *can* she do to protect them?

---

[9]See also footnotes 7 and 16 on the subject of adoption.

Maata intends, I think, to test the limits of Chubby Maata's attachments to home, to Puppy, perhaps to Maata herself—to test whether she knows what is hers and how determined she is to keep those possessions. In testing, she may create or heighten Chubby Maata's emotional awareness that she has a home and wants to stay there, and that she has a puppy and wants to keep him.

Maata is surely also testing—it's one of the usual motives for enacting these dramas[10]—to see whether Chubby Maata will take her questions and actions seriously. And Chubby Maata does indeed seem to half know that Maata is playing—but only half! Her laughter when she tries to pull Puppy away is strained. She doesn't trust Maata to put Puppy down of her own accord, nor does she rely on the effectiveness of a direct verbal request. She tries a manipulative ploy that she has heard adults use when they want her to avoid some object or place—"it's all shitty"—and at the same time she counters physical force with physical force. Neither tactic works. Maata doesn't take her warning seriously; she overrules Chubby Maata's attempted construction of the situation by ignoring it. Moreover, she is physically stronger than Chubby Maata and chooses to exercise that strength. She holds onto Puppy. Chubby Maata has only succeeded in demonstrating her own childishness.

But is Maata the only person she doesn't trust in this situation? At one revealing moment, Chubby Maata gives us a hint that she is, after all, tempted by Maata's offer or seduced by her voice. "Oops! I almost agreed!" she exclaims, standing guard over her feelings. Perhaps some of the force with which she pulls Puppy away is directed against herself.

Maata hears Chubby Maata's self-observation and immediately seizes her advantage: "Oh, you *agree!*" Attributing the decision to Chubby Maata, pretending that she is only carrying out Chubby Maata's will, she swings the little girl into her arms and heads for the door. Chubby Maata, alarmed at this development, struggles, protests, and succeeds in regaining her freedom. For the moment, she has extricated herself from her predicament—autonomously, as far as she knows—but she seems to

---

[10]The judgment that testing is going on is based on several kinds of evidence. The most direct evidence is that adults will sometimes state explicitly, in answer to my questions about motives, that this is what they are doing. Once I heard a teenager comfort a friend with whom she had been "playing" in this way, by saying: "I was only testing you." Sometimes, too, adults, observing a child's refusal to be drawn by one of these playful questions, remark with satisfaction: "She/he knows." And finally, as I said, when a child can no longer be drawn into a particular drama, adults stop enacting that drama with that child.

doubt whether she can do it again. Does she realize that she got herself into the predicament in the first place through her own feelings and her own words? Perhaps she only fears that Maata may prove physically stronger than she in the end. In the tug of war over Puppy, Maata has already demonstrated that her strength will make any struggle a close one. In any case, Chubby Maata looks for a protector to save her in case of further attacks — from Maata and perhaps also from her own mixed feelings.

Her mother is her first line of defense, but Liila does not seem inclined to help her, to reward her for having chosen her own home over against Maata's. She ignores her daughter. Perhaps she wants to see what Chubby Maata will do next, and whether she can solve her own problem. Perhaps, too, she is curious to find out how determined Chubby Maata will be, in the absence of maternal succor, to retain what is hers — whether, indeed, she will recognize what is hers without her mother's acknowledgment.

Her uncle Juupi is more supportive. He picks Chubby Maata up and sets her on his lap, giving her the protection that enables her to feel that she has won the battle — a protection that *may* even enable her to recognize that Maata *was* playing, even if dangerously. She laughs, in a manner that seems to say: "Ha ha! You can't catch me!" Danger can be fun when one feels safe.

Chubby Maata has won this particular battle with Maata; Maata stops playing this game for the moment. Nevertheless, it seems to have left a powerful impression. The next thing I notice is that Chubby Maata, all by herself, is running back and forth, back and forth, between her protector and the door. She says: "One, two, talee, GO!" each time she leaves Juupi, and flings herself across his lap every time she returns. It looks very much like a reenactment of Maata's drama, but this time under Chubby Maata's own control. It is she who decides to run to the door and she who decides to return, and her protector is always there, waiting for her, albeit passively and in silence. She is Maata and Chubby Maata, aggressor and prey. She can act out Maata's wish to take her home and her own wish to be persuaded by her friend — or her involuntary response to the dangerous seduction of Maata's voice — and yet be sure, this time, of winning against both aggressors, outer and inner. She may also be acting out escape from this difficult situation, without having to really escape because Juupi is there to protect her when she comes back. Finally, the very energy exerted in the rerunning of the drama must help to relieve the tension caused by the original performance[11] — tension created by the experiences of being attacked and of feeling conflicted in ways that might have had dangerous consequences.

Chubby Maata has showed no signs of tiring of her game when Juupi suddenly, rudely, interrupts it by hitting her lightly on the bottom. Is it just an affectionate tap? Or does Juupi intend it to have the effect it does have? Chubby Maata cries out — the wordless cry of protest that is characteristic of Qipisa (and other Inuit) children, both small and not-so-small. Juupi protests his innocence: "It wasn't me, it was Yiini [the anthropologist]." Is he testing to see whether Chubby Maata can distinguish truth from fiction? I *could* have hit her; I was sitting well within reach of her bottom when she was lying across Juupi's lap. There might also have been a message for Yiini in that touch on Chubby Maata's bottom: a naughty desire to get *my* social relations with Chubby Maata into turbulent waters? a vicarious pat on *my* behind? Juupi was one of several young men who descended on me regularly and en masse in the evenings for the purpose of playing explicit and persistent sexual games, dramas which I enjoyed not at all but didn't know how to avoid.

Chubby Maata looks at me intently — trying to judge the truth of Juupi's accusation? Trying to imagine why I might have done it? Or just displeased that I did it? She must be puzzled. Ordinarily, I was good to her. I welcomed her very frequent visits to my tent and gave her all the tea with milk and bannock and jam that she wanted, which was considerable. When I first arrived in her camp, she was very afraid of me and clung, wide-eyed, to her mother whenever I appeared; but by this time, so far as I could see, she had completely lost her fear of me. She appeared, all alone, in my doorway several times a day, her round face beaming with friendly confidence, and she didn't wait to be invited in. I loved her, and I'm sure she felt it. Unless she had come at her mother's request just to fetch a little bannock to eat at home or a little milk for her bottle, she came directly to me, where I sat leaning against my rolled-up sleeping bag, settled herself comfortably beside me, often nestled trustingly against me as she did against her mother, and began to play and talk with me. She inspected my fingers one by one, noticing the arthritic bumps ("What's that?") and the ancient scars ("Who hurt you?"), ordered me to cross and uncross my feet as she did hers, to cry, to jump with fear when she tickled my face with a caribou hair pulled from my sleeping hide, or to draw her a picture of my (nonexistent) baby daughter, and I happily obliged.

---

[11] I owe this point to Dr. Inge Lynge, in conversation, 1989.

Her mother was not so happy about her small daughter's familiar ways with me, and she did not approve of my encouraging them. Once when Chubby Maata approached me and began to chatter, I heard her say, irritably, under her breath, "Yiini, as usual!" Partly, I think, she thought Chubby Maata's behavior rude: inappropriately forward and demanding, lacking in *ilira-*, a feeling of respectful restraint motivated by fear of disapproval, which her mother thought appropriate to her daughter's relationship with me. I wondered sometimes whether Liila was also a bit jealous of Chubby Maata's affection for me. If so, Maata's playful attempts to "steal" her daughter from her might have reminded her of *my* seductive offers of chocolate and jam. In any case, when Chubby Maata turns to look at me solemnly, Liila asks her, "Do you like Yiini?" and Chubby Maata, with an air of embarrassment, avoiding my eyes, wrinkles her nose in denial. Has she changed her mind? Is she lying? Liila could have scored an easy victory at this point, confirming that Chubby Maata was right to dislike me and that she should be a little careful of me; one never knew what I might do. But she does no such thing. Instead, she asks, "Why on earth *don't* you like her?" Her amused voice says clearly, "what a strange notion, not to like Yiini."

Chubby Maata is nonplussed. Is it so strange to dislike someone who has hit her? But *had* I hit her? I had never hit her before. Does she or doesn't she — should she or shouldn't she — like me? The problem is too hard for her; there is something in it that she doesn't understand, perhaps a hidden message that she can't find. She puts her head down on the couch and hides her face in her hands. But her inquisitors are relentless. Now it is Maata who takes up the attack: "[If not Yiini] then who *do* you like?" The open-ended question is even harder than the other. Having begun to perceive that the obvious and natural answer does not always satisfy the questioner, Chubby Maata is becoming cautious. She needs a clue to an appropriate response and none is forthcoming. She doesn't venture out on the unfamiliar ground; she is silent. But Maata is as persistent in her pursuit of this question as she was in pursuit of her first one about Chubby Maata's coming to live with her. She tries a different tack: "Do you like *me?*" Oh dear. Maata, like Yiini, is often a good companion, warm and friendly, but today she is being troublesome — and, besides, if Chubby Maata says she likes her, perhaps Maata may try again to take her home with her. Does Chubby Maata like her or doesn't she? And whatever her feelings may be, what is it safe to say?

This time, instead of hiding her head, Chubby Maata tries to regain control of the situation, as she did the first time Maata tormented her: "One, two, talee, GO!" As before, the great burst of energy with which

Chubby Maata shoots toward the door expresses and relieves her discomfort, and again, as before, the race may represent to her a much needed escape. Moreover, if her anxieties about Maata's intentions have been rearoused by the latter's new question, the race may still enact the conflict of deciding on a home, and may again represent an attempt to master that situation. But the new question may be giving the original dilemma an additional dimension, or underlining one that was before only dimly visible in the background. If Chubby Maata says she likes someone, is she giving that person permission to possess her and take her away? In order to be safe, does she have to control only the behavior of others, or also her own feelings? She has already received a hint that the latter may be the case in Maata's vigorous response to her slip: "I almost agreed!" So, the race with herself may have shifted meanings slightly, in accordance with a new perspective or a new emphasis. And whatever else is going on in her mind, Chubby Maata may hope that her loud exclamation and the activity that follows it may distract the attention of the adults and make them stop questioning her; certainly it expresses the wish that they stop.

Alas, the game that gave her a sense of control the last time she played it is not so successful this time. The questioning continues. But perhaps she has gained something, nevertheless? At least now it is her friend and protector Juupi who asks the question: "Do you like *me?*" The answer seems easier this time; after all, he *is* her friend and protector. Chubby Maata ventures to say yes, she does like him. Oops! She is undone again. He does not accept the natural answer but continues in a saccharine, seductive voice: "Just me alone, yes?" This time Chubby Maata recognizes the betrayal. Juupi has trapped her, and she responds again with: "One, two, talee, GO!" Let me out of here! Both Maata and Juupi press her for an answer, but now Chubby Maata is aware that she has no idea what answer will satisfy—and probably no idea, either, who she does or doesn't like at this moment. Her "one, two, talee, GO!" now seems only a release for confused feelings, a desperate perseveration of a strategy that once worked to give her mastery over a difficult situation and other confused feelings, and an equally desperate attempt to distract her tormenters and make them stop.

The question of who Chubby Maata likes is not resolved, but she is saved for the moment by the fortuitous arrival of two new visitors: Saali and his mother Rota. The focus shifts to them—though not altogether away from Chubby Maata. When the visitors appear in the doorway, Liila draws her daughter's attention to Saali's shirt. She may be trying to distract Chubby Maata from her noisy game, or merely taking advantage of a new situation to start a new drama. The topic she introduces is one of the familiar themes in the repertoire of dramas in which she engages Chubby Maata, but it may have been suggested to her at this moment by the first drama, in which Maata tried to "steal" Chubby Maata from her, and Puppy from Chubby Maata.

The shirt had probably been a Christmas present to Saali from Chubby Maata. It was the custom for everyone in the camp to give a present to everyone else, and on Christmas Eve sacks upon sacks of used clothing were pulled out from under beds and from storage bins, and suitable items chosen for distribution. But Liila doesn't remind Chubby Maata of this fact, she pretends that Saali has stolen the shirt. It's another test; will Chubby Maata recognize the truth? Liila's voice is excited, but this time Chubby Maata doesn't take the bait. Either she is wise enough to know that her mother is lying, or the question of who owns the shirt doesn't exercise her. Who possesses *her*—and *Puppy*—those are the problems of ownership that occupy her at this moment. Liila, seeing no sign of concern in Chubby Maata's manner, drops the subject, and Chubby Maata continues to run energetically back and forth from the door to the couch, where Juupi is still sitting.

Three-year-old Saali, standing, as three-year-olds do, between his mother's legs, watches Chubby Maata and the others for a few minutes and then, perhaps in need of a little reassurance—he is, after all, on "foreign" soil, and Chubby Maata's activity is certainly not calming—he turns to his mother and demands that she nurse him. But Rota is not willing to gratify his baby wish; she tells him, in effect, to go and be a child, to run with his peer instead of retreating into the soft comfort of his mother's body. At the same time, she condemns that childish activity, too, labeling it wild, mindless, confusing, meaningless. *Uimak-*, the word she uses, is disparaging. It is usually said as a prohibition: *"Don't uimak-!"* To an adult ear, it doesn't sound as though Rota considers the "child" a more attractive creature than the "baby", and, oddly, the behavior that she is recommending to her son is the very antithesis of the reticence expected of a well-behaved visitor. On the other hand, it effectively distracts him from his baby wish.

Saali does not appear to have any negative associations to his mother's instruction. Showing no sign of being offended, he joins Chubby Maata in her race; and in the enjoyment of its vigor, he seems to lose any feelings of unease that might have afflicted him on entering the room. And of course he also ceases to behave with the decorum that those uncomfortable feelings engender.

But now Rota has an idea that will, at one and the same time, escalate and "civilize" the fun by giving social form to the idiosyncratic wildness of the two running children. "Play that you are an evil spirit," she suggests to Saali. It is a favorite entertainment of children of all ages. Titillated by the fear that is aroused by the distorted face and body and the strange manner of locomotion adopted by the "evil spirit," they run, screaming with delight, to a safe distance or a secure hiding place, from which they can laugh at, and with, the evil spirit, who thoroughly enjoys the dramatic effect of his or her performance. Adults, too, hearing the excited laughter of the children as they flee, stop and turn and smile, sometimes even open doors and look out to see the evil spirit.

But it is the fear of real evil spirits that gives spice to these performances, and that fear is a much heavier matter. Few, if any, Qipisa people of any age are altogether free of it, and many children, even teenaged girls, are nearly paralyzed by it after dark. Teen-aged boys keep their fear under closer control,[12] but children refuse—even 10-year-old Juda refuses—to go from house to house unless an adult watches them to make sure that they arrive safely at their destination; and girls, going out to urinate, to fetch meat or water, or to visit after daylight has faded, travel in pairs or groups, and express astonishment at anyone—like the anthropologist—who doesn't share the fear. "It must be very convenient," said one girl, wistfully, seeing me set out alone at dusk toward the waterhole on the edge of camp. But at the same time, I have the impression that it is considered a little "mindless"[13] *not* to be afraid of a presence that is so patently real.

Saali's performance probably evokes the real evil spirit in a scary way only for Chubby Maata and her four-year-old sister Rosi, the youngest of his spectators. These two small girls do flee the miniature monster with gratifying cries of alarm and excited laughter, and huddle together at a distance, poised to run again as soon as he comes too close. The others, however, may have another mixture of feelings. For one thing, Saali is so small a monster that, for an adult, he is a comical contradiction in terms. Only a child nearer his size could identify *him,* in a threatening way, with the invisible shapes that skulk in the darkness, scratching on lit windows and ever ready to grab the back of one's jacket as one runs. But he himself clearly imagines that he is big and scary when

---

[12]Boys are by no means free of fear, however. One young man was so alarmed on one occasion when I was playing the role of evil spirit that he became convinced that I had stolen his soul. Ten years later he would still not speak to me.

[13]The word that, here and throughout, I translate as "mindless" is *silait-*. The *silait-* qualities of babies and small children are often spoken of as charming, but in older children and adults, *silait*-ness is strongly disapproved.

he swells himself up into monstrous forms. Moreover, he enjoys being big and scary, his eyes gleam with delight; and to see both his "misunderstanding" of his nature and his pleasure in his phantom self must amuse the adults mightily.

There is another contradiction, too, in the children's game. I pointed out that Rota, in suggesting to Saali that he play evil spirit, is at the same time escalating the excitement, the wildness, of the children's play and "civilizing" it, in the sense that she is turning Chubby Maata's game, which she perceives as lacking in shape and meaning, into a socially patterned form of "mindless" behavior, which does have meaning for her, and I think that the adult viewers of the small monster are probably enjoying both the impropriety of the game and its propriety, its antisocialness and its socialness. It is not right to aggress against people and frighten them, nor is it right to escalate excitement. Souls can fly out of people who are excited.[14] On the other hand, the aggression of the pretend evil spirit is controlled by Rota, who pulls the strings; it is standardized, one might even say ritual, in form; and it is far too small to really frighten adults. Unwittingly, small Saali may be showing the adults their own monsters—their own aggressive feelings and their own fears—allowing them vicariously to make those monsters stalk the floor with clawed fingers, and at the same time, allowing them to reassure themselves, because the bugaboos are all so insignificantly tiny. The children, who run and squeal, are not so easily reassured. Nevertheless, they are not seriously frightened, either. Serious fear would elicit not squeals but cries, not laughter but tears or frozen silence.

Perhaps, with repetition, the game loses its vividness; in any case, it comes to an end, and the monster shrinks back into a baby, who needs the presence of his mother. (Had he perhaps frightened *himself* just a bit?) Now it's Chubby Maata's turn to attack. Is it revenge? Or just the fizz of aggression in the air? Perhaps both—compounded by the turbulence of the feelings so recently roused in her. She comes up behind him, grabs him, pulls his hair, and says happily: "I'm attacking [*ugiat*-]!" This time she herself "civilizes" her extravagant behavior by giving it a socially acceptable label. She may or may not know that *ugiat*-ing is done, properly, as an expression of affection; she does know that adults—occasionally even children—get away with aggression against children when they call it *ugiat*-ing and do it with good humor. But it doesn't work. Her definition of the situation is not accepted. Saali cries out in protest, and Liila tells Chubby Maata to desist. She obeys; but

---

[14]See footnote 12 for an example of this phenomenon.

now Saali really does need comfort, and he asks for it, and receives it, in
the form in which it is most commonly offered, the form of mother's
milk.

Alas for his infant peace, the dyadic intimacy of a loved baby with his
mother. Juupi sends it crashing. First, he asks Saali if Saali will allow
*him* to be the baby: "Shall *I* nurse?" He is pretending to compete with
Saali as one baby with another, on equal terms. Then, suddenly, he is not
a baby but a grown man—"Shall I kiss it?"—and is competing on very
unequal terms. Not only is he a socially powerful adult competing with
a socially weak baby, he also has much greater physical strength and can
easily take Saali's possession away from him—as he demonstrates by
acting out his suggestions.

Juupi's motivations for this interference are probably mixed, and so
too are the messages that are sent in Saali's direction. First, as to
motivation: it is clear that, 27 years old and still unmarried, he has a
young man's sexual interest in Rota's breast. I imagine that he also
thinks, as Liila does of Chubby Maata, that it is beginning to be time for
Saali to give up nursing. His drama doesn't take the form of "Wouldn't
you like to nurse from *another* woman?"—a drama that is enacted with
younger children; it is "Let *me* do it instead of you."

At the same time, at some level, Juupi may also retain a baby's interest
in the breast. Inuit men as well as women often feel very strongly
attached to their mothers in a dependent way throughout their lives; and
men's love for their wives tends to acquire some of the same character.
It is a common sight in Qipisa to see a married man of any age lying
relaxed in his wife's lap, while she grooms his head or face. Food and
drink, too, being fed, typically carry, for adults as for children, powerful
messages of affection, of being nurtured and cared for. Two incidents I
observed speak with exceptional clarity of this dependent relationship
and its association with mother's milk. On one occasion a middle–aged
man was lying in his wife's lap while she searched his dark hair to pluck
out the tell–tale grey of age—which is said to "itch." As she worked, he
picked up his little son's bottle of milk, which lay discarded beside him,
and sucked. There was no evidence that he was doing anything unusual.
On the other occasion, it was a young man who curled around his baby's
back as they lay on the sleeping platform while his wife, curled around
the other side of the baby, nursed the child to sleep. Son and father fell
asleep together, and when Liitia rose, she looked down at the two of
them and remarked in a disgruntled voice: "My two sons."

When Juupi, then, says to Saali: "Shall I nurse?" the potential
messages for Saali are complex. What he may intend to convey is: "See

how silly I (and therefore you) look, nursing in this babyish way." He is not the only person who is beginning to send Saali this message in one form or another. But feelings born out of his own concerns may shift that message subtly, or add to it another: "I want the breast — and I want to torment Rota — and therefore you can't have it."

Saali doesn't have the experience that would enable him to pick up Juupi's meanings very accurately, but his own concerns, resonating with Juupi's, may help him to glimpse some of the vibrations or to feel possessive strains that in part resemble Juupi's.

What are Saali's concerns? For Saali, as for other children his age, milk sucked from a bottle, or better, from mother's breast, spells comfort. And the contented and peaceful way in which he leans against Rota while he sucks tells us that the milk he imbibes is part of a special and very important relationship with his mother: a baby relationship — and perhaps soon, or even now, a bit more than that.

I have no evidence that Saali at this moment has oedipal feelings — a little boy's fantasy of taking his father's place — but I think it probable that he may object to his father's interfering with *his* place; and I wonder whether the two forms of possession, linked, as we have seen, in adults, are not similarly linked in three-year-olds. This question was raised for me by another Qipisa boy, who was a little younger than Saali and who was, like Saali, still nursing. Luki's father had playfully pulled his wife onto his lap and was holding her there. Luki, catching sight of them, let out an angry shriek, ran over, and tugged strenuously at his mother's skirt. Luki's mother, like Rota, took her son's side. She laughed at him with affectionate amusement, got off her husband's lap, and picked him up (Briggs, 1975, p. 174). Although I think that Luki, at that moment, was jealous not so much of his father's mature, husbandly role as of an interloper's interference with his own baby role, the links between baby and adult roles seem presaged in the little boy's behavior. Indeed, it is hard to know how the elements of baby and adult are distributed in this scene.

Whatever the exact nature of Saali's emotional involvement with mother, milk, and breast at the moment when Juupi interfered, the message that he is most likely to pick up is that he is in danger of losing something valuable. Juupi's sudden competitive head thrust may heighten Saali's awareness of what it is he values, as well as intensifying the value itself, both because it is clearly something Juupi also wants, and because Juupi is threatening to take the valued something away from him. Juupi is demonstrating that the outer world of other people exists and has the power to disrupt Saali's private enjoyment of babyness within the protective circle of his mother's arm. This, together with Juupi's competitiveness, Saali can hardly help but see; and the interference stimulates him to defend what he values, impulsively and vigorously.

The "models" that Juupi, wittingly or unwittingly, is providing for Saali may be harder for the little boy to see. I already suggested that Juupi may be showing Saali how silly it looks for a big boy to nurse. At the same time — although perhaps both he and Saali are unaware of it — he may be teaching Saali that the breast, and the closeness to a nurturant body, are not really lost when one stops nursing. The baby relationship can be replaced by an adult sexual one. Nursing and kissing are linked, and Juupi, consciously or not, demonstrates this very clearly and shows Saali how to relate as an adult man to an adult woman. Moreover, because he himself is gleefully enjoying that relationship, he makes the appropriate "feeling-tone" potentially available to Saali, too. Saali may not be very far away from a cognitive appreciation of sex, either; his four-year-old sister Miika, like other four-year-olds of both sexes, is already very aware of sex and takes a salacious delight in talking about it.

Now Rota defends herself against Juupi's play-acting and its painful consequences and Juupi, perhaps titillated by her cry, perhaps taking it as an invitation, continues his "attack" on Rota, more aggressively and more sexually. And again, he asks Saali's "permission".

If Saali had perceived Juupi's questions as a threat to Rota, he might have been impelled to protect his mother, and perhaps on some other occasion he will be so motivated, but at this moment, he perceives the questions as threats only to himself. Most concerned to protect his milk supply, he demonstrates clearly to his audience how much of a baby he still is. Rota is left to defend herself and him. In protecting herself, telling Juupi not to interfere, and removing herself from his vicinity, Rota incidentally protects her son. And so, in spite of his big, forceful competitor, Saali wins — as Chubby Maata, with Juupi's help, won against Maata.

At this point, one of the other two young women, Maata or Liila, suggests to Chubby Maata that she turn in circles. Their intent is to bring her to grief — playfully, of course. They hope she will make a comical fool of herself, be charmingly mindless. Their intent may also be to protect Rota, though perhaps they are only seeking new and more vivid diversion in the wild and mindless spirit of the preceding events. Whatever the intent, the effect of protection is achieved, because now all attention is focused on the new game, and Juupi stops tickling Rota.

Chubby Maata's performance is, indeed, comically mindless, and so is her enjoyment of the performance. All the other children join in the fun—in Saali's case, despite his mother's warning. Rota, although she didn't explain it to Saali, has foreseen exactly what will happen: After a few minutes of riotous fun, in which the children probably enjoy both the odd bodily sensations and the laughter of the adults—which they fail to interpret as being at their expense—somebody falls too hard, and the game ends in tears. As it turns out, it is not Saali who is the victim, after all, but Chubby Maata, the child whose mindless lack of foresight allowed the game to start in the first place. She cries and seeks comfort in her baby bottle of milk and in her mother's near, but passive, presence. So ends the sequence of dramas for this evening.

## THE DRAMA ANALYZED: THEMES AND PLOTS

It is clear that dramas grow spontaneously out of ongoing social activities and are woven into these activities in ways that seem fitting to the players, one drama following the next with an emotional–cognitive logic that is sometimes obvious, sometimes not. There may be, indeed, more than one logic in any given case. I have suggested already that adult actors may have a variety of reasons for initiating a particular drama with a particular child at a particular moment. Some of these reasons have to do with aspects of the child's behavior or with an event in the child's life that makes the drama appropriate, whereas others have to do with events in the adult's own life. Adults are testing, experimenting with, and seducing the child, dramatizing the plots of their own lives, and expressing their own feelings and wishes all at the same time. So, at one level, the logic of any drama concerns the motives of the adult actors. Any one actor may have several motives, simultaneously or sequentially, in the same interaction, as well as in different instances of the same drama; moreover, the motives of each actor may differ from those of others.

Idiosyncrasy is, of course, not allowed free sway; there are disagreements about how dramas should be enacted—ideas about rightness and wrongness. I saw this one day when Maata was playing "want to come live with me?" with a four-year-old. Thinking, I judge, about her own future motherhood, Maata suggested to the little girl that she come and be Maata's baby. Thereupon, an old lady in the audience said to the child, "You'll carry Maata's baby on your back, won't you?" Maata's personal motives led her astray from the plot acceptable to the old lady, and the latter corrected her. The logic here is provided by a sense that I would hesitate to call motivational or intentional; it is, rather, a sense of the fittingness of certain responses or questions, as opposed to others, the appropriateness of certain sequences of events, certain outcomes, as distinct from others.

Each of these levels of logic, the motivational and the sense of the fitting, contributes something to the structure and the coherence of individual dramas. Both levels also contribute to the structure of the sequences in which the dramas are played. It is the interweaving of these levels of logic, together with the child's understanding — or lack of understanding — of the associated messages, that creates the plots of the dramas and the lessons for the child.

It is characteristic of these dramatic sequences that they do have structures — perhaps more than one when turned about and held at different angles, like an Inuit sculpture, which may represent human, animal, or spirit, depending on how one looks at it. Some sequences cohere more tightly than others. The dramas that comprise the sequence that I present here are relatively disparate; there is no single refrain that links the whole and presses us to search for a cumulative meaning to that whole. Nevertheless, there are themes that recur in various forms throughout the sequence, and each recurrence of a theme adds elements to the plot concerning that theme. Moreover, for the most part, one drama seems to grow naturally out of the previous one. So, again it may make sense to look at the sequence as a whole.

I have already talked about some of the probable motives of the actors in the sequence. Now let us move to the other logical level I mentioned, take one theme at a time, and see what culturally fitting plots concerning that theme are created over the course of the sequence, what lessons may be contained in them, and how they are communicated.[15]

For me, just now, the most striking theme in the sequence concerns issues of belonging, possession, and attachment. A number of questions are raised about Chubby Maata's relationships with other people in her community. Who does she belong to? Who does she *want* to belong to? Who are her friends and allies? Who does she like, and who *should* she

---

[15]I am not implying that there is somehow a "total" number of themes. However, an analyst, looking at the same sequence on different occasions, may perceive different themes, depending on what is, for the moment, foremost in her or his mind. And, of course, the perspectives of the actors and of the various members of the audience concerning salient themes also vary, depending on their concerns and on the accumulated experiences they utilize in making their interpretations.

like? Who can she trust? And closely related to these questions: What does she own? And can she keep her possessions?

The dramas enacted with Saali in the second half of the sequence point him toward questions on the same subjects. Let's see how these themes are developed throughout the sequence and what the children are likely to learn from them.

In the first scene, the first three paragraphs, of the drama, the plot concerning attachment seems simple. Maata tells Chubby Maata through tone of voice and words that she loves her and her puppy and would like them to come and live in her house. She asks her if she would like to come, but when Chubby Maata refuses, Maata escalates her offer and turns the invitation into a threat by starting, still with tender mien, to execute the plan, first against Puppy and then, when Chubby Maata hesitates, against Chubby Maata herself. Chubby Maata has to exert increasing energy to make her point of view prevail, and she has to find an ally; but in the end, she is allowed to win, and she can laugh at Maata's threat.

But is Chubby Maata's situation really so simple? She is confronted with two questions in this first scene, both of them potentially dangerous. The first, in order of presentation (and my own logic) is: How do I feel about going to live with Maata and her family? The second is: Regardless of how I feel, can I control the situation? Can I prevent her from taking me to live with her? In whose hands is the initiative?

I have the impression that, notwithstanding the slip — "Oops! I almost agreed!" — that tells us that Chubby Maata is keeping guard over mixed feelings, it is the second question that presses most on her in this scene. When she catches her slip, her tone is cheerful — she doesn't perceive her own feelings to be very problematic — whereas the energy with which she pulls herself and Puppy away from Maata, her cries, and her attempt to alienate Maata from Puppy all betray a good deal of anxiety. It is *Maata's* intentions that are problematic.

We have seen that, in vividly dramatizing the consequences that would follow Chubby Maata's acceptance of her invitation, Maata has turned that invitation into a threat. The dramatization certainly makes the threat seem very real, and if Chubby Maata is sufficiently aware of events in the world about her, she may find evidence there, too, to support her anxiety. As must already be clear, a great many children in Qipisa are adopted. Among these are Chubby Maata's own younger sister and a cousin, her favorite playmate. Both of these children were given, as babies, to their grandparents — Chubby Maata's own grandparents — and they live with the latter, next door to Chubby Maata. Chubby

Maata may already know this. She is often present when dramas that comment on their adoption are enacted with them.[16]

Maata is testing Chubby Maata to see if she understands enough to resist her invitation consistently. At the same time, in picking up first Puppy and then Chubby Maata, she is structuring the situation in such a way that it is likely to elicit and strengthen exactly the feelings that will produce the negative answer. This is very helpful of Maata. Chubby Maata doesn't have to think very much about what to do; her reactions are immediate, spontaneous, and strong.

Nevertheless, Chubby Maata *is* confronted with a dilemma created by the juxtaposition of forceful action with a tender voice. The one arouses her resistance, whereas the other — we can assume from "Oops! I almost agreed!" — seduces her. Perhaps the tone recalls other times when people, using it, have offered her things she wants: comfort, closeness, food, a bottle . . .; or perhaps it reminds her specifically that she likes Maata and has had good times with her. Chubby Maata enjoys very much being the focus of affectionate attention, and her enjoyment of affection is not confined to her relationships with her parents. The latter are very important to her, but she also enjoys being cuddled and cooed at by her maternal grandparents, by various aunts and uncles, by Maata, and by me. She responds affectionately to many of the people who offer affection. So, by any of several routes, Maata's inviting voice brings Chubby Maata, potentially, face-to-face with the first of the dangerous questions I mentioned: How does she feel about Maata's offer? And about Maata?

The fact that soon after Maata stops her game, Chubby Maata begins one of her own, which symbolically and with great energy recapitulates the game of the older girl, strongly suggests that the questions Maata raised have not been resolved for Chubby Maata. The dangers are still present. It is a highly charged moment, a moment in which loving and being loved by one object, Maata, has become associated with the possibility of losing other loved objects: home, mother, puppy. And now, at the very moment in which Chubby Maata is working to gain control of these threats, a second interrogation begins, resonating with

---

[16]When Qipisa people adopt children in infancy, the adopted children tend to be very much loved — perhaps even more so than if they had not been adopted. Nevertheless, I have never seen a child respond positively to a playful offer of adoption, like the one dramatized in this sequence. Indeed, dramas about adoption are designed to discourage any desire to be adopted. Maata herself was very much loved by her adoptive family, but it may well be that her own history of adoption may be another factor in her liking for this drama and may influence her understanding of it.

the first in various ways and elaborating its theme in such a way that the perils associated with attachment proliferate.

In the first scenario, the message, from Chubby Maata's perspective, seemed to be: "Maata loves me and is trying to possess me—and if I give any sign at all of acceding to her wish to possess me, my puppy or my home is lost." The second scenario—the interrogation about whom Chubby Maata likes—brings the little girl's feelings about Maata under closer scrutiny. Instead of being elicited spontaneously and in the right direction through dramatic action, the feelings are called up verbally, to be analyzed by Chubby Maata herself, and clues to "right" answers are extremely subtle or altogether lacking. Chubby Maata is pressed to label the feelings and to take responsibility for them publicly, while Maata still looms dangerously on the horizon, ready to pounce if Chubby Maata gives her a chance.

If Chubby Maata says she likes Maata, will Maata pounce? Might such an admission be similar to "almost agreeing" to go to live with her? That possibility might incline Chubby Maata to say she doesn't like Maata—but when, just previously, she said she didn't like Yiini, her mother was amused—a sure sign that Liila considered the answer "mindless." Chubby Maata has experienced other very powerful interrogations on the subject of her likes and dislikes concerning the people around her and must already have discovered that there are no easy answers. In this case, too, it is clear that all her attempts to find acceptable answers to the question fail—under circumstances in which it seems to her extremely important to find a right answer, because she has already, in scene one and on other occasions, experienced hairbreadth escapes as consequences of a wrong answer.

In other words, whereas scene one might dispose Chubby Maata to a spontaneous gut resistance to being loved by Maata and to loving her in return, scene two, the second interrogation, forces her to take conscious possession of her reactions and at the same time, it calls those reactions into question, without suggesting any easy alternative responses and without spelling out the consequences of possible answers. Both the answers and their consequences are left to Chubby Maata's imagination—an imagination tutored both by the vivid drama in scene one and by past experiences.

Another thing that scene two does is to expand the number of relationships in which Chubby Maata has to define her position and make public her feelings of attachment or the reverse. Now it is not just Maata but also Yiini, Juupi—even Liila, when she participates in the questioning—who threaten her. Indeed, potentially, it is anybody or everybody, as Maata's open-ended question "Who, then? Who do you like?" hints. What will *they* do to her if she says she likes them — or, for that matter, if she says she doesn't? What if she likes *one* and not others? These are difficult problems indeed for a three-year-old — especially while doubts, engendered by scene one, concerning her ability to control others' behavior by her responses are still alive. No wonder she races back and forth with a "One, two, talee, GO!" She is running between the frying pan and the fire.

Yet another way in which later events build in an unsettling way on the first scene concerns the matter of alliances. In that first scene, Chubby Maata tries briefly and unsuccessfully to enlist her mother as an ally against Maata, but her failure doesn't defeat her; she simply tries somebody else and without much trouble finds — she thinks — a secure protector in Juupi. We have seen that she is sufficiently confident of his support to be able to laugh at the danger she was in.

The alliance is of short duration, however. When Juupi hits Chubby Maata, he undoes her feeling of being protected, even though he denies having been the aggressor. At the end of scene one, it must have seemed to Chubby Maata that if her resistance were sufficiently single minded and vigorous, and if she had an ally, she could keep what she valued — provided only that she knew what that was. A few lines later, however, just before she is interrogated about who it is that she values, her alliance begins to come apart at the seams, and she is left alone facing a phalanx of adults who attack her verbally, if not physically. When she feels herself hit on the bottom, she has two choices as to how to interpret the situation: She can either perceive her former protector as well intentioned but more ineffectual than she imagined; or, in spite of Juupi's protestations of innocence, she could suspect, on the basis of past experience with similar dramas, that he is the real aggressor. At the same time, she is given reason to doubt the simple benevolence of another important person in her world: Yiini, her substitute mother and playfellow.

As the story line develops, then, other people besides Maata begin to appear complex and unpredictable. Nobody can be trusted consistently to support and not to attack. The problems inherent in attachment to people are proliferating, and the waters of understanding are becoming increasingly muddier as simple superficial solutions disintegrate in them. By the time Rota and Saali come in, a number of questions have been raised concerning Chubby Maata's relationships with the other people in her world, people outside her immediate family, and with regard to all of these relationships, it must be less clear to Chubby Maata than at the close of scene one what the dangers are, what the right answers are, and what will be the consequences of a wrong answer. The possibilities opening to imagination are broad indeed.

But there is still more to the problem. So far, I have treated scene one as though it were about *people,* pure and simple, but in fact Puppy plays quite a sizable role in the drama. What is the nature of that role? First of all, Maata involves him as though he were part of a unit that includes both him and Chubby Maata. She says, "You–and–Puppy," and the assumption is that where Puppy goes, Chubby Maata will follow. The same threat is extended to both, and the same fate will be experienced by both. Puppy is a "person," too. And conversely, Chubby Maata is a "possession."

To the extent that Chubby Maata perceives an identity or sympathy between herself and Puppy, the dramatized removal of her pet must help to make vivid the danger of her own removal. At the same time, Puppy is also a possession of hers, which could be separated from her, and to the extent that she perceives *this,* Maata's treatment of Puppy adds another dimension to Chubby Maata's dilemma and to the lessons that she learns. Now she will perceive herself as having two possessions, Puppy and her home, both of which can be lost, and she has to choose between them. In either case, Puppy, an actor in the drama as innocent as herself, helps to enliven and develop two lessons that we have already seen in this drama: first, that she and her possessions are very attractive to others, and second, that what others want, they'll try to take, regardless of the owner's wishes, if the object is not given voluntarily. In other words, people are viewed as possessions. Consequently, both *being* desirable and *having* desirable things create situations that are dangerous, in that they can bring about the loss of what one values.[17]

The lessons about possession are not cumulative in this sequence of dramas, separately from those concerning attachment: Indeed, when possession — the matter of Saali's shirt — comes up for discussion in a context divorced from problems of attachment, Chubby Maata pays no attention at all. This doesn't necessarily mean that problems concerning the possession of objects are meaningless for her except when they are tangled up with problems concerning affection. Other dramas show that

---

[17]On the other hand, the right to belong, even the right to exist, may be contingent on the wish of someone to possess one, so *not* being desirable could be even more dangerous. This is another dilemma that Chubby Maata may confront sooner or later, if she hasn't already, but I don't see it in the present sequence of dramas.

property rights are an important issue for Chubby Maata, quite apart from the question of who owns *her*. But they also show that she is beginning to be wise when her mother playfully tests her knowledge of who owns what. She is no longer easily fooled, as she once was. So it is possible that when her mother warns her that Saali has stolen her shirt, she recognizes in Liila's tone of voice, or in the form of her remark, a clue to the fact that she is being given false information. In addition, or alternatively, she may at this moment be so absorbed in the other problems that are being presented to her that she has no emotional space left over for shirts, the more so as the latter issue is not acted out on this occasion in a way that compels her attention.

Later in the sequence, another drama concerning possession occurs in a form that once more meshes it thoroughly with attachment to people. This time the contested object is a breast, and Saali is the child protagonist-victim, but if Chubby Maata is watching, and if she has eyes to see, she may find the plot in some respects familiar. As in the first scene of the sequence, an adult pretends to value for himself, and to take away for his own use, something the child also values — a something that is attached to a whole complex of values surrounding self, mother, and home, so that the theft threatens the child with the disruption and loss of his entire, familiar, safe world. This time, too, the attacker asks the child's permission for his invasion, but at the same time he overrides the child's resistance with his greater physical force, and the child "wins" only by his own vigorous effort, and with the help of an adult ally.

There are differences, too, of course, between the first possession drama and the last. In the first one, Chubby Maata is threatened with losing both her puppy and her home, whereas in the last one, Saali is threatened with the loss not of his home but of the breast. He can keep the possessor of the breast.

Chubby Maata, however, is not likely to perceive such differences. She is much more likely to see similarities between her situation and Saali's. In the first place, she, like Saali, is being weaned, so she herself is sometimes the protagonist in dramas like the one Juupi plays here with Saali, dramas that may resonate with this one in her mind. In the second place, Chubby Maata's behavior on other occasions demonstrates clearly that home for her is still imbued with baby meanings and that the special dyadic baby relationship with her mother continues to be very important to her. One of her refrains, whispered to Liila when they are out visiting, is: "Let's go home to have a bottle." So, loss of the breast, separation from mother's body, may seem to her not so very different from loss of home. And for that matter, the same may be true of Saali. He, too, may still be young enough so that the breast embodies his mother and his mother embodies home.[18] Both children, then, are likely to feel at the end of this sequence that their secure, but babyishly unthinking, attachment to mother has been called into question by the intrusion of the larger world, and that the larger world is somewhat menacing.

In the long run, one of the lessons of dramas like this will be that the two extremes of attachment are both inappropriate. On one hand, it is dangerous to respond indiscriminately to all offers of affection. Such response might cause one to lose the most important and legitimate source of love and nurturance: one's home. Chubby Maata and Saali are learning early to recognize who it is that takes care of them, who they belong to, and they are learning to respond with powerful and unquestioning devotion. In dramas like these, which test a child's progress in this domain, the key adults in the child's life are likely to take a back seat at the performance, to offer no support, but, instead, to watch with absorption to see whether the child will reward their affection and their care by clinging to them or by stating clearly and firmly her or his allegiance, while other adults in various indirect but forceful ways push the child toward deciding in favor of home.

At the same time, the children are learning that exclusive relationships are also inappropriate or even dangerous. In this sequence, Juupi is the carrier of this lesson, both to Chubby Maata, when he disturbs their alliance, and again when he asks her if she likes him alone, and to Saali, when he intrudes between the little boy and his mother. Neither the reasons for the prohibitions nor their full dimensions are spelled out in this series of dramas, however. To discover these things, the children will have to draw on other experiences, both playful and serious.

---

[18]There is evidence that the connection between mother and home often lasts well beyond babyhood. Much older children, too—up to age 10 or 12 in my observations—may come to fetch their mothers, when the latter are out visiting. "Mother, come home," they plead. When mother asks whether anything is wrong, the answer is "no", and if she asks why she should come, the answer may be a self-conscious smile and a repetition of the demand: "Come home!" Mother may "moo" at the child: "Always following mother!" but after a few minutes, if she can't distract the petitioner, she often gives in and goes home. I judge, therefore, that the child wants her not because something has happened at home that requires her attention, but simply because home is not home without her. I have also seen husbands go out to seek company, or even follow their wives on a visit, "because it's lonely at home when my wife is out." I have already pointed out the association between wife and mother.

# THE LESSONS OF THE NATURAL
# HISTORY MODE

I said at the beginning of this essay that I was learning a great deal more through studying the experience of one child than I learned by making more fragmented analyses of the same dramas, taking little or no account of the actors. Just what am I learning?

First of all, I think the example I have given of the natural history mode of analysis has demonstrated that these dramas, like any other aspect of culture, can be analyzed from different angles or at different levels, more and less "abstract"; that is, more and less distant from experiences that the actors in the drama might recognize or verbalize. In the terms Geertz (1983) uses, "experience–near" and "experience–distant." At the "near" end, one can look for the motives and intentions of each actor, adult and child, the messages they probably mean, wittingly or unwittingly, to send. One can also look for clues that might tell us the fate of the messages sent. Which ones were received? Which not? What transformations do they seem to have undergone in their passage from adult to child or child to adult? And how do the motives, the intentions, the understandings of the various actors interact to create new understandings — and misunderstandings?

A surprising amount of information on these difficult questions can be gleaned from a line–by–line analysis of what each actor says, combined with data about the actors' life situations and about the background knowledge on which they can draw in interpreting one another's words and actions. When we want to know what prompts Maata to repeatedly ask her three–year–old namesake, Chubby Maata, (and another little girl, as well) the standard question "Do you want to come live with me?" it is helpful to know that Maata is 20 years old, has just been married, and is looking forward (she says) to having a daughter of her own. When Chubby Maata remarks, "Oops! I almost agreed!" we can guess that she imagines herself to be an autonomous actor who is making real decisions about her life, but the vigor with which she beats off Maata's advances tells us that she fears Maata might really take her away, regardless of, or in accordance with, her own wishes. When she runs to the lap of her uncle and laughs at Maata over her shoulder, we can see that she believes she will be safer in the arms of a protector. On the other hand, both the laugh and the light tone in which she comments on her own behavior — "Oops . . ." — suggest that she may be beginning to suspect that Maata's question was, after all, "just play".

Looking at intentions, motives, understandings, and misunderstandings, then, teaches us a lot about the cognitive–emotional–social development of one child. More than that, a complex knowledge of one child's vicissitudes allows us to ask questions about the experience of other children, which we would not otherwise have grounds for asking. Chubby Maata can be compared with Saali and with others to produce eventually a densely textured picture of similarities and differences among individuals — similarities and differences, not merely in behavior and in the substance of attitudes, but also in the structure of understandings and motivations, the thought–and–feeling processes that support the visible and audible behaviors and attitudes. I think we know intuitively that the two levels of phenomena are not likely to be related in a one–to–one way, but that similar inner processes may result in a range of emotional and cognitive outcomes, whereas similar outcomes may be underlaid by a variety of motivations. Chubby Maata and her peers may help us to test those intuitions.

My picture of the processes that Chubby Maata engages in in the building of her world and, simultaneously, my sense of the way in which Inuit, brought up in this manner, may experience their culture is furthered by another perspective, as well. This perspective is more distant from what the actors in the dramas — even the adult actors — might formulate; it concerns the themes or issues around which the various dramas cluster.

The dramas that are played with Chubby Maata raise questions on a number of closely related subjects. For ease of reference, I have labeled some of these — loosely and probably temporarily: identity, belonging, attachment, possession, nurturance, and aggression. All of these subjects appear, in one form or another, in the drama I have described, although I have analyzed only the plots concerning belonging, attachment, and possession. Dramas concerning these three themes place Chubby Maata in her social network and point out to her its boundaries. They teach her the advantages and disadvantages of belonging, the feelings appropriate to attachment, and the dangers of loss, as well as investigating her possessive wishes, appropriate and inappropriate. What rights does she have to objects and to people? Who and what does she *want* to possess? What would happen in the event of loss?

We have seen that these issues develop, combine, and conflict in various ways, creating plots, which are never simple. Often the plots take the form of dilemmas — problems of how to act — which Chubby Maata has to find a way to deal with. The following are some of the dilemmas that might be awakened or strengthened by the drama I have described.[19]

(1) Chubby Maata might want to be loved (we know from other dramas played with her that she does), but at the same time, she may perceive being loved as dangerous too: People might steal her or carry her away.

(2) She may be drawn toward liking people (she is very affectionate), but at the same time, she may fear that liking people might be dangerous, too, either because (a) she might be asked to make a choice between "liking" one loved person and another; or because (b) admitting to liking someone might be tantamount to giving that person permission to carry her away.

(3) She might also have to decide whether she likes or dislikes someone, and that could tear her in two directions, if (a) she both likes *and* dislikes that person (or is both drawn toward *and* fears him or her); or if (b) the consequences of liking and disliking are equally dangerous (or unknown).

Plots can be found in the development of a single theme or issue in the course of a single drama or sequence of dramas. They can also be found in the interrelationships among themes within a single sequence. Plots may accumulate over time, both forward, as the same issue is developed differently in different dramas on different occasions, and backward, as each drama adds to, and changes, the child's understanding of previous dramas. Take, for example, the dramas based on another question that is often asked of Chubby Maata: "Are you a baby?" In one drama, babyness is warmly rewarded, even celebrated, unconditionally. On another occasion, it is celebrated, but at the same time a price is attached to the status: "Your sister is expressing her affection for you in that exaggerated way, by pinching you, because you're such a darling little baby." Sometimes, when the question is a commentary on Chubby Maata's babyish, disapproved behavior, it seems aimed to humiliate. On still other occasions—indeed, quite frequently—the intent behind the question and the ensuing drama seems ambiguous, designed to leave Chubby Maata wondering about how her babyness is regarded, and what advantages and disadvantages that status may have for her.

Now, what are we to make of all these plots? My notion is that the kernel questions, frequently repeated and often dangerous from the

---

[19]I say that the drama "might" awaken these dilemmas because I can't be sure that Chubby Maata actually formulates matters in this way at this moment, though she certainly gives evidence at several points of being torn in two directions. The important point is that the drama creates or strengthens the potential for these dilemmas to materialize.

point of view of the child, will be perceived by the child as important problems to be solved. The child will focus on questions when they occur, and they will act like magnets, drawing his or her attention to any events that might provide clues to their meanings, and to appropriate ways of dealing with the problem. The plots, themselves often dangerous, constitute such events, and I suggest that every time the question occurs, it will resonate with other occurrences, so that each plot will provide additional clues to how to deal with the problem. Meanings will cumulate, and in this way, little by little, children will create for themselves worlds that contain variants of the plots of their parents' worlds.

In addition to tracking key questions from one interaction to another, I think it is also possible to find links among interactions by tracing the tones of voice in which messages are delivered. In this case, I am speaking of ordinary "serious" interactions in addition to the playful dramas with which I have dealt so far. Inuit children are often spoken to, using a limited repertoire of exaggerated voices, and the use of these voices by no means matches tidily the verbal content of what is said. Loving words may be uttered in a disgusted or a cold, rejecting voice and hostile words in a loving voice. Not always, of course — which adds to the child's problems of interpretation.

The process of tracing out all these interrelationships, recognizing at the same time that there must be many others that I cannot trace, which are created by associations in other communicative modalities — facial expressions, gestures, touches, smells — makes me aware of a labyrinth of potential meanings that children have to thread their way through, meanings that they have to trace out repeatedly, and repeatedly try to make *temporary* sense of, by selecting links, codifying perceptions, forming and revising hypotheses about relationships, consequences of action, and so on.[20]

Of course, my image of the world that a child is building will never match exactly that of the child. One reason for this discrepancy is that I can never have access to all the material out there in the world that the child has to build with; I can never see, hear, smell, and feel all that happens to the child. Secondly, and more fundamentally, I am not that child; I do not have the child's accumulated store of thoughts and feelings with which to meet events, react to them, create them, and build on them. Moreover, not only do I not have the child's thoughts and

---

[20]I think this paragraph applies not only to the situation in which Inuit children find themselves but, more broadly, to the processes through which all of us create meaning.

feelings, I have a great many of my own, which interfere with my perceiving accurately those of the child. Nevertheless, by analyzing what I can see of the messages, the plots, simple and complex, cross-cutting and contradictory, that these dramas contain, and by cross-checking what seem to me to be the messages with the clues that the child gives me to the way *she* reads or fails to read the messages, I can, I think, glimpse something of the shapes, always changing, always incomplete, of the world the child is building. And more important, I think I can see and understand a good deal of the building process.

So, at one pole of analysis, I have acquired a richly textured picture of one individual's world and of the processes by which that world is constructed. And I think I can extrapolate from knowledge of this one person in several ways. True, I cannot assert that the worlds of all other Inuit children must be just like hers, and I certainly cannot conclude that she embodies all there is of Inuit culture; but I am led to a view of culture—Inuit culture, and perhaps culture in general—which is quite different from the one I started out with 20 years ago. My focus is on the ways in which culture may be organized and created in the minds and bodies of those who participate in it. I see culture now as a bag of ingredients that are available for selection, that is, available for being invested with affect, hence meaning. And I think I see one of the processes through which this emotional investment may occur: the creation of a sense of problem, a personally relevant and even dangerous problem, which focuses, first, attention and then efforts to solve or cope with the problem.

I see Inuit culture experienced by one three-year-old—and, by extrapolation, other Inuit—as a mosaic of dilemmas, which echo, cross-cut, confirm, and negate one another; which are never totally resolved, and which always have to be juggled, rearranged, repeatedly dealt with and redealt with. The fact that the Inuit adults I know are continually watchful, constantly testing the responses of others, argues that a habit of living with dilemmas—continually constructed and reconstructed as experience changes—carries over into adulthood and, indeed, lasts a lifetime.

These dilemmas are, of course, not created for children entirely through the medium of challenging questions and playful dramas. The dramas grow out of, and enact the plots of, everyday life, and children have experiences in everyday life that support and confirm the messages contained in the dramas. At the same time, the dramas are a vital force in maintaining those everyday plots; indeed, they re-create them cognitively and emotionally in every new generation. By presenting issues, usually emotionally dangerous ones, in exaggerated and personally relevant form, by blowing up the alternatives monstrously — not "Would you like to come visit me?" but "Would you like to come live with me?"; not "Why don't you give me a present?" but "Why don't you die so I can have your new shirt?"; not "Are you angry with your baby brother?" but "Why don't you kill him?" — the dramas make the plots visible and salient to the child. More than that, by presenting the issues in such emotionally forceful ways, they help to create the thoughts, feelings, and motives that support the culturally appropriate plots, the dilemmas. The dramas create the child's sense of "being-in-the-world," the nature of his or her experience of the world.

From a child's point of view, the plots are real, they are facts of culture, which she or he has to learn to deal with, in playfully dramatic interactions and in all others. Because children are initially unable to distinguish "playful" statements and questions from "serious" ones, they experience through these emotionally powerful dramas, in intensified and vivid form, the power of others to control their lives, to act on them in dangerous ways. At the same time, and paradoxically, because the dramas present children with questions and not answers, because they allow them to make what they perceive to be their own decisions, they enable each child to experience him or herself as responsible for his or her own fate. In other words, exactly because children are manipulated as unwitting objects in these dramas, they can experience themselves as efficacious actors, as subjects, helping to create the plots of their lives. For the uninitiated, the dramas are everyday life. And even when they have learned to recognize playful messages as different in some way from serious ones, the dramas remain continuous with everyday life, for all players. The point where serious ends and play begins, and the particular mix of serious and play in any one interaction become matters for negotiation: "I was just playing."

I can't make generalizations across individuals about the specific understandings and the specific forms of dilemma that each acquires, because, obviously, the details of experience — the child's family environment and daily experience in the serious realm, the particular structures of the dramatic sequences that are enacted with each child, the actors' motives for enacting a certain drama with a certain child at a certain moment in a certain way, that child's accumulated potentials for understanding the adult's words and actions, and the adult's ability to understand the child's responses — vary in each case. And here again, the fact that, in both serious and playful modes, the child is asked questions and not given answers is important. Although, of course, adults manipulate the costs and benefits in the dramas so as to point children in the direction of unremarkable responses—responses that "it's not fun any more" to play with—nonetheless, ultimately, every child finds, or fails to find, his or her own answers, by his or her own route.

## CONCLUSIONS: THE MODES
## OF ANALYSIS COMPARED

To conclude, let me briefly compare my two modes of analysis and recapitulate the important lessons I learned by switching from the analysis of semidecontextualized messages and arbitrarily selected dramas to detailed analyses of dramas in their naturally occurring contexts.

First, the noncontextual mode helped me to form an idea of how Inuit children acquire motives for learning appropriately Inuit values, attitudes, and behavior. Using this mode, looking at the questions asked, the themes dealt with, I saw the emotional power of the dramas that adults enact with children, and I was reminded that a certain amount of danger in a situation can stimulate learning and motivate the selection of what to learn, drawing attention to anything that will help one to deal with the danger. Juxtaposing one drama with another, however arbitrarily, also made me aware of the possibility that the emotions and thoughts that underlie and, in some circumstances, support values may sometimes be less straightforward than we imagine—indeed, downright contradictory. But it was only when I switched to the natural history mode that I saw what densely textured, richly tangled structures people in interaction may create from the cultural bits and pieces they select to work with.

The latter mode also increased my sense of the potentials for diversity in the structures, the worlds, that individuals within one society may build. I stress the *potentials* and not the *fact* of diversity, about which I am not yet prepared to speak. Working in the noncontextual mode, I began to distinguish the social, cognitive, and emotional *processes* involved in the acquisition, the management, and the *experience* of culture from the *substance* of culture, that is, the values, attitudes, and behaviors that are created and manipulated in these processes. I also learned to distinguish the *overt substance* of values, attitudes, and behaviors—"Inuit are generous"; "Inuit value autonomy"—from their *psychodynamic functions and meanings,* that is, the emotional resonances and motives that underlie generous or autonomous behavior. But taking the dramas out of the distinctive contexts in which they occur, as I did at first, perceiving them only as products of generalizable situations—adoption, the birth of a sibling, weaning—and assigning meanings to the words and gestures of the drama according to my own logic and sense of likelihood, instead of observing the child's reactions to the messages and the adult's responses to these reactions, allowed me to slip easily into the assumption that all children understood the messages in the same way—in the way *I* analyze them. I suspect that this is an illusion.[21] The natural history mode leads me to a more complicated notion of the nature of "sharedness" in society. Looking at the dramas in their natural contexts, retaining all the details of the interactions in those contexts, I suddenly saw the possibilities for individual variation with respect to all of the variables I had previously distinguished: the overt substance of values and behaviors, their underlying meanings, and the processes by which they are acquired and maintained. Perhaps some of these variables may be shared to some extent by some individuals some of the time, but the nature and extent of this sharing must remain an open question. Not only may individuals differ among themselves, but also any one individual may differ from himself or herself at different points in time. For example, the "same" value may be psychodynamically different and may play different roles in the psychic economies of different individuals, or for the same individual at different points in the life cycle—or even at different moments in the day—because it is associated with different tangles of experience. "Honesty" means something different to me on a day in which I have been robbed than it meant when I learned "Thou shalt not steal" in Sunday school, and it means something different when I am afraid of being "caught" in a lie to an anonymous bureaucrat than it means when I am lied to by someone I love and trust. On all these occasions the value I place on honesty is underlaid and supported by different emotions, associations, beliefs, and motives, and it gives rise to different behavioral tendencies.

In addition to giving me a richer and more complex picture of the psychological structure of values, attitudes, and behaviors, and of the

---

[21]Duckworth (1987) vividly describes individual learning processes among our own children—the very different routes by which children may learn to solve the problems with which they are presented in school, under the nose of the unsuspecting teacher, who assumes that everyone learns (or fails to learn) in the same way.

Of course, an observer's logic and sense of likelihood influence the way in which she/he interprets one child's interactions, too, but in the latter case, the availability of detail, strictly attended to, reins in galloping hypotheses at every turn.

possibilities for individual diversity at various levels of analysis, the natural history mode, unlike the noncontextual one, allows me to see how *actively* emotions, values, and attitudes, as well as behavior, are negotiated in the learning of them, through question and answer, response and counterresponse. Consequently, it makes clear the possibilities for flux and change in any individual's understandings of his or her world. The natural history mode allows me to watch meanings being constructed contextually, with the help of patterns of resonance—among phrases, questions, tones of voice, and so on—patterns that shift continually as each new repetition of a question modifies, even kaleidoscopes, the lessons contained in previous dramas, and creates new lessons. So I realized the impossibility of a child's acquiring a total and fixed set of understandings concerning his or her world.

At the same time, I realized the impossibility of *my* acquiring a total and fixed set of understandings. As Robert Paine put it: "In the noncontextual mode one's data self-destruct, but in the natural history mode they regenerate themselves." In other words, when one generalizes too soon and too neatly, one can make only a limited number of generalizations. On the other hand, when one opens one's eyes to the multifaceted and untidy interrelationships that characterize everyday life, there are always new angles from which the data can be analyzed. One question leads to another—for me as well as for Chubby Maata, because there is no totality and no permanence to the structures of meaning that she is building.

BIBLIOGRAPHY

BRIGGS, J.L. (1975), The origins of nonviolence: Aggression in two Canadian Eskimo groups. *The Psychoanalytic Study of Society,* 6:134–203. New York: International Universities Press.
_____ (1979a), *Aspects of Inuit Value Socialization.* Ottawa: National Museum of Man, Mercury Series.
_____ (1979b), The creation of value in Canadian Inuit society. *Internat. Soc. Sci. J.,* 31:393–403.
_____ (1982), Living dangerously: The contradictory foundations of value in Canadian Inuit society. In: *Politics and History in Band Societies,* ed. E. Leacock & R. Lee. New York: Cambridge University Press, pp. 109–130.
_____ (1983), Le modèle traditionnel d'éducation chez les Inuit. *Recherches amérindiennes au Québec,* 13:1.
_____ (1991), Expecting the unexpected: Canadian Inuit training for an experimental lifestyle. *Ethos,* 19:259–287.

DUCKWORTH, E. (1987), *"The Having of Wonderful Ideas" and Other Essays on Teaching and Learning*. New York: Teachers College Press.
GEERTZ, C. (1983), From the native's point of view: On the nature of anthropological understanding. In: *Local Knowledge: Further Essays in Interpretive Anthropology*. New York: Basic Books, pp. 55–70.
STAIRS, A. (1989), Self-image—world–image. Presented at First Conference of the Society for Psychological Anthropology, San Diego, CA.

# 8

# Rorschaching in North America in the Shadow of Hallowell

## GEORGE AND LOUISE SPINDLER

Our research with the Menominee Indians of Wisconsin (1948–1954) and intermittently, since that time, was inspired by A. Irving Hallowell's earlier studies in the 1930s and 1940s of the Chippewa of Northern Wisconsin and the Ojibwa of Canada (Hallowell, 1955, 1956, 1976).[1] The Ojibwa, Chippewa, and Menominee are closely related culturally and were, at the time of the studies, distributed acculturatively from a culturally intact baseline among the Inland Ojibwa to a virtually culturally assimilated Menominee socioeconomic elite. At the time, it was thought that the projective techniques, and particularly the Rorschach ink blots, could be used to define personality structure cross-culturally, because the ink blots were thought to be "culture-free" (Henry et al., 1955). This assumption did not long remain unchallenged, as was the case with most of the assumptions of the personality and culture movement that flourished in the 1940s and early 1950s.

Although many of us who were part of that movement have remained in psychological anthropology, only a few have remained steadfast in their continued use of the projective techniques (DeVos and Boyer, 1989; Suarez-Orosco, 1989; Boyer et al., 1990). We the authors have moved on to other interests (L. S. Spindler, 1978; G. D. and L. S.

---

[1]Others who were part of the Flambeau study (of Chippewa) and whose data Hallowell used in addition to his own include: John Gillin, Victor Raimey, Victor Barnouw, Maude Hallowell, Blanche Watrous, Erika Bourguignon, Beatrice Mosner, Melford Spiro, Ruy Coelho and William Caudill. Stephen Boggs and Thomas Hays worked later (1951–1952) at Flambeau and Berens River.

Spindler, 1989a, b), though we are still working with Menominee data (G. D. Spindler, 1987a, b; G. D. and L. S. Spindler, 1990).

The conjunction between Hallowell's research and ours is one of the few examples in the behavioral sciences of interrelated, comprehensive, long-term, field-based research that produced accumulative results. The results seem worth reviewing for their historical significance in a volume dedicated to Hallowell; this work grappled with problems in the articulation of sociocultural and psychological processes that have not, as yet, been resolved. Although this chapter is not expressly intended as a defense of the Rorschach in cross-cultural or culture change studies, the results of this combined research appear to justify further consideration of it and other projective techniques by psychological anthropologists.

The "lot" of the Rorschacher in professional anthropology is not an easy one. When we were at the Center for the Advanced Study of the Behavioral Sciences in 1956–1957, just after George Spindler published his first major monograph on the Menominee (1955) a widely respected senior anthropologist took him aside to tell him "everyone here thinks that you are intelligent and have a bright future ahead of you in anthropology, but that you are hooked on the Rorschach and this will not be to your advantage." This was discouraging indeed, for Spindler made a very considerable investment in learning these techniques in the seminar offered by Klopfer at UCLA. In the 2 years that Spindler participated in this seminar, all of the projective techniques, but especially the Rorschach, were presented, practised, defended, and interpreted. And the many seasons of field work with the Menominee, although by no means exclusively devoted to collecting Rorschachs were focused on exploring the relationship between psychological and sociocultural adaptation.

In Hallowell's introduction to *Culture and Experience* (1955, p. xi) he refers to our use of the Rorschach "in an investigation of acculturation in relation to personal adjustment on the Menominee Reservation," as indicating the kind of potentialities inherent in projective techniques "when used systematically in a well designed project." The faith that Hallowell had in our work, which he expressed, both in professional contexts and personal relationships, constituted a major source of inspiration and reinforcement for us.

Using an "experimental" research design urged upon us by Walter Goldschmidt, George Spindler's UCLA mentor, we were able to: (a) establish a sociocultural continuum of adaptations; (b) confirm a northeast woodlands personality type; (c) establish a "systematic deviation" for the peyotists; (d) establish that there was a personality reformulation at the "elite," acculturated, adaptive level; and (e) establish specific differences between males and females as they struggled with the exigencies of sociocultural change (G. Spindler and Goldschmidt, 1952). We also did a thorough ethnography of the Menominee reservation community and applied an "expressive autobiographical interview" technique (developed by Louise Spindler) to selected cases among the women and the men, thus giving us a person-centered view of the acculturative process that we would have otherwise missed (G. D. and L. S. Spindler, 1970; L. S. Spindler, 1978).

The rest of this chapter will be devoted to a summary discussion of each of these major moves developed in our research with the Menominee and their relationship to Hallowell's work.

## ESTABLISHING THE SOCIOCULTURAL CONTINUUM

The major categories of Menominee adaptations in the sociocultural dimension are presented in Fig. 1.

By the end of our first summer of field work, we had an impressionistic grasp of the major dimensions of the sociocultural variable, but we had no defined categories. During the academic year at UCLA, as part of our general preparation for return to the field, we developed a

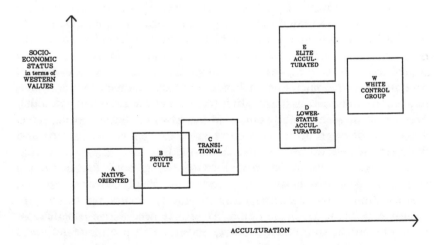

**Figure 1**
Acculturation and Socioeconomic Status.

sociocultural index schedule. This schedule contained 180 coded items under 20 major headings. These headings were: name (has or has not Indian name), age, "blood" (degree of Menominee descent), location, marital status, education, subsistence (including income), home (including type, condition, sanitation, furnishings), automobile, political activity, language, type of reading, parental status (blood), education, occupation, language, religion, knowledge of native lore and belief, utilization of medical services, recreation, group membership (including ceremonial organization and informal friendship groupings). The complete schedule can be found in G. D. Spindler (1955) and L. S. Spindler (1962). This schedule was filled out for every respondent and it became an essential part of their case data. Very often the schedule could not be completely filled out until a second or third visit. Many items, such as indoor toilet, lack of running water in the home, heating and cooking facilities, condition and type of home and furnishings, could only be recorded on the basis of direct observation. Other items, such as parental status, recreation, knowledge of native lore, income, participation in groups, could only be known by direct questioning or prolonged acquaintance. We found it expedient to limit direct questioning although for some items on the schedule it could not be avoided. This direct questioning was used only after good rapport had been established.

The items on the sociocultural index were selected to allow us to place individuals and households on the continuum that we surmised, through our first summer of work, to exist on the reservation. We also posited a socioeconomic differential for the categories within the continuum. The relationship is expressed in Figure 1. The schedule forced us to searchingly look at each case and to collect data that could be coded, then treated statistically. It also gave us a qualitative grasp of the sociocultural configuration characterizing each person in our sample. Our sociocultural continuum was established first for the males alone (68 individuals). The sample of Menominee women (61 cases) was taken somewhat later. A white control group of 12 men married to Menominee women and living on the reservation was also established.

We tried various initial groupings of the persons in the sample according to their sociocultural indices and finally selected religious identification (or absence of it) and membership as points of entry in groups such as the Medicine Lodge, Dream Dance, Native American or (peyote) Church, and the Holy Name Society. This procedure defined a native-oriented, peyote, transitional, and two acculturated categories. It was then necessary to establish the validity of those groupings by testing statistically the distribution of the sociocultural indices that we had collected. To do this, we applied the *chi-square* and the *tetrachoric r*. By using these techniques, we were able to demonstrate that the degree of association for each item with the posited categories was sufficiently high to indicate the presence of a continuum of sociocultural adaptations, and also establish the points at which the various sociocultural categories were distinguished from each other. This required the application of over 500 statistical tests of differentiation and association. When we finished with this fairly complex process, we were able to describe with confidence the nature of our sociocultural variable.

Our problem was to determine the psychological adaptation made by individuals as they adapted to culture change. We used the Rorschach as the major index of psychological adaptation though we had a plethora of data collected through participant observation, interviewing, and the application of the expressive biographic interview before our field research was ended. We feel, in retrospect, that the firm establishment of the sociocultural continuum was absolutely essential to the success of our research and it represented one of the ways in which our work differed from that of Hallowell's and most other researchers concerned with the same general problem. For Hallowell's purposes, the establishment of this continuum was not as critical because he was comparing groups who lived in quite different areas, which were characterized as wholes at different acculturative levels. His "Lakeside" Berens River (Manitoba) group of Ojibwa was manifestly less acculturated than the "Native-oriented" group of Menominee, although there were some aspects of self-selection in this group that we did not understand until years after our initial field research with them (G. D. Spindler, 1968).

## A NORTHEASTERN CULTURE AREA PSYCHOLOGICAL TYPE

The typical psychological structure indicated by the Rorschach for the native-oriented group (Figure 2) is characterized by the striking lack of overt emotional responsiveness.[2] That which is present is highly controlled and quite tentative. This is indicated by the lack of main responses

---

[2]There have been significant improvements in scoring and interpretation of the Rorschach. We cannot rescore and reinterpret the data for this paper. There is also some risk in presenting modal psychograms of this sort, because many readers will not know what they represent. By "modal," we mean both the scores and their quantitative relationships that were critical in establishing the differences in the distribution of scores and relationships among the Menominee sociocultural categories.

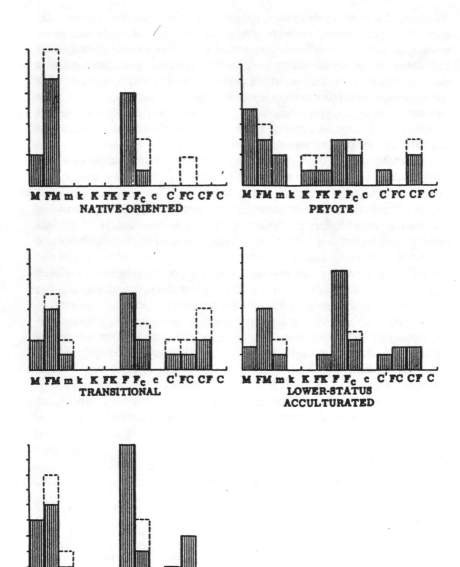

**Figure 2**
Group Psychograms for the Acculturative Continuum.

using bright color and the concentration of the "additional," or second-ary, responses of this type in the controlled color scoring category (*FC*). A slow reaction time further supports this interpretation. Standard Rorschach interpretations characterize this as a type of adjustment that does not allow the variability of the environment, either interpersonal or impersonal, to affect personality equilibrium very directly. This is clear in the ratio of human and animal movement (*M, FM*) to color and shading responses (*FC, CF, C, Fc, c, C'*) and the general emphasis on the determinants to the left of *F* in the psychogram as compared with those on the right. At the same time, a subtle responsiveness to the environment and some suppression of it, especially in interpersonal relationships, is suggested. This is indicated by the presence of controlled shading responses (*Fc*) in all but three cases, and the greater productivity exhibited in proportionate responses in the total record to the chromatic cards (those with bright color) without the explicit use of color in percept formation.

The reader familiar with Rorschach scoring and interpretation will see that all of the aforementioned statements are direct applications of standard Rorschach procedure at the time of the study. There are a myriad of questions that can be raised about these procedures that would take us well beyond the scope of this chapter. What surprised us then and still surprises us is the integrative configuration thus produced fits the culture and observed behavior of the native-oriented Menominee group very well.

Where such a striking lack of overt emotional responsiveness and high degree of rational control over whatever responsiveness is exhibited appears in European or American protocols, one expects to find compensations in an emphasis on a rich fantasy life revolving around the self, as indicated by human movement responses. This is not the case. The imaginative resources are drawn into the production of animal movement responses instead, with this determinant dominating any other single response.

The characteristic intellectual approach is expressed in simple, but adequate (in terms of fit of percept to form), whole percepts and large, usual, detail responses. Small detail responses, and percepts involving unusual relationships or white spaces, are relatively infrequent. The accepted interpretation for this pattern is that the tendency is to approach problems directly and simply, and in practical terms.

The marked absence of indications of overt emotional response and the exercise of constraint over that which does appear, the relatively little emphasis on self-projective, imaginative creativity, especially in an intratensive (inward-oriented) setting, and the limited range of intellectual interests expressed in content, would be accompanied by indications of rigidity and constriction, as this configuration usually appears in Euro-American protocols. This is not true of the typical native oriented Menominee type. Apparently, this psychological structure achieves a balance that is predicated on quite different terms then is usually the case in Western culture. This balance, it seems, is not achieved by rigid defenses. These Menominee function adequately in terms of the demands placed upon them within their own cultural setting and apparently do not need to resort to this type of defense.

The preceding psychological construction from the Rorschach protocols served as the psychological base line for further analyses of the various sociocultural categories on the continuum. This construction also served as a comparison with Hallowell's sample of 44 adult Ojibwa from the Inland group. The native-oriented characteristics are more clearly represented among the Ojibwa because they are less acculturated than the Menominee group (Hallowell, 1955).

The Ojibwa psychological type is indeed very like that derived for the Menominee. A most striking similarity is in the near absence of the explicit use of color. Given a standard interpretation, then, neither the Ojibwa nor the Menominee are given to free overt emotional response and are not subject to mood swings reflecting changes in the interpersonal environment. This similarity is accompanied also by the same high degree of intratensiveness exhibited in the proportions of $M$ and $FM$ to the determinants on the right of $F$. There is no evidence, likewise, of diffuse or intellectualized anxiety, internal tension or conflict awareness, or introspection as anxiety resolution.

Even in the location of percepts there is similarity. Both emphasize the usual large detail $(D)$ and whole $(W)$ approach, with the Ojibwa group producing 52% $D$ and 24% $W$, and the Menominee group 59% $D$ and 32% $W$. The location areas in the inkblots for percepts are therefore the same and the relative emphasis upon those areas is similar. This suggests that the Menominee and Ojibwa groups exhibit a similar intellectual orientation.

Although there are some differences, the native-oriented Menominee and less acculturated Ojibwa share a psychological structure that is highly intratensive, lacking in overt emotional response, given to exercise of a high degree of control over affect when it does appear, and lacking in at least the codifiable evidence of anxiety, tension, or conflict.

This comparison of the Ojibwa and Menominee Rorschach data seems to demonstrate the existence of a broadly similar psychological structure that conforms to the general cultural unity of the two tribes. They share much in ritual, cosmology, and sociopolitical structure. In our view, it is not strange that they should share psychological characteristics. It seems probable, as Hallowell suggested, that a psychological type of this kind is generic to most of the northeastern North American culture area, and may extend over much of the native eastern woodlands area.

This interpretation, however, was subjected to harsh criticism by some anthropologists, who saw this psychological commonality, if indeed the commonality could be granted at all, as the result of sociopolitical oppression and economic deprivation; some even saw it as a form of "cultural" racism (G.D. Spindler, 1975). The connection between psychological structures of this kind and such posited variables is very hard to construct, even at a hypothetical level. The view taken by both Hallowell and ourselves was that culture determines more of what we regard as personality or perceptual structure than do sociopolitical and economic conditions that have not become institutionalized as tradition (and have not become culture). Even the most poverty stricken of the native-oriented Menominee never seemed to be people who had institutionalized their poverty or their oppression. Their world view and concept of themselves, as supported not only by Rorschach responses, but all of the other kinds of data that we collected over seven intensive seasons of field work, indicated that the Menominee culture was very much alive in the native-oriented group, and that it survived, though attenuated, under the conditions of life imposed by the Euro-American domination. In fact, the adaptation of the native-oriented group to that domination was to work at maintaining this culture (G.D. and L.S. Spindler, 1984). We came to regard this group and its culture as a kind of reaffirmative movement (G. and L. Spindler, 1989b).

## PEYOTISM AND PSYCHOLOGICAL PROCESS

One of the ways in which our research differed from Hallowell's was due to the fact that we had a well-defined peyote group in the reservation community. Though there was some peyotism among the Flambeau Ojibwa in Wisconsin that constituted Hallowell's most acculturated sample, he and his co-workers did not separate them out for special study. We became interested in the peyotists very quickly (G.D. Spindler, 1952). When we started collecting Rorschach responses from them, we discovered that nearly all of the members had experience in some depth with the traditional Menominee culture, but during their lifetimes also had fairly intensive contact with Catholicism and its representatives. They were people who had found neither the traditional religious forms nor Catholicism satisfying and who felt a deep need for a religious "home." Peyotism seemed to be the answer for some persons of this kind, for it provided a supportive ingroup experience and was culturally a medley, or synthesis, of traditional and mainstream cultural patterns. The symbolism of the peyote ritual is clearly syncretistic. The 13 poles of the tepee within which the peyote rituals are held represent Jesus Christ and the twelve disciples. Sometimes a Bible is present in the meetings though never read, but rather serves as a symbolic representation of Christianity. Artwork given to us by peyotist friends usually showed the figure of Christ in some form, along with the tepee and the circle of participants within it, seated on cedar boughs, and passing a staff carved with crosses and a peyote drum around as songs were sung during the meetings. The fire, the embers of which were arranged by a ritual fire tender, would be, by morning, either a thunderbird or a dove, depending upon the character of the particular meeting. The peyote cult, in effect, rationalized and synthesized the culture conflict that its members were encountering.

The peyotists are highly deviant within the Menominee Rorschach sample. Their Rorschach responses differentiate consistently from every other acculturated category, and they are internally (as a group) homogeneous. Only the native-oriented group is as frequently differentiated from other groups. The peyote group is, however, distinguished from all other groups in different ways than is the native-oriented group (G.D. Spindler, 1952, 1955; as see Figure 2).

The Rorschach responses of the peyotists are distinguished from those of all other Menominee groups in the high proportion of responses concerned with human movement (for example, "there's a person walking up that trail, up toward this other crowd up here"). It is also the only group in the sample that consistently exhibits a predominance of such responses as compared to animal movement responses. The peyotists also produce responses that are scored for diffuseness as a prevailing characteristic more frequently than any other group in the sample (for example, "all this part here is smoke"). Likewise, they produce more responses that require three-dimensional views of the two-dimensional ink blots (as all flat "pictures" are). (For example, "there's a tepee way back in there and a path to it from here with those rocks on the sides.") They also show some signs of what is regarded as looseness in perception — their responses sometimes disregard obvious features of the outlines and relationships among different parts of the ink blots. They exhibit strong responses to color, (for example, "here's a big explosion, all fiery.") As they see it, color often dominates other possible qualities of the form or outline of the blot.

In these last two indices, perception and color, the peyotists are not distinctive from the transitionals. The peyotists are more like the transitionals than they are like the native-oriented. But unlike the peyotists, the transitionals have no single primary group to which they belong and they do not exhibit the same degree of deviation from the rest of the sample as do the peyotists; and they are not as internally homogeneous.

There seems to be a strong relationship between the perceptual structure revealed by Rorschach responses and the behavior of the peyotists, as well as statements that can be construed as indicative of their world view. For instance, the percent of human movement responses and predominance of human over animal responses may be considered together as indicating an usually high degree of concern with the human world as against the animal or object world. The quality of the human movement responses of the peyotists frequently exhibits a tendency toward concern with motivations and feelings, which is entirely foreign in the native-oriented context. "Right here, it looks like two people here. They kinda join hands together. It seems like it makes these dark clouds up here light up like if those two people did join hands them clouds would disappear. Like if they understood each other . . . they're getting mighty close to it . . . the light is coming down." The peyotists also exhibit intense self-concern and this is decidedly reinforced by the peyote ritual and setting. The mescaline in the peyote also has the effect of turning one in upon oneself, at least in this ritual context, aided by the hypnotic drumming and singing, staring at the chief peyote or into the fire, and being surrounded by others praying in their various private ways to Kesemanetow (see the "Peyote Road" in G. D. and L. S. Spindler, 1984). There is ample evidence of anxiety in the statements and behaviors of peyotists as well as in their Rorschach responses. The reason most peyotists are peyotists is because of anxiety. The anxiety indicators, particularly the free-floating kind of anxiety, exhibited in the Rorschach responses, are notable (see Fig. 2).

The peyotists' Rorschachs also include a deviantly large number of three-dimensional responses, usually suggesting tendencies towards introspection. Peyote ideology specifically sanctions introspection, aided by the "medicine," as a means to knowledge and power. Much of the behavior at meetings is introspective in nature; this seems closely related to the self-projective fantasies suggested by the proportion of human motor responses and also in the high number of three-dimensional Rorschach responses. Again, there seems to be a strong relationship between the peyote experience and the psychological characteristics of peyotists as inferred from Rorschach responses. The tendency for color to dominate other qualities in peyotists' responses (when bright color is present in the ink blots), and the tendency towards looseness in perception of structural forms, is also suggestive. The first may be interpreted as suggesting a less controlled emotional responsiveness and the second as a looseness of control in the perception of ordinary reality. The relative looseness in emotional control seems supported by behavior at meetings. For example, crying when praying or speaking is not only sanctioned but virtually required. It is a way of expressing sincerity and asking for help. This tendency has been noted by others who have worked with peyotists. It is in sharp contrast to the controlled composure of the native-oriented.

The possible looseness in "reality control" is more problematic. It is a logical but not necessary corollary of looseness in emotional control. There are no specific concomitants in behavior or idealogy, and if anything, peyotists appear to have the rational for their ritual worked out better than the native-oriented. Perhaps peyotists become less concerned with "ordinary" reality as they become more concerned with "nonordinary" reality, or perhaps this looseness in reality control is the product of unresolved conflict. We conclude that ruminative, self-projective concern, introspection, diffuse anxiety, relative looseness of affect control, and possibly looseness in the perception of ordinary reality are the distinguishing psychological features of peyotists.

It is important that the transitionals and peyotists do share some psychological features, and particularly important that in their sharing of them, they are together distinctive from either the acculturated or native-oriented group. Looseness of affect and reality control are distinctive features of both peyotists and transitionals; these features are what one might expect among people who have lost faith in traditional cultural norms for behavior, and who don't think that the culture of their parents and grandparents works anymore. Nor have the transitionals found or created a new culture. The committed peyotists have. In fact they created it out of the materials at hand. They became so closely identified with the culture that they and their "self-created" culture seem inseparable. Their present adaptation is a result of this close interdependency, and in both its sociocultural and psychological dimensions is a response to cultural, socioeconomic, and political displacement and destruction resulting from Euro-American domination.

When we look at the total relationship between peyote experience and peyote psychology, we are led to the inference that the peyote itself and the mescaline it contains are almost incidental. What is important is the existence of a tightnit, responsive, supportive primary group, and an organized system of meanings that is dramatized again and again at every meeting, and the fact that these meetings are in themselves a dramatization of the dilemma of the uprooted human. The "peyote road" is the path to salvation and redemption, but salvation is a metaphor for a satisfactory, secure, and knowable way of life (G. D. and L. S. Spindler, 1984). The road itself is the trail between fire and darkness, but fire and darkness are metaphors for an unknowable past and an uncertain future. The peyote church is a kind of semipermanent, "encounter" session where one's deepest secrets and feelings can be shared with the company of others, and where the usual norms concerning control and autonomy are dispensed with. Peyote meetings are more effective than most encounter sessions, however, because peyotism has an internally consistent culture of its own that can be acquired by the seeker and, once acquired, continues to solve problems.

The conclusions described were very important to us in our study of the relationship between sociocultural and psychological adaptation because of the tight nexus between the two in the peyote case. If we had simply included the peyotists, as we might have, in the broader transitional sample, we would never have seen this nexus. It is imperative for the kind of study we were engaged in to make this separation. Careful attention to the sociocultural variable made it possible.

## THE ELITE ACCULTURATED

The psychogram drawn for the elite acculturated Menominee represents accurately a modal number of 8 out of the total of 13 males in this category (see Fig. 2). These persons are not only alike psychologically but are similar in age, social and occupational position, and cultural experience. They represent the presumed end point of the acculturative continuum in both social and psychological dimensions. The other 5 men in this category share many significant psychological features with this modal type, but they also exhibit variations away from it that are worthy of separate treatment. We will deal with these variations later.

The elite acculturated sample was not available in comparable form among the most acculturated Ojibwa at Flambeau (Wisconsin) for Hallowell and his co-workers. The Menominee situation made it possible for such a category of persons to emerge. By the time we were doing our field work with the Menominee, lumbering on the reservation was already a large scale industry that employed about 500 people, mostly males, year-round. Both the experience in a modern industrial complex and the wages and positions that the industry made available enhanced lifestyles that created the basis for the emergence of a mainstream American social and fiscal elite.

The psychological configuration represented by the psychogram drawn for this group (Fig. 2) is keynoted by the fact that open emotionality, as indicated by the direct use of bright color in percept formation (*FC, CF, C*), is characteristic, but this open responsiveness is subject to rational considerations and is intellectually controlled, as indicated by the relative emphasis on *FC*. This combination clearly distinguishes the elite acculturated from the native-oriented baseline and from the transitionals.

The elites are not "stoics" like the native-oriented personnel. But they are not emotionally disturbed and they are able to use their emotions in the attainment of goals they hold important. The peyotists and transitionals exhibit explosiveness, irritability, and anxiety in their emotionality. The elites control and channel it. Where the intermediate types exhibit regressive trends in respect to control functions, the elites exhibit what we called in our analysis a "reformulation of personality structure."

Some other characteristics of this configuration deserve attention. There is evidence of considerable self-projective fantasy, but the content of these self-projections is not morbid, depressed, or disturbed, as it frequently is among the peyotists and transitionals. The content of human movement percepts is vigorous, in contrast to the passivity expressed in the native-oriented responses of the same type. The configuration represents a successful adaptation, as perceived in the framework of mainstream American culture, to the exigencies of life under conditions brought about by the impact of Euro-American culture.

The most typical elite acculturated configuration represents an end point of the acculturated continuum represented within the contemporary Menominee population, as contained within this sample of male personnel. The progressive shift from something that may be called "quiescent stoicism," represented by the native-oriented psychological configuration, through the disturbed emotionality and regressive breakdown of control functions particularly characteristic of the transitionals and to a lesser extent among the peyotists, to the controlled and channelized emotional responsiveness characteristic of the elites, appears to be the most consistent and dramatic aspect of the psychological adaptation accompanying the sociocultural changes represented in the continuum of acculturation. The modal elite acculturated Menominee type is, in effect, a successfully adjusted middle-class American with practically nothing identifiable as "Menominee." Despite the extensive research carried out with the Rorschach and other projective techniques on acculturating American Indian populations, no group has been isolated that represents a parallel psychological reformulation comparable with that represented by the elite acculturated Menominee. In contrast, Hallowell came to the conclusion that there was a persistent core of psychological characteristics sufficient to identify an Ojibwa personality constellation, aboriginal in origin, that was clearly discernable through all levels of acculturation studied. (Hallowell, 1955).

American Indian reservation populations are, on the whole, depressed minorities. Avenues to successful economic adaptation, and therefore to successful adoption of a congeries of associated values in an economy-oriented society, are largely denied them. The Menominee situation is relatively favorable, due to the lumber industry on the reservation and attendant possibilities for responsible self-government. It is possible for a member of the tribe to occupy a social and economic position that is comparable in almost every respect with that of the successful, middle-class mainstream American represented in the nonreservation areas close to the Menominee community. It must be upon this experience that the reformulated personality configuration of the elite acculturated is based. Where this experience is not available, there is little reason why a minority population of any kind should undergo a reformulative psychological adaptation, despite whatever changes in dress, speech, or habitation take place; and there is nothing to prevent whatever psychological changes that do occur from taking a regressive and disorganized form, as they did among the Flambeau Ojibwa that Hallowell (1955) and his co-workers studied.

This leaves unanswered the question as to whether or not an ethnic identity can be preserved at the same time that a successful socioeconomic adaptation takes place. Some light is shed on this question by the five variant cases in the elite acculturated male sample. These five, the exceptions to the rule, appear to represent a native-oriented psychological type surviving at the level of most successful adaptation to Western values.

All five of these cases represent a high degree of occupational success and have attained positions of prestige among other elites. They have good incomes and nice homes by middle-class mainstream standards. The age range is 33–79, but three are over 60.

What is interesting about their Rorschachs is that their inclusion among those of the native-oriented group would not disturb statistical patterns of differentiation in the comparison of codified indices with other Menominee groups; that is, with one exception, which we will discuss in a moment. The most striking similarity is in the area of emotional control indicated by responses to bright color and the general intratensive versus extratensive balance in Rorschach responses. This means that at the deeper levels of personality organization, these men are essentially native-oriented Menominee. The exception is in the form of the inanimate-movement factor. This score is interpreted to signify "conflict awareness." It is presumed to indicate a certain degree of tension that is not quite anxiety, and does not necessarily suggest a destructive factor unless accompanied by other indications of disturbance. This may be an indication that this native-oriented personality structure is operating under some stress. What is particularly important with respect to these five cases is that all of them were raised in traditional style and spoke Menominee when they were children. But all of them went on to school and seemed to have been imbued with the work–success ethic, which was not by any means lacking among tradition-oriented Menominee. The grandfather of one of the men was named "Anxious-To-Go-Ahead." The man himself, a successful farmer, says, "If you plant good and work hard, God will give you a good place forever."

These men represent a variant adaptation that suggests that under certain conditions, preserving a traditional ethnic identity and achieving socioeconomic success by mainstream standards is quite possible. What is particularly important is that the Rorschach was sensitive to this variant adaptation. We were not alerted to these cases through the sociocultural index schedule, but rather through their Rorschachs.

## MALE/FEMALE DIFFERENCES

Up to this point, we have dealt exclusively with a male sample. The reason we have done this in both this chapter and other publications is because inclusion of the female sample with the male sample would have blurred the significant and interesting difference among the male acculturative categories. The women, even a preliminary examination showed, were responding to somewhat different aspects of the total situation of change.

In a general way, the Menominee data fit the model of male–female differences in culture change suggested by other studies, including Hallowell's (1955). Menominee males appear to be more anxious and less controlled than do the women. And the women are psychologically more conservative, that is, they exhibit more of those attributes established for the native-oriented group. This suggests that the disruptions created in rapid culture change hit the men more directly, leaving the women less damaged and less anxious. It is interesting that, despite the psychological conservatism of women, they tend to make a better adaptation to the exigencies of culture change than do men in most native American samples. They seem to be both psychologically conservative and flexible.

Standard statistical techniques such as *Chi-square* and *exact probability* were applied to the Rorschach data for the male sample to discover what statistically significant differences existed in the distributions of various Rorschach scores and combinations of scores among the acculturated categories. The differences revealed for the males were numerous, highly significant statistically, and "made sense" with respect to convergences between psychological and sociocultural process.

We initially anticipated that this same order of differences would be exhibited by the females. The same statistical procedures were initially applied to the Rorschach data. The laborious process of applying exact probability and *chi-square* tests to all possible comparisons of acculturated categories among the women and between comparable categories of men versus women, revealed very little by way of either statistically significant or logically consistent differences. Apparently, the females were a sample of a universe that was not responding to the same forces as the males; or they were responding to same forces, but differently (L. S. and G. D. Spindler, 1958).

In an attempt to discover statistically the differences in the distribution of Rorschach responses between the two sexes that we hypothesized as existing on the basis of participant observation, autobiographies, and interviews, we applied *chi-square* tests to the Rorschach data of all females compared to all males, in a massive test of difference without respect to acculturative categories. Significant differences were revealed by this method that indicated that women exhibited less loss of emotional control and yet expressed their emotions more openly. They exhibited a narrower range of interests and experience as indicated by the content categories of their responses. There seemed to be more involvement on the part of women with biologically oriented drives. Women exhibited fewer tension and anxiety indicators than did the men, less conflict awareness, and fewer attempts at introspection as a possible resolution of personal problems. Women as a whole also showed a higher degree of reality control than did the men and responded to ink blots with quicker reaction time. In brief, women appeared to be more controlled both intellectually and emotionally, and yet retain enough open affect to be flexible — which presumably permitted them to adapt with less difficulty than males to the exigencies of culture change.

We developed and applied other statistical techniques to the construction of modal psychograms for the males and the females that permitted us to locate a "psychocultural center of gravity" in the acculturative continuum for the males and for the females separately. These procedures are somewhat convoluted and extend beyond our present concerns. Interested readers may wish to look at G. D. Spindler and L. S. Spindler (1958) and L.S. Spindler (1962).

In general, the picture is of disjunctive, psychological adaptation for the males and continuous adaptation for the females within the posited acculturative continuum for the Menominee. Without regard for the specific, psychological interpretation of Rorschach responses, these statements can be made on the basis of statistical analysis of the distribution of Rorschach scores. In fact, it is possible to take this position with respect to the analysis of the entire spectrum of differentiations exhibited by the Menominee sample as a whole. For some purposes, what is important is that there is a distinguishable native-oriented, Rorschach configuration, a systematically deviant, and homogeneous pattern for the peyotists, another pattern for the transitionals that looks like a native-oriented configuration undergoing breakdown, and a reformulated, at least drastically changed, elite acculturated configuration. When we looked at the male/female differences in this same way, we found, as stated, that, whereas the males are sharply differentiated with respect to Rorschach configurations at different acculturated levels, females are not.

If we had used the Rorschach in the whole study simply as an indicator of perceptual configurations that differentiate acculturative groups without regard for any specific interpretation of their presumed psychological meaning, we would have avoided a host of problems that follow from those interpretations. And yet, those interpretations, based on Rorschach responses, seem to fit the ethnography of each of the acculturative categories well.

Louise Spindler worked further to research, in depth, 46 cases from her female sample to explore the relationships between the perceptual structure as revealed by the Rorschach, specific Menominee versus mainstream values revealed in expressive autobiographic and other interviews, and expressions of self–other relations; for example, between mother and child. Her monograph on Menominee women and culture change (L.S. Spindler, 1962) explores these relationships in detail.

She found a tight correlation between role taking, values, the Rorschach, and self–other relations. The tight nexus among these different variables suggests that each of them is an indication of the same underlying process. What we call *psychological, cultural, role-taking,* and *self* are the constructions that we, as analysts, place upon phenomenona. The underlying processes defy direct description. They are products of the intermediation of the inner world of fantasy and imagery and the outer world to which individuals must adapt. This is the basic problem that Hallowell was engaged in and in which we are engaged as well.

In all of our research with the Menominee, the Blood, the Mistassini Cree, and in our most recent work in Germany, we have found that gender-related differences in responses to culture change and to our various techniques of inquiry are the most consistent and outweigh relationships to such variables as socioeconomic status, religion, or age. We have explored these differences in a recent paper included in a festschrift for Melford Spiro (G. and L. Spindler 1990).

## MENOMINEE INDIVIDUALS AND THEIR ADAPTATIONS[3]

So far in our discussion, we have proceeded almost as though individuals did not exist. We wish to correct any impression that we think individuals are unimportant by ending with attention to two persons, one male and one female, who happen to be in the transitional, acculturative category. It is within individuals that the intermediation of the inner and outer worlds occurs, and it is through the study of their behaviors and the choices that they make in a conflicted environment that we come to some understanding of adaptation to cultural change. The two persons we will

---

[3]Some anthropological postmodernists might criticize these short autobiographies as a product of our interaction with the informants. Although we would be the last to deny that any interaction has consequences, we would reply that the convergence of observations of each person over several years, the characterizations by others of each of them, and in many action settings, as well as the projective data, make a strong case for their validity as credible personal documents.

discuss are among those for whom we have expressive autobiographic interviews, in addition to the whole complex of observational, interview, and projective data.

### Maggie

Maggie's great-grandmother was a famous medicine doctor (her term, meaning *shaman*) who used both black (*evil*) and white (*good*) medicines and influenced her greatly during the early stages of her development. She taught her to fast and to isolate herself during menstruation, and how to use herbal and other medicines. This great-grandmother was respected by others for her power.

Maggie relates:

> My great-grandmother earned her witchbag by fasting. She laid in a hammock in the sun for ten days without eating and held her hand up like this (demonstrates). The bag was a gift. She made a bag of medicines. She went to work and got parts from serpents. She had so much Power! She got bones from children buried — I seen them. At night she would talk to her bag and disappear. I cried. She scared me. She could turn into anything — a dog or anything. When someone got her mad, she turned into a turkey and made a lot of noise. Then she'd witch them and fight and they wouldn't live — or she would cripple them and make them sick. She turned into a cat. Sometimes when she was come'n there would be a fire come'n. She'd pass me out so she could go.

Maggie was baptized Catholic. She interiorized a set of basic Menominee assumptions about power and one's relationship to the universe. Her parents were from a farming section of the reservation where some of the initial stages of acculturation, such as membership in the Catholic Church, were accomplished by the settlers at a very early date. In this geographically isolated area, the farmers were able to retain a large share of Indian beliefs and observe some Indian customs, even though they attended the Catholic Church on Sundays.

Therefore Maggie had alternatives from both cultures presented to her. She choose, self-consciously, to identify with her great-grandmother and found Menominee values and beliefs compatible with her highly individualistic orientation. However she never identified with the native-oriented group. She lived in a frame house near Neopit, the central sawmill town, with her husband, who had a pension and drank heavily. Maggie was quite socially isolated. The native-oriented group rejected her for her expedient, aggressive manner and said she always tried to "steal the show" when they were putting on their dances. The women in the acculturated groups identified her as "queer" because of her attempts to maintain a traditional posture with respect to medicines and witchcraft. She said, "I can cure anyone of sickness. When my great-grandmother died, she said, "Here's a seed, eat it and dream of medicine I know." When someone is sick I know what's wrong. Then I go out and pick it. She said I would know what she knowed."

White people on and off the reservation who saw her dressed in buckskin for tourist occasions as a "real" Indian furnished an important audience for her. At one time, she told fortunes to tourists using a crystal ball. The roles of mother and wife were never all-absorbing for her; however, she showed great resourcefulness in her ability to support her family when her husband would spend time and money drinking. She had little respect for her children, who lacked her motivation and abundant powers of endurance; she was always ready to help them, however, when they were in trouble. At the time the expressive autobiographic interview was taken, she was caring for her grandchildren.

Her Rorschach faithfully displays her unique combination of traditional and mainstream attitudes and customs. She sees "Indian spiders," "thunderbirds," "bears," " a big woman eater," "stone axes and arrowheads like they used in the Black Hawk war," "Indian butterfly," "deer horns," "Indian lynx," and so on. But she also sees "high-collared men," "two canaries," "a wishbone," "a bowl." The native-oriented content does, however, significantly outweigh the mainstream content. Her Rorschach psychogram exhibits a traditional intratensive orientation but includes explicit, though controlled, responses to color.

Her Rorschach protocol reinforces and extends the kinds of materials drawn from the autobiographic interview and from observation of her behavior. These are the major functions that we regarded the Rorschach as fulfilling in individual case studies.

*Frank Bear*

Frank Bear, a vigorous man, age 56, lived alone in a log cabin some distance off the main road. He was a full-blooded Menominee, raised by

conservative grandparents. He occasionally worked in the logging operations, sometimes farmed a small garden, hunted and fished, and did
dynamiting of stumps, old buildings, and so forth, both on and off the
reservation. He drank heavily, had bad dreams, and seemed suspended in
a psychological and cultural "no man's land."

He spoke Menominee well and expressed himself in English with a
wide and complex vocabulary. He attended off-reserve Indian boarding
schools to the equivalent of an eighth grade level. He read a wide variety
of magazines and welcomed copies of *Time, Life, Newsweek,* and
particularly *Readers Digest* that we brought him from time to time.

He was not a practicing Catholic nor a member of any native-oriented
ceremonial group, but had been marginal to the medicine lodge, one of
the most important, traditional, religious organizations. He, too, is
isolated; although having many acquaintances and a great deal of
experience outside the community, he has no close friends.

He said of himself at the start of this autobiographic interview:

> I was brought up by my old grandparents. The first thing I was
> taught was respect for older people. We had to show courtesy—
> never listen to conversations of older people; never interfere with
> the conversations of guests. I always had a respect for older people.
>
> They tried to inspire respect for spiritual things by fasting. Then
> we was taught to fear nothing—particularly the darkness. It didn't
> mean nothing. If we was afraid at night why not be afraid in the
> daytime?
>
> "When I was compelled to go the government school, I heard
> more about witchcraft and fear and everything else. That was the
> first time I became aware that there was differences in people's
> beliefs. Some was pagans and some Catholics. I was considered a
> pagan because my grandparents could speak only Menominee and
> was not Christian. And in summer vacations I was taught different
> things while I lived with them. At school they tried to teach us all
> that was wrong. I asked my grandmother if there was anything like
> hell or heaven. She said that there was for the white man, but I
> should always remember that there was different kinds of men.
> What was true for the white man was not true for us. And so when
> I went back to school, there was conflict between those beliefs. I
> had an intense desire to prove that the pagan Menominee was just
> as good as the Catholic. My grandma proved to me that these
> half-breeds were nothing. Neither white nor Indian.

His story goes on to develop a picture of deep cultural conflict that has become personal conflict for him. He feels that the old traditions are dying; he has ambitions to revitalize the medicine lodge and bring back some of the old customs. He says, "I think the old people lived a much more beautiful life. They appreciated thunder and lightning and they took a man for not what he had, but the truthfulness in him. That old order of the Menominee had the principles of what made great people."

He dreamed about the medicine lodge and believed that the portent of one dream was that he would be invited in. In another instance, he dreamed about nuns, and dogs, both of which tried to drag him from his bed and out of his home. Nothing could symbolize more dramatically the conflict that Frank had experienced all his life and that was deep inside of him. The nuns represent Catholicism — the focal point of the demands of Western culture (as Frank saw it), and they are dragging him off to the Catholic Church and the white man's world. The dogs represent the traditional Menominee culture. The dog is the "gatekeeper" to the afterworld in traditional belief; dogs are eaten ceremonially in the medicine lodge, and Frank is called a "dog eater" by some of his more acculturated acquaintances. Frank struggled against both the nuns and the dogs in his dreams. He woke up and made a traditional tobacco propitiation to the spirits. There is no reasonable compromise for him.

His Rorschach, like his dreams, showed how deep the struggle went in Frank Bear's thoughts, fantasies, and feelings. His Rorschach responses were elaborate, with a wide range of imaginative content and considerable lively action in both human and animal spheres. There is one constant thread that runs through his responses, however, and culminates in his response to card VI. In the first ink blot he sees the "topography of an aerial sketch — lakes and heavy woods, planes, gulfs, peninsulas, islands — a dark mountain slope along the coast. Looks like a couple lakes been drying out . . ."

In card II he sees a channel going into a lake, with rocks or sand that have been eroded by water and wind. In response to card IV, he says, "simply can't get away from the idea it is an aerial picture of an island — and all those terrains — leaves marks that's been there for years and years; the water eroding — rock solider in some places — sticking out some places — and some deposits of what is eroded in dark spaces. . ." (there are other similar responses).

For card VI: "This looks like an old injun symbol — (sighs) like a totem pole — yes, sir, like a thunderbird totem pole, an old ancient one driven into the ground. Yah — the pole looks like they had a lot of regard for the sacred past—like symbolic evidence. They seemed to have marked each mark a symbol—to know them you'd need to understand some stories or . . . to me seems awful good . . . like in the center—all the stories you would have gotten . . . and it all requires more than just a lot of thought. It seems to tell the story of a country—them symbols are up here (top of card)—the rest of the people down here (lower part of the blot) are all dead, like a dead planet. It seems to tell the story of a people once mighty, that have lost . . . like something happened—and all that's left is the symbol.

Frank Bear seems to have literally projected identification with the dying traditional culture, and he is preoccupied with the process of decay and disintegration that he has seen taking place. This becomes explicit in the response to card VI, but seems to be present in his consistent tendency to perceive erosion in the land and rocks—that he sees, appropriately enough, from a distance, as in an "aerial sketch."

His response to card VI can be seen as a culmination of a process that started as soon as he began to fantasize in response to the first ink blot. It is an indication of the extent of his preoccupation with the disintegration of the traditional Menominee way of life. His response constitutes a pervasive set toward the world. He is preoccupied with disintegration and deterioration processes, and he explicitly links these processes with "a people once mighty" of which nothing is left but the symbol. One can see in Frank Bear's responses the pathos of the position of the individual caught up in deep cultural conflict. The autobiographic interview, his dreams, and his Rorschach all tell the same story but in different ways. Our understanding would been incomplete without the Rorschach, for it indicated that in a foreign medium like the ink blots, he saw his own fate so clearly—in the fate of his culture—disguised as eroding terrain and drying lakes.

This use of the Rorschach for individual cases is very different than our use of it as a source of indices that distinguish perceptual configurations characterizing the various categories within the acculturative continuum. It is less abstract and of course more personal, but it also deals with rather different data. Dealing with content, imagery, symbolism is quite different than dealing with Rorschach scores and treating the distribution of those scores and their interrelationships statistically. Both approaches seem to us to be worthwhile if the basic purpose of the research is, as we said, to try to understand the relationships between the inner world of the psyche and the outer world of reality, as people adapt to the exigencies of life brought about by culture change and sociopolitical domination.

## CONCLUSION

What we have tried to show is how our work with the Menominee both confirmed and extended the research among the three acculturative levels of Ojibwa that Hallowell and his co-workers studied.

The Menominee research confirmed Hallowell's hypothesis that there was a northeast woodlands psychological configuration. Whether or not one accepts the specific interpretation of Rorschach indices, it is significant that samples quite unrelated to each other excepting through the sharing of a cultural tradition should produce similar kinds of responses and relationships between categories of response—that is, response to an unfamiliar problem, the ink blots of the Rorschach.

Our research also confirmed Hallowell's observation that an eroded, native-oriented, psychological configuration persisted through, in our case, the transitional acculturative level of Menominee.[4] For Hallowell, there was nothing more beyond this acculturative level; but for us, there were the elites.

The data from the elite sample indicate very clearly that a reformulation of psychological structure is possible when there are socioeconomic supports for it. But just as important is the observation that, for a few individuals whose early socialization was traditional Menominee, the baseline psychological structure persisted, but without the signs of decay and maladjustment characteristic of the transitionals.

The peyote cult group, who either were not among the Ojibwa Hallowell studied or whom he did not distinguish, provide us with other information relevant to the transitional phase of adaptation. The peyote psychological configuration is like that of other transitionals, except for the specific reflections of peyote ritual and theology. When a cultural solution to a problem of culture conflict becomes specific and shared, it appears to directly influence the perceptual organization displayed in responses to the Rorschach.

One of the major differences of our work in comparison to Hallowell's was the precise definition of the acculturative categories. The fact that these acculturative categories exist within one larger community is impressive. The tight relationships, particularly between the male re-

---

[4]We wish to make it clear that we regard all of the psychological configurations of the Menominee as adaptive, including those expressed in the behaviors and by the Rorschach responses of those we have categorized as *transitionals*. The elite, acculturated adaptation is successful, as judged by criteria furnished by the socioeconomic structure and mainstream culture of the non-Menominee American society outside the reservation community.

sponses to the Rorschach and the sociocultural positions ascribed by placement on the acculturative continuum is made possible only because both major variables are sharply defined and statistically treated.

The male/female differences are something that Hallowell (1955) did pay some attention to, but without particularly significant results. His conclusion was that females were somewhat better adjusted than males, and we found that to be the case also, but he used an "adjustment" measure that tended to obscure, we feel, the extent and character of male/females differences for his samples. The observation that females tend to be somewhat better adjusted may be quite important, but it is probably of greater significance for an understanding of the psychology of culture change, to be able to point to the ways in which the psychological configurations of males and females are differently distributed within the acculturative continuum. This is what our methodology permitted us to do.

And lastly, our autobiographical "cases" permitted us to go with some depth into the struggles of individuals to make sense out of their situations. Hallowell also collected material of somewhat the same order and he included occasional references to such individuals in his writings. To study individuals in this manner without the contextualization afforded by careful sociocultural as well as psychological work would be, in our opinion, fruitless. In this, as in many other matters, we are in whole-hearted agreement with Hallowell.

*In Retrospect*

This revisit to our Menominee research, its relationship to Hallowell's work, and the questions that our researches were attempting to answer suggests to us that so-called, sociocultural adaptation goes deep into the biopsychic organization and adaptive processes, by means of which individuals survive in a changing environment. If this is so, we can never hope to understand sociocultural change if we ignore this dimension of process. Nor are we dealing with a simple "inner" and "outer" dichotomy of adaptation, as both we and Hallowell were wont to do. These data suggest that there is a holistic, selective, adaptive process of great complexity and subtlety taking place, for which analytic models then and now are inadequate. We are not seeing these processes with sufficient scope or with sufficient understanding of the interrelatedness of biopsychic and sociocultural processes. Perhaps an evolutionary perspective would serve us better or, an in-depth study of selected individuals over a significant time period would be useful.[5]

The studies by Hallowell and ourselves that have been the object of this integrative summary can be seen as steps, although inadequate ones, given the complexity of the problem, in the direction of an understanding of processes of great importance in our world today, as we seem to be heading toward Apocalypse. A renewal of interest, not in the relationships of Rorschach or other projective data to sociocultural continua, as such, but in the complex, holistic relationships among phenomena that we have, probably mistakenly labeled "psychological" and "sociocultural," seems imperative. This chapter is intended as a minor contribution in that direction.[6]

# BIBLIOGRAPHY

BOYER, M., DITHRICH, C.W., HARNED, H., HIPPLER, A.E., STONE, J.S., WALT, A., & BOYER, L.B. (1990), Australian Aborigines: The Volgnu, The Pitjatjara and the "dark people" of Bourke. *The Psychoanalytic Study of Society*, 15:271–310.

DEVOS, A., & BOYER, L. (1989), *Symbolic Analysis Cross-culturally: The Rorschach Test*. Berkeley: University of California Press.

HALLOWELL, A.I. (1955), *Culture and Experience*. Philadelphia: University of Pennsylvania Press.

_____ (1956), The Rorschach technique in personality and culture studies: In: *Developments in the Rorschach Technique*, Vol. 2, eds. B. Klopfer, M.D. Ainsworth, W.G. Klopfer, & R.R. Holt. New York: Harcourt Brace Jovanovich pp. 115–225.

_____ (1976), *Contributions to Anthropology: Selected Papers of A. Irving Hallowell*. Chicago, IL: University of Chicago Press.

HENRY, J., NADEL, S., CAUDILL, W., HONIGMAN, J., SPIRO, M., FISKE, D., SPINDLER, G., & HALLOWELL, A. (1955), The use of projective techniques in cross-cultural research. *Amer. Anthropol.*, 37:245–270.

SPINDLER, G.D. (1952), Personality and peyotism in Menomini acculturation. *Psychiat.: J. for the Study of Intraper. Proc.*, 15:151–159.

_____ (1955), *Sociocultural and Psychological Processes in Menomini Acculturation*.

---

[5]We have, in fact, made preliminary inquiries about possible foundation support for a revisit to both the Menominee and the Blood Indian communities (we carried out a major similar research with the Blood Indian from 1958 to 1966) to locate and study individuals surviving from our early samples.

[6]These comments in retrospect reflect a "conversation" George Spindler had with Gregory Bateson in a dream on the night of June 5, 1990. The setting was a cocktail party at the Center for Advanced Study in the Behavioral Sciences at Stanford, so the discussion was less coherent that might otherwise have been the case. Gregory, however, appeared to be in excellent spirits.

University of California Publications in Culture and Society, Monogr. 5: Berkeley: University of California Press.

_____ (1968), Psychocultural adaptation: In: *The Study of Personality: An Interdisciplinary Appraisal,* eds. E. Norbeck, D. Price-Williams, & W. McCord. New York: Holt, Rinehart & Winston, pp. 326–347.

_____ (1975), A man and a book: A review essay on A. I. Hallowell, *Culture and Experience.* Philadelphia: University of Philadelphia Press, 1974 (first published in 1955). *Reviews in Anthropology,* 2, 144–156.

_____ (1987a), Joe Nepah, ein schizophrener peyote-esser der Menomini: In: *Die Wilde Seele: Zur Ethnopsychoanalyse von George Devereux,* ed. H.P. Duerr. Frankfurt am Main: Suhrkamp, pp. 294–315.

_____ (1987b), Joe Nepah: A schizophrenic Menominee peyotist. *The Journal of Psychoanalytic Anthropology,* 10:1–16.

SPINDLER, G.D., & GOLDSCHMIDT, W. (1952), Experimental design in the study of culture change. *Southwestern J. Anthropol.,* 8:68–83.

SPINDLER, G.D., & SPINDLER, L. (1970), Fieldwork among the Menomini: In: *Being an Anthropologist: Fieldwork in Eleven Cultures,* ed. G. Spindler. New York: Holt, Rinehart and Winston, pp. 267–301, 1984.

_____ ,_____ (1984), *Dreamers with Power: The Menominee Indians.* Prospect Heights, Illinois: Waveland Press, 1971.

_____ , _____ (1989a), The self and the instrumental model in the study of cultural change and modernization. *Kroeber Anthropological Society Papers* 69–70:108–116. Berkeley: University of California.

_____ , _____ (1989b), Instrumental competence, self-efficacy, linguistic minorites, and cultural therapy: A preliminary attempt at integration. *Anthropol. and Ed. Quart.,* 20:36–50.

_____ , _____ (1990), Male and female in four changing cultures. In *Personality and the Cultural Construction of Society: Papers in Honor of Melford E. Spiro,* eds. D.K. Jordan, & M.J. Swartz. Tuscaloosa: University of Alabama Press pp. 182–200.

SPINDLER, L.S. (1962), Menomini women and culture change. *Amer. Anthropol. Assn.* 64: Memoir 91, Vol. 64, no. 1, Part 2.

_____ (1978), Researching the psychology of culture change and urbanization. In: *The Making of Psychological Anthropology,* ed. G. Spindler. Berkeley: University of California Press pp. 174–201, 1980.

_____ , & SPINDLER, G.D. (1958), Male and female adaptations in culture change. *American Anthropologist,* 60:217–233.

SUAREZ-OROZCO, M.M. (1989), *Central American Refugees and U.S. High Schools: A Psychosocial Study of Motivation and Achievement.* Stanford, CA: Stanford University Press.

# 9

# Behavioral Evolution Beyond the Advent of Culture

THEODORE SCHWARTZ

## INTRODUCTION

Hallowell pioneered in the conceptualization of "behavioral evolution" leading to the emergence of a species possessing the capacity for culture. He was clearly among the "incompleteness" theorists and philosophers (Schwartz, in press), who conceived of human nature as incomplete without the inclusion of social and cultural components. However, Hallowell did not pursue the further behavioral evolution of human nature through the evolution of its cultural constituent. I will consider the difficulties that Hallowell found with cultural evolution and its implications for the further cultural evolution of human intellect and personality. I will argue that these difficulties have been, or can be, overcome and I will indicate some of the lines of that further behavioral evolution from which Hallowell appears to have recoiled.[1]

Although the foundations existed from which one could have ex-

---

[1] In 1950–1952, I took several courses with Hallowell. I went to the University of Pennsylvania with the intention of studying physical anthropology. Hallowell's influence decided my career in psychological anthropology, and influenced my interests and perspectives within that field. Although I was preparing for field work in Africa, Hallowell one day asked me if I would like to go to New Guinea with Margaret Mead. Needless to say, I was ready to leave immediately. On his recommendation, I was one of those interviewed by Mead to assist her in her field work in Manus in 1953, as she returned to the scene of her 1928 fieldwork. I am deeply grateful for his intellectual guidance and his personal kindness to me. If I seem critical of one aspect of his work, it is not to detract from his broad achievements but only to urge us to cross the threshold to which he brought us in the study of behavioral evolution.

tended the study of behavioral evolution along its cultural dimension, a number of objections to the idea of cultural evolution itself led Hallowell to reject the enterprise. To argue with Hallowell's objections and try to show that they could have been answered might seem both anachronistic and futile were it not that his position, articulated at midcentury, remains in effect and hence, will serve well as a point of departure. With some important exceptions,[2] much of recent writing on cultural evolution derives from sociobiology and responses to it.[3] Around the time of the Darwin centennial, there seemed to be a revival of interest in cultural evolution, but it amounted to little in the area of postcultural behavioral evolution.[4] Sociobiology stimulated recent theoretical work on models of cultural evolution that are not themselves sociobiological; that is, these models refer to the specific nature of cultural process and transmission and their divergence from the most comparable biological/genetic processes but may, nevertheless, attempt to see how far a Darwinian model may be carried in cultural evolution (Boyd and Richerson, 1985; Cavalli-Sforza and Feldman, 1981).[5] I am not dealing with attempts to extend a neo-Darwinian model to culture in this chapter but rather, the evolution of culture, with its own special characteristics and consequences, many of which are importantly non-Darwinian. The program that I see implied in Hallowell's work but not brought to fruition there — the study of the behavioral evolution of the human mind and personality as both contributor and consequence to cultural evolution — is the concern of few current scholars.

## BEHAVIORAL EVOLUTION AND THE BEHAVIORAL ENVIRONMENT

Although Hallowell spoke of behavioral evolution and the behavioral environment, he was not referring to behaviorist psychology. His psychologizing was phenomenological, gestaltist, comparative, and to a limited extent, psychoanalytic. Behavior, for Hallowell, included implicit as well as explicit acts, states, and processes; mental, perceptual, symbolic and linguistic, as well as motor acts. The term *behavioral* was intended to contrast with *morphological* rather than with *mentalistic*.

---

[2]See discussion of Carneiro's work below.

[3]See Durham (1990) for a survey of recent work concerned with cultural evolution of varying degrees of emulation of biological models.

[4]See Goody (1977) and Horton and Finnegan (1973) for some important work.

[5]See Durham (1990) for a survey of the literature and extensive bibliography.

Keeping this broad sense of *behavior* in mind, evolution, viewed in its morphological and behavioral aspects, moved in parallel, one dependent on the other, at least to the point where the capacity for culture was established. Behavioral evolution shifted attention from a succession of animal morphologies to the evolution of behavioral systems. Hallowell, who eschewed formalism, did not speak of *systems* in spite of the fact that this period was the heyday of *general systems theory,* a forerunner of current *cognitive science.*

In his lectures, Hallowell traced the evolution of the complexity and versatility of the behavioral repertoires of animal species and reciprocally, the increasing richness and differentiation of the behavioral environments that corresponded to the capacities of each organism to respond differentially to potential features of the environment. For each organism there was a different behavioral environment. The behavioral environment also could be said to evolve as the sensorium and response repertoire of animal species evolved. As intervening variables between stimulus and response assumed ever-increasing importance, responses became less stimulus-bound; stimuli themselves became less discrete and more presentational, more dependent on interpretation in terms of stored past experience, as organisms, from the start, increasingly incorporated their histories. The most important of these intervening variables or processes evolved in the increasing capacity of organisms to represent and store experience. Explicit symbolism, employing personal and conventional meanings, not only forms the demarcation between pre-human protoculture and human culture, but also, and by the same means, is the point of emergence for conscious and self-conscious thought by enabling internal communication (thought) and external communication. Not until quite late in the development of representational means does this capacity become self-reflexive, making possible self-objectification, self-consciousness, and self-monitoring as a basis for the development of moral, social, norm-related behavior. This emergence of self was of great importance to Hallowell (1954). He stressed that this evolution takes place in an indispensable social context.

For the human species, culture must be added to the structures and capacities defining the behavioral environment. Culture segmented, and selected for relevance potential features of the physical environment. Culture added the figmentary to the physical — a new (in the evolutionary sense) kind of object, blending the physical, biological, and cultural. Thus, for example, a human behavioral environment included other objects and beings, both actual and imagined, and excluded features of the actual environment of which members of the culture were unaware (such as the iron ore deposits of the great lake area to pre-Columbian Indian populations). Of course, behavior can be affected by elements of the environment of which people are unaware, but this would not be a part of the behavioral environment in Hallowell's sense, perhaps better termed a *phenomenological ecology.*[6]

# THE INCOMPLETENESS THESIS

It is apparent that one does not have a human nature without biology — a human body and brain. It may have been less apparent that one does not have human nature, one that behaves as a human being, without the implementation of that body and brain, through learning a specific human culture. It is not only the biochemical commonality and uniqueness of the individual but also this enculturative specificity, formed in interaction with specifically enculturated, not generalized, others, that constitutes an individual. The "incompleteness thesis" (Schwartz, 1989, in press) asserts that human nature is radically incomplete; much of that nature consists of the capacity to complete itself in the enculturative process through the acquisition of a culture. Hallowell's position on "incompleteness" is clear. In his presidential address to the American Anthropological Association in 1949 (Hallowell, 1950), he states:

> The assumption is that the individual functions as a psychobiological whole, as a total personality. Behavior has a structural basis, but this structuralization has arisen in experience and cannot, therefore, be reduced to an inherited organic structure. "Intelligence," "reason," or other mental traits then become specific functions of the personality structure. Thus, the distinctive psychological organization of the human being, whether described as mind or personality structure, is just as much a function of his membership in a social group as it is a function of his inherited organic equipment [p. 5].

And further:

> To behave humanly as an adult the individual must become psychologically organized in a socialization process. His biological equipment is only *one* of the conditions necessary for this [p. 5].

---

[6]See discussion of terminology and literature cited by Hallowell (1988, p. 388, note 33).

As Kroeber stated it: "To look for 'unconditioned human nature' is paradoxical because the essence of human nature is that it is conditioned" (cited in Róheim, 1950, p. 5). It is necessary, then, to consider why, if culture — the preeminent human species adaptation — is an indispensable constituent of human nature, Hallowell did not pursue, (in fact, may have rejected), the further behavioral evolution of human nature through the process of cultural evolution.

Hallowell interweaves culture and personality structure so intimately and essentially, that again, it would seem to me that cultural evolution must entail the evolution of personality itself — an evolution that Hallowell traced for us, up to and just beyond the threshold of culture but no further. To emphasize the cultural component, as Hallowell does, does not mean that he saw it replacing the biological, but the value of his contribution lies not in his "interactionism," which in itself would be trivial — who is not an interactionist? (Schwartz, 1983) — but in specifying the interactions. To this end, for example, Hallowell (1955) stated:

> The individual was forced to make his personal adjustment to life by means of the symbolic system provided by his society. But no culture frees the infant from the fundamental conflict arising from the biologically rooted impulses on the one hand, and the demands of parents or parent surrogates on the other, nor the need for some internal resolution of such conflicts. But the demands of the parents and the manner in which children are handled are not identical in all societies; hence the crucial importance of the socialization process in relation to the differential strains and stresses that account for the personality structure under one set of conditions as compared with another [p. 13].

One cannot disagree with this statement, but it seems to me not to go far enough on the side of culture. Like much of the literature of psychological anthropology, discussion of the influence of culture as a variable is confined to socialization (the manner in which children are handled). Elsewhere (Schwartz, 1981) I have stressed the distinction between socialization and enculturation, the former, behaviorist in origin, employs an animal training model. In the socialization model, child-rearing practices shape personality through the culturally shaped patterning of reward and punishment, gratification and frustration, attachment, and more complex, but generally, behavioristically conceived processes. Enculturation, on the other hand, focuses on the individual (in childhood and beyond) as a sentient human being, acquiring, reconfiguring, and applying a specific culture. This ideational environment makes up much of the content and context of personality, not in the form of pure cognition, but in a perceptually, behaviorally and cognitively relevant blend of form, meaning, affect, motive, aesthetic, value, and moral components. An emphasis on enculturation is a corrective complement, not a substitute for the processes designated as socialization. It is to indicate this fuller scope that I prefer to speak of an "experience-processing" rather than an "information-processing" model of culture. It is clear from Hallowell's writings that his interest was most directly in culture and its phenomenological implications for perception and behavior—its effect in constituting a behavioral environment. In fact, he offers little observation or comment on Ojibwa childhood or socialization.

If one takes human nature as specifying the basis for human behavior, then it is clear that human biology plus socialization still leaves an incomplete specification of human nature, to which enculturation must be added. It now is quite well understood that culture impinges on child rearing practices, which have their effects on personality, and that these effects may be projected in institutionalized, symbolic forms, which can be used as symbolic resources in the maintenance and defense of the personality. Psychodynamics, in the form of conflict between drives and norms, has further occupied much of our attention. Less well attended, at least in our theoretical models, although well described in the literature in some of its most striking, exotic forms, is the direct effect of culture as an ideational and orientational environment, having direct implicational force in the form of assumptions and beliefs, underlying the affective tone of personal experience as well as interpersonal relations. At this level, culture is both the source and palliative of fear, anxiety, stress, trauma, and aggression as well as a source of a degree of real gratification and security. Culture defines the radius of the circle of trust and of the moral community, as well as the measure of our achievements and aspirations. In these direct effects of culture, we can trace evolutionary trends that have greatly altered the behavioral environment in which some members of advanced cultures live. It was the utopian hope of the 18th century philosophers of the enlightenment that such trends would soon prevail. We have come to realize that evolutionary processes are historically complex, subject to differentiating contingencies, and pervaded by massive continuities of earlier cultures that are far more persistent than we might once have believed.

## PERSONALITY IN EVOLUTION.
## THE PLACE OF PSYCHOANALYSIS IN
## HALLOWELL'S THOUGHT

Hallowell derived ego and superego as the personality structures both required and engendered by the evolutionary emergence of society and culture, rather than from specifically Freudian, psychodynamic processes. In the early 1950s when I was in his classes, Hallowell's lectures were rich in allusion to comparative and phenomenological psychology. He accepted the psychoanalytic model of psychic structures, (including their cultural structuring), as a pseudostructure—an analog device for representing dynamic relations at a functional level and a way of talking about the conjoined evolution of culture and of personality. Mammalian and primate childhood dependency and primary attachments, increasingly prolonged while reproduction is delayed, allowed both for the lengthy development of personality structure as well as for the acquisition of cultural competence. I am not aware of his making use of the Oedipus complex, for example, and I will discuss his rejection of recapitulationism in psychoanalytic thought. For these reasons, I believe that Hallowell's use of psychoanalytic theory was quite limited. It contributed to his definition of generic, human, psychobiological nature and to his development of the idea of culturally institutionalized defense mechanisms. In yet another major contribution to psychology and culture, Hallowell examined the social functions of anxiety—an idea with functionalist origins in anthropology (Hallowell, 1941). Thus culture can create sources of fear and anxiety, pattern them, for example, into a fear of sorcery, use anxiety for social control, and offer some means of defending against anxiety, which may nevertheless leave it as a pervasive feature of life in many cultures. It is not the purpose of this chapter to discuss Hallowell's many important contributions to psychological anthropology, however, and I will confine myself to his thinking about behavioral and cultural evolution.

Issuing from the foundation laid by Hallowell, the following statement by Bourguignon (1979) illustrates the direction that would seem to be implicated by those foundations.

As culture changes and evolves over time, so does the world that is experienced by human groups. Its complexity is related to an increase in empirical knowledge and in practical skills, or a shift in the types of knowledge and skills that are required under new circumstances. At the same time, in ideological or metaphysical terms, it also reflects the image of a more complex social organization. To function effectively personalities must be adapted to this changing behavioral environment, which yet, to some extent, is itself a reflection of the personality type fostered by the group's life style. . . . We have attempted to relate this evolution of personality types to an evolution of both culture and of the culturally constituted behavioral environment [p. 73].[7]

Perhaps I have overlooked it, but I do not find such a statement or interest coming from Hallowell. It would have required the recognition of types of societies and of evolutionary process in typological transformations, however complex and locally diversified that process may have been. Hallowell stood with his contemporaries, the students of Boas (though he was not directly one of them) in the early culture and personality school, in recognizing an integration of personality in culture, although denying that cultures could be validly subsumed under larger types. Benedict (1934) denied that her "configurations" were types or part of a typology. Even Devereux in seeking social/cultural types for his "type disorders" felt that cultures were so diverse that only the broadest types, *Gemeinschaft and Gesellschaft,* were valid (Devereux, 1956). Even if drawn in such broad and dubious speculations (hysteria with *Gemeinschaft;* schizophrenia with *Gesellschaft*) Devereux did take an evolutionary perspective on culture and psychopathology.

## HALLOWELL'S OBJECTIONS TO RECAPITULATIONISM AND CULTURAL EVOLUTION: HOW THESE OBJECTIONS MIGHT HAVE BEEN ANSWERED

Hallowell concluded his presidential address by saying that we study cultural diversity in order to extract the generic. This aim would not satisfy me, and I think this aim does not represent the scope of Hallowell's own interests. For one thing, the diversity of human culture and experience may be as important as the common denominator. More to the point, the generic would disregard the evolutionary differences

---

[7]Bourguignon refers to Robert LeVine's (1973) model that attempts to account for the "fit" between personality types and an evolutionary array of societal and subsistence types. LeVine's model is exceptional, psychologically oriented, and evolutionary in its inclusion of ontogenetic factors in relation to subsistence types.

among cultures and miss the evolution of human nature, mind, and personality in their emergent and therefore variable, not generic, properties.

Hallowell's writing gives us the benefit of his conceptualization of behavioral evolution and of the trends coalescing into a human nature that both enables, and is extended by, culture. It does not indicate the richness of the terrain through which he guided his students through the various "levels of integration,"[8] and by which the "grades" of behavioral evolution could be traced. His ethnographic writing is more representative of his theories of Ojibwa culture, which embody his understandings of the phenomenology of cultures. His course on the ethnography of the self satisfied the appetite for diversity that had brought many of us into anthropology. One wants more than final theoretical formulations to feed this appetite. Hallowell's course on the history of anthropology introduced me to the literature (most of the 19th and early 20th century writers in anthropology) of cultural evolution. Regardless of criticisms of these early formulations of the course of cultural evolution, it is obvious where human beings began culturally and where we are, or rather, where we are going, as we participate in the dizzying process of exponentially accelerating cultural evolution. From our evolutionary perspective, we look back on the adaptive radiation of human cultures as humankind spread over the earth at an as yet early, primitive stage of cultural evolution; and then, ever more rapidly we see the spindle close in a convergence of cultures to the point that it may be becoming difficult to believe in their earlier diversity. Given Hallowell's concern with behavioral evolution and his own position with respect to the incompleteness thesis, what were the theoretical and philosophical problems that led him on another path, together, I must add, with most other anthropologists.[9]

Some of these problems have to do with a perception that cultural evolutionism was associated with racism, ethnocentrism, unilineality, superorganicism, recapitulationism, and that, moreover, it was empirically incorrect. In spite of these not inconsiderable difficulties, we must assume that Hallowell accepted the fact of cultural evolution in some form, (left unstated), that somehow we had gotten from small scale, simpler, social and cultural beginnings to the recent mosaic of cultures in the process of converging to a world culture. Hallowell's chosen role was that of critic. We find indications of his reservations about cultural

---

[8]Schneirla's (1949) term; Hallowell (1988, p. 367).
[9]Sapir, for example, wrote, "[e]volutionism as an interpretive principle of culture is merely a passing phase in the history of thought . . ." (1920, p. 378).

evolution in his article, "The Recapitulation Theory and Culture" (Hallowell, 1939).

## THE QUESTION OF A BIOLOGICAL OR RACIAL BASIS FOR CULTURAL EVOLUTION

Hallowell (1955) argued that the idea of unilineal cultural evolution was, implicitly or explicitly, linked to the belief that cultural evolution depended on biological evolution and that the level attained culturally by a people was "interpreted as an index of their limited mental capacities" (p. 15). The literature of that period is full of references to the "inferior races" based on their "level of cultural attainment." He further stated:

It was thought that mental development paralleled the organic in the hierarchy of evolutionary stages beginning with the lowest stages of animal mind and gradually ascending to human mind; the latter, in turn, developing through a succession of stages in the history of the race to the apex reached by the adult "rational" mind of occidental man [p. 15].

In this century, American anthropology took it as a fundamental social responsibility to combat the blatant errors of racism, offering many arguments and abundant evidence against the widely prevalent folk identification of cultural difference, perceived invidiously, with race. The issue seems never finally laid to rest. Racial inequality as a basis for judging social and cultural attainment is periodically asserted with claims of support from scientific evidence, such as differences on average group scores on IQ and other tests. (for example, Jensen, 1969, 1979).[10] No matter how decisively opponents of "scientific" racism (among whom most anthropologists and psychologists are numbered) feel that they have refuted its claims and revealed its biases, scientific racism seems always to return. From what we know from history, and what we have experienced in this century, a high degree of sensitivity and vigilence is justified. But where race and culture *are* clearly distinguished and cultural evolution is *not* seen as dependent on differential biological capacities, need we continue to reject cultural evolution because of the existence, (past and present), of a false biological reading of it? Even

---

[10]See Gould (1981) for general treatment.

where the two levels or processes are distinguished, a discomfort persists — a contamination that is difficult to expunge.

As for those who have been called, "Our Primitive Contemporaries," (Murdock, 1934) it has become clear, if more proof were needed, from the rapid pace of acculturation around the world, that whereas there are relatively primitive cultures, there are no primitive peoples. When I first went to New Guinea in 1953, still under a classical colonial system with only a scattering of mission schools in the villages, it would have seemed incredible that in 20 years Papua, New Guinea would be a self-governing country with a large, English-speaking and literate population, and with many university graduates who were born in villages — some having come into contact with the outside world only in the 1960s — incredible that the system would change so rapidly, not that New Guinea "savages" would be capable of it. No one living as an anthropologist, among the people of a nonliterate population could doubt that he or she was among people manifesting the usual range of intelligence, capable of mastering any culture under the right circumstances.

## EVOLUTION AND ETHNOCENTRISM

Even where a theory asserts that cultural evolution does not depend on biological differences, there is still the problem of ethnocentrism. As the theory arises in European-derived cultures, it has the self-congratulatory effect that the evolutionary theorist just happens to find himself at the pinnacle, the latest and highest stage of cultural evolution. After all, what could be more evolved than the production of theories of evolution or even more so, a theory of evolutionary thought? But again, this ethnocentric view, in favor of particular populations, is not a necessary or accurate account of the history of cultural evolution. It should be apparent that the relative, cultural evolutionary status of peoples and regions has shifted from one historical period to another in a process that Sahlins and Service likened to a "relay race" manifesting a "law" of limited local evolutionary potential, in which the baton is passed on, often unwillingly, from the civilized to their barbarian clients or conquerors (Sahlins and Service, 1960; Service, 1971). At an earlier time, when the Mediterranean, the Indus Valley, and other seats of early civilizations were advanced, the "savages" were the Europeans. The relative, evolutionary status of individual genetic populations changes over time. Culture has always been leaky, seeping across cultural boundaries or obliterating them in a torrent. The "advanced" attributes of Euro-American culture and its further advancement is increasingly less geographically and racially bounded. Further, if we don't abort the process and the species, we will ourselves, in this period of history, be regarded as relatively primitive by later generations. Our ethnocentrism is complicated by the fact that it coexists in our culture with exocentrism, a kind of romanticism and cultural rejection that sees the evil of our own culture and the virtue of others, especially if these cultures are exotic or remote in time and space. I encountered this in institutionalized form in some recent research of mine on New Age religion. Anthropology itself draws on such sentiments, it is to be hoped in a balanced form in which the extremes of ethnocentrism and exocentrism neutralize each other.

## REJECTION OF THE SUPERORGANIC

As Hallowell and most other anthropologists did not confound race and culture, this cannot be the only deterrent to their exploring the implications of cultural evolution for the further evolution of human nature. It is a seeming paradox that at the same time that Hallowell opposed taking culture as biology, he also rejected superorganicism, as represented by Alfred Kroeber (1952) and Leslie White (1959, 1973), which most radically separated biology and culture. Yet Hallowell's position differed in some important ways from that of the superorganicists. In a manner reminiscent of the way in which Hallowell abstracted behavior from morphology (but as a perspective rather than as an assertion of their independence), Kroeber and White, following Spencer (Carneiro, 1967), argued, in effect, that once culture came into being (and they would agree with Hallowell on how this came about), it became a new order of being—the superorganic, that would henceforth evolve *sui generis,* although carried by human beings through whom culture flowed, mutated, and recombined. Major innovations may occur in individuals with exceptional capacities if they are standing in the right historical time and place. But as the evidence of independent invention and the many voices of the *Zeitgeist* would indicate, advances in culture presumably depended on no one individual, group, or race. For the segment of evolution in which he was interested, that leading up to the emergence of human personality and its culture-generative capacity, Hallowell readily adopted the notion of emergent "levels of integration" manifesting new properties, so that the process, of evolution itself evolved as in the emergence of photosynthesis or of sexual reproduction to which the emergence of culture is comparable. He did not accept the notion of culture as a new phenomenal order, the superorganic, except in its most basic sense that culture is not genetically transmitted (though it is, in a sense, organically transmitted through learning with appropriate transductions that bridge the interpersonal synapse).

As far as the general proposition that cultural variation was not to be explained by biological variation, Hallowell and probably most American anthropologists would have agreed. White took the fact of cultural variation and the doctrine of psychobiological unity of the human species to be sufficient proof that culture cannot be derived from biology, except in a general, enabling way—thus his dictum that "a constant cannot explain a variable." This applies to biology, as a constant, but also to human psychology—taken as a constant, reducible to biology; to an extent, they were talking past one another. Both would agree in not explaining cultural variation by biological variation and that culture is super- or non-organic in the sense that it is learned, not inborn. But in arguing pro and con on the relevance of psychology and culture, White was speaking of generic psychology; Hallowell, of personality, a resultant of biology and culture, mediated by psychological processes acting within the experience of individuals. Human psychology, therefore, in its end product, the behaving, culture-competent personality, is not a constant but a variable, depending on local environmental, historical, and cultural circumstances that shape the life experience of the individual. Psychology, as a behavioral system, must be taken in its phenotypic sense as personality, taken in its formation and in its realization in behavior, implicit and explicit, contributing interactively to the structuring of events. "Personality" is taken here in its most inclusive sense, as the entire stored and secondarily organized set of the residues of experience. It is not merely that which is unique to the individual but also that which is shared; not only the motivational, affective and evaluative, but also the cognitive, intimately co-mapped and intersubstantiated with the other components of experience and behavior (Schwartz, 1976). It was unclear at the time of Hallowell's writing and obscured by then current conceptual models of culture, society and personality, that personality and culture are not two separate, interacting systems, but are extensively, mutually constitutive[11]

In any case, I do not see Hallowell's opposition to superorganicism to have been a necessary obstacle to placing culture and personality in an evolutionary context. Cultural evolution without experiential process is comparable to biological evolution viewed from a morphological,

---

[11]See Spiro (1951), as an important exception the the prevailing tripartite model.

palaeontological, and taxonomic point of view, a succession of forms, without understanding of the processes that shape and animate them – an "origin of species" without physiology, biochemistry, and genetics. For White, cultures could be arrayed in evolutionary sequence on a set of descriptive, and perhaps, explanatory variables, such as energy consumption per capita, or the size of artifact inventories, or the size of the largest polity sustainable. For Hallowell, this sort of superorganicism, separating culture from its actors and creators, was unacceptable. I recall his objecting, for example, to the expression "culture contact," saying, "cultures don't contact, people do." This was not a cause that enlisted me, as I could see utility and appropriate or necessary circumstances for both perspectives (Schwartz and Mead, 1961). It is another instance where Hallowell may have been impeded from a more consistent evolutionary view by a widely shared reading of humanistic values that linked the superorganic to current cultural evolutionism, as devaluing and depersonalizing the individual.

## THE OBJECTION TO A UNILINEAL SEQUENCE OF EVOLUTIONARY STAGES

For Hallowell, unilineality posed a further problem in accepting cultural evolution. In the 1939 article on recapitulationism, and seemingly persistent in his thinking, he held that recapitulationism depends on the idea of unilineal evolution – that everywhere human cultures went through the same stages of development that reappear in ontogeny. Against this he argued that there are no invariant evolutionary stages, and that primitive cultures are too diversified to be subsumed under such unitary stage characterizations. In short, there are no stages and no universal sequence of stages. This objection might have led to the adoption of a multilineal evolutionary model of the sort Stewart (1949, 1955) developed in the late 1940s and the 1950s. Such a model already was characteristic of biological evolutionary models where grades (evolutionary levels) were perceived as superimposed on a phylogenetic tree with multiple branches (clades). This sort of resolution was later developed by Sahlins and Service (1960).[12] Certainly, the problem of unilineality need not be a final impediment.

   Critics of psychological evolution, including Hallowell, in attempting to refute the ideas of Lévy-Bruhl (1985; Cazeneuve, 1972), argued that

---

[12]See also Schwartz and Mead (1961).

alleged primitive traits of thought are not confined to primitive cultures but are found as well among modern peoples. One might conclude from this that such traits are not primitive. Or one might argue that primitive traits persist in otherwide modern cultures that are, therefore, not evolutionarily homogeneous—that the primitive is represented more in some domains of culture than in others, in some individuals or subgroups more than in others, and in some mental states more than in others. This is my view (Schwartz, 1973, 1989). One could hold the view that the primitive outcrops here and there among the modern or else that it is the modern that exists as islands in a sea of primitivism. Such primitive persistences are not only found as "recapitulations" in modern children, but are variably distributed and institutionalized in modern cultures themselves, manifested in the behavior of adults as well as of children. In any case, is the persistence of the primitive in modern cultures a problem for cultural evolutionary theory? Aside from explaining such persistences as recapitulations, I will mention other possibilities. An early approach from which something may yet be derived is the "doctrine of survivals." More recently, the method of "scaling" offers useful results. The possibility that the persistence of "primitive" features represents regression, reversion, truncation or arrested development may be noted. Finally, Tuzin's suggestion that the primitive or childlike in adult behavior and thought points to childhood as a cultural source will be mentioned.

The concept of "survivals" was popular among anthropologists and folklorists of the late 19th century (Hodgen, 1977). One looked for fossils of earlier cultures and beliefs that persisted, though changed, into modern times. Traits largely had to have lost their original functions, to have become peripheral (at least relative to the observer, rather like "superstition") for them to be considered survivals, like the cuff buttons on men's jackets or archery surviving as a sport. The concept of survivals was largely descriptive rather than explanatory. It did, however, suggest a process of change. A survival may undergo change in form (transformation); it may undergo a change of function (transoperation or transtructuration); its place in the culture relative to other traits may change (transposition); its hierarchical position may change (transcendence or subsumption); it may change its type or level of abstraction (metageny); or its frequency of occurrence (transiteration); or its cultural value (transvaluation); it may undergoe a change of meaning including a literal/figurative switch (transfiguration); further, it may be transmogrified. Clearly traits do not merely persist without such rearrangements.

The application of the method of Gutmann scaling to culture traits to arrive at evolutionary sequences carries with it a conception of cultural evolution that embodies directionality and steps of cultural advancement under certain criteria in place of the older model of a sequence of stages as clusters of traits that replace each other in time. The approach is primarily due to the work of Carneiro, who pursues a Spencerian rather than a Darwinian model of cultural evolution. I find his arguments for a Spencerian model persuasive (Carneiro, 1962, 1973, 1974, among others). Many culture traits can be sequenced in such a way that a culture having any one of them will also have all of the others below it in the sequence and lacking any one of them will lack all others in the sequence above it. Carneiro used a list of hundreds of traits (methodological problems such as trait independence cannot be discussed here). Simply counting the number of such traits each culture has allows a rank ordering of evolutionary "advancement." I mention this model because of the feature of cumulativeness. Traits are added even as most previous traits are retained; for example, people don't cease to use copper once they have learned to use iron (though any of the changes discussed under "survivals" may come into play). Rather than a few broad stages, one sees an inverted pyramid with many steps. The traits cut across various social and cultural domains (I would argue against a sharp separation between social and cultural, the social seen as a cultural artifact). The structure takes the form that it does because of functional prerequisiteness, the dependence of later forms on earlier ones. This is a model that accounts in a functional way for the prevalent survival of earlier forms into later cultures. As far as it has been developed, the model says little about the relations among co-occurring traits. It does show directionality in lines of development of complex traits or domans, such as political organization or architecture. It demonstrates a number of the trends attributed to evolution, particularly increased complexity and integration. Such a trend is transmodal, that is, it shows continuity from biological to cultural evolution.[13] Such directionality, argues Carneiro, in concordance with Spencer's view, is definitive of evolution. Whether one speaks of stages or cumulativeness, there seems to be little use in calling it evolution without directionality. Durham (1990) follows a Darwinian model of "descent with modification." In a survey of recent "advances" in evolutionary theory, he is exclusively interested in phylogenesis, the differentiation of cultures while retaining traits that indicate

---

[13]"Transmodality" (my coinage) would indicate that a directional trend is systemic rather than only biological. Transmodality applies also to retardation/acceleration of ontogenies. See discussion of heterochrony.

their common ancestry with other cultures in a monogenetic tree while rejecting any consideration of grades, levels, advancement, or trends, including the trend to complexity — perhaps out of decency or delicacy, since he labels the Spencerian model as "archaic and prejudiced" (Durham, 1990, p. 8). I think it erroneous to speak of evolution without addressing the question of how we got from there to here.

Cultural evolutionary theory is advancing, though much of it in recent decades has been based on adaptations of biological models rather than on properties and processes specific to culture. But traits such as "craft production for exchange" or "monumental architecture" seem remote from psychological evolution, although I am prepared to see such traits in a psychological perspective among other perspectives. External complexity reflects internal complexity of the internalized enculturative structures of individuals (see also Levy, 1973, Ch. 8). The culture's mass and complexity is not so much collective as it is distributive over a population. If we are (in part) what we know, then it makes a difference what knowledge resources of a specific culture we have acquired. Only a thin line of descent exists of scholars who have pursued psychological evolution and, more broadly, the behavioral evolution of homo sapiens based upon cultural evolution. This failure amounts to a psychological equivalence of "creationism" in the behavioral sciences.

## THE OBJECTION TO RECAPITULATION

The main purpose of Hallowell's recapitulation article was to refute the application of Haeckel's doctrine, that "ontogeny recapitulates phylogeny" (Haeckel, cited by Gould 1977, pp. 76–77) to evolutionary comparisons among cultures.[14] There are various weaker and stronger versions of the doctrine of recapitulation. In general, it meant that the immature forms (before and, perhaps, after birth) of a more evolved life form, go through stages in development in which they manifest structures homologous to those of less evolved, or earlier members of, their own clade or phylogenetic line. Thus, in the most often cited example, the human embryo briefly displays undeveloped gill slits that are homologous to those of our gilled aquatic ancestors. These develop not into human gills but into later structures in the vocal and auditory apparatus. Not all later structures are more complex in an obvious way, for example, the number of bones in the skull decreases as we trace them

---

[14]For a book length treatment of this doctrine, including its attempted applications in biology, psychology, psychoanalysis, and the social sciences, see Gould (1977).

from fish to man, but embryonically, many of the originally, more numerous bones appear as separate centers of ossification. Recapitulation remains one kind of evidence for evolution; it does not require a complete reenactment of earlier morphological forms, rather, it is more like a reminiscence on the history of the phylogenetic line as later forms build on past structures, discontinue some, and adapt others to new uses.

But the idea of recapitulation was extended from its empirical, biological bases by analogy equating stages in the evolution of culture with stages in the postnatal development of the child. This meant that one could assert that childhood development among the members of more evolved cultures reenacted the stages of cultural evolution through which human cultures had passed. Further, it meant that under mental or neurological disease or impairment there could be reversion or regression, not only to an earlier mode of adaptation from one's own childhood, but in doing so, one reverted to the "cultural childhood" of the species, exemplified by "primitive" or "savage" cultures.

Hallowell, and later, Gould, documented the prevalence of recapitulationist notions applied in psychology, psychoanalysis, and by some social scientists. Of greatest influence in developing and disseminating the recapitulationist equation were Freud and many other psychoanalysts and various stage-theorists of child development, such as Piaget. Thus, citing Freud (1938):

> The era to which the dream-work takes us back is "primitive" in a two-fold sense: in the first place, it means the early days of the individual—his childhood—and, secondly, in so far as each individual repeats in some abbreviated fashion during childhood the whole course of the development of the human race, the reference is phylogenetic [p. 77].

And further, Freud (1939), wrote:

> The archaic heritage of mankind includes not only dispositions but also ideational contents, memory traces of the experiences of former generations. [p. 157].

Recapitulation as Hallowell (1955) perceived it, probably correctly, in Freud and others was based on the inheritance of mind "Thus, mind, whether viewed individually or racially is primarily if not solely, a function of organic structure, of inherited dispositions and tendencies. Consequently, experience counts for very little as an important constituent of mind" (p. 20). Such an organic view of mind could be discarded and still leave external, nonorganic processes for the persistence of the "primitive", for example, the scaling model or the notion of survival with altered cultural status, or stratification in cultures — for example, a Moslem Java with a Hindu imagination and religious consciousness. But all continuity requires some effective form of transmission. Specificities of retention in comparison of childhood traits in one culture with adult traits in another culture are not accounted for by childhood perceptions and imagination alone. If we eliminate biological transmission of cultural content, then an alternative mode of transmission or retention must be proposed. Furthermore, the question of recapitulation must be recast into a broader examination of possible relations between ontogenies and phylogenies at the cultural level.

Hallowell appears to reject recapitulationism in any form, without compromise and without offering any alternative formulation that would indicate that there is anything to be salvaged in what others professed to see in the comparison of the child, the savage, and the mentally ill (sometimes the "schizophrenic," or the "neurotic" or, for that matter, any regressed mental state). His reaction is like that of many ethnographers who have come to know individual members of a "primitive" culture closely. One's informants and members of the group in general are clearly intelligent adults — different from ourselves but not so much that there is not a basis for a human relationship with some degree of mutual understanding. We often identify with and befriend those who permit us to live among them and put up with our endless inquiries. On the issue of recapitulation, Hallowell clearly separated himself from psychoanalysis. It seems to me that Hallowell could have rejected recapitulationism in the forms that then prevailed without rejecting cultural evolution. Was it necessary to see the child in more advanced cultures as evincing the primitive traits, modes of thought, and belief of adults in less advanced cultures and to equate both with the thought of psychotics? The parallelism seemed to imply a biological basis for complex behaviors, ways of thinking, and beliefs. It equated a stage of maturation (as Piaget believed "childhood animism" to be) with a stage of cultural development, one spontaneous, the other institutionalized.[15]

Hallowell further rebuts recapitulationism with the argument that children in a primitive culture may be less childlike than children of

---

[15]Hallowell (1988, p. 28) cites Susan Isaacs and Nathan Isaacs arguing for the distinction between spontaneous impulse or fantasy in the child and institutionalized belief of the adult member of a primitive culture.

Western civilization. Our children are said to be more childlike because we keep them that way, following our conception of childhood (but see also discussion of foetalization). Yet, under recapitulationism, we compare not these unchildlike children but the adults they become with children in our own society. Hallowell seems to rely here on Mead's report that Manus children, when asked such questions as why someone's canoe had drifted and been lost, gave practical and secular answers such as it hadn't been tied properly, whereas adults gave "animistic" answers, for example, attributing it to the malice of a ghost (Mead, 1932). Mead's study was intended as a refutation of Piaget's recapitulationist, ontogenetic scheme of stages in child cognitive development, including an early animistic stage. Mead, applying her "Yes, but the Eskimo" method (Schwartz, 1983), believed her brief inquiry among Manus children to have shaken the foundations of recapitulationist stage theory. In her later work in Manus and elsewhere, Mead did not attempt to replicate her study and I know of little else that bears on it. But taking it at its face value and in its broadest implications, it would support the view that childhood may be undeveloped in some respects but is not specifically "primitive" in terms of the many traits such as animism that have been attributed to children and to primitives or savages, which now would be more exactly attributed to primitive cultures. Children were less or not animistic because they had not yet learned to be. Either they had not absorbed that part of the culture, or, as Mead says, speaking of a discontinuity in Manus socialization, they were not yet responsible for responding in terms of that domain of Manus culture. Although Manus children were present and witnesses to seances and other scenes of adult religious life and their own well-being depended on adult morality and its ghostly supervisors, they were passive and irresponsible spectators until early adulthood. One sees in this discussion the reality of a complex interweaving of maturation, socialization, and enculturation, and a life cycle as a sequence of statuses, to which some of what we may have attributed to maturation is attached. Mead often made the point that our own culture animates the universe for our children to a degree extraordinary among cultures; in play, in serious, or both, depending on subcultures. Is this a set of transformed survivals, converted by adults into benign boogeymen? There is much that could be said on the nature and effects of play-animism in our culture, but not here.

Accepting the idea that there are resemblances between the behavior and thought of children and that which we associate with primitivism but seeking an alternative to genetic explanations involving inheritance of mind or recapitulation of earlier evolutionary stages, Tuzin (1990) developed the idea that the resemblence between adult and child is derived from the fact that much of culture is learned in childhood from other children and perhaps is a product or creation of childhood. Adults learn these primitive/childlike traits from children, either from their own and other children or they carry them into adulthood with them from their own childhood. I will not try to replicate Tuzin's intriguing arguments, which undoubtedly supply a neglected part of the picture. My own interest here is on the evolutionary process that involves the whole life history and offers another part of an explanation of both similarities and differences between child and adult in primitive and, for the time being, modern cultures.

## CULTURAL HETEROCHRONY: INNOVATION, ACCELERATION AND RETARDATION

For the evolutionary biologist, the interest in recapitulation has been a question of what can be learned about phylogeny from ontogeny, from the evidence of embryology continued into the entire life cycle. A particularly important phrasing is that phylogeny is a sequence of ontogenies undergoing modification (Gould, 1977, p. 212). For the purposes of cultural evolution we must add — an intercommunicating population of coeval ontogenies (individual maturational/enculturative life histories). To put that together, we must say that cultural evolution is a sequence of populations (a population flow through time) of coeval, intercommunicating, individual maturational/enculturative life histories. Under this formulation, one is liberated from imagining evolution only as a sequence of adult morphologies or adult personal versions of cultures. Such a view is complementary to a superorganic perspective of the transformation of culture, viewed in terms of its forms or artifacts. Every artifact (anything to which culture gives form, material or not) to be produced, used, or "read" (found intelligible) has its counterparts in the enculturative structures of individuals. We must examine the analogic yield for human enculturated behavior and its disanalogic limits, because, in certain crucial ways, biological and cultural evolution are different and non-Darwinian in many ways — in modes of transmission, intentionality, goal projection, effects of consciousness, among others. The ontogenetic model has special importance for culture. For biology, the population is a set of reproducing organisms characterized by gene frequencies controlling the rates of developmental processes and the sequence and timing of the emergence of structures. For culture it is something more than this—the analogy to a set of trait frequencies in some biologically-derived, cultural models misses much that is specific to culture.

An ontogenetic view such as that synthesized by Gould (1977) provides the broader context in which the discussion of recapitulation should be carried forward. Although in later writing on behavioral evolution, Hallowell gives strong emphasis to the importance of the immaturity and long dependency of the human infant, which provides the setting for personality formation and, in traditional societies, much of the setting of enculturation, he does not adopt the framework of foetalization as a kind of inversion of recapitulation. Róheim's (1950) extensive treatment of foetalization or paedomorphosis complement's Hallowell on recapitulation but something more must be done to consider the two together.[16] Foetalization and recapitulation are inverse forms of heterochrony. In general, the immature forms of related species resemble each other more than do their mature forms. Ontogeny produces differentiation. If there is acceleration or retardation of ontogeny between two related species (heterochrony), then there is the possibility of the immature form of one resembling the mature form of the other. Where recapitulation finds a parallel between the infant (or, biologically, also the embryo) of a more advanced species or culture and the adults of the less advanced, foetalization sees foetal or immature characteristics of a less advanced species being retained as the adult form of the more advanced species.

Thus it is argued that in many respects, morphology and growth rates, including the rate of growth and the proportion of the brain to body size of the human adult resemble those of a foetal or immature ape.

> But if axolotl represented a juvenile stage of higher salamanders, then the perennibranchiates had merely gone a step further and committed themselves to permanent youth by dispensing entirely with their adult form—an undoubted exception to recapitulation [Gould, 1977, p. 179].

The parallel is incomplete, of course. The more specialized structures of the less advanced forms develop with maturity. The more advanced form is ontogenetically retarded. The human being, of all mammals, has the slowest rate of maturation with the consequence of long dependency

---

[16]Foetalization, paedomorphism, and neoteny are not distinguished in this chapter, but see Gould, (1977, p. 179, footnote).

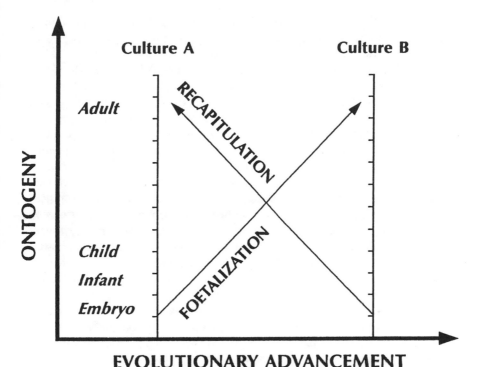

**Figure 1**
Foetalization and Recapitulation

and a very long period of learning readiness related to the need for the acquisition of culture. Róheim (1950) makes a further important point that relative to its slow development, not in absolute time, human beings are sexually precocious. "Most significant, however, is the fact that the Soma is more retarded than the Germa so that within the frame of our general retardation *our sexuality is relatively precocious*" (p. 402.)

From these ontogenetic features, Róheim derives the family, the need for repression, and the origins of culture. His richly suggestive theory is not entirely consistent. He sees the possibility for both recapitulation and foetalization to co-occur but does not really consider them in a single framework. At times he draws on recapitulation, although he cites others who see the two as incompatible. Foetalization results in a more generalized organism. The human is specialized as a generalist. But Róheim is also a cultural evolutionist who draws on recapitulation. He points out that we can be specialized in some respects, as in the human foot and generalized in others, as in the human hand.

Foetalization, as much as recapitulation, as doctrines, can be tainted with racism. Róheim seems to take seriously authors he cites to the effect that the various human races represent different degrees of foetalization or retardation—the more retarded ontogenetically, the more advanced evolutionary. Physical anthropologists have also noted the morphological part of this assertion—Australian aborigines are the most gerontomorphic; caucasians fairly gerontomorphic; Africans the most paedomorphic, at least with respect to the cranium. White skin is cited as a paedomorphic feature found in fetuses and neonates of all anthropoids and human races (Roheim, 1950, p. 403). Not quite explicitly, physical features seen as paedo- or gerontomorphic are linked in discussions of cultural advancement or retardation, even when, as the previously mentioned characterization of races would indicate, they are not well correlated. One needn't argue that it is a spurious correlation when in fact it is a noncorrelation. The casual slippage from race to culture seems now less likely than in the first half of the century.

Hallowell's (1955) discussion of the drawings of children in advanced or modern industrial societies compared with "primitive art" (the art of adults in primitive cultures) offers a basis for discussion of the appearance of parallels, sometimes asserted to be recapitulations (p. 24). Hallowell mainly saw the argument as dismissing the idea that recapitulation is involved in any resemblences between primitive and children's (not to mention "schizophrenic" art). But it could also be used as part of a cultural evolutionary account of recapitulation that fits well with a scaled trait model of cultural evolution. At least it seems to be so for negative traits, and features of advanced art techniques, such as single point perspective drawing. It is not clear what positive resemblances there are that are not reducible to negative ones. Without resorting to inheritance of mind, the appearance of recapitulation can be accounted for by a combination of maturation and enculturation but depending on the latter. The children of the two cultures are similar (though early childhood is not acultural, some differentiation may begin early) but the adults of the less advanced culture share with the children of both cultures a lack of some inventions, knowledge, or skills of the more advanced culture. The children of the more advanced culture have not yet acquired these features through enculturation, and both adult and child of the less advanced culture have not yet acquired them through evolution or acculturation. The child of the less evolved culture may be less primitive than adults of that culture (Mead's claim for Manus children) because primitivism is not just an absence of advanced traits (although it is this in part) but also the development and elaboration of traits that explain what is not yet known and an attempt to produce magically what cannot yet be produced or controlled effectively.

On the cultural level, the fact that primitive traits persist in advanced cultures does not make them *not* primitive traits but part of the heterogeneity of evolutionary status in modern populations. Advances produce a set of cultural properties variously interrelated, differentially distributed among the members of a population, and not yet acquired and available to children and others. Within the individual, primitive and modern can coexist, sometimes in different domains or situations, sometimes hierarchically. To understand the cultural evolutionary status of a population more fully and not just in an abstract ranking of the whole, it would be necessary to examine the structure of a culture within the population and within the individual. The "ethnography of the individual" (Schwartz, 1989) would have to be a hybrid of ethnographic, biographical, and clinical inquiry seen in a theoretical context that spans (at least) these three aspects.

Much of Hallowell's argument is against alleged cultural and psychological parallels to the biological doctrine of recapitulation. Are there also cultural and psychological parallels to foetalization? Paedomorpism may be one of the evolutionary trends that shows transmodal continuity — the trend seeming to continue from the biological mode to the cultural mode. One might look at the timing of social maturity and see it in general as being increasingly deferred in more advanced and complex societies. (At the same time, to follow Róheim's suggestion for the biological process, social, sexual (and perhaps, biological sexual maturity) becomes even more precocious. Róheim (1950) mentions play as a characteristic of immature mammalian forms. If one may generalize from play to leisure, perhaps generalize also to education, exploratory, expressive, and other nonsubsistence forms of behavior, these may also be extended into or through the life span. One may also question whether more immature ego development goes along with deferred social maturity in our own "advanced" society. Much of recent cultural criticism of what appears to be institutionalized narcissism, if the observation is correct, may also be a consequence of retardation of maturity in personality formation. Other social problems may relate to the sexual precocity (relative to retarded maturity) which Róheim identified. It is possible that the alleged, endemic narcissism may be a misreading of a culturally extended evolutionary process. We may simply be like Gould's perennibranchiates seeking to extend youth further and further into the lifespan. Perhaps this trend is antidotal to the danger that extending life expectancy could produce an arthritically rigidified gerontocratic culture. Although it is interesting to speculate on mutations or culture changes affecting ontogenetic/enculturative rates, I must limit myself to these few remarks.

## BEHAVIORAL TRENDS RESULTING FROM AND CONTRIBUTING TO CULTURAL EVOLUTION

We are what we know, and as Hallowell has shown, we are also what we don't know but think we do. Cosmology is an internal event about an external event, some, but not all of which, is projection or error. Consciousness externalizes the internal, makes it objectlike, and adds to our inner cosmology the domain of the self. Knowledge is of different kinds, with different implications for behavior. This must have been intuited in primative cultures from the start. Except for certain extreme circumstances, as in religious cults at the moment of their most excited sense of imminence of fulfillment, when they must further force the hand of God by acting as if they believed their beliefs, almost all of magic supplements rather than substitutes for subsistence activities (Schwartz, 1962). The primitive cosmology was hyperdeterministic, intentional, and moral; accident, impersonal causation, and ignorance are modern discoveries.

Consciousness not only expands through the growth of knowledge but it comes to know itself. Evolution is growth and differentiation but also transcendence through the creation of metalevels of thought and representation — a continuation of the process that Hallowell described in the evolutionary emergence of the self. It is one thing to have knowledge of spatial relations and another to abstract and systematize that knowledge as Euclid and his predecessors did, and yet another to make of knowledge itself an object of knowledge; yet another to engage in this discussion of the phenomenon of "metageny," to put a label on this process. A youth contemplating infinities of time, space, and numerosity, may comparably experience a metagenous vertigo in climbing the hierarchy of consciousness. The growth of knowledge and its internal self-transcendence is an evolutionary process transforming its creator-possessors. All of this is built on the same biological base the human species possessed for at least tens of thousands of years. That base, originally evolved in adaptation to quite other circumstances, contained a huge surplus preadaptation, only in part because of its own built-in capacities, but also in large part because of its dependence on the cultural implementation and extension of those capacities. In simplifying things, (which I try to avoid), I sometimes tell students to think of intelligence as the *genotype* and intellect as the *phenotype*. But as a set of capacities, intelligence is culturally extended. Culture does not just supply content, as important as specific content is, for example, a mythic versus a scientific cosmology, it also informs the structure and process of the basic capacities that we think of as intelligence. For example, it does this through the use of more general, context-free cultural heuristics in problem solving. Human nature evolves not only as a realization of the initial human biological potential but as an exploration of the potential of culture itself.

## CONCLUSION

The errors that Hallowell and others correctly exposed—a false link between cultural evolutionary status, biological evolutionary status, and race, need not forever keep us from a correct formulation recognizing the role of cultural evolution as constitutive of the evolution of human personality, intellect, and behavior. Nor need the fact so many have pointed out, that primitive or earlier cultural traits persistent among us lead to a denial of cultural evolution; we know that we got from there to here. "Here" is a transitory point on a trajectory, at present exponential, but of unknown future contour. There remains the fact of cultural evolution and its constitutive effect on human nature. The growth and structure of consciousness has consequences for the world of the *évolué*. To make conscious is to render problematic. Literature, more than behavioral science concerns itself with exploring the consequences of manifold consciousness.

Neither racism nor cultural ethnocentrism need be inevitable concomitants of cultural evolutionary theory, nor insurmountable obstacles to the exploration of the fullest implications of the fact of cultural evolution and its consequences for human nature, mind, and personality. Cultural evolution can be studied; individual cultures as well as emergent world cultures can be evaluated in evolutionary terms without sacrificing the "cause" or the "message" for which anthropological relativism and antievolutionism were intended. Perhaps reconciliation is possible through a kind of evolutionary relativism in which cultures, embodied in human artifacts that are substantial, mental, relational, moral, and aesthetic, are evaluated relative to their evolutionary status and history.

We are no longer in the position of Hallowell in the 1940s of confronting a single sequence of broadly sketched, evolutionary stages, not much better than "savagery," "barbarism," and "civilization." I referred to Julian Steward's work on multilineal evolution, regionally differentiated under diverse ecologies. Another line of development of our understanding of evolution sees cultures as a bundle of variables interlinked in relations of lead and follow. In Morgan, Marx, Engels, and White, the consequences of technological change and changes of economic organization as they reverberate throughout culture were explored. Gradually, during this century, our thinking about evolutionary models changed away from monodeterminism, away from the expectation of a high degree of integration and adaptatedness, continuous and gradual change; away from efficient homeostasis and equilibria, all driven by a prime mover in measured responses. In place of this, systems theory led us to think of systematicity as a variable, a matter of degree, at times minimal; of systems that may not only be self-excitatory, but that supply self-perturbations without which they would be lifeless mechanisms. Our ontologies have come to include the probablistic along with the deterministic. In the past decade, nonlinearity and chaos have been a focus of much attention with diverse applications in the physical and biological sciences. Their application in the behavioral sciences is to be expected. Anthropologists make tentative use of models derived from "fuzzy" set algebras and decisions under uncertainty and risk. In biological evolution, the new catastrophism is established; gradualism is replaced by "punctuated equilibria." Extinction is now known to have been the rule. In the place of a teleology, at first of intent, later of immanent process leading in necessary directions, we are left, supposedly, with a "quirky" nature in which, perhaps, other outcomes may have been likely (Gould, 1989). In place of a doctrine of progress, we are offered not even directionality, derived from system/process properties, but only local adaptation — modification in place of evolution. All of this defines a cosmological mood, perhaps inhospitable to rationality as we once knew it. This perception is, perhaps, based on moral disappointment. Direction defined by complexity and other such parameters, does not mean necessary progress. Gould mentions wars, pollution, and the whole litany of our modern woes. It is hard to accept that the formulation and realization of values is in our own hands, no more assured by nature than it was by the supernatural. But the mood depends partly in our construal of these events and their implications. "Chaos," for example, is inappropriately named when it, in fact, reveals order of a particular sort in what we once would have found to be chaotic. Each of the aforementioned changes describes a new, deeper, more complex perception of reality in which we are learning to think. It is, in short, evolution in response, not to an environmental change, but rather, behavioral evolution in a behavioral environment transformed by our own new understandings — a response to further cultural evolution that continues the ongoing reconstitution of human nature. In the perspective of this chapter, the obstacles that Hallowell faced are seen to be transcendable. Under current understandings of the history and process of cultural evolution, the study of its consequences for the further evolution of human nature can go forward without the impediments of racist and nationalist competition for evolutionary prestige. Hopefully, the climate, at least among the disciplines that are the organs of human consciousness, has changed to where we can now go beyond the point to which Hallowell's seminal studies led us.

## BIBLIOGRAPHY

BENEDICT, R. (1934), *Patterns of Culture.* Boston: Houghton Mifflin, 1961.

BOURGUIGNON, E. (1979), *Psychological Anthropology: An Introduction to Human Nature and Cultural Differences.* New York: Holt, Rinehart & Winston.

BOYD, R. & RICHERSEN, P.J. (1985), *Culture and the Evolutionary Process.* Chicago: University of Chicago Press.

CARNEIRO, R.L. (1962), Scale analysis as an instrument for the study of cultural evolution. *Southwestern J. Anthropol.,* 18:149–169.

———— (1972), The devolution of evolution. *Social Biology,* 19:248–58.

———— (1973), Structure, function, and equilibrium in the evolutionism of Herbert Spencer. *J. Anthropolog. Res.,* 29:77–95.

———— (1974), The four faces of evolution. In: *Handbook of Social and Cultural Anthropology.* ed. J.J. Honigmann. Rand McNally, pp. 89–110.

CAVALLI-SFORZA, L.L. & FELDMAN, M.W. (1981), *Cultural Transmission and Evolution: A Quantitative Approach.* Princeton, NJ: Princeton University Press.

CAZENEUVE, J. (1972), *Lucien Lévy-Bruhl* (trans. P. Riviére). Oxford: Basil Blackwell.

DEVEREUX, G. (1956), Normal and abnormal. In: *Basic Problems of Ethnopsychiatry,* Chicago: University of Chicago Press, pp. 3–71, 1980.

DURHAM, W.H. (1990), Advances in evolutionary culture theory. *Ann. Rev. Anthropol.,* ed. B.J. Siegal. Palo Alto, CA: Annual Reviews, Inc., pp. 187–242.

FREUD, S. (1916) *Introductory Lectures on Psychoanalysis. Standard Edition,* 16. London: Hogarth Press, 1961.

———— (1938), Moses and monotheism. *Standard Edition,* 23:1–137. London: Hogarth Press, 1964.

GOODY, J. (1977), *The Domestication of the Savage Mind.* Cambridge: Cambridge University Press.

GOULD, S. J. (1977), *Ontogeny and Phylogeny.* Cambridge, MA: Belknap Press of Harvard University Press.

———— (1981) *The Mismeasure of Man.* New York: Norton.

_____ (1989), *Wonderful Life: The Burgess Shale and the Nature of History.* New York: Norton.

HALLOWELL, A.I. (1939), The child, the savage, and human experience. In: *Culture and Experience.* Philadelphia: University of Pennsylvania Press.

_____ (1941), The social function of anxiety in a primitive society. In: *Culture and Experience.* Philadelphia: University of Pennsylvania Press, 1955.

_____ (1950), Personality structure and the evolution of man. In: *Culture and Experience.* Philadelphia: University of Pennsylvania Press, 1955.

_____ (1954), The self and its behavioral environment. In: *Culture and Experience.* Philadelphia: University of Pennsylvania Press, 1955.

_____ (1988), *Culture and Experience.* Prospect Heights, IL: Waveland Press. Originally published 1955, University of Pennsylvania Press.

HODGEN, M. (1977), *The Doctrine of Survivals: A Chapter in the History of Scientific Method in the Study of Man.* Folcroft, PA: Folcroft Library Editions.

HORTON, R. & FINNEGAN, R., ED. (1973), *Modes of Thought.* London: Faber & Faber.

ISAACS, S. (1930), *Intellectual Growth in Young Children.* London.

JENSEN, A.R. (1969), How much can we boost IQ and scholastic achievement? *Harvard Ed. Rev.,* 33:1–123.

_____ (1979), *Bias in Mental Testing.* New York: Free Press.

KROEBER, A.L. (1952), *The Nature of Culture.* Chicago, University of Chicago Press.

LEVINE, R.A. (1973), *Culture, Behavior, and Personality.* Chicago: Aldine.

LEVY, R.I. (1973), *Tahitians: Mind and Experience in the Society Islands.* Chicago: University of Chicago Press.

LEVY-BRUHL, L. (1985, orig. Eng. trans. 1926). *How Natives Think.* Princeton, NJ: Princeton University Press.

MEAD, M. (1932), An investigation of the thought of primitive children, with special reference to animism. *J. Royal Anthropolog. Insti.,* 62:173–90.

MURDOCK, G.P. (1934), *Our Primitive Contemporaries.* New York: Macmillan.

ROHEIM, G. (1950), *Psychoanalysis and Anthropology: Culture, personality and the unconscious.* New York: International Universities Press.

SAHLINS, M.D. & SERVICE, E.R, ED. (1960), *Evolution and Culture.* Ann Arbor: University of Michigan Press.

SAPIR, E. (1920), Review of Robert H. Lowie, *Primitive Society. The Freeman,* 1:377–379.

SCHNEIRLA, T.C. (1949), Levels in the psychological capacities of animals. In: *Philosophy for the Future,* ed. R.W. Sellars, V.J. McGill & M. Farber. New York:

SCHWARTZ, T. (1962) The Paliau Movement in the Admiralty Islands, 1946–1954. *Anthropolog. Papers of the Amer. Museum of Natural History,* 49:211–421.

_____ (1973), Cult and context: The paranoid ethos in melanesia. *Ethos,* 1(2).

_____ (1976), Where is the culture? In: *The Making of Psychological Anthropology,* ed. G. Spindler. Berkeley: University of California Press.

_____ (1981) The Acquisition of Culture. *Ethos.* 9:4–17.

_____ (1983), Anthropology: A quaint science. *Amer. Anthropol.* 85:919–929.

_____ (1989), The structure of national cultures. In: *Understanding the USA: A Cross-Cultural Perspective,* ed. P. Funke. Tbingen: Gunter Narr Verlag.

_____ (in press), Psychology and anthropology: An unrequited relationship. In *The Social Life of the Self: Issues in Psychological Anthropology,* ed. T. Schwartz, G. White & G. Lutz. Cambridge: Cambridge University Press.

_____ MEAD, M. (1961), Micro- and macro-cultural models for cultural evolution. *Anthropolog. Ling.* 3:1–7. Also in M. Mead, *Continuities in Cultural Evolution.* New Haven, CT: Yale University Press, 1964.

SERVICE, E.R. (1971), *Cultural Evolutionism.* New York: Holt, Rinehart & Winston.

SPENCER, H. *The Evolution of Society: Selections from Herbert Spencer's Principles of Sociology,* ed. R.L. Carneiro. Chicago: University of Chicago Press.

SPIRO, M.E. (1951), Culture and personality: the natural history of a false dichotomy. *Psychiat.,* 14:19–46.

STEWART, J. (1949) Cultural causality and law: A trial formulation of the development of early civilizations. *Amer. Anthropol.,* 51:1–27.

_____ (1955) *Theory of Culture Change: The Methodology of Multilinear Evolution.* Urbana: University of Illinois Press.

TUZIN, D.F. (1990), Of the resemblance of fathers to their children: The roots of primitivism in middle-childhood enculturation. In: *The Psychoanalytic Study of Society,* 15:59–103. Hillsdale, NJ: The Analytic Press.

WHITE, L.A. (1959), *The Evolution of Culture: The Development of Civilization to the Fall of Rome.* New York: McGraw-Hill.

_____ (1973) *The Science of Culture: A Study of Man and Civilization.* New York: Farrar, Straus & Giroux.

# 10

# Idiosyncrasy and the Problem of Shared Understandings: The Case of a Pakistani Orphan

## KATHERINE P. EWING

From the vantage point of the present, Hallowell's writings form a remarkable and valuable bridge between the questions asked by the early students of culture and personality and current interest in the subjective experience of individuals as actors who are actively engaged with the anthropological researcher. Although Hallowell shared the early culture and personality studies' experience-distant concerns with how specific features of a culture correlate with aspects of adult personality organization, the primary thrust of his research was to develop concepts that would enable him to capture, and accurately convey in immediate terms, the interpretive world of the culturally "other." The title of one of Hallowell's major works, *Culture and Experience* (1955), stresses his concern with understanding and communicating the lived world of his informants. My own earliest efforts at articulating Pakistani Muslim concepts of self were directly guided by his papers on the cultural shaping of the Ojibwa self (Hallowell, 1954a, b) an approach that, although unacknowledged by Geertz in his often-quoted formulation of the

The research for this project, conducted in Lahore, Pakistan, in 1975–1977, and in 1984–1985, was funded by two grants from the American Institute of Pakistan Studies. Some of the material in this paper was first presented at the second Workshop on the Family in South Asia, sponsored by the Social Science Research Council and held at the University of Chicago, September 6-7, 1981. I would like to thank members of that workshop, as well as Bryce Boyer, Ruth Boyer, Bertram Cohler, Gilbert Herdt, McKim Marriott, Ralph Nicholas, Naomi Quinn, and Melford Spiro for helpful comments on earlier drafts of this paper. I would especially like to thank the Pakistani women who patiently sat with me for many hours and revealed their lives to me.

problem of the culturally shaped self (Geertz, 1973a, 1983), anticipated it by nearly two decades.

Although my argument in this chapter has benefitted from recently developed conceptual tools that were unavailable to Hallowell, my concern with drawing the idiosyncratic experience of the individual informant into a cultural analysis, and taking into account how that experience might be affected by the researcher, was also sensitively anticipated by Hallowell, particularly in his paper, "Fear and Anxiety as Cultural and Individual Variables in a Primitive Society" (Hallowell, 1938). I can only hope that my own efforts to convey the idiosyncratic experiences of a Pakistani woman in a culturally sensitive way meet the standards set by Hallowell so many years ago.

## INTRODUCTION

Individuals participate in a social world of shared understandings and activities, yet they organize their experience idiosyncratically. Over the years, anthropologists have put forth a variety of arguments for ignoring these idiosyncrasies, focusing only on the symbols that constitute "culture," that is, shared understandings.[1] Even culture and personality studies of the past approached the problem of personality by limiting the studies to those aspects of personality regarded as culturally shaped and shared; the result was an analytic chasm between the cultural and the psychological.[2] Paradoxically, the psychological became even more

---

[1]Geertz's justification for ignoring the idiosyncratic and the psychological seems to be the one that continues to be popular among anthropologists today. Along with articulating for his colleagues a valuable and widely accepted definition of culture as a system of symbols and meanings, Geertz asserted that symbolic activity occurs, not inside people's heads, but rather in the public arena (see Geertz 1973b, p. 91). On the basis of this definition, one could safely ignore anything that was not symbolically articulated, and one could assume that anything articulated was communicable and, therefore, symbolic and cultural. By his reasoning, if it was cultural, it was not psychological (see Ewing, in press).

[2]The culture and personality studies that had their heyday in the 1930s, 1940s and 1950s established a conceptual separation between the individual psyche and an abstract, culturally shaped personality or "basic personality structure" (Kardiner, 1945). This conceptual separation created theoretical difficulties that anthropologists found impossible to overcome, as long as they assumed culture to be an enduring complex of patterns and institutions, a cohesive entity that consists only of those elements and experiences that are shared by all. These studies abounded with unsolved technical and conceptual difficulties, not the least being that only a small percentage of individuals studied in a particular society corresponded to the hypothesized "modal personality" of that group, and that the range of personalities within the society appeared to be greater than

impenetrable for those ethnographers so concerned with being true to the interpretive worlds of individual informants that they can assert only the essential untranslatability of the other's experience. Certain anthropologists have denied the validity of the ethnographic text itself as a statement about one's informants.[3] Anthropologists are reexperiencing the dilemma of philosophers such as Leibniz (1714) who, beginning with the premise that humans are windowless monads, could not reason themselves into the possibility of a social world, despite the evidence of their senses.

Notwithstanding this dilemma, the common sense of the anthropologist who becomes a participant in the culture he observes tells him that he *does* understand the feelings, the reactions, and the experiences of his informants — even if he cannot articulate how or why he understands. There are anthropologists who have recently asserted the wisdom of their intuitions about their informants and have thrown over the traces of a cultural relativism tightly bound to the analysis of linguistic forms.[4] But tools for specifying the sources of one's intuitions, for looking at phenomena other than the abstractable linguistic content of informants' utterances, have not yet been systematically developed by

---

differences between societies (Dubois, 1961, p. xx). More relevant for present purposes, these early studies lacked the conceptual tools, including a useful definition of culture or a concept of symbol, that would enable them to interpret the significance of observed practices for those experiencing them, thus making highly speculative their interpretations of the correlations between psychological organization (such as an organization of defense mechanisms typical of individuals of a particular society) and cultural practices that they did identify. Concerned with establishing correlations between cultural institutions and adult personalities that were cross-culturally valid, anthropologists chose to study specific personality factors rather than individuals as complex entities (Dubois, 1961, p. xix), and thus downplayed or ignored the lived experience, the interpretive world, of the informant. It was this interpretive world that became a central focus of cultural anthropology, beginning in the 1960s. The prestige and influence of culture and personality studies then waned, as anthropologists declared issues of individual psychology irrelevant to their study of symbols and meanings.

[3]See, for example, Tyler (1986). One reaction to this questioning has been a retreat to minimally edited field notes (for example, Dwyer, 1982). Ethnographies of this genre are intended to capture the uncertain nature of the anthropologist's knowledge, demonstrate the impossibility of accurately representing the other's experience, and illustrate how an interpretive world is constructed between anthropologist and informant (Crapanzano, 1980).

[4]If they are correct about the intuitive sources of understanding, a retreat such as Dwyer's, away from interpretation into transcript, is an abdication of responsibility for interpreting, because it leaves the job to readers who lack the intuitions based on first-hand experience.

anthropologists.[5] The result is an interpretive lacuna as anthropologists strive through ad hoc means to communicate their nonverbal insights into the lives of their informants.

The problems and the possibility of understanding another are not limited to cross-cultural encounters. The interaction between a psychoanalyst and patient of the same cultural background exposes the extent to which shared understandings are problematic in a way that is not normally observed in ordinary communication, where our errors of interpretation are not usually highlighted. Reflecting on psychoanalytic technique, Gedo (1987) has observed that only through a slow and painstaking process does the analyst pick up what he calls the patient's "personal dialect," that is, his preferences and capacities for receiving information (p. 7).[6] Even psychoanalysts who focus most of their attention on uncovering the possible multiple significances of every utterance learn how to conduct a psychoanalysis more as an art than as a specifiable body of techniques (see Ewing, 1987, pp. 18–19).

As I see it, the primary task facing us today is to develop more sophisticated tools for identifying how we do actually move through our own experience of another's expressions, both linguistic and nonverbal, to an apprehension of that other human being's experience and thence to generalizations that are valid across persons and across cultures. I suggest that one of the key ways in which we do this is by hearing the idiosyncrasies in that other human being's ways of using language. We listen to their efforts at communicating until, at last, we understand; until, that is, we perceive the regularities in their peculiarities. We identify patterns of communication and interpret them. Some of these regularities can be identified as cultural patterns, which we discover by comparing what appear to an outsider to be peculiarities of action, with the actions of other informants, and find that they are shared. Other regularities are idiosyncratic to an individual. Our awareness of cultural patterns enhances our ability to listen for the peculiarities in an individual's modes of expression that go beyond the cultural differences that separate anthropologist and informant.[7]

---

[5]Wikan (1990) represents one recent effort to move beyond the constraints of linguistically oriented analyses.

[6]From this perspective, a criterion for determining the development of the psychoanalytic relationship is the extent to which the analysand expresses the feeling that the analyst "sounds like myself talking." An important aspect of the analytic process involves extending the analysand's potential for developing shared understandings with others, though Gedo does not limit psychoanalysis to this hermeneutic project.

[7]Hallowell (1955) made a similar point in his consideration of the relationship between

Another important strategy for apprehending and interpreting the communications of the people encountered in fieldwork is not only to observe patterns in the other's varying responses to the ongoing interaction, but also to monitor carefully one's own emotional reactions and apparently stray thoughts, because these may provide important clues to the significance of the other's communications that go well beyond the referential content of his utterances (see Crapanzano, 1980). In the clinical situation, a patient typically transfers onto the psychoanalyst unresolved conflicts first experienced in relationship to primary caregivers in childhood. Reciprocally, the transferences of the patient may stimulate countertransference responses in the psychoanalyst, in which the psychoanalyst experiences himself as the patient sees him and acts in ways that affirm the patient's misperceptions and projective identifications (Klein, 1946).[8] Traditionally, countertransferences were regarded by psychoanalysts as "blind spots," unconsciously motivated responses triggered by resonances with issues in the psychoanalyst's own past that prevent the psychoanalyst from effectively interpreting the transference. Recently, however, psychoanalysts have recognized that countertransferences, when identified, can be an invaluable source of information about the patient and his conflicts (see Searles, 1979; Boyer, 1989). Though full transferences usually do not develop in nonclinical situations such as fieldwork, unconscious processes such as projective identification do occur and do stimulate countertransference responses in the anthropologist. Anthropologists can also learn to draw systematically on their emotional responses, including anxiety, as a source of information about their informants (see Devereux, 1968).

In this chapter, I draw on these two distinct sources of information, idiosyncratic usages of specific symbols on the one hand and interactive patterns of transference and countertransference on the other, in order to articulate the process of interpretation. I demonstrate that individuals use cultural symbols idiosyncratically and that these idiosyncrasies are

---

individual and cultural factors in the experience of fear and anxiety. He carefully identified evidence of severe neurotic conflicts in individuals he personally observed and demonstrated how these conflicts, though not directly arising out of culturally shaped concerns, were expressed and justified in cultural terms by the informant. As he put it: "Their phobias are personal and have no culturally phrased causes. Individuals subject to such phobias often rationalize them in terms of whatever beliefs seem appropriate" (p. 261).

[8]Projective identification is a strategy by which a person strives to distance himself from a threatening aspect of his own personality, particularly aggression, by attributing it to the other.

indicators of how the individual organizes his or her social and personal experiences. Issues of transference and countertransference are used to aid in the interpretation of the idiosyncrasies. Focusing on idiosyncrasies of communication in terms of both their referential content and their pragmatic functioning in the relationship between anthropologist and informant, against a background of cultural practice, thus provides a way of specifying our window into an individual's interpretive world.

Though idiosyncrasies may be linked with a wide range of individual strengths as well as weaknesses, when a person's functioning in the social world is disturbed,[9] the ways in which the person's usage of symbols differs from the usage of others may parallel symptoms of a psychological disorder as identified in Western clinical populations. Specifying idiosyncrasies in the communicative process provides a basis for making clinical generalizations and diagnostic assessments of the individual, and permits a consideration of the relationship between cultural processes and personality organization.

## THE IDIOSYNCRATIC USE
## OF CULTURAL SYMBOLS

I take as a starting point for my analysis the position that the individual is an active interpreter and constructor of symbols, continually modifying the cultural symbols that constitute received wisdom. Individuals create communicative patterns, habits, and personal understandings out of their experiences of interactions with particular others, who themselves organize their experiences idiosyncratically. As Spiro (1951) observed, "[T]he cultural heritage is inherited by learning, and learning is not a uniform process, but one which varies considerably from individual to individual . . . Not only do different children assign different meanings to the cultural heritage, resulting in qualitatively different cultural heredities, but the degree of acceptance and resistance differs as well" (p. 39). These individuals, who have widely differing experiences, social roles, and personality organizations, participate in various ways in this ongoing process. They use shared symbols (which have histories of their own) as vehicles of communication, but they interpret these symbols in more or less idiosyncratic ways.

---

[9]As a participant observer, the anthropologist usually forms intuitive impressions about a person that are based on diverse experiences with that person in a variety of social contexts. Assessments of disturbed functioning can be made on the basis of these experiences.

I am using the concept *symbol* in the broadest sense, to mean anything that serves as a vehicle for the communication of a concept. Furthermore, in the search for idiosyncrasy, I focus on how symbols function personally for those using them, following Obeyesekere's development of the concept of "personal symbol" (1981).[10] But my usage differs from Obeyesekere's. Obeyesekere privileged certain classes or types of symbols as operating at the juncture of culture and personality. I argue that it is arbitrary to privilege certain symbols in this way. From the perspective of the individual actor's usage, all semiotic signs are organized self-referentially. In other words, referential meaning cannot be divorced from pragmatic messages; every communication, whatever the content, is simultaneously a statement about oneself (Labov and Fanshel, 1977), and thus in some way is idiosyncratic. Freud addressed this issue in his discussion of dream work. He noted that even the most insignificant "day residue" is broken apart and used as a vehicle for the expression of latent dream thoughts; in other words, is used as a personal symbol.[11] Any symbol may, therefore, act as highly condensed vehicle for drawing together personal, idiosyncratic experiences and culturally shared meanings, allowing the expression, management, and perhaps resolution of conflict, both intrapsychic and social, in specific situations.

But it is important to point out that we cannot, therefore, simply label the idiosyncratic as private, "subjective" meanings that can be distinguished from the public, "objective" meanings of a symbol (see Lakoff and Johnson, 1980, pp. 226–228). People reveal in dialogue a tendency to conceptualize their experience in terms of images, themes, schemata,

---

[10]See Crapanzano's (1980) discussion of "symbolic-interpretive elements," as well as Obeyesekere's (1981) formulation of the concept "personal symbol" for differing perspectives on this issue. I was also inspired by Poole's discussion of Obeyesekere's (1987) concept and his demonstration of its application to children in Papua New Guinea.

[11]Freud's effort to privilege certain "typical" dreams or symbols pushed early studies of dream interpretation in a direction that continues to color studies of cultural "projective systems." Anthropologists violently rejected psychoanalytic interpretations of cultural symbols as manifesting typical unconscious images or conflicts, a rejection epitomized by Leach's (1958) paper "Magical Hair." Efforts to bring the psychological back into cultural studies show the effects of this polarization. Obeyesekere (1981), for instance, has distinguished between "personal symbols" and "psychogenetic symbols." According to Obeyesekere, both are psychological symbols, but the former involve "deep motivation," whereas the latter do not (p. 13). Obeyesekere's intention was to protect psychoanalytic studies of cultural symbols from anthropologists' accusations of reductionism and the consequent banishment of the psychological from the study of culture. But Obeyesekere's distinction privileges certain symbols and has the effect of drawing anew the boundary between culture and personality in an arbitrary way.

and metaphors. Many of these metaphorical structures are culturally shaped, linguistically established, and serve to organize shared experience for members of a society (Lakoff and Johnson, 1980, pp. 13–16). Furthermore, there are variations within a society as to how and when certain metaphorical structures and images are used. Luborsky, for instance, argued that American men and women differ in their "conceptual templates" for interpreting certain types of experiences and thus tend to differ in their choice of images for expressing those experiences (Luborsky, 1987). Taking this approach further, I argue that all communication involves a level at which understandings are idiosyncratically organized, and that the choice and use of imagery to express and organize experience differs. There is a point at which understandings are not shared, at which meanings do not overlap. In everyday communication, we assume, not completely accurately, that we understand the other, and we assume that we are understood. Simmel recognized the ambiguities of communication resulting from the fact that we project understanding onto the other and that "we cannot fully represent to ourselves an individuality which deviates from our own," so that "the picture of another man . . . is based on certain distortions" (Simmel, 1965, pp. 342–343). By careful examination of my informants' use of signs in dialogue with others, I demonstrate how, despite their shared "habits" and background, there are significant discrepancies in the understandings of the participants. How misunderstandings and discrepancies are managed is highly dependent, I argue, on the individual's psychological organization.

The problem of moving beyond the interpretive world of the informant or analysand to cross-cultural comparisons and experience-distant statements about things like psychological organization is one that has been a locus of controversy among anthropologists (see Geertz, 1984; Spiro, 1986). Thanks to Ricoeur, (1970), psychoanalysts have also become aware of the interpretive leap that they regularly confront clinically. Although Ricoeur identified symbols as having a double meaning, determined on the one hand by their past, which can be uncovered by means of a reductive hermeneutic of cause and effect, and constituted on the other hand through a progressive, problem-solving trajectory that can only be apprehended through an interpretive hermeneutic, anthropologists such as Geertz took up the problem of explanation versus interpretation in terms of a chasm as broad as the one that has traditionally divided culture and personality. Spiro (1986) and Poole (1987) tried to bring the two modes of inquiry together for anthropologists by identifying them as appropriate to different stages in the research process, corresponding to a "context of discovery" and a "context of validation." But this model still requires an epistemological leap between the hermeneutic process of data collection and hypothetico–deductive process of data reorganization and inference.

I would argue that both interpretation and comparison go on at all levels of analysis and theory building. Waelder (1962) thoughtfully characterized the nature of inference and theory building in psychoanalysis by distinguishing six levels of explanation and theory, all of which involve the reorganization and comparison of data.[12] Formulations such as Waelder's suggest to me that the dichotomization of hermeneutic and hypothetico–deductive modes of inquiry is not inevitable. Beginning with the identification of idiosyncrasy, I demonstrate how the interpretation of elements of dialogue itself rests on a process of comparison and generalization that is essentially the same process by which one makes both clinical assessments and generalizations about cultural forms. An understanding of another develops only by recognizing patterns in their efforts at communicating. Patterns and their significance are recognizable by comparing utterances and actions that share some features with other communications of that individual and with the communications of others. One may proceed from an identification of idiosyncrasies in the use of cultural symbols within the context of dialogue to a consideration of the pragmatic functions of such usages in the communicative process (including the countertransference reactions these usages stimulate in the interlocutor), to motive, and, finally, to models of both psychological functioning and cultural processes.

To illustrate this strategy for examining how individuals express their unique experiences through culturally shared signs in terms of their particular psychological organization, I have chosen the case of a young Pakistani woman who lost her mother in early childhood and her father a few years later. Because her experiences are quite atypical for Pakistanis of her background, it is not difficult to demonstrate that her uses of imagery and her understandings of social issues such as motherhood and marriage are idiosyncratic. Yet this woman, whom I shall call Nilam, illustrates how shared understandings and personal experiences are drawn together and communicated simultaneously in a socially acceptable way. Her experiences are atypical, but she is not regarded by others as being in another world. Though she experiences considerable stress, she (for the most part) communicates in terms shared and

---

[12]He also recognized that the process of data collection is inevitably shaped by clinical theory.

understood by others and uses culturally established solutions and ideals
for the management of socially organized conflicts.

I begin the process of interpretation by organizing the narrative
material in terms of particular images that struck me as being important
symbols in terms of which Nilam herself organized her experiences and
her self concepts, attending to instances of misunderstanding and their
role in the semiotic process. I selected four symbols that have clearly
identifiable culturally shared referents. In each case, I discuss the
referential content of each sign and describe how Nilam pragmatically
uses the sign in our conversation and what this usage suggests to me
about her subjective experience, thus moving me cautiously into an
interpretation of motive. The idiosyncratic components of each symbol
include variations in specific details, in the organization of components,
or in the relationship of the individual to the symbol, including how the
symbol is used pragmatically.[13] When considering her pragmatic use of
these symbols, I draw on my countertransference reactions as a source of
data for interpreting the personal significance of the symbols. Analysis at
this level corresponds roughly with Waelder's second level of "clinical
interpretation." As Waelder (1962) described the process, the observed
data "are. . . made the subject of interpretation regarding their interconnections and their relationships with other behavior or conscious content" (p. 620). In my discussion of the symbol "mother," I begin to draw
more heavily on psychoanalytic clinical theory (Waelder's fourth level),
in particular, the concepts of defense and identification, to explain
Nilam's pragmatic usage of the symbol.

## NILAM'S LIFE STORY

Nilam was one of several urban women of marriageable age whom I
interviewed during my fieldwork. Nilam, as well as most of these other
women, had some college education but was no longer in school, and
thus was waiting in a kind of limbo before marriage. I met Nilam
through one of her neighborhood friends, a young unmarried woman
who I knew quite well. I visited with her more or less weekly over a
period of a few months early in the course of my fieldwork in the city of
Lahore. During the first interview, Nilam, her two sisters, and my
research assistant were present. During most subsequent interviews,

---

[13]In many cases, such discrepancies may be discerned by contrasting my informants' use of
a symbol with my own "generalized" (if limited) knowledge of how other informants of
similar background have used such symbols.

Nilam and just one sister, Bushra, were present, though neighbors often drifted in and out of the house. The conversation shifted frequently between an account of Nilam's and Bushra's lives and more general discussions of subjects such as marriage. Our final conversation was at the home of one of Nilam's neighbors, another unmarried woman of the same age. This was the only time when 19-year-old Bushra was not there.[14] When Bushra was present, our conversations would begin calmly, with Nilam taking the lead. Gradually, Bushra would interrupt frequently and loudly. They would both become increasingly excited, telling me the horrifying story of their lives, until finally Bushra dominated the conversation. My final interview with Nilam in the neighbor's home was quite different. This setting stimulated in Nilam nostalgia about how a family should live, which she perceived as contrasting dramatically with her own situation.

At the time, I did not set out to conduct psychologically diagnostic interviews, and clearly, the setting, with other people drifting in and out, was far from that of the clinician's office. Nevertheless, Nilam's personality and, undoubtedly, the depth of her conflicts and pain, led her to be so open about her experiences that it is possible to assess aspects of her personality organization even on the basis of the limited contact I had with her. This fact is itself diagnostic: From a psychoanalytic perspective, both she and her sister could be said to draw on rather immature, and thus readily visible, defenses for mediating between conflictual intrapsychic processes and the outside world.

When I met her in 1975, Nilam began telling me about herself readily, beginning with her parents' marriage:

My parents were first cousins[15] before marriage. They got married in 1950. They lived in Karachi, and my father had a good job in government service. But then the children started coming—every year. I was the oldest. We were seven in all, and I was like a mother to the others. Then when I was eight, my mother committed suicide, by pouring oil over herself and igniting it. Then our lives became a real tragedy, when our father died in 1971. He was in Dacca [East Pakistan] just before the war which divided Pakistan. It seems that the Bengalis mixed poison in his tea, which broke a

---

[14]The interviews were in Urdu, though Nilam heavily sprinkled her speech with English, perhaps for my benefit, but undoubtedly also in order to present herself as an educated woman.

[15]This is the preferred form of marriage among Muslims.

vein in his head. When he died, four years ago, we were forced to move from Karachi, because we had no relatives there. We came to Lahore where my uncle [mother's brother] lived because Eastern girls can't live alone. But now we want to get our own house, because really, our uncle is not human. It will be hard for me to get married, but now I am working to arrange Bushra's marriage.

This story, with which Nilam began her account of herself, corresponded closely to the description of Nilam and Bushra that our mutual friend had given me before our meeting, suggesting that it was essentially the story that a benign third person would repeat to someone wanting to know about Nilam. After providing me with this orienting, rather schematic summary of their lives, Nilam and Bushra elaborated their account, primarily by focusing on the cruelty of their relatives and the hardships orphans face.

Nilam's childhood experiences were clearly atypical. In addition to the tragic loss of both parents, there is considerable evidence, on the basis of this story, as well as subsequent narratives, that her mother and other relatives displayed extensive psychopathology that affected the childhood experience of Nilam and her siblings. But at the level of content — the details of her life in relation to the typical Pakistani family — Nilam communicated her situation in terms readily comprehensible to other participants in the culture. Her difficulties were the typical fate of an orphan.

I included the preceding narrative (which Nilam told me virtually without interruption, except for my occasional requests for clarification), because it does a remarkably good job of orienting the reader to the basic outline of Nilam's life. Unlike many people, Nilam evidently had organized a "story" about herself even before the anthropologist's request for one, suggesting that she tended to see herself from the outside, defined as a social anomaly in the eyes of others. Certain key themes are embedded within this fairly brief narrative, although their complex significance was not readily apparent to me when I first heard the account. But as we talked further about her life and as I observed her activities in the interview situation, the layers of significance embedded within the narrative became increasingly evident. Other themes and images could also form the basis for organizing the material that emerged in our interviews, but I selected four signs that seemed to be particularly salient in the context of our discussions. The first is a specific image, *fire,* which represents both sexual passion and a link to the death of Nilam's mother. The second is a symbol representing a conceptual distinction that recurs in several different contexts, namely the relationship between "outside" and "inside" (*zahir-batin*). The third is a complex symbol representing the normative idea of proper family, and the fourth is the symbol "mother," which inevitably draws together emotionally charged personal experiences with culturally shaped expectations and ideas. Examination of each of these symbols demonstrates aspects of the process by which Nilam both used culturally shared symbols and experienced them idiosyncratically, to the point where she often experienced tension and miscommunication.

*Fire*

Unfortunately, I cannot provide here all the narratives on which I base my inferences, but I will demonstrate the outcome and something of the process of a first level of data organization. At this level, I pulled out certain images and themes that recur in Nilam's narratives and actions, noting interconnections among themes and relationships of these themes with other behaviors and thoughts. I approach the task of interpretation by organizing the material around central themes that, I argue, emerged as personal symbols for Nilam but that are also cultural symbols forming the basis of understandings shared with others.

The image of fire and burning came up repeatedly in Nilam's communications, as well as erupting vividly in action. "Fire" appears to be a highly charged symbol for her that merged several layers of significance, ultimately leading to confusion. In the symbol of fire, Nilam experienced the merging of an important and pervasive culturally shared meaning, sexual heat, with an even more vivid personal meaning with quite different implications: that of danger, death, anger, destruction, and chaos.

In our conversations, Nilam described her perception of a ceaseless tension in her sister Bushra, a constant pressure, a kind of "heat." She complained that her uncle repeatedly accused Bushra and her of being "the fire of Karachi," that is, corrupt women. Her uncle used the culturally popular image of fire to describe sexual passion. According to this popular image, corruption is equated with sexual heat. The sexual fire of women is contained by the veil, which must always be worn in the presence of men.[16] The restrictions imposed by society, as presented in

---

[16]For a discussion of Muslim ideas of female sexuality that explicitly contrast a Muslim image of the active, passionate female with Freud's equation of femininity with passivity, see Mernissi (1987).

the Qur'an, are intended to control the unruly, hot passions. Those who follow these rules are successfully shaped by them and "cool" with age.

In our dialogue, Nilam repeatedly protested, as if to justify herself, that she and Bushra were pure, not obsessed with sex in the way that her uncle accused them. The repetition of this theme of protest and outrage suggested that Nilam herself was confused, because she did vividly experience the image of fire and burning, yet she did not feel herself to be consciously preoccupied with sex or sexually provocative. Her uncle had projected an image onto her that created conflict and confusion because it partially reflected her experience while, at the same time, misrepresented it. The cultural image of fire did represent her understanding of sex and her experience of sexual fantasy. At the same time, Nilam's pragmatic use of the image of fire in other communications and actions suggests that superimposed on (or underlying) this culturally articulated metaphor was an even more vivid and concrete experience that represents a fundamentally different personal issue.

Moving from the referential content of utterances to the specification of the pragmatic functions of an utterance involves a process of inference. When we look at how informants pragmatically use symbols and consider the observable, social, or personal effects of such use, we have stepped outside of the informants' conscious frame of reference, which is heavily dependent upon culturally articulated ways of describing a particular phenomenon. When interpreting the ways in which informants use symbols, we are not necessarily describing these symbols or communications as the informants would describe them, but rather as they demonstrate them. As Freud argued, through such demonstrations, a person may communicate a conflict that he is not able to remember or articulate consciously. Freud distinguished "remembering" from "repeating" and saw both as important components of the curative process of "working through" in a clinical setting (Freud, 1914).

What kind of data are used to make this type of inference? Turner (1967), in identifying the meanings and functions of ritual symbols, juxtaposed informants' statements about the meanings of such symbols with how they acted with respect to such symbols. Actions are also a form of communication usually intended to be experienced by others. Mead (1934) and Peirce (1940) stressed that an important component of the meaning of an action is the kind of reaction it stimulates in the other.[17] In the clinical setting, psychoanalysts repeatedly observe actions

---

[17]An example of how an anticipated reaction is imbedded as a component of the meaning of an act, occurs in Crapanzano's (1980) hermeneutic study of a Moroccan informant,

that, though ostensibly private, may be revealed to have a communicative function (see Freud, 1914). Nilam's behavior with respect to fire seemed to serve a communication function of this sort. During the first interview, Nilam acted out her experience of fire and burning concretely. Shortly after telling me that there would be confusion in the household if she left to get married, smoke began pouring into the sitting room. Both Nilam and Bushra jumped into frantic activity. There was chaos as they tried to put out the fire. A few minutes later Nilam returned and explained that she had put rice on the fire to cook and had forgotten about it. It had been her duty to watch it. Nilam was visibly agitated; she had just acted out her reaction to fire and her experience of chaos in front of me, demonstrating the affect that had been missing in her account of her mother's suicide.

Because the (anticipated) reaction of the other can also be considered a part of the meaning of her act of burning the rice, I will explore for a moment my reaction to the situation (countertransference). I felt the eruption of chaos and a desire to help contain and organize the situation, as if I should take charge, but I also felt that I was too much of an outsider to do anything helpful. Only after others (my readers) pointed out to me what was missing from my account, did I realize that I also felt guilty for having distracted Nilam with my questions, for having disorganized her, for "causing" the fire. My failure to recognize this guilt suggests a countertransference reaction, a "blind spot" in my perception of anger that Nilam may have been experiencing toward me. Ultimately, I just stood at the door near the smoking rice and watched. My expected role was perhaps clarified for me a short while later, when Nilam told me a story about the principal of the boarding school she had attended when younger who had taken in all of the siblings, even those who were too young for the school, and provided them with a surrogate home. This woman was English. All this suggests to me that Nilam and Bushra were reenacting their experience of helplessness at their mother's death by fire and that they were placing me in the role of potential rescuer. Yet this caretaker ultimately disappointed and destroyed. Like her mother, I had caused a fire; hence, Nilam's anger was unconsciously directed at me, in transference.

Drawing yet another inference, one that brings us closer to Nilam's psychological organization, we can conclude that Nilam's experience of herself (and of Bushra) "on fire" was also an identification with her

---

when Crapanzano observed that "by means of the performance, he [the informant] is transformed from an ordinary social personage into either a pilgrim or a bard" (p. 86).

burning mother and her mother's anger. Without apparently realizing consciously any connection to her mother's fate, her descriptions of the emotional agitation that she and Bushra constantly experienced recreated her mother's death. For instance, during the interviews, Bushra became increasingly agitated and emotional and gradually dominated the conversation with her outbursts. Nilam, who also became more excited, described Bushra's behavior as habitual and out of control, "as if she were on fire." Identification with a lost "object" (the image of a person to whom one has had a strong and developmentally significant attachment) is a common strategy for avoiding the experience of loss by incorporating the loved one into oneself (Freud, 1915).[18] Nilam thus implicitly recognized that Bushra's fire and her own preoccupation with fire were not primarily "sexual heat,"[19] but the cultural imagery that others had provided her with (and taunted her with) forced her to organize her perception in these terms.

## Inside and Outside

Although it might be possible to penetrate the significance of fire for Nilam more deeply, and even to organize much of our thinking about her in terms of this image, it will, I believe, prove to be more useful to highlight a few other themes that were prominent in Nilam's self presentation, and then to explore their interconnections, rather than giving what may be excessive weight to a single image.

Prominent in Nilam's thinking was a pervasive distinction that she made between what is outside or visible (*zahir*) and that which is inside or hidden (*batin*). This *zahir–batin* distinction is central in Muslim Sufi thought and penetrates much of Pakistani life. Reality, for Pakistanis, is to be discovered in the inner states of persons and of situations. A distinction is made, for instance, between esoteric Sufism and the exoteric aspects of Islam. There is a clear link, however, between inner and outer, and the two are usually thought to be in harmony. For instance, the exoteric and esoteric meanings of the Qur'an do not contradict each other. It is thought that the external habits of a person shape his inner character, so that great importance is placed on external

---

[18]I will show further evidence for this interpretation in my discussion of *mother* as a personal symbol for Nilam.

[19]Although the central issue in this context is not sexuality, it is undoubtedly the case that their experience of sexuality has itself been shaped by this trauma. Nilam's fantasies of marriage, for instance, highlight a reproduction of her relationship with her mother.

behavior. In child rearing, parents place emphasis on shaping the habits and hence the character of the child. Most Pakistanis feel that they can read the "inner" man with great accuracy.

By articulating a distinction between outer phenomena and inner reality, Nilam thus drew on culturally established and organized imagery. But, as with the image of fire, the ways in which Nilam used this distinction to organize her experience were also idiosyncratic. Specifically, instead of assuming a continuity between outer and inner experience, Nilam described many different types of phenomena in terms of a distinction between outer appearances and inner reality, and in each case, she assumed the existence of an irreconcilable discrepancy between the two. Nilam's perception of discrepancy and unpredictability can be seen in her perception of central cultural symbols such as the Qur'an: "If sometimes we read Qur'anic verses, it is good, but other times everyone feels fear. There are special, dangerous verses of the Qur'an. My mother recited a verse and became crazy [pagal]." According to Nilam, palmistry, too, has two sides that are inconsistent: "The lines on the palm reveal the future, past and present. The back of the hand can reveal dangerous qualities."

She spoke of her family in terms of the discrepancy between inner and outer. From the outside "in the eyes of the world. . .," her uncle is her guardian. "But if you want to know the secret, he is not." She described her sister from both the inside and outside. Bushra rushes around, as if she were on fire. Yet, "her heart is clean." The tension caused Bushra to be what Nilam called a "psychological case." Her sister Bushra's description of her mother's death reinforces this imagery of discrepancy between inner and outer that is evident in Nilam's communications. Bushra's account suggests a linkage between this disjunction and the image of fire, both having their source in the sisters' experience of their mother and the threat of chaos. Bushra's account is striking in its eerie juxtaposition of external order and an inner, destructive power: "The house was very clean even though there were seven children. . . . Before the suicide she cleaned the house and put water on the fire for her bath after death."

We can see here a pattern that seems to organize Nilam's (and Bushra's) thinking, especially when they moved close to emotionally charged issues. In general terms, there is a discrepancy between appearances and inner, hidden qualities. In terms of Nilam's experience of the world, this pattern of organization suggests a fundamental experience of unpredictability and danger — ultimately, of chaos and rage. This perception is certainly not shared by all Pakistanis, although her sister seemed to experience it, and perhaps her mother (about whom we will hear more later). This pattern of thinking is clearly based on culturally shared assumptions; yet, at the same time, it is idiosyncratic. Most Pakistanis feel that they can predict the nature of reality on the basis of appearances. For Nilam, there was no predictable relationship between appearance and reality. The world was, therefore, a dangerous place, which she was doing her best to control. But because her own inner qualities were unpredictable, chaos always threatened to break through.

Nilam even experienced herself in terms of a discrepancy between inside and outside: "My name means sapphire wrapped in a sheet. I have qualities that people cannot see."[20] A serious issue for Nilam was whether the hidden quality behind the appearance of things was valuable, like the sapphire, or dangerous, (even life-threatening). She was ambivalent about her inner qualities; she experienced her inner states as unpredictable. In other contexts, she discussed her uncontrollable anger, which ruined her relationships with others. As in the rice-burning episode, internal chaos and destructive anger always threatened to break through her efforts at organization.

From this experience of self, as revealed in her idiosyncratic use of the *zahir–batin* distinction, it is possible to make a diagnostic inference concerning Nilam's psychological organization. The unpredictable relationship that she experiences between inside and outside suggests a lack of integration of her various experiences of self and a difficulty regulating states of tension. This unintegrated self-experience had a grandiose quality that emerged in her descriptions of her childhood: "My childhood was special. When I was nine months old, I started to walk. . . ." She claimed to have been doing all the housework when she was only four years old. In childhood, she could read palms, even without having read books on the subject. With respect to palmistry and dream interpretation, she expressed an atypical (though culturally patterned) claim of power to foretell the future, which seemed to be the expression of a grandiose fantasy. She explained her ability to do this as coming from divine nature (*qudrati tor pur*). Nilam seemed to be assuring herself that such divine powers would enable her to control and anticipate even the most violently chaotic experience. But even her fear of creating disaster and of the destructive potential of her rage, which she expressed in several contexts, had a grandiose component to them. Nilam thus displayed a grandiose sense of her inner power and uniqueness that was juxtaposed against, and was perhaps an effort at compensating for,

---

[20]This quotation has been altered to preserve her anonymity and maintain consistency with the pseudonym I have chosen, but it retains the structure of the original utterance.

her sense of impending chaos and her feelings of inadequacy in dealing with it.

## The Concept of Proper Family

Perhaps because of the extreme nature of her family's deviation from a typical family environment, the fact that her family was far from her conception of a "proper family" was one of Nilam's preoccupations during several of our meetings. She drew the contrasts sharply. It could be argued that the image of a proper family was a major organizing theme of her life story, at least as she presented it in this context. Given its personal salience for Nilam, we may identify the concept as another personal symbol for her. Proper family is, of course, a complex symbol, and may perhaps best be understood as a culturally organized schema (see, for instance, D'Andrade, 1984). This schema is a frame of reference in terms of which Nilam interpreted the actions of various relatives and family friends; it also provided a rationale for many of her own activities.

Nilam has an image of proper family relationships that in many respects corresponds with that of other women her age. In the Pakistani family, every relationship is defined hierarchically, so that every individual is subordinate to some members of the family and dominant over others. Proper behavior involves the submission and obedience of juniors to elders. Elders are expected to discipline their juniors, but they must do so with love. Juniors are expected to obey and respect their elders and to offer them service.[21] Children can expect of their parents food, love, a good environment, prayers for their well-being, rational control and guidance, and education. Traditionally, the choice of a spouse is the last major decision that parents make for their daughters, the fulfillment of their duties as parents. Once a daughter is married, her husband and in-laws become her guardians and providers. After her marriage, it is the bride's duty to respect and submit to the wishes and authority of her in-laws and to produce children, especially sons, for her husband. A young woman should strive to control her own feelings, especially anger, and to act with reason in all her relationships. In the ideal family, those with authority over her will respond with a love that will give her satisfaction in the performance of her duties. She, in turn,

---

[21]Inden and Nicholas (1977) articulated Bengali kinship expectations in similar terms.

will respond with love to her own children in this ever-renewed, hierarchy of relationships.

Nilam did not state the propositions of this "cultural account" directly. They were implied in her complaints about the behavior of her elders and in her expressions of concern about the life situation and living conditions of her brothers and sisters. She expressed sadness that her parents had not lived to fulfill their duties to their children, thus forcing her to deal with things on her own. I heard similar criticisms of elders expressed by other Pakistanis and thus inferred a cultural patterning of expectations along the lines previously described.

Nilam and her friends drew on this background of shared understandings, as they formulated many aspects of their current situation in similar ways. For instance, one important experience that they communicated (and helped define for themselves and each other by communicating) was the social stress of the particular phase of their lives, the anticipation of marriage. This stress, however, impinged on each of them uniquely, although all anticipated with apprehension the adjustment to a new family.

Certain aspects of Nilam's account suggest that even before her mother's death, her parents did not adequately fulfill their duties: "Every year I prayed that there would be no more children, because I had to do all the work, even when I was four. When I was eight, my mother died. I don't know how people play in this life." But Nilam's overt anger, mixed with contempt, was directed at her *mamu* (her mother's brother) and *nani* (her mother's mother). In cultural terms, she complained that proper relationships between remaining elders and their juniors were not maintained. In particular, her uncle and grandmother imposed arbitrary restrictions but failed to perform their duties, a violation of culturally specified proper behavior. Thus, she did not consider her uncle a "real" guardian. Her grandmother should have been arranging her marriage and her sister's marriage, but instead told them that she wished they would die. Nilam, the eldest daughter, must therefore marry off her younger siblings first, because the responsibility of looking after them has fallen upon her.

Even many of the negative aspects of her own family life Nilam understood in culturally shared terms. Specifically, emotional/physical health is thought of in interpersonal terms. The disobedience of a child, especially an adult child, may damage the health of a parent. A parent's improper control or lack of love will ruin a child. More generally, improper control, or teasing done out of passion or selfish malice, exercised by any elder over a junior, may "break" the mind of the junior.

As Nilam put it, "Now Bushra is a psychological case because she spent a year with our grandmother. If I had been in her place, I would be in a mental hospital." When I saw Nilam again nine years later, Bushra had actually been admitted as a psychiatric patient, and was staying at an in-patient facility at the time of my visit. At this later time, Nilam's description of her relatives drew on the cultural model of improper control to explain the fate of her siblings:

> My *nani* and *mamu* were very strange people. They tortured us and teased us. That had an effect [*asar*] on the minds of most of my brothers and sisters. Their minds didn't stay perfect. The effect on three of them was so great that it weakened their minds. It was very excessive for two of them (alluding to a brother who committed suicide and to Bushra).

Interpreted in cultural terms, her grandmother and uncle deliberately imposed arbitrary restrictions but failed to perform their duties as elders. Her grandmother was the source of her mother's troubles and sabotaged her parents' marriage. She interfered with the initial marriage arrangements and then caused her to become insane by urging her to read a Qur'anic verse one hundred thousand times. Nilam described that, more recently, Bushra had also been driven close to suicide because she had lived with her grandmother for a year. She repeated what she had said nine years earlier, "If I had lived there for a year, I would now be in a mental hospital."

Despite the culturally organized aspects of her account, Nilam was unusual in her willingness to freely make such direct criticisms of her own elders in a social situation with several others present, suggesting that in this case, though the referential content of her utterances was constituted of culturally shared ideas, her pragmatic usage of such ideas was idiosyncratic. Returning to the image of outside–inside for a moment, it would appear that having found no safety or refuge inside the family, Nilam looks outside for help, making family secrets public. She has inverted the typical Pakistani orientation, in which a strict "veil"[22] demarcates the private, inner world of the family and the public outer world, (from which women must be protected).

Nilam's characterizations of her relatives can be used as a marker indicating a major component of her psychological organization, the

---

[22]The Urdu word for the seclusion of women, *purda,* literally means veil.

degree of maturity[23] demonstrated by the nature of her intrapsychic
representations of others, which we can infer from the structure of her
discourse about her relatives. We can ask whether her description of
another conveys a sense of a real, complex individual, demonstrating
mature object relations. During the course of our interviews, Nilam spent
most of her time talking about four people: her mother, father,
grandmother, and uncle. Nilam's images of her parents were idealized,
and she was detached affectively from her conscious memories of them.
Although she clearly had experienced profound disappointment in the
failure of her family, she never expressed anger directly at her parents or
pinned the blame on them. In contrast, she directed her rage overtly and
unambivalently against her grandmother and her uncle, whom she
depicted as being inhuman tyrants. Nilam's descriptions of people were
vivid, but the characters she described were one-dimensional. For
instance, with great vehemence she recounted incident after incident that
revealed her grandmother's bizarre cruelty. Based on the idealization of
her parents, and the negative characterization of her other relatives, there
was little evidence that she was able to integrate positive and negative
qualities into a single representation. This suggests that she made heavy
use of the device of "splitting,"[24] a developmentally early type of defense
against anxiety or other overwhelming affect such as rage.

Her conviction that her relatives weakened the minds of her brothers
and sisters fits with cultural ideas of the shaping of children, a result of
improper hierarchical relationships, but Nilam also uses it as a defense
against her rage at the failures of her parents. From this point of view,
we can see a "gap" in her discourse: She argues that because her relatives
were strange people, they had an "effect" on the brothers and sisters; by
means of this explanation she is able to omit any suggestion that the loss
of their parents affected them. The striking gap is any mention of
reaction to their death, except in terms of logistics.

## Image of Mother

Like the idea of *proper family,* the image of *mother* is a complex symbol
with multiple layers of culturally shared meanings, many of which, of

---

[23]From a psychoanalytic perspective, a mature object relationship is characterized by the
ability to maintain a love relationship in the face of frustration and to accept the
limitations and separateness of the loved object.

[24]This concept was described and incorporated into a model of psychological development
by Melanie Klein (1975, p. 153).

course, overlap with the complex of ideas constituting proper family. The idea of mother also carries multiple layers of emotionally charged personal meanings. Exploring the significance of the idea for Nilam, as well as how she organized her feelings about her own mother, provides us with data that suggest important aspects of her psychological organization, particularly the nature of her defenses and the ways in which early identifications with this parental figure appeared to shape her self-experience and behavior.

For Nilam, the image of mother evoked powerful feelings of absence, loss, and anger. But these feelings were detached from her descriptions of her explicit memories of her mother, indicating that she defended herself against the intensity of feelings associated with her mother. The affective side of Nilam's maternal idealization emerged in her fantasies about her imagined future mother-in-law:

> I love to visit homes where mothers are present. I will marry a person who has a mother. I love to hear the call of "daughter." (She cries.) I don't win the love of other mothers. I feel inferior because my mother isn't here. My desire in life, more basic than other desires, is to win the love of my husband's mother.

Nilam's focus on her mother-in-law is not unusual, given the structure of marriage in the Pakistani family. Anticipation of a mother-in-law is a normal preoccupation of young women not yet married, who frequently discuss their feelings in culturally established imagery. The bride is expected to come into her husband's family with a feeling of antagonism toward her mother-in-law. The mother-in-law is expected to be a harsh taskmaster, exerting control, not just over the daughter-in-law's performance of household tasks, but even over her access to her husband.[25] Nilam's expectations of her relationship with her mother-in-law were thus unusual. Girls express intense longings about marriage, but they usually express these longings in romantic terms about their future husbands, rather than toward a mother substitute.

In contrast to the affect that Nilam demonstrated in her fantasies about a mother-in-law, the account she gave me of her own mother had a peculiar, detached, affectless quality. But like the image of a mother-in-law, her conscious image of her mother is an idealized one.

---

[25]Folk songs, for instance, often dwell on the theme of the ever wakeful mother-in-law who prevents the bride from going to her husband at night (Kakar, 1978, p. 74).

Our mother died when Nargis, the youngest, was six months old. My father saw my mother before marriage. It was a love marriage.[26] She was very pretty, but her mother (my grandmother) was not ready to arrange her marriage. We believe that when she went to her husband's house, the house was haunted and that she came under the influence of something.[27] She would give away all the money her husband gave her to beggars. She was always absent minded. One day she called her neighbor. She asked the neighbor to write a note saying that she excused her parents and her husband, but that she was tired of this world. She said, "When my husband has to care for the children, he will come to know how to care for them." Then she poured oil over herself and burned.

This description of Nilam's mother was expressed in terms of cultural imagery, including elements that might be found in an account of a revered elder, even a saint. In particular, she emphasized her mother's generosity and religiosity, evidenced in her giving money away to beggars. Embedded also in this account is another cultural ideal: the passive submission of the perfect wife who responds to the cruelty and neglect of her elders (which could include her husband) with quiet submission and withdrawal.[28] The idea of passive obedience was particularly evident in Bushra's account of the same episode: "Before the suicide she cleaned the house and put water on the fire for her bath after death." Nilam attributed her mother's failures to influences beyond human control, most explicitly, to spirits that haunted the house, an attitude that helped her to maintain her idealization of her mother.

These idealizations of other mothers and of her own mother are an important component of Nilam's articulated concept of mother, and they conform to culturally established imagery, such as that found in Indian films.[29] But observing Nilam's actions, her pragmatic use of the symbol mother, suggests other, less positive dimensions of mother's significance

---

[26]This is in contrast to an arranged marriage and is traditionally considered reprehensible.

[27]This is a way of describing an experience of possession.

[28]The most popular guide to ideals of proper behavior for Muslim women gives the following advice on conjugal and family relations: "Anger must be firmly checked. To check it, immediately remove from your sight anyone with whom you are angry. If the person does not go away, you should leave. Then reflect that however much you may hold this person to blame, Almighty God holds you at fault even more" (Metcalf, 1990, p. 190).

[29]Pakistanis avidly watch Indian films, which are broadcast from Amritsar, India, and are readily received on Lahore television sets.

for her that profoundly shaped Nilam's life. Her actions reveal the ways in which she internalized many aspects of her experience of her mother, to the extent that she experienced herself as her mother.

Acting successfully as a "mother" for her siblings was one of Nilam's explicit aims. It is an indication of one of the ways in which she internalized the image of her mother. One of the first things she told me when we met was that she is like a mother to the others. She felt that she acted like a mother to them throughout their childhood, and now she was fulfilling one of the primary duties of a mother by trying to arrange the marriages of a sister and two of her brothers before she thought about her own marriage. I asked her why she was postponing her own marriage, and she explained, "The system of housework [ghar ka nizam] is under me. If I leave, there will be confusion." She thus presented herself as a kind of martyr, as she feels her own mother was, fending off chaos, nobly carrying out a role thrust upon her because her elders have failed her, carrying on the "housework" her mother abandoned at her death.

But according to Nilam's first-hand childhood experience, a mother is someone who cannot fulfill an impossibly demanding role. Nilam demonstrated this aspect of motherhood in the interview situation, showing me in her actions her inability to keep the household running smoothly. This was particularly vivid in the rice-burning episode. Nine years later, when we met again, she gave me another less dramatic but even clearer demonstration. Now married, with an infant of her own, she received me graciously. She served tea and sent her young nephew out to buy a cake in the bazaar.[30] Serving tea is a ritual that is performed whenever anyone pays a visit — it may occur several times in a single day. Despite her concern that I be impressed with the tea, positively displayed through the cake purchase, she forgot to serve the sugar and milk until I reminded her — when the tea had already gotten cold (in Pakistan, *nobody* drinks tea without milk and plenty of sugar). Given the fact that the style of serving of tea is in Pakistan extremely standardized and routinized, her omission was a particularly striking communication, demonstrating to me in an instant that she found the task of motherhood overwhelming, as her own mother had. As in the episode of the burnt rice nine years earlier, she was also demonstrating her anger at my failure to nurture her.[31]

---

[30]Serving cake was a way of telling me that I was an honored guest. It is a common practice to send a young child for sweets in such circumstances.

[31]Milk and sugar are also the ingredients of baby formula. During the course of my

Unconsciously, Nilam appeared to be keeping her mother alive by experiencing herself as her mother. She struggled to fend off the chaos that followed her mother's suicide, yet she simultaneously perpetuated it through reenactment. According to Freud, this is a way of avoiding the experience of overwhelming loss: Instead of completing the work of mourning, she internalized the image of her mother, and continued to express this identification in ways that prevented her from functioning effectively in the present.

## UNCOVERING UNDERLYING CONFLICT

The analyses of these four symbols—fire, inner/outer, proper family, and mother—stress different facets of Nilam's experience. I now ask whether my interpretations of these symbols, particularly my identifications of the idiosyncratic in Nilam's usage, when taken together, seem to point persistently to the expression of an unresolved conflict that played a role in organizing Nilam's experience. Though I am not working from a single text, as Freud did when interpreting a dream, I will adopt a procedure similar to Freud's (1900) strategy in *The Interpretation of Dreams*. Freud relied on the technique of free association as his basic source of data for interpreting dream symbols. He then looked for themes that seemed to recur in association to several dream symbols. These points of convergence were taken to be indicators of an underlying conflict that motivated the dream (and that motivated the allegedly "free" associations). In the case of my dialogues with Nilam, what she expressed to me and how she expressed it can be understood as a reenactment of themes and issues that organized at least certain sectors of her experience.

Nilam's idiosyncratic usage of the image of fire suggests that a basic issue for her was her traumatic experience of her mother's suicide, which she continued to relive in the form of imminent chaos and destructive rage, experienced both externally and internally. Her experience of inner fire as chaos and rage suggests that issues of sexual conflict, which are

---

nine-year absence, Nilam and I had each had a child. At my departure following this second stint of fieldwork, I was perhaps unconsciously striving to compensate for the failures in nurturing she had projected onto me by giving her the diapers and baby bottles I brought with me from the states. Consciously, I was concerned for the welfare of her bottle-fed daughter, who appeared to be a "failure to thrive" baby. As I write, I am aware of guilt at not having given her formula to put into the bottles, a symbol that condenses and expresses a basic aspect of our relationship.

often intended when fire imagery is used by Pakistanis, are for Nilam secondary to issues of tension regulation and the integration of her experiences of self. Nilam's use of the image of fire also suggests that she had internalized images of her mother, and experiences herself as her mother in ways that were overwhelming for her.

These themes of the threat of chaos, the destructive power of her anger, and difficulties integrating various aspects of her self-experience are also evident in her understanding of the culturally articulated distinction between inner and outer, which organizes many areas of Pakistani experience. Nilam's perception of lack of predictability between inner and outer made her suspicious of others and led her to misread the communications and intentions of others. It also reflects an element of grandiosity in her self-experience, which may have been a strategy for preventing herself from being overwhelmed by her fear of chaos. This grandiosity oscillated with a despairing image of herself as deficient and unable to control her own impulses, such as rage.

Nilam relied on the concept of proper family to help her orient herself with respect to her experience of loss and lack of love. But her use of this concept as an ideal had as its underside the depiction of those with whom she was actively interacting as inhumanly evil — an indication that she relied on a developmentally early defense mechanism known as "splitting." As is the case with her disparate images of herself, she appeared unable to integrate negative and positive images of others into single, more complex, and realistic representations.

Her use of the concept of *mother* further demonstrates her difficulties with the integration of her various experiences of self and of other. It also highlights how her feelings are not always congruent with her cognition. This disjunction is revealed by means of a consistent gap in her accounts: Overtly, she expressed no affective response to memories of her mother. She presented herself as if she were in complete control of her images of her parents, a self-presentation resting on a kind of distortion. It is a distortion because, as I demonstrated earlier, the missing affect, primarily anger, intruded itself indirectly into our dialogue, in the form of burning rice, cold tea, and emotionally dramatic stories about her inhuman relatives. I believe it is possible to identify this distortion as evidence of a kind of psychopathology without imposing my own values arbitrarily on her, by tracing out the effects of such a distortion on her life. At the most superficial level, her inability to experience and regulate her anger directly and, therefore, to maintain control over situations, means that she was not able to act as an efficient and courteous hostess or, more critically, to be an adequate mother for her own daughter (the child was obviously malnourished and unkempt). In effect, she was acting to perpetuate chaos and destruction.

Nilam's inability to accept and integrate her feelings about the loss of her mother into her conscious self-experience resulted in an immaturity that disrupted her current relationships. Nilam was aware of this disruption but was unable to understand its source. For instance, Nilam's idiosyncratic longing for a mother-in-law was, as we have seen, a displacement of longing for her mother, a longing that could never be satisfied. After expressing an intense desire to win the love of her future husband's mother, she observed: "If I desire and that desire is fulfilled, it becomes of no importance. I get a desire and work hard for it to be fulfilled, and then it is nothing—it is my psychology." Her fear of marriage was, in part, a realization that the same thing would happen to her longing for a mother-in-law. In some sense, she knew that her image of marriage as the route to being a "proper" woman in a proper family and, behind that, a satisfaction of her impossible longings for her mother and her father, was illusory. In fact, in our meeting nine years later, following her marriage, she expressed an intense hatred of her mother-in-law, which seemed to have more to do with her once-again disappointed expectations than it did with the particular characteristics of her mother-in-law.

In addition to avoiding recognition of her traumatic feelings of loss and longing for her mother, Nilam tended to idealize her mother. This idealization can be seen as covering another gap in her self-presentation, hiding what can be hypothesized as conflictual feelings about her mother. But that which was hidden continued to shape her experience, unmodified, her traumatic feelings of loss went because unacknowledged. The unacknowledged disappointment and rage that she experienced in relationship to her mother were split off from her image of her mother and displaced onto others, thereby distorting her perception of them and making realistic relationships with others difficult.

Nilam clearly always experienced difficulty maintaining satisfying relationships with others, and had considerable difficulty functioning effectively as a wife and mother. It is possible to state in diagnostic terms, by shifting levels of inference, the characteristics of her interpersonal relationships that give rise these difficulties. Nilam's explicit descriptions of her relationships with others may be examined to determine whether her representations of significant others were multifaceted or unidimensional, indicating a tendency to perceive others either as separate people with their own motivations and needs or merely as extensions of her own needs (representing an earlier, developmentally more egocentric perspective). A further strategy for assessing her psychological organization in terms of developmental level is to determine whether she was concerned with, and capable of, experiencing triangular relationships and the conflicts associated with oedipal issues, or whether she continued to be preoccupied exclusively with the dyadic issues characteristic of the earlier mother–child bond. Other criteria for making a diagnostic assessment include the organization of defenses, which are revealed in her strategies for handling conflictual and stressful material, and her ability to integrate her experiences of self and regulate tension in the face of threats to self-esteem.[32]

I have moved through several stages of interpretation. Beginning with Nilam's patterns of expression, I pinpointed several idiosyncrasies in Nilam's communications. I then made inferences about underlying conflicts that would account for these idiosyncrasies. Now I will briefly consider how these conflicts would be labeled from a diagnostic point of view, jumping for a moment fully into the jargon of the clinician. Putting together the quality of her experience of others (that is, her object relations) and her experience of self, we could describe her problems as being primarily preoedipal in nature: She relied heavily on primitive defense mechanisms such as splitting, and showed evidence of a severe narcissistic personality disorder in her unstable, unintegrated grandiose self and parental imagoes. This lack of integration was associated with a failure to develop stable object relations. We can speculate that her oedipal attachment to her father rested on an unsteady foundation, based primarily on identifications with a mother who was herself highly unstable.[33]

---

[32]A Kohutian self psychologist would argue that the ability to maintain a cohesive self in the face of stress is a diagnostic criterion for establishing the presence or absence of a narcissistic personality disorder (see Kohut, 1977). Although I agree that the self psychologists are describing a clinically observable phenomenon that is associated with tension regulation, I question the underlying metapsychological assumption that there is single "cohesive self" which develops in normal individuals (see Ewing, 1987, 1990).

[33]In this and other accounts, there was evidence of her experience of oedipal wishes in early childhood, their reactivation in adolescence, and her defenses against them. "When I was in ninth class, my father gave me my mother's bra. Then I had reason (ᶜàql). I became embarrassed." We can surmise that the image of filling her mother's bra encapsulated her oedipal strivings. Nevertheless, these oedipal wishes were colored, if not overshadowed, by the reminder of her mother's death and the threat of chaos or

# CONCLUSION

The idiosyncrasies discernable in a person's use of cultural symbols may act as markers of particular ways of organizing experience. I demonstrated the possibility of identifying idiosyncrasy and the utility of this approach for specifying how the anthropologist comes to understand the experiential world of another. By focusing on idiosyncrasies as a marker of personality organization, I suggest a way of moving through culture to personality and intrapsychic conflict that assumes no necessary causal relationship between culture and personality. This approach avoids any assumption that specific developmental immaturities, intrapsychic conflicts, or clinical syndromes are characteristic of certain societies because of their cultures, or that the culture itself (its myths, rituals, and so forth) provides evidence of a modal personality or conflict.

Rather, analysis of the idiosyncrasies of communication allows the researcher to focus both on cultural patterns and processes and on the broad range of personalities and disorders observable in any society. Expressing themselves by means of culturally organized symbolic systems, people exhibit a wide range of personal concerns, conflicts, and disturbances. Some of their concerns are largely shaped by the vicissitudes of early experiences; others may be issues arising out of current social and economic pressures. Prominent among these experiences are the accidents of human existence that can happen to anyone, regardless of one's cultural upbringing — accidents such as losing a parent, a home, a job, or being the oldest or youngest sibling, experiencing a major illness, having parents who are themselves psychologically disturbed and emotionally unavailable, and even being born with a particular temperament. Though the interpretation, and thus the impact, of such events is, of course, culturally shaped, humans appear to have a repertoire and range of basic psychological responses, defenses, and ways of coping with experiences of deprivation and distress that are recognizable cross culturally. The idiosyncrasies in an individual's communications reveal aspects of one's ways of perceiving and organizing experience that can be interpreted in terms of categories that facilitate the formulation of hypotheses about the person's intrapsychic organization. It is thus possible to move from interpretation of individual experience to clinical generalization.

In Nilam's case, markers of idiosyncrasy point to the organization of

---

disintegration associated with destructive anger that was a more basic aspect of her psychological organization.

psychological defenses, intrapsychic conflict, and immaturities that impair her adult functioning—in other words, psychopathology. I chose to discuss a person with evident psychopathology because, in her case, idiosyncratic usages stand out sharply and can be easily articulated and interpreted in terms of features associated with Western diagnostic categories.

But the approach may be used with any individual and data may be interpreted in terms of other, nonclinical frames of reference. Idiosyncrasies are not only markers of psychopathology. In other cases, the significance of idiosyncrasies may be different—as in the case of an individual who has successfully and creatively resolved a conflict (see Ewing, 1990). In such cases, the idiosyncrasy may mark a new interpretation of a cultural symbol, resulting in a usage that may be adopted by others experiencing similar conflicts. Idiosyncrasy may be the mark of a cultural innovator, a social or political leader, and the innovator's peculiarities of usage may be an important place for anthropologists to look in order to further our understanding of culture as a dynamic process.

## BIBLIOGRAPHY

BOYER, L.B. (1989), Countertransference and technique in working with the regressed patient: Further remarks. *Internat. J. Psycho-Anal.* 70:701–714.

CRAPANZANO, V. (1980), *Tuhami: Portrait of a Moroccan.* Chicago: University of Chicago Press.

D'ANDRADE, R.G. (1984), Cultural meaning systems. In: *Culture Theory: Essays on Mind, Self, and Emotion,* eds. R.A. Schweder & R.A. LeVine. Cambridge: Cambridge University Press, pp. 88–119.

DEVEREUX, G. (1968), *From Anxiety Method in the Behavioral Sciences.* The Hague: Mouton.

DUBOIS, C. (1961), *The People of Alor: A Social-Psychological Study of an East Indian Island.* New York: Harper & Row.

DWYER, K. (1982), *Moroccan Dialogues: Anthropology in Question.* Baltimore: Johns Hopkins University Press.

EWING, K.P. (1987), Clinical psychoanalysis as an ethnographic tool. *Ethos* 15:16–39.

_____ (1990), The illusion of wholeness: Culture, self, and the experience of inconsistency. *Ethos* 18:251–278.

_____ (in press), Is psychoanalysis relevant for anthropology? In: *The Social Life of the Psyche: and directions in psychological anthropology,* ed. T. Schwartz, G. White & C. Lutz. Cambridge: Cambridge University Press.

FREUD, S. (1900), The interpretation of dreams. *Standard Edition,* 4 & 5. London: Hogarth Press, 1953.

_____ (1914), Remembering, repeating and working-through. *Standard Edition,* 12. London: Hogarth Press, 1958, pp. 145–156.

―――― (1915). Mourning and melancholia. *Standard Edition,* 14. London: Hogarth Press, 1957, pp. 243–260.

GEDO, J. (1987), The art of psychoanalysis as a technology of instruction. Presented to the Chicago Psychoanalytic Society.

GEERTZ, C. (1973a), Person, time, and conduct in Bali. In: *Interpretation of Cultures.* New York: Basic Books, pp. 360–411.

―――― (1973b), Religion as a cultural system. In: *Interpretation of Cultures.* New York: Basic Books, pp. 87–125.

―――― (1983), "From the native's point of view": On the nature of anthropological understanding, In: *Local Knowledge: Further Essays in Interpretive Anthropology.* New York: Basic Books, pp. 55–70.

―――― (1984), Distinguished lecture: Anti anti-relativism. *American Anthropologist* 66:263–278.

HALLOWELL, A.I. (1938), Fear and anxiety as cultural and individual variables in a primitive society. In: *Culture and Experience.* Philadelphia: University of Pennsylvania Press, 1955, pp. 250–265.

―――― (1954a), The self and its behavioral environment. In: *Culture and Experience.* Philadelphia: University of Pennsylvania Press, 1955, pp. 75–110.

―――― (1954b), The Ojibwa self and its behavioral environment. In: *Culture and Experience.* Philadelphia: University of Pennsylvania Press, 1955, pp. 172–182.

―――― (1955), *Culture and Experience.* Philadelphia: University of Pennsylvania Press.

INDEN, R.B., & NICHOLAS, R.W. (1977), *Kinship in Bengali Culture.* Chicago: University of Chicago Press.

KAKAR, S. (1978), *The Inner World.* Delhi: Oxford University Press.

KARDINER, A. (1945), *The Psychological Frontiers of Society.* New York: Columbia University Press.

KLEIN, M. (1946), Notes on some schizoid mechanisms. *Internat. J. Psycho-Anal.* 27:99–110.

―――― (1975), *The Psycho-analysis of Children.* (trans. A. Strachey). New York: Dell Publishing Company.

KOHUT, H.1977, *The Restoration of the Self.* New York: International Universities Press.

LABOV, W., & FANSHEL, D. (1977), *Therapeutic Discourse: Psychotherapy as Conversation.* New York: Academic Press.

LAKOFF, G., & JOHNSON, M. (1980), *Metaphors We Live By.* Chicago: University of Chicago Press.

LEACH, E.R. (1958), Magical hair. *J. Royal Anthropolog. Inst.* 88:147–64.

LEIBNIZ, (1714), The Monadology, In: *Leibniz: Selections,* ed. P.P. Wiener. New York: Charles Scribner's Sons, 1951, pp. 533–552.

LUBORSKY, M. (1987), Analysis of multiple life history narratives. *Ethos* 15:366–381.

MEAD, G.H. (1934), *Mind, Self and Society from the Standpoint of a Social Behaviorist,* ed. C.W. Morris. Chicago: University of Chicago Press, 1962.

MERNISSI, F. (1987), *Beyond the Veil: Male-Female Dynamics in Modern Muslim Society.* Bloomington: Indiana University Press.

METCALF, B.D. (1990), *Perfecting Women: Maulana Ashraf ᶜAli Thanawi's Bihishti Zewar.* Berkeley: University of California Press.

OBEYESEKERE, G. (1981), *Medusa's Hair.* Chicago: The University of Chicago Press.

PEIRCE, C.S. (1940), Logic as semiotic: The theory of signs. In: *The Philosophical Writings of Peirce,* ed. Justus Buchler. New York: Dover Publications pp. 98–119.

POOLE, F.J.P. (1987), Personal experience and cultural representation in children's 'personal symbols' among Bimin-Kuskusmin. *Ethos* 15:104–135.

RICOEUR, P. (1970), *Freud and Philosophy*. New Haven: Yale University Press.

SEARLES, H.F. (1979), *Countertransference and Related States: Selected Papers*. New York: International Universities Press.

SIMMEL, G. (1965), How is society possible? In: *Essays on Sociology, Philosophy, and Aesthetics*, ed. Kurt H. Wolff. New York: Harper & Row, pp. 337–356.

SPIRO, M.E. (1951), Culture and personality: The natural history of a false dichotomy. *Psychiatry* 14:19–46.

_____ (1986), Cultural relativism and the future of anthropology. *Cultural Anthropology* 1:259–286.

TURNER, V. (1967), *The Forest of Symbols*. Chicago: Aldine Press.

TYLER, S.A. (1986), Post-modern ethnography: From document of the occult to occult document. In: *Writing Culture: The Poetics and Politics of Ethnography*, eds. James Clifford and George E. Marcus. Berkeley: University of California Press, pp. 122–140.

WAELDER, R. (1962). Psychoanalysis, scientific method, and philosophy. *J. Amer. Psychoanal. Assn.* 10:617–637.

WIKAN, U. (1990), Culture and translation: Insights from Bali. Paper presented to the Duke University Department of Anthropology. Durham, NC.

# 11

# Circumcision and Biblical Narrative

## MELVIN R. LANSKY
## BENJAMIN KILBORNE

## THE PROBLEM

The practice of circumcision as a Jewish ritual reconfirming the covenant of Abraham has remained ubiquitous, not only among observant Jews, but among Jews who have given up synagogue affiliation, dietary laws, and observation of the Sabbath. Stripped of its ostensible religious meanings, circumcision has become a widely practiced, neonatal surgical procedure practiced by Jews and non-Jews alike.

Often, circumcision is given a hygienic rationalization. The circumcised male is felt to be clean, healthy, and even civilized. Indeed the terms, *uncircumcised,* or *Philistine,* usually connote barbarism, a lack of polish, and animal-like, unbridled lust or aggressiveness.

Today, however, the hygienic justifications for the practice of circumcision are largely without convincing scientific foundation (Apfel, 1951; Morgan, 1965; Gellis, 1978). Not only are penile malignancies rare, some cervical malignancies, which increase in prevalence in women with uncircumcised sexual partners, have been seen to result from a lack of hygiene, correctable by simple cleansing.

Considered apart from its supposed hygienic value, the practice of circumcision must recapture our amazement. The common consciousness is deflected from the stark reality of the attack on the penis. Such rationalizations make circumcision a practice of particular interest for psychoanalytic investigation. Circumcision, a ritual mutilative attack on the genitals rationalized by hygienic and medical mythology, remains widespread even outside religious custom and is also experienced as a healthful or celebratory event. How this can be so constitutes the subject of this paper.

Psychoanalytic literature on the topic is relatively sparse, consisting of clinical studies and studies of the ritual itself. What clinical literature there is centers around traumatic circumcision in childhood, not ritual circumcision shortly after birth. The latter is, of course, early in the preverbal part of life, before the age at which psychoanalytic treatment becomes possible and before convincing, direct clinical inference or plausible reconstruction can be made. Glover (1929) describes a traumatic recollection, an injury to the hand, which serves as a screen memory warding off even more disturbing recollections of traumatic circumcision in the childhood of one of his patients. Nunberg's (1947) classic paper on the meaning of circumcision points to the significance of the foreskin both as part of the penis and as something into which the penis is inserted, hence, bisexual in its intrapsychic significance. Interesting though this material may be, it is unclear that associations to the surgical procedure in Nunberg's patient reflect more than an understandably acute activation of preexisting castration anxiety and bisexual conflict. The same considerations apply to Bird's (1958) elegantly reported study on the significance of circumcision on a latency age boy in psychoanalytic treatment. These papers point to the limitations of the conclusions drawn from the strictly clinical psychoanalytic setting in illuminating the significance of circumcision as a cultural ritual. Clinical material, however interesting, is of limited use for the psychoanalytic study of the significance of circumcision. When reported in case histories of persons in treatment, the circumcisions in question are in sharp psychoanalytic focus because they are highly traumatic and probably occur in the presence of pathologically severe castration anxiety. The clinical evidence from these reports, then, reflects an activation of castration anxiety and bisexual conflicts in individual patients and does not adequately examine the meanings of the ritual act.

Other psychoanalytic authors attempted to study ritual itself. Róheim (1939) focused on circumcision in the context of adolescent rituals of manhood in Australia. He suggests that the practice of infant circumcision marks the end of reparation for a previous phase of hostility. Malev (1966) suggested that, in the circumcision ritual, the father's ambivalence is played out with the grandfather and son in the circumcision ritual. Reik (1915) and Bettelheim (1954) emphasized the castration motif in circumcision rituals, but fail to do more than establish a linkage of the specific rituals to the castration complex. Schlossman (1966) speculates that circumcision may be seen as a punishment for the Israelites' return to the unbridled sexuality of orgiastic Canaanite rites. It is hardly surprising that both clinical and anthropological studies convincingly link circumcision to the castration complex. Neither method of approach seems, however, to provide an adequate psychoanalytic understanding of the mutilative act of circumcision that is both a ritual and a compromise formation. Like any ritual, circumcision has both manifest and latent meanings. Such manifest and latent dimensions reveal and conceal different elements of shared ambivalence that are enacted in the ritual. Ambivalence toward the male newcomer—together with fear of his power and potential sexual rivalry—are symbolized by the ritualized attention to the penis.

In this chapter, we approach circumcision psychoanalytically as both ritual and compromise formation. To complement clinical and ethnological perspectives, we suggest another perspective: the study of narrative sequences, in references to circumcision in the Hebrew Bible. By examining the context of narratives concerning circumcision, we approach narrative structure using a kind of associative method. The Biblical narrative points to the latent meaning of the act of circumcision; it illuminates the circumcision ritual as a compromise formation involving both expression and defense. We will consider the six major narrative sequences in the Hebrew Bible dealing with ritual circumcision: two from Genesis and one each from Exodus, Leviticus, Joshua, and I Samuel. Although our observations from these often startling ancient texts concern a very limited aspect of the whole scope of ritual circumcision, their implications are, we feel, important for any psychoanalytic understanding of circumcision.

## THE NARRATIVES

### The Covenant (Gen. 17)

Abram, uprooted from Mesopotamia, is a foreigner in the land of Canaan. He has no progeny (Gen. 15). He feels uprooted and weak before hostile forces and wants offspring for power and continuity. The lack of fertility creates intrafamilial conflict (Gen. 16). Sarai, who is barren, gives the octogenarian Abram her servant Hagar so that he may have children. Hagar conceives and then despises her childless mistress. Sarai drives Hagar out of the household; she returns only after an admonition from an angel. Ishmael is born when his father is 86 years

old. Within the family, fertility brings not only power but also faction-
alism, conflict and clan fragmentation. Abram, renamed Abraham,
receives the covenant at the age of 99:

> (9.) And God said unto Abraham; "And as for thee, thou shalt keep
> My covenant, thou and thy seed after thee throughout their
> generations. (10.) This is My covenant, which ye shall keep,
> between Me and you and thy seed after thee; every male among you
> shall be circumcised. (11.) And ye shall be circumcised in the flesh
> of your foreskin; and it shall be a token of a covenant betwixt Me
> and you. (12.) And he that is eight days old shall be circumcised
> among you, every male throughout your generations, he that is
> born in the house, or bought with money of any foreigner, that is
> not of thy seed. (13.) He that is born in thy house, and he that is
> bought with thy money, must needs be circumcised; and My
> covenant shall be in your flesh for an everlasting covenant. (14.)
> And the circumcised male who is not circumcised in the flesh of his
> foreskin, that soul shall be cut off from his people; he both broken
> my covenant" [Gen. 17:9–14].

The establishment of the covenant is followed (Gen. 18) by a visit from
three angels, who tell Abraham that Sarai (renamed Sarah) will have a
child. Sarah laughs. The narrative theme then switches abruptly (Gen.
19) from fertility and continuity to variations on licentiousness and
sexual iniquity. The angels go to Sodom. With God's help, Abraham
intervenes in an attempt to save any righteous inhabitants of the city.
When not enough righteous men can be found, the city is doomed. Lot,
Abraham's nephew, is visited in Sodom by two angels. During this visit,
men of Sodom demand the two angels for sexual purposes. Lot,
however, offers his daughters instead. God smites the Sodomites with
blindness. Although angels warn Lot of the impending destruction of the
city, his sons-in-law refuse to accompany him in his flight. He therefore
flees with only his wife, who is turned into a pillar of salt because she
disobeys instructions and looks back on the destroyed city. Escaping to
the mountains, Lot is given drink by his daughters, both of whom have
intercourse with him and become pregnant. From these incestuous acts
issue the Moabites and Amorites, respectively.

Uprooted again, Abraham (Gen. 20) fears Abimelech, the local king,
and says that Sarah is his sister, not his wife. (This is partially true
because Sarah was a close relative before marriage, but it reflects an
aspect of castration anxiety—Abraham, out of fear of sexual competi-

tion, disowns his role as her sexual partner.) God intervenes through a dream in which Abimelech is told that Abraham is a prophet and Sarah his wife. Fertility, suspended in Abimelech's domain while the king was pursuing Sarah, is restored to Abimelech's people when the king returns Sarah to Abraham. This scenario, of the vulnerable and uprooted Abraham, is followed immediately (Gen. 21) by the birth and circumcision of Isaac and the subsequent interfamilial strife that results in the expulsion of Hagar and her son, Ishmael. Abraham makes a treaty with Abimelech, who leaves the area.

Chapter 22 concerns the test of faith in which Abraham is ordered to sacrifice Isaac. Manifestly pious and faithful in his obedience to God, Abraham in action in the test of faith enacts (without acknowledging the wish) the filicidal aspects of the ambivalence toward the son and successor. This conflict ritually represented, the text moves on to the death of Sarah and the end of Abraham's uprootedness when he purchases a burial ground, the cave of Machpelah, near Hebron. He becomes legitimized as a land owner with progeny and power.

The text surrounding the covenant of circumcision, then, deals with a great variety of struggles in which the newborn male is central: fertility and continuity; power or weakness of the clan in relation to outsiders; power and value of the women as childbearers; the prospect of licentiousness, incest and sexual iniquity; fear of sexuality in the presence of rivalrous males and outsiders; lines of succession; filicide; and the end of the period of uprootedness through the purchase of land and the birth of progeny.

### The Rape of Dinah (Gen. 34)

Jacob, in the land of Horan, (Syria) is called by God to return to Canaan (Gen. 31). He is pursued by his father-in-law, Laban, who subsequently gives him leave to return to the land of his birth. Jacob, preparing to face his brother, Esau, whom he treated deceitfully, divides his family into two groups, lest Esau try to destroy them. Alone at the river Jabbock, Jacob meets an angel and wrestles all night with him. Jacob is injured but blessed by the angel and renamed Israel. The meeting (Gen. 33) with Esau is friendly. The hostilities that Jacob feared do not ensue, and the clans of the two brothers rejoice together. Esau goes to Seir, leaving his repatriated brother and his family alone in Canaan. Jacob (Israel) goes to Succoth, then to the city of Shechem, where he buys land and erects a pillar.

Shechem, son of Hamor the Hivite, ruler of the city of Shechem, rapes Dinah, Jacob's daughter (Gen. 34). Shechem is in love with Dinah and asks his father to get Dinah for him in marriage. Hamor pleads his son's case. Jacob's sons say, guilefully, (Gen. 34:14–31) that all of the inhabitants of Shechem must be circumcised for intermarriage to be permissible.

> (13.) And the sons of Jacob answered Shechem and Hamor his father with guile, and spoke because he had defiled Dinah their sister, (14.) and said unto them: "We cannot do this thing, to give our sister to one that is uncircumcised," for that were a reproach unto us. (15.) Only on this condition will we consent unto you: if ye will be as we are, that every male of you be circumcised; (16.) Then will we give you our daughters unto you, and we will take your daughters to us, and we will dwell with you, and we will become one people. (17.) But if ye will not heathen unto us, to be circumcised; then will we take our one daughter, and we will be gone." (18.) And their words pleased Hamor and Shechem Hamor's son [Gen. 34:14–18].

All the men in the town of Shechem are circumcised:

> (24.) And unto Hamor and unto Shechem his son harkened all that went out of the gate to his city; and every male was circumcised, all that went out of the gate of his city. (25.) And it came to pass on the third day, when they were in pain, that two of the sons of Jacob, Simeon and Levi, Dinah's brethren, took each man his sword, and came upon the city unawares, and slew all the males. (26.) And they slew Hamor and Shechem his son with the edge of the sword, and took Dinah out of Shechem's house, and went forth. (27.) The sons of Jacob came upon the slain, and spoiled the city, because they had defiled their sisters [Gen. 34:24–27].

Jacob reproaches them. God calls Jacob to Bethel (Gen. 35). He leaves foreign gods and jewelry buried in Shechem. His nomadic existence continues until after his wife Rachel dies giving birth to Benjamin.

In this disturbing narrative sequence, circumcision, which within the clan is the badge of inclusion for sexual acceptability, does not promote the inclusion of the outsiders in the clan of the uprooted Jacob. The ritual fails to resolve the issues of sexual transgression (rape) and foreignness. Jacob's demand that the men of Shechem undergo circumcision sets the stage for guile, murder, and plunder, not intermarriage and stable relationships outside of the clan. Although the clans of Jacob and Esau overcame their previous hostilities, the Israelites and the Shechemites could not do so after Shechem's rape of Dinah. The circumcision ritual, although it mitigates the ambivalence about the power and sexuality of a young male within the clan, does not resolve the tensions between the two unrelated clans.

## The Threat of Filicide, Authority and the Call to Leadership (Exodus 4)

The Book of Exodus begins after a sojourn of 400 years in Egypt. The Israelites have multiplied so much that the current Pharoah fears their power and orders the death of all newborn Hebrew males (Exod. 1). The filicidal theme with murderous intent is displaced outside of the Israelite group onto the Egyptian overlords.

The birth lineage and royal upbringing of Moses are then described (Exod. 2). Moses slays an Egyptian, who is beating a Hebrew. His authority is challenged later when he tries to mediate a quarrel between Hebrews. Fearing punishment for the murder, Moses flees to the land of Midian. There, he rescues the daughters of Reuel (Jethro) from oppression and is given Zipporah, Jethro's daughter, in marriage. Soon thereafter, Zipporah gives birth to Gershom, Moses' firstborn son. In the meantime, in Egypt, Pharoah dies and God remembers his covenant with the patriarchs when he sees how the burdened Israelites suffer in bondage.

Moses, tending his father-in-law's flocks, beholds a burning bush that is not consumed in the flames. This begins the call to leadership to which Moses responds with great reluctance, for he wonders whether the Israelites can accept his authority to lead them out of Egypt. Doubting that Pharoah will accept his authority (Exod. 4), Moses is given two signs: his staff will turn into a serpent, then back into a staff, and his hand will become leprous as he puts it into his bosom, and later returned to normal when he puts it into his bosom again. Furthermore, water from the river will become blood. Moses balks again and protests that he has difficulty speaking. God is angry. Moses is told that his brother, Aaron, is to be his mouthpiece. Moses takes his leave of Jethro. God says that he will harden Pharoah's heart. Israel, God's "firstborn" must be freed, or God will slay the Egyptian's firstborn. Themes of power, authority, fear of the younger males, and filicide dominate the chapters in Exodus that precede the deliverance.

Near the end of the account of Moses' struggle over accepting his call to leadership comes the astonishing passage dealing with circumcision.

> (21.) And the Lord said unto Moses: "When thou goest back into Egypt, see that thou do before Pharaoh all the wonders which I have put in thy hand; but I will harden his heart, and he will not let the people go. (22.) And thou shall say to Pharaoh: Thus saith the Lord: Israel is My son, My first-born. (23.) And I have said unto thee: Let My son go, that he may serve Me; and thou hast refused to let him go. Behold, I will slay thy son, thy first-born." (24.) And it came to pass on the way at the lodging-place, that the Lord met him, and sought to kill him. (25.) Then Zipporah took a flint, and cut off the foreskin of her son, and cast it at his feet; and she said, "Surely, a bridegroom of blood art thou to me." (26.) So He let him alone. Then she said: "A bridegroom of blood in regard of the circumcision" [Exod. 4:21–26].

However enigmatic the narrative, several themes are clear: Moses' reluctance to accept God's call, God's "filicidal" attack on Moses, stopped by Zipporah's circumcision of her son, and the resolution of Moses' ambivalence toward leadership. Aaron is sent to meet Moses. The brothers confer with the elders of Israel, who accept their authority.

The ensuing chapters concern the dealings of the united Israelites, led by Moses and Aaron, with the oppressive Pharoah. At first (Exod. 5) they ask to leave for a three-day feast. Pharoah retaliates by increasing the Israelites' burden. They are to receive no straw to help them make bricks. The people question Moses; Moses questions God.

Circumcision is referred to later in the book of Exodus, this time metaphorically, when Moses is again sent forth to deal with Pharoah. He says: (Exod. 6:12): "Behold the children of Israel have not harkened unto me. How shall Pharoah hear me, who am of uncircumcised lips?" Here, as with many other metaphoric usages of circumcision in the Hebrew Bible (see also Lev. 26:41) circumcision connotes that which is accepted, authoritative, entitled, or holy. Pharoah's refusal to allow for the feast escalates the struggle between the masters and slaves, a struggle that culminates, not merely in freedom of worship, but in total separation — the Exodus. Chapters 7 to 10 detail the signs and the first nine plagues shown to Pharoah to attain deliverance. Chapter 11 recounts the death of the firstborn and Chapter 12, with the Passover itself, that is, the blood from the sacrifice that protects Israelite households from the filicidal plague (compare the bloody sacrificial circumcision that saves Moses in Exod. 4:24–26).

The narrative of the political and religious deliverance is highlighted by two bloody sacrifices somehow granting entitlements to sons and warding off filicide. The first is circumcision, the second the Passover itself. In both, the "children" are saved from murderous parents. In the entire narrative, filicide is referred to frequently, but each time the filicidal threat is *displaced* outside of the clan: fathers do not kill their own sons. Pharoah, feeling the Israelites' strength, kills *their* firstborn males. God's firstborn (Israel) is threatened. God will retaliate by striking the *Egyptian's* firstborn. Threatened by God, Moses is spared because of the bloody circumcision of *his* firstborn (Gershom); and finally, all the Egyptian firstborn are slain by God's angel in the last plague except those exempted by virtue of the bloody sign—the lamb's blood smeared on the door of Israelite households. What all of the themes have in common is the unacknowledged (displaced) filicidal wishes of the fathers and the compromise formation—the bloody sacrificial resolution—that represents both the expression of, and defense against, the filicidal tendencies that threaten the tribe. The opening lines of Exodus remind us that continuity and power depend upon the increase of progeny. The Exodus (separation) itself can take place only when the intraclan and familial ambivalences are reduced by the two bloody sacrificial compromise rituals that (in like fashion to neurotic symptoms) express an impulse, deflect it from its original devastating path, and portray it as a harmless symbolization of a destructive impulse.

### Cleanliness and Ritual Circumcision (Leviticus 12)

Guilt and sin are offerings of the book of Leviticus *after* the Exodus, after the giving of the Ten Commandments and before the portions on mercy and holiness and the injunction to "love thy neighbor as thyself." (Lev. 19:18). Sin and guilt offerings are described in detail, but transgressions for which these acts are expiations are not spelled out. It is clear that ritual offerings must be performed in exact detail. Two sons of Aaron are killed by God for incorrectly performing an incense offering (Lev. 10)—another resonance of the filicidal theme. Moses himself was angry about the manner in which sin offerings were performed. The narrative notes that, after Aaron's sons are slain, offerings are performed correctly. The separation of clean from unclean is carried further when the dietary laws are put forward (Lev. 11).

The following chapter (Lev. 12) details periods of uncleanliness after childbirth. After delivering a male child, the mother is unclean seven days. Circumcision is performed on the eighth day (see also Gen. 17).

> (12.) And the Lord spoke unto Moses, saying: "(2) Speak unto the children of Israel, saying: If a woman be delivered and bear a man child, then she shall be unclean seven days; as in the days of impurity of her sickness shall she be unclean. (3) And the eighth day the flesh of his foreskin shall be circumcised. (4.) And she shall continue in the blood of purification three and thirty days; she shall touch no hallowed thing, nor come into the sanctuary, until the days of her purification by fulfilled. (Lev. 12:1–4)

For a female child, there are two weeks of uncleanliness and 66 more days blood of purification, a total of 80 days. The narrative continues with laws regarding lepers (Lev. 13 and 14).

The circumcision ceremony, then, follows an allusion to displaced filicide in the context of ritual carefully devoted to separating acceptable from unacceptable. Here in the narrative, circumcision is clearly in the context of injunctions that separate the acceptable, clean, healthy, obedient, and holy from the unacceptable, unclean, diseased, or forbidden.

### Preparation for the Conquest (Joshua 5)

Joshua and the book bearing his name and recording the conquest of Canaan are alike in their one dimensionality. Unlike the wily Jacob, the narcissistic Joseph, and the sometimes timid and abashed Moses, Joshua is not shown as a man with flaws and inner imperfections and struggling for a more complete moral perfection. His personality, his mission, and his accomplishments are entirely externally directed, without significant inner conflict and without ambivalence. The absence of inner turmoil and strife means that Joshua can transmit unity to the group—those of the Israelites who survived forty years' wandering in the desert and who crossed the river Jordan. In the narrative dealing with the conquest and partition of Canaan, this transmission is exemplified by two episodes.

The first unifying act, occurring right after the Israelite host has crossed the River Jordan, confirms the impending prospect of war with the Amorite and Canaanite occupants of the land. Joshua orders circumcision by flint knives (Josh. 5:2–9), because circumcision was apparently not done on newborns in the desert during the 40 years during which the older generation, already circumcised in Egypt, died out.

> (2.) At this time the Lord said unto Joshua: "Make thee knives of flint, and circumcise again the children of Israel the second time." (3.) And Joshua made him knives of flint and circumcised the children of Israel at Gibeath-ha-araloth (That is, the hill of the foreskins). (4.) And this is the cause why Joshua did circumcise: all the people that came forth out of Egypt, that were males, even all the men of war, died in the wilderness by the way, after they came forth out of Egypt. (5.) For all the people that came out were circumcised; but all the people that were born in the wilderness by the way as they came forth out of Egypt, had not been circumcised. (6.) For the children of Israel walked forty years in the wilderness, till all the nation, even the men of war that came forth out of Egypt, were consumed, because they harkened not unto the voice of the Lord; unto whom the Lord swore that he would not let them see the land which the Lord swore unto their fathers that he would gives us, a land flowing with milk and honey. (7.) And he raised up their children in their stead; then did Joshua circumcise; for they were uncircumcised because they had not been circumcised by the way (8) and it came to pass, when all the nation were circumcised, every one of them, that they abode in their places in the camp, till they were whole. (9.) And the Lord said unto Joshua: "This day have I rolled away the reproach of Egypt from off you" [Josh. 5:2–9].

This rededication of the covenant takes place in the face of uprootedness and impending war in the land of Canaan. It is at Gilgal, at the "hill of the foreskins," that Passover was observed, the manna ceased, and Joshua prepared for the conquest.

The second unifying act occurs after the sole Israelite defeat: at Ai. Assuming that the defeat must have resulted from a lack of holiness or lack of obedience to the law, Joshua made an inquiry of God. The curse was explained, and ultimately the transgressor, Han, confessed to burying plunder in his tent. He was stoned to death. The forces of Joshua went on to conquer Ai and possess the entire promised land.

Like the stoning of Han, the circumcision was an act conferring holiness, dedication, and specialness on the insiders (the Israelites) to prepare them for the war against the hostile outsiders, the occupants of the land of Canaan. Circumcision in this narrative sequence reaffirms holiness, purity of purpose and specialness within the clan in the specific context of war and uprootedness.

## David and Saul (1 Samuel 18)

The complex relationship of Saul to David provides the setting for the last major narrative reference to circumcision in the Hebrew Bible. David is introduced twice (this inconsistency undoubtedly reflects a blending together of two separate narratives) first as a harp player and singer who can soothe Saul's melancholic moods, and later as the young brother of two of Saul's soldiers, the youth who slays the giant Goliath. (1 Sam. 17)

David is, at first, beloved of Saul and his son Jonathan, with whom David makes a covenant (1 Sam. 18). Saul's envy of his young, newly appointed officer is kindled when the women, coming out to greet the troops, are heard singing, "Saul has slain his thousands. David his ten thousands." (1 Sam. 18:7) Melancholy and rage overtake Saul and he tries twice to kill David with a spear. Saul sees that the Lord has departed from him and is now with David. Both the northern tribes of Israel and the southern Judeans love David. Saul guilefully offers David first his eldest daughter, Merab, and, later, his younger daughter, Michal, in marriage, if he will fight the Philistines and produce 100 foreskins in payment for his bride:

> (20.) And Michal Saul's daughter loved David; and they told Saul, and the thing pleased him. (21.) And Saul said: "I will give him her, that she may be a snare to him, and that the hand of the Philistines may be against him." Wherefore Saul said to David: "Thou shalt this day be my son-in-law through one of the twain." (22.) And Saul commanded his servants: "Speak with David secretly, and say: Behold the King hath the delight in thee, and all his servants love thee, now therefore be the king's son-in-law." (23.) And Saul's servants spoke those words in the ears of David. And David said, "seemeth it to you a light thing to be the king's son-in-law, seeming that I am a poor man, and lightly esteemed?" (24.) And the servants of Saul told him saying: "On this manner spoke David." (25.) And Saul said: "Thus shall ye say to David: The king desireth not any dowry, but a hundred foreskins of the Philistines, to be avenged of the King's enemies." For Saul thought to make David fall by the hand of the Philistines. (26.) And when his servants told David these words, it pleased David well to be the King's son-in-law. And

the days were not expired. (27.) And David arose and went, he and his men, and slew of the Philistines two hundred men; and David brought their foreskins and they gave them in full number to the King, that he might be the King's son-in-law. And Saul gave him Michal his daughter to wife [I Sam. 18:20–27].

The narrative chronicling the older man's envy of the younger displays the destructive ambivalence toward the younger man. Saul has offered his daughter in marriage in an attempt to get rid of David. The dowry of Philistine foreskins underscores the death wish accompanying Saul's invitation into the family and promotion overtly offered to David. In this text, the *wish* is not displaced, but Saul's plans are so constructed that they conceal his murderous intent; the Philistines will commit the actual *act* of murder.

David, himself, represents a displacement figure to handle Saul's ambivalence toward his own son, Jonathan. In 1 Sam. 19 and 20, Jonathan's intercession for David fills Saul with such rage that Saul throws a spear at Jonathan in an attempt to kill him. Ambivalence toward the son and filicidal conflict reach their most profound representation in the depiction of the volatile king beset by wars with the Philistines throughout his reign, and his envious attacks upon David and Jonathan. The covenant of circumcision, which ritually binds internal strife and ambivalence, undergoes a strange transformation that highlights the perversity of the internal discord: It is the circumcision of dead Philistine men, not live Hebrew babies, that becomes the vehicle of David's entrance (however tenuous) into the family of Saul.

## DISCUSSION

These reflections on the "associative" context of narratives dealing with circumcision in the Hebrew Bible differ from the psychoanalytic understanding gained either from the study of clinical material derived from traumatic circumcision procedures in childhood or from examination of the meaning of ceremonial rituals abstracted from their communal or interfamilial conflictual context. Indeed, ceremonial rituals presumably rose as compromise formations out of conflicts like those found in the Biblical narratives.

It is not our purpose to propound a detailed method of narrative analysis. Rather, we have attempted to place the Biblical texts dealing with circumcision in the context of narrative sequences so that themes surrounding these narratives can appear in a perspicacious light. As one would consider a clinical phenomenon in the light of its associative context, we are presuming that the context of narrative sequences reflects preconscious and unconscious preoccupations that illumine the manifold meanings of the material in question.

Perhaps the most striking overall features of these narratives, considered as a whole, are the number of allusions to murders of sons and the astonishing degree and extent of savageness, both sexual and aggressive. These features are, of course, more pronounced when the narrative sequences are abstracted and juxtaposed for comparison.

In the Biblical texts, scenes of uprootedness in the land, together with fear of warfare and attack mingle with scenes of interfamilial ambivalence toward the feared and needed newcomer and with a need for the circumcision ritual to demarcate the circumcised male as healthy, clean, sanctified, and acceptable and not diseased, unclean, uncouth and hostile. Ritual circumcision shares certain structures in common with neurotic symptoms. The ritual expresses as well as defends. It has a manifest and a latent content. In the *conscious experience of the adult,* the newborn male is welcomed, sanctified, made special, and accepted. What is kept latent, that is, out of immediate awareness, is the significance of the actual mutilative attack on the genitals; or, if the Biblical texts reflect general human conflicts, the filicidal wish itself. So the circumcision ritual may screen the castration wish or even the wish to murder the potentially powerful and rivalrous young male newcomer. Narratives dealing with the sacrifice of Isaac, the murder of the men of Shechem, and Saul's plan to have the Philistines slay David point to this quite clearly.

Group cohesiveness, that is, exclusivity as regards intermarriage and rites of succession, is enhanced by distinguishing the circumcised as opposed to the noncircumcised male. The circumcision ritual affirms the group fantasy, in which traits threatening the group's cohesion, for example, filicidal impulses from father or unbridled sexuality from son, can be split off, projected, and experienced as coming from the outside group.

These feared, projected traits include not only filicidal aggressivity and unbridled sexuality, but also uncleanliness, lack of civility, or lack of status (take careful note the Biblical and current connotation of the word "Philistine" or "Uncircumcised" in the symbolic sense noted in Exod. 6:12; Lev. 26, 41, and throughout the Hebrew Bible). This phallocentric ritual, which separates clean, holy, and acceptable from dirty, unacceptable and forbidden, has its mamocentric counterpart in the dietary laws (See Lev. 12:3).

Particularly strong in these disturbing passages from the Hebrew Bible is the relation of circumcision in the text preceding and following fear of impending sexual or aggressive chaos within the family or from other peoples of the same land. The original covenant follows Sarai's expulsion of the pregnant Hagar (a conflict over fertility, entitlement, and power) and precedes the attempted sodomy of the angels and Lot's incest with his daughters (uncontrolled sexuality, sexual iniquity, incest). Isaac's circumcision follows Abraham's denial to the neighboring people of Abimelech that Sarah is his wife (Abraham's castration anxiety). Isaac's circumcision, in turn, precedes the expulsion of Hagar and Ishmael and the sacrifice of Isaac (intrafamilial conflict over fertility, and succession of generations). Circumcision and slaughter of the men of Shechem follows the rape of Jacob's daughter, Dinah, after the recent migration to the region of Shechem. Circumcision in this text symbolizes the sexually available insider, as opposed to the hostile and unacceptable neighbor. The gory episode is a grim commentary on the limits of ritual as a symbolic compromise formation avoiding overt conflict. Zipporah's bloody circumcision of her son proceeds the confrontation with Pharoah leading to the Exodus (circumcision as the sacrifice appeasing filicide and granting authority and status). After the Israelites' crossing of the Jordan, the children of the desert, following Joshua's orders, are circumcised before warring with the occupants of Canaan and the conquest of the promised land. Circumcision reaffirms inner cohesion, purity, and specialness of the group faced with hostile outsiders. Split off aspects of intrafamilial conflicts — Saul's murderous wishes toward David/Jonathan in 1 Sam. 18 — are projected onto the Philistines in the narrative in which Saul sets of a price of 100 Philistine foreskins for Michal's hand in marriage. Philistine foreskins symbolize the ambivalence over power and sexuality within the Israelite camp. The young male (David/Jonathan) is needed by the father for the battle with the outsiders but feared and plotted against in a way that utilizes the ongoing war with the Philistines as an opportunity for displacement.

These themes, which emerged from the psychoanalytic scrutiny of text sequences in Biblical narrative, do not exhaust the meaning of circumcision that has been practiced in many lands and in many eras. Nonetheless, examination of the narratives in this manner does heighten our awareness, both of the specific texts themselves and of the conflictual issues that so clearly emerge from the narrative sequences seen as "associative material." Whereas many of these conflicts exemplify the castration complex, the theme of displacement of disowned filicidal impulses is at least as prominent. A study of associative detail found in the Biblical texts provides a valuable complement to anthropological and clinical perspectives on ritual circumcision and constitutes an important contribution to our understanding of its deepest meanings.

## SUMMARY

Circumcision of the newborn male is usually given a hygienic justification, which is inadequate for a psychoanalytic understanding of ritual attack on the penis. The authors supplement clinical and anthropological studies of ritual circumcision with a study of the six major passages concerning circumcision in the Hebrew Bible and the narrative sequences that provide the context of these texts. Considered together, the texts reveal an astonishing number of references to displaced filicidal wishes and to sexual and aggressive savagery. Analysis of Biblical texts in the context of narrative sequences provides a method akin to the associative method that supplements clinical and anthropological investigations.

## BIBLIOGRAPHY

APFEL, H. (1951), Ritual Circumcision. *Arch. Pediat.* 68:427–30.
BIRD, B. (1958), The bisexual meaning of the foreskin: *J. Amer. Psychoanal. Assn.,* 6:287–304.
BETTELHEIM, B. (1954), *Symbolic Wounds.* Glencoe, IL: Free Press.
GELLIS, S. (1978), Circumcision. *Amer. J. Dis. Child.,* 132:1168–1169.
GLOVER, E. (1929), The screening function of traumatic memories. *Internat. J. Psycho-Anal.,* 10:90–93.
MALEV, M. (1966), The Jewish Orthodox circumcision ceremony, *J. Amer. Psychoanal. Assn., 14:*516–517.
MORGAN, W. (1965), The rape of the Phallus. *J. Amer. Med. Assn, 193:*123–124.
NUNBERG, H. (1947), Problems of bisexuality as reflected in circumcision. *Imago,* 1949.
REIK, T. (1915), *Ritual Psychoanalytic Studies.* New York: International Universities Press, 1958.
RÓHEIM, G. (1939), The covenant of Abraham. *Internat. J. Psycho-Anal.,* 14:516–517.
SCHLOSSMAN, H. (1966), Circumcision as a defense. *Psychoanal. Quart.,* 5:340–356.

# 12

# Cultic Elements in Early Christianity: Rome, Corinth, and the Johannine Community

## W. W. MEISSNER

In previous essays, I discussed the cultic aspects of the origins of Christianity, particularly as they relate to and derive from extant Palestinian religious movements (Meissner, 1988), and the early manifestations of the cultic process in the evolution of the churches of Jerusalem and Antioch (Meissner, 1989). This analysis will follow further variations of the cultic process as it evolved in the emergence and forming of the Christian communities within the hellenistic culture of the first century Mediterranean basin and within the political structure of the Roman empire. Christian communities of the first centuries experienced periods of instability and unrest, marked by the ebb and flow of various ideological influences, which gradually evolved in the direction of a common orthodoxy and delimitation of the limits of heterodoxy. The pressures of persecution called for a degree of unification in the face of a common enemy, but internal factions and their divergent understandings of the nature and direction of the new church set the stage for the dynamic progression from a collection of contending cultic groups toward a organized, structured, unified, and universal church. I will argue that, even in the face of persecution from a common enemy, the cultic process created splits and divisions within the Christian community that threatened the very existence of the nascent church.

## ROME

When we turn to the early development of the church in Rome, the picture has many similarities to that found in Antioch (Meissner, 1989), but also some critical differences. In Brown's (Brown and Meier, 1983) reconstruction, he argued that the dominant form of Christianity at Rome in the early days (in the 40s and early 50s) was closer to the Jerusalem and Judaic model. Similar to the Antioch story, the church underwent progressive changes, moving through a phase reflected in Paul's epistle to the Romans (circa AD 58), through an intermediate period, covering most of the last third of the first century and evolving in the direction of the structures reflected in the letter of Clement, written from Rome to Corinth (circa 96 AD). Thus, Roman Christianity was transplanted originally from Jerusalem and reflected the Jewish–Gentile Christianity associated with the pillars of the Jerusalem church. Peter and James. They represented a group of Jewish Christians and Gentile converts who did not follow a hard Judaizing line of insisting on circumcision for all converts, but wanted to hold tightly to other traditional observances, particularly the dietary prescriptions.[1] James' followers had created a stir at Antioch over the issue of Jewish Christians eating with Gentiles and so not observing the dietary laws. The story of the development of Roman Christianity then is one of the gradual integration and reconciliation of the Christianity of Paul with a more developed Petrine tradition that allowed the two apostles to join forces in the establishing and consolidating of the Roman church.

There is good evidence to suggest that the ultraconservative Jewish Christians made life difficult for both Peter and Paul in the decades of the 40s and 50s, especially in Jerusalem. Peter's attitude toward maintaining the Jewish tradition was somewhat more moderate, although more conservative in tone than Paul's. If the majority position in Rome was primarily identified with Peter, it is not unlikely that a minority of more radically conservative Jewish Christians were also on the scene. Despite his attempts to hold to a moderate line in the epistle to the Romans, Paul repeats his opposition to any demand for circumcision among Gentile converts. The possibility exists that, insofar as the Jews were exempted from the persecution of Nero, the Jewish Christians and their circumcised Gentile converts may have represented themselves as Jews and tried to distinguish themselves from the Gentile Christians who had been converted without circumcision. One can guess that Peter's more moderate position may have been the predominant one, forcing Paul to moderate his earlier more radical repudiation of the Judaic traditions.

---

[1]This would represent Brown and Meier's moderately conservative group. See Brown and Meier (1983), or my previous discussion of these groupings, Meissner (1989).

At the same time, the direction of Roman thinking did not favor a radical rejection of the Jewish heritage. The issue surfaced again in the middle of the second century in the teaching of Marcion. Although Paul had taught a basic opposition between the law and the teaching of Christ, he still maintained that the law came from God. Marcion, however, took an extreme position, declaring that the law was the creation of a demigod, who was not the true God who sent us Christ as his emissary. Marcion's adoption of, and reliance on, Paul as the basis of his teaching did not save him from expulsion from the community of believers (circa AD 144). Thus, the Paul of Romans represents a much more moderate and conservative view regarding the relationship between Christianity and the Jewish heritage than the Paul of Galatians.

Certainly, Paul's more moderate attitude would have made it more possible for his teaching to be accepted by the Roman church, which had itself been founded by Jerusalem Jewish Christians of a somewhat more conservative stance. The presence of elements of Paul's theology in the first epistle of Peter becomes understandable, if in fact the Roman church had accepted some of the main lines of Paul's thinking, at the same time maintaining its primary adherence to Peter. The Pauline derivatives are primarily from the epistle to the Romans and reflect Paul's more moderate position.

External events must have played their part; the fall of Jerusalem and the destruction of the temple must have had a profound affect on Roman Jews, who had witnessed Titus' triumph and the parading of the sacred liturgical vessels from the temple. The Judaean campaign was something of an embarrassment to Rome, the Roman military juggernaut forced to go to extreme lengths to "swat a fly." Propaganda made up the difference, however, so that for many years afterward coins were struck celebrating the defeat of the Jews—a continuing daily reminder to the Roman Jews of their humiliation. The great arch of Titus portraying the destruction and sacking of the temple was completed in AD 80. In addition, a special "tax" for the support of the Roman temple of Jupiter Capitolinus was imposed.

By the end of the first century, the forces of moderation and consolidation reached a new level reflected dramatically in the first letter of Clement to the Corinthians. Viewed against its historical background, it may well have been the difficulties in the Corinthian church that prompted this consolidation in the Roman church. By the time of its writing, Roman Christians had already felt the sting of persecution and even execution in the time of Nero and Domitian. Christianity was regarded as a "foreign superstition." The issue of survival in the face of social disintegration was acute and prominent in the minds of the Roman community. The greatest danger for Clement was internal disorder, the jealous opposition of Christians against fellow Christians. Clement's remedy was an appeal to order based on the twofold themes of a strong Jewish heritage and a respect for imperial authority.

Clement argues in support of the ecclesiastical structure that had already developed in many of the major churches by the end of the first century—the tripartite structure we have already identified in the church of Antioch (Meissner, 1989). Clement's claim of divine approval for this hierarchical structure carries with it a demand for solid allegiance with the bishops and presbyters, a call for unity, and for a closing of ranks in the face of a looming persecution that would last for 200 years.

But the implications of this argument reach far beyond the Jewish heritage. Clement's admiration of Roman military discipline made him realize that the fortunes of Christianity were limited unless Christians could learn to take advantage of the strengths of its adversary. Christianity was not destined to be just another oriental mystery religion; it was destined to establish itself as a society with exclusive claims that were basically antithetical to those of the absolute state. Earlier Christian works (Romans 13:1-7; 1 Peter 2:13-17) demanded obedience to Roman authority, but Clement tried to establish the same argument and the claim of a similar obedience for church authorities. The future of Christianity depended on the success of the structure and integration of its communities and its ability to retain converts. Its organization and structure prove superior to the empire and would provide better motivation for its members. Clement's letter thus offers a formula not only for overcoming persecution, but for defeating the persecutor.

Commenting on this view, Harrington (1982) summarizes the argument as follows:

> . . . orthodoxy or ecclesiastical Christianity represented the type supported by the majority of Christians in Rome at the end of the first century and the beginning of the second century. The Roman church then gradually extended the boundaries of its influence to Corinth (see 1 Clement), Antioch, and other places. . . . Orthodox and heretical groups used similar tactics; e.g., repeating false rumors, not recognizing false believers as fellow believers, not admitting anything good about opponents, emphasizing their weaknesses and inadequacies, and supporting or even falsifying their views. But in the course of the early Christian centuries the so-called heretical groups remained divided and even fought among

themselves. They were finally routed, one after another, by so-called orthodox Christians [p. 163].

Thus, even in the face of external persecution, the divisive influence of the cultic process had its identifiable effects that had to be countered in order that the internal unity of the church be established and preserved. The tendency to unite in the face of a common enemy was not sufficient.

Brown (Brown and Meier, 1983) argued that Clement's letter was in fact continuing a trajectory that had its proper antecedents in earlier Christian attitudes toward the conversion of Rome. The Acts of the Apostles dramatically begins the story of the church in Jerusalem, but closes its account with the establishment of the church in Rome. Even in Acts, the Christian destiny was cast with Rome and the Gentile world it represented. The church's hopes were centered on Rome, rather than Athens, the great museum of classical antiquity, or Alexandria, the repository of classical learning. These early Christians understood that the power to change the world lay not in the museum or in the library, but in the capitol of political power, the center of the Roman empire. As Brown commented, "If there was a Christian 'drive toward Rome,' in part it was because centered in that city was the machinery that ruled the known world and through which that world could be claimed for Christ" (p. 181).

The pattern of contending forces, divergent interests, and splits that took place between various segments of the primitive Christian church, particularly among Jewish Christians and their Gentile converts, reflects a pattern of gradual withdrawal and separation of the nascent Christian community from its dependence on, and ties to, the Jerusalem church. At Antioch, the beginnings of the Christian movement there saw face-to-face confrontations between Paul and the Hellenists on the one side, and Peter and the followers of James on the other (Meissner, 1989). The strains posed by the issue of the relationship between the gospel and its Jewish heritage continued, so that even after the destruction of Jerusalem, the splits between the more conservative and liberal groups would have continued to exercise a powerful influence, despite the increasing majority of Gentile Christian converts. In this context, Matthew attempted to mold this *mixtum gatherum* into a consistent Christian identity. His view mediated between the more liberal outlook of Paul and the more conservative exclusionary attitude of the James faction. Peter was caught in the middle, pressured from the one side by the followers of James, but also realizing the implications of Paul's mission and the importance of extending the gospel message to the rest of the non-Jewish world.

It was presumably to overcome these persistent tensions and divisions, and probably in response to the external forces of Jewish persecution that the Antioch community evolved a more firm, authoritative structure under the headship of a single teacher–bishop. Ignatius of Antioch propounded this structural solution as a response to the divisive forces within the Christian community. The more liberal factions were more open to hellenizing influences, including gnostic influences toward a "high" christology (a view of Christ emphasizing his divine origin) that in its extreme form tended to evacuate the humanity of Christ (docetism). The conservative Judaizers maintained a powerful influence, even though their numbers were diminishing. In the time of Ignatius, things had not yet come to a point of schism, but Ignatius seems to have found it necessary to find a mediating middle ground for the sake of preserving the integrity of the Christian community.

The situation was roughly similar in Rome where the dominant influence from the beginning was exercised by Judaizers, espousing the views of James and, to a certain extent, Peter. Thus, the early Roman converts would have been more attached to the Jewish heritage than Gentile converts converted elsewhere by Paul. Paul's approach to Rome in the late 50s, when he was making a collection on behalf of the Jerusalem church, was considerably more moderate toward the Judaic question than earlier. Although this may have gained him greater acceptance in Rome, his martyrdom may have resulted from a reaction on the part of extremely conservative Jewish Christian zealots. In any case, this more moderate Paul took his place along with Peter as one of the pillars of the Roman church.

After the destruction of Jerusalem, the Roman church assumed the rights of preeminence that belonged to the older Jerusalem church and became the leader, guide, and teacher of the other churches. By the end of the first century, Clement had already wedded the levitical heritage to the Roman heritage in an insistence on the authority of the bishop and the necessity of obedience to his prerogatives based on the model of Roman imperial order and authority. Thus, the organizational and structuralizing tendencies that arose in the context of the Antioch controversies found their logical extension in the evolution of a Roman hierarchy and the notion of apostolic succession.

## CORINTH

In Corinth, the divisive social forces that emerged as aspects of the cultic process centered around issues of social stratification. Social stratifica-

tion and the conflicts and tensions associated with it played themselves
out in particular fashion in the Corinthian church. The social composition of the Corinthian community included a strong, socially dominant
group of Christians drawn from higher social levels. Although the
majority of the church members may have come from lower and
middle-class strata, they stand in marked contrast to the more influential
members, probably fewer in number, who were drawn from higher social
strata. Paul himself described some aspects of the social structure as
follows:

> Take yourselves for instance, brothers, at the time when you were
> called: how many of you were wise in the ordinary sense of the
> word, how many were influential people, or came from noble
> families? No, it was to shame the wise that God chose what is
> foolish by human reckoning, and to shame what is strong that he
> chose what is weak by human reckoning; those whom the world
> thinks common and contemptible are the ones that God has
> chosen—those who are nothing at all to show up those who are
> everything. The human race has nothing to boast about to God,
> . . . [I Corinthians 1:26–29].

Theissen takes the references to the wise, influential, and noble as
referring to a social stratification that contrasts this level of social status
with those who are lower born, despised, or dispossessed. If there were
not many in the Corinthian church who could be regarded as wise,
influential, and nobly born, then certainly there were some. Their
influence must be counted as significant, insofar as Paul seems to feel it
necessary to devote the better part of his letter to dealing with their
supposed "wisdom." Paul even draws a rather strong contrast with his
own circumstances, for example, the fact that he earns his bread by the
work of his hands, experiences hunger, has no permanent home, and is
persecuted, whereas those who are powerful and honored occupy the
opposite end of the social scale. If the upper class members of the church
constituted a minority, it seems likely that they must have formed an at
least prominent and probably influential minority. Certainly the majority of the Corinthians who are known to us by name seem to have
enjoyed such elevated social status and probably represent the more
active and important portion of the Corinthian church.

The stratified composition of the Corinthian community probably
reflects a more advanced stage in the development of primitive Christianity. The oldest forms of church structure were found in Palestine,

where the movement originated. The transition from the more rural and agrarian world of Palestine to the more highly urbanized and hellenistic world of the Mediterranean basin was accompanied by a social shift, in which the influence of Christianity penetrated more deeply into higher social strata. Paul's collections for the poor in Jerusalem were based on support gathered from these more influential and well-to-do classes. As Theissen (1982) commented:

> The history of primitive Christianity was thus shaped even in the first generation by a radical social shift which altered important socio-cultural, socio-ecological, and socio-economic factors through the processes of Hellenization, urbanization, and the penetration of society's higher strata. If this is taken into account it can hardly be deemed an accident that the Hellenistic congregations only hesitantly accepted Palestinian traditions, which came from an entirely different social world. As is generally acknowledged, Paul knows only a few of the sayings of the Lord. And even if he had known more, the ethical radicalism of the Jesus tradition, with its ethos of surrendering family, property, and home, would have found little room to survive in the congregations founded by him [p. 107].

The divisive implications of such social stratification focused around the issue of eating meat. Meat was relatively rare in the diet of the lower classes, since they depended in large part on the public meat distributions on certain official ceremonial occasions. In addition, meat was included in pagan religious celebrations, so that not only would such celebrations have provided the context in which the lower classes might have had contact with meat, but also established a close connection between eating meat and the religious worshipping of idols. In contrast, the upper classes would have had much greater access to meat supplies and would have been much more accustomed to consuming it (Theissen, 1982).

These social differences were introduced into the Christian community by the conversion of upper class Gentiles, creating difficulties both for Jewish Christians and lower class Gentile Christians. The resulting conflicts created inevitable tensions within the Christian community. Former pagans would have difficulty in seeing meat independently of its ritual setting, but they would not have wanted to lose out on the meat offered in the pagan feasts. If they did eat meat, it would have been with a guilty conscience. Converted Jews, who had been liberated from mosaic dietary restrictions, would have been tempted to eat the public meats as well, but would have found difficulty in abandoning old taboos. None of these inhibitions would have had much effect on higher class converts.

In contrast, higher class Christians would have enjoyed a greater degree of integration into the surrounding pagan society. One of the characteristics of these church members from higher social strata was the place of *gnosis* in their approach to religion. It was their special knowledge or understanding that allowed them to transcend the obsolete religious restrictions that seem to have been matters of conflicted conscience for the less privileged. As Theissen (1982) suggested, the only comparable position regarding the eating of meat sacrificed to idols among the Christians arose from more explicitly gnostic groups of a later date. The eating of meat sacrificed to idols was certainly not a common characteristic of the gnostic movement, but it was one typical behavior among others. The prohibition against eating such consecrated meat was more uniform in orthodox Christianity.

The connections between such Corinthian "gnosis" and later Christian gnosticism are both controversial and scarcely direct. But the analogies persist. In both instances, we can see a reshaping of the Christian faith in connection with the inclusion of higher social classes. Along with higher levels of social stratification comes certain other characteristics, including a higher intellectual level, an emphasis on knowledge, a form of elite self-consciousness, and a greater openness to interchange with the surrounding social environment. The gnostic system of thought emphasized special knowledge and a high degree of intellectual capacity. The gnostic impulse, with its emphasis on knowledge and the power of understanding as vehicles of salvation, is also an upper class characteristic. Salvation takes place in these terms less through the power of a deity than through the inner possession of understanding. The failure of the educated classes to shape the world in political terms is usually compensated for by a more radical turning to ideas. Salvation is gained through true understanding and true knowledge.

The Corinthian gnostics believed that idols do not really exist — a form of demythologization. Such knowledge is liberating and tends to be associated with a somewhat superior attitude that looks down on and devalues those who do not possess it. Gnostic writings tend to reflect an acutely elitist consciousness that drives a wedge of separation between those who possess true knowledge and understanding as opposed to those who believe only by faith. Normal Christians, in this perspective, are second-class citizens. This reflects the degree of internal stratification in hellenized Christian communities, as for example Rome and Corinth, where upper class Christians self-consciously set themselves apart from the everyday Christian community. The distinction between the "strong" and the "weak" at Corinth, or references to the spiritualists and the worldly seem also to be based on the possession of special wisdom.

In addition, the gnostics tended to be much more open to and involved in the cultural ethos of pagan antiquity. Much of the complaint against the gnostics on the part of church fathers was really only common behavior for that period. The gnostics tended to take part in the delights of the day, banquets and theatrical performances, engaged in the social life of the city, and tended to be no more strict about sexual morality than the rest of the community. Nor were they enthusiastic about martyrdom. This liberality obviously also included a lack of scruples about eating meat offered to idols.

Thus, the Christian gnosticism of the second century was in large degree a theology of the upper classes. The same characteristics found in later gnosticism also played a role in the Corinthian community. As Theissen (1982) commented:

In the case of the Corinthian gnostics we also find a certain level of education, the significance of knowledge and wisdom for ethics and salvation, and an elitist self-consciousness within the community which goes hand in hand with a considerable liberalism about associating with the pagan world. In both instances these characteristics taken together point to an elevated social status [p.136].

The split and the tension of powerful ideologies within the Corinthian community seemed inevitable. On the one hand, the more hellenistically inclined upper class Gentile converts were strongly influenced by the gnostic ideology and social attitudes. But at the same time, there persisted a powerful and pervasive influence of older traditions, derived from both pagan and Jewish sources, that played a role in the more numerous, if less influential and prominent, members of the lower classes. The evolving life of the nascent church was caught between these powerful ideological forces representing the derivatives of an earlier, possibly obsolete, protest movement on the one hand, and the more sophisticated, enlightened, adaptive and upper-class influence stemming from the increasing surge of hellenistic converts.

In the middle of all this, Paul seems to have tried to weave a conciliatory course. He does not consistently support the position of the enlightened and the strong, even though he seems to have been in basic agreement with it. He tries to seek a reevaluation of the norms of social rank and dominance, including the aspects of higher knowledge and wisdom, in terms of the preaching of the cross. It is a plea for the higher classes to accommodate to the needs of the lower classes, and for the allowance for the acceptance and tolerance of more than one tradition. Although the privileges of status of the higher classes are preserved, for example, in allowing private meals with consecrated meat (1 Corinthians 10:23ff), emphasis is placed on the undesirable effects of scandalizing the weak by this practice. Paul's attempt at solution reflects what Theissen (1982) described as the "love-patriarchalism" of the Pauline letters. He writes:

This love-patriarchalism allows social inequities to continue but transfuses them with a spirit of concern, of respect, and of personal solicitude. Concern for the conscience of the other person, even when it is a "weak" conscience and obedient to norms now superseded, is certainly one of the congenial characteristics of this love-patriarchalism [pp. 139–140].

The social stratification of early hellenistic Christian congregations was characterized by a dominant and influential minority of those who were wise, powerful and noble, in marked contrast to the majority of church members who came from much more humble origins and enjoyed much lower social status. The problem was in balancing and integrating socially differentiated expectations and class-specific demands. It is probable in the Corinthian context that the well-to-do provided the means for the eucharistic feasts. In so doing, however, they may have followed a practice common to their social group of bringing special food that they partook of separately from the rest of the congregation— a kind of private meal eaten at a separate table from the others. Theissen (1982) summarized the situation in these terms:

It is worth summarizing once again our reconstruction of the behavior of those Christians who consume their "own meal" in the congregational gathering. Some wealthier Christians have made the meal itself possible through their generosity, providing bread and wine for all. What was distributed is declared by means of the words of institution to be the Lord's and given to the congregation. Thus, in conjunction with this common meal there could have taken place a private meal because the starting point of the Lord's Supper was not regulated, and up to this starting point (that is, until the words of institution) what had been brought and provided was private property. More importantly, this distinction was possible because the wealthier Christians ate other food in addition to the bread and wine, and the words of institution made no provision for sharing this with the fellowship [p. 160].

It is not difficult to see how such a practice would have sown the seeds of division and contention. The obvious danger was that the Lord's Supper, rather than being the point of unity and common sharing in the Body of Christ, ran the risk of becoming the basis for internal division, envy, and antagonism within the Body of Christ.

# THE JOHANNINE COMMUNITY

A special case in the evolution of church doctrine and structure is provided by the Johannine church. Questions have arisen regarding the connection of the Johannine community to the rest of the church organization. Certainly the Johannine community, centered around the figure and the teaching of the author of the fourth gospel, manifested certain definite sect characteristics, particularly the opposition to outsiders, whether they be the world, or the Jews, or even other Christians.

Brown (1979), following the lead of Scroggs (1975), takes the position that the entire early Christian movement was itself sectarian in character: It emerged out of an agrarian protest movement; it set itself in opposition, at least in its early stages, to establishment claims (the claims of family ties, of religious institutional affiliation, of wealth, and even of theological intellectuality); it claimed to be egalitarian; it offered special acceptance within the community; it was voluntary in character; it demanded total commitment from its members; and it taught a basically apocalyptic doctrine. Thus the Christian community, as it is revealed to us through the fourth gospel and the Johannine epistles, must be regarded as a sect, but at the same time as part of the larger sectarian movement of Christianity.

The sectarian or cultic quality of early Christianity, at least in its Jewish Palestinian form, set itself in opposition to other Jews who did not believe in Jesus. In Acts (24:5, 14) such nonbelieving Jews were regarded as forming a deviant group sect, a *hairesis,* the same term used to describe other Jewish sects. Despite these sect characteristics, the further question of the extent to which the Johannine community had actually broken communion with other Christians remains a matter of controversy (Brown, 1979).

The development of the Johannine community can be traced though a series of phases. The first phase represents the pregospel era and reflects the origins of the community and its close relations to mid-first-century Judaism. By the time the gospel was written, the antagonism between Johannine Christians and the synagogues had been exacerbated because of the teachings about Jesus. The expulsion of the Christians from the synagogues was a natural outcome of this continuing conflict. This first pregospel period probably covers several decades, extending from the mid-50s to the late 80s. The community at this juncture consisted primarily of Jews whose adherence to the cause of Christ was cast in terms of a relatively low christology (a view of Christ emphasizing his humanity rather than his divinity). The gradual emergence of a higher christology (emphasizing the divine origin of Christ) brought the Johannine faction into increasingly sharper conflict with the Jews, who would have regarded such a view as blasphemy.

The second phase would involve the situation in the Johannine community around the time of the writing of John's gospel, around AD 90. The period was one of continuing persecution and the persistence of deep antagonisms between the Johannine community and the Jews. These conflicts reinforced the Johannine insistence on a high christology, an emphasis that had further implications for the relationships between the Johannine faction and other Christian groups who did not share the Johannine christological ideology to the same extent.

The subsequent phase would reflect the situation at the time of the writing of the Johannine epistles, probably around the end of the century. Brown (1979) offered the hypothesis that this period was marked by a struggle within the Johannine community between two groups of disciples who interpreted the gospel in quite divergent ways. The reverberations from these splits in the community are decisive in the epistles.

The last phase was marked by the dissolution of the Johannine church after the writing of the epistles. The more radical secessionists broke off communion with the more conservative faction in the Johannine community, and probably drifted in the ensuing years of the second century into docetism, gnosticism, Cerinthianism,[2] and Montanism.[3] They car-

---

[2]Cerinthus was a gnostic heretic who taught that the world was created by a demiurge, not by the supreme God, and that Jesus was a mere mortal on whom the spirit of Christ descended at baptism. Thus, in the crucifixion, only Jesus suffered because the Christ could not suffer.

[3]Montanism was a gnostic, illuminist heresy, originating in the second century, based on the teachings of Montanus. He preached a spiritualist doctrine, calling his followers to a renewal of primitive simplicity to form a spiritual elite under the direct guidance of the Holy Spirit.

ried with them the teaching of the fourth gospel, which thus came to have a central place in influencing heterodox views. The followers of the author of I John seem to have gradually merged with the "church catholic" of Ignatius of Antioch somewhere in the early second century. This shift was marked by a gradually increasing acceptance of the higher Johannine christology, but at the price of the acceptance of the authoritative teaching structure of the church. As Brown (1979) commented:

> Much of this recognition shows a community whose evaluation of Jesus was honed by struggle, and whose elevated appreciation of Jesus' divinity led to antagonisms without and schism within. If the Johannine eagle soared above the earth, it did so with talons bared for the fight; and the last writings that were left us show the eaglets tearing at each other for the possession of the nest. There are moments of tranquil contemplation and inspiring penetration in the Johannine writings, but they also reflect a deep involvement in Christian history. Like Jesus, the word transmitted to the Johannine community lived in the flesh [p. 24].

The origins of the Johannine community were probably no different than the origins of the Christian movement in general, except that the followers of John were probably more likely to draw their converts from the Jews who came to Jesus with high messianic expectations and found in him the messiah of their hopes. Their claim was that "We have found the one Moses wrote about in the Law, the one about whom the prophets wrote" (John 1:45). Even so, the titles attributed to Christ in John are also familiar in the synoptic writings, Acts and Paul, suggesting that, to a certain degree, the attitudes toward Jesus in the Johannine community were not significantly different from those of other Christian groups.

Question had also been raised regarding the influence on the fourth gospel of the thought of the Essenes of Qumran (Meissner, 1988). There is in fact no convincing evidence that the Qumran influence on John was in any sense direct. If there was any influence at all, it had to be indirect, probably through the conversion into the Johannine community of Jewish Essenes who would have brought with them ideas that can be found in the Qumran literature, for example, the dualisms of light versus darkness, truth versus falsehood, the notion of an angelic Spirit of Truth who leads the sons of light against the sons of darkness, et cetera. These ideas would have been readily incorporated into the Johannine christology as reinforcing the divine origin of Christ. Possible links have also been suggested between the mission of John the Baptist and the Essenes, because John would have operated in the vicinity of the Qumran settlement and his preaching contained certain features in common with Qumran viewpoints. The Essene influence may have been carried into the Johannine community by the followers of John who joined the community.

The christological developments may also have been triggered by the conversion of a large group of Samaritans. This integration of the two groups and the acceptance of the new converts by the majority of the Johannine community would have elicited the suspicion and hostility of the synagogue leaders. The conversion of the Samaritans in John 4 marks a turning point, after which the gospel focuses increasingly on the rejection of Jesus by the Jews. Whether the newly converted group consisted entirely of Samaritans or not can be argued, but they probably included Jews of particular views antagonistic to the Jerusalem temple, who had incorporated some aspects of Samaritan teaching, including a christology that was not based exclusively on the notion of a davidic messiah (Brown, 1979).

The antagonism with the Jews and the expulsion from the synagogue probably drove the Johannine community increasingly toward the Gentile world, and resulted in an adaptation of Johannine thought so as to make it more intelligible and acceptable to this wider context. Thus there is a strain of universalism that enters the gospel, such that Christ's mission was divinely ordained to all men who would come to believe in him. But this attitude is qualified by a dualism that divides the human race into those who believe against those who do not believe, into the followers of darkness and the followers of the light, into those who are condemned and those who are saved. To this extent, then, the Johannine community increasingly defined itself in oppositional terms, establishing its claims to divine truth and salvation by way of opposition to other external groups. The various groups of opposing forces are detailed in the accompanying table (see Table I), together with their characteristics and the rationale of rejection. The spectrum of opposition and rejection underlines the inherent sense of specialness, privilege and elitism that permeated the Johannine community.

The increasing rejection by the Jews and by the world in general contributed to a major theme of Johannine thought. The theme is consistent: "To his own he came; yet his own people did not accept him" (John 1:11); "God so loved the world that He gave His only son . . . but men preferred darkness to the light" (John 3:16–19). The Johannine Christians also shared in this fate of rejection: "If the world hates you,

TABLE 2
The Johannine Outgroups

### Non-Christian

| I. The World | II. "The Jews" | III. Followers of John the Baptist |
|---|---|---|
| These preferred darkness to the light of Christ because they were evil. They are unbelievers, who are condemned by their choice and under the power of Satan. This reflects pagan persecution and antagonism against the cultic exclusivism of the JC. Hatred of Christ and his disciples who were not of this world. The Johannines were strangers in the world, alienated. "World" broader than but included "the Jews." | Jews of the synagogues who rejected Christ and decided to expel from the synagogue all who thought him to be the messiah: particularly the Jewish authorities. Points of dispute: (a) claims about the oneness of Christ with the Father, making himself God's equal; (b) claims that the worship of Christ replaces the Jewish feasts and temple worship. Persecuted and executed Johannine Christians. | Some of John's followers joined the community, some did not. Claimed that John > Jesus. Gospel insists that the Baptist decrease while Christ increased. John's adherents misunderstood rather than hated Christ; some hope for conversion. |

### Christian

| IV. Crypto-Christians | V. Jewish Christians | VI. Christians of Apostolic Churches |
|---|---|---|
| Christian Jews who remained in the synagogue, but could not admit their belief in Christ. Prefer the praise of men to the glory of God. Tried to maintain private faith in Christ with Jewish heritage. Choose Moses over Christ. Lumped with "the Jews," but way still open to confess faith publicly. | Converts who had left the synagogues but whose faith did not measure up to Johannine standards. May have represented followers of James at Jerusalem. Held low christology between IV and VI: Christ not divine, eucharist not Jesus' flesh and blood. For John, not true believers. | Mixed communities of Jews and Gentiles, separated from the synagogues, regarded themselves as followers of Peter and the Twelve. Moderately high christology: Christ was the messiah, born of davidic descent, the Son of God, but without a clear notion of the pre-existence of the Word. Saw Christ as founder and institutor of the sacraments, and the church as the legitimate of apostolic teaching and pastoral mission. For John they did not understand Christ's true nature or the teaching function of the Paraclete, but they were the only other Christian group to whom the JC could look for unity. |

bear in mind that it has hated me before you. If you belong to the world, the world would love its own; but the reason why the world hates you is that you do not belong to the world, for I chose you out of the world" (John 15:18–19). This sense of earthly alienation and yearning for a heavenly home pervades the Johannine ideology. It would seem more than likely that this ingroup solidarity and exclusivism, and the contemptuous oppositional tone of the relationships between the Johannine community and outside groups would have increased the likelihood of hostility, antagonism, and even persecution.

Thus there is considerable evidence that reinforces the cultic dimensions of the Johannine movement. The hostility expressed in the gospel account toward other groups is directed not only against the synagogue and the Jewish leaders, but also involves a sense of estrangement and alienation even from other Christian groups (see Table 1). While the theme of accusations against other Christian groups is not exclusive to the Johannine faction, in the Johannine documents the sense of exclusion of other groups from the Christian fellowship is more telling. Beyond these oppositional attitudes and the concurrent definition of the ingroup of believers in opposition to various outgroups of nonbelievers, John's gospel expresses a sense of alienation and superiority that sets the Johannine community apart. The Johannine Jesus is a stranger in the world, who is misunderstood and rejected, even by those whom he came to save. It is the Johannine Christians who really understand Jesus, for they share with him the rejection and persecution of this world. They possess a unique grasp of the truth, and a more meaningful and more significant christology to which they have been guided by the illumination of the Spirit.

If these cultic and sectarian tendencies were allowed to run to an extreme and remained unmoderated by other influences, the Johannine community would very likely have drifted in the direction of complete separation from the body of the church into heresy. Yet the price of unity for the Johannine Christians would have been an acceptance by the church of the higher Johannine christology of the preexistence of the Word. History spares us any speculation about what might have happened, if this theoretical possibility of the rejection of the Johannine christology by the church had been realized, for in fact the wider church did adopt the Johannine perspective. To the extent that the Johannine view "carried the day," it would seem to reflect a more general sense of higher christology even in other non-Johannine segments of the early church, and indicate that despite the cultic and sectarian influences operating within the Johannine community, the major group of Johannine disciples were able to achieve some meaningful degree of rapprochement with other Christian groups. Presumably, this reconciliation was made possible by the splitting within the Johannine community that siphoned off more radical and recalcitrant groups who would have followed the divisive path of sectarian development.

The pessimistic outlook of the author of the epistles seems to have been in some degree prophetic ("the last hour" of I John 2:18). The splits between his own adherents and the secessionists became definitive. After the writing of these epistles, there is no further trace of a distinct Johannine community. The likelihood is that the contending groups were incorporated into the wider church on the one hand, and into the gnostic movement on the other.[4]

As the orthodox group merged with the church, it carried with it the high Johannine christology of the pre-existence of the Word, the basic theological ideology that they so stoutly defended in the struggle with the secessionists. They also preserved that christology from any tendencies toward docetism or monophysitism. In fact, the threat of heresy and the inability to protect against the threat of schism ultimately drove the orthodox faction to accept the authoritative structure, which had come into being in the church of the second century, and in which the authoritative teaching figure was the presbyter–bishop. This structure was quite foreign to the Johannine tradition.

The secessionists, on the other hand, freed from the moderating influence of the more orthodox perspective, drifted even further in the direction of an ultrahigh christology. If Jesus' earthly career had no real salvific impact, they now thought of it as having no reality at all. Thus the Johannine influence entered the currents of docetism and gnosticism, and created the basis for a new theology.

On the orthodox side, the church of the second century was at first wary of the fourth gospel and the Johannine tradition, because it had given rise to heresy and was being used so assiduously in the support of heresy. The addition of the epistles, however, offered a guide to a more correct interpretation that allowed the church to champion the Johannine view as orthodox over against its more extreme gnostic interpretations. Ultimately, writers like Irenaeus would use the gospel in attacking gnostic doctrines that were, in fact, derived from the teachings of the

---

[4]The fragmentation of the gnostic movement provides another interesting arena for the playing out of the cultic process, both in its derivation from the Johannine community and in its later divisions and multiplications. I hope to explore this phenomenon more deeply in a subsequent essay.

heterodox secessionists from the Johannine community. The contribution of the author of I John may thus have been to save the fourth gospel for the church.

## THE CULTIC PROCESS

Examination of these early sectarian currents in the early Christian church bring into focus the lines of opposition and cleavage that arose within the respective communities. Each had its historical, situational, cultural, and sociological differences that determined what differences played a role and what divisions arose in the respective contexts. In Rome, it was the issue of Judaizing influences and the identification with the Jerusalem church; in Corinth, the issue was more socioeconomic, but still connected with the observance of dietary laws; and in the Johannine community, the central focus seems to have been the question of a high versus low christology. In both Corinth and the Johannine community, the religious grouping contained significant gnostic elements that reflect the basic characteristics of a gnostic cult (Meissner, 1987) with its connotation of gnosis and a higher understanding that set the group off from other orientations. These sectarian dynamics reflect the workings of the cultic process as respective ideological groupings that struggled to establish and maintain their respective claims.

In each case, the gradual evolution of a central orthodox church structure and belief system came about through the continued workings of the cultic process (Meissner, 1987). As divergent groups split from the central structure, they drifted into various more-or-less heretical formations, leaving the central organization in a more advantageous position to gain a stronger and more consolidated footing. Church unity was purchased at the price of heretical diversity.

In the context of such struggles and oppositional divisions, powerful psychological forces were at work that contributed to the polarization and concretizations of doctrinal positions and led to the exclusivism among factions. The dynamics were radical and uncompromising: You are with us or against us; you believe as we believe or you are a heretic. The historical accounts provide us with no more than a pale reflection of these ordeals, cast usually in the palid terms of doctrinal divergence. The human drama of opposition, argument, antagonism, political maneuvering, at times violence and brutality, that accompany such sectarian struggles is lost behind the veil of time. But we can infer that the psychological dynamics were no different then than we know them today—the dynamics of the ingroup versus the outgroup, of us versus them (Group for the Advancement of Psychiatry, 1987), of the need for enemies (Meissner, 1978; Volkan, 1985, 1986, 1988), reflecting the implementation of the paranoid process that plays such a central motivational role in these expressions of the cultic process (Meissner, 1984, 1987).

It is important to remember that these cultic divisions and realignments took place in a context marked by the continuing persecution of the Christian communities by hostile outside forces—at first Palestinian Jews and later the Romans. Persecutions persisted through the first three centuries, at least until the time of Constantine (AD 312)(Hughes, 1962). Christians in Antioch, Corinth, and Rome suffered from the persecutions that extended throughout the Roman Empire. One would have anticipated that the common cause of confronting a common enemy would have acted to unify and consolidate the church internally—one predictable outcome of the paranoid process. And this was not an inconsiderable factor—the blood of martyrs became the seed of Christians. But what is also remarkable about the data from these early Christian communities is that, despite these consolidating pressures, divisive cultic processes played out their influences in such a way as to threaten the lives of these communities from within. The strength of these forces testifies to the power of the cultic process and of the dynamisms of the paranoid process undergirding it, regardless of extrinsic circumstances.

A particularly important chapter in the evolution of the Christian church and in the further elaboration of the workings of the cultic and paranoid processes lies in the development of gnosticism. The account of these developments thus far bring us to the threshold of that fascinating period, to the origins of gnosticism within the Johannine community, where the drift toward orthodoxy and toward integration with the church of Rome could only be realized in the face of heretical divergence in the spawning of gnostic subdivisions. These splinter groups came into being as radicalizations and more extreme forms of expression of the gnostic strains inherent in the Johannine community itself and in its theology, especially the higher christology of the gospel of John.

## BIBLIOGRAPHY

BROWN, R.E. (1979), *The Community of the Beloved Disciple*. New York: Paulist Press.
_____ MEIER, J.P. (1983), *Antioch and Rome*. New York: Paulist Press.
GROUP FOR THE ADVANCEMENT OF PSYCHIATRY (GAP). (1987) *Us and Them: The Psychology of Ethnonationalism*. New York: Brunner/Mazel.

HARRINGTON, D. (1982), *The Light of All Nations: Essays on the Church in New Testament Research*. Wilmington, DE: Glazier.

HUGHES, P. (1962) *A Popular History of the Catholic Church*. New York: Macmillan.

MEISSNER, W.W. (1978), *The Paranoid Process*. New York: Aronson.

_____ (1984), The cult phenomenon: Psychoanalytic perspective. The *Psychoanalytic Study of Society*, 10:91–111. Hillsdale, NJ: The Analytic Press.

_____ (1987), The cult phenomenon and the paranoid process. The *Psychoanalytic Study of Society*, 12:69–95. Hillsdale, NJ: The Analytic Press.

_____ (1988), The origins of Christianity. The *Psychoanalytic Study of Society*, 13:29–62. Hillsdale, NJ: The Analytic Press.

_____ (1989), Cultic elements in early Christianity: Antioch and Jerusalem. The *Psychoanalytic Study of Society*, 14:89–117.

SCROGGS, R. (1975), The earliest Christian communities as sectarian movement. In: *Christianity, Judaism and Other Greco-Roman Cults—Studies for Morton Smith at Sixty*, Vol. 2, ed. J. Neusner. Leiden, Holland: Brill, pp. 1–23.

THEISSEN, G. (1982), *The Social Setting of Pauline Christianity: Essays on Corinth*. Philadelphia: Fortress.

VOLKAN, V.D. (1985), The need to have enemies and allies: a developmental approach. *Political Psychol.*, 6:219–247.

_____ (1986), The narcissism of minor differences in the psychological gap between opposing nations. *Psychoanal. Inq.*, 6:175–191.

_____ (1988), Nuclear weapons and the need to have enemies: a psychoanalytic perspective. In: *Psychoanalysis and the Nuclear Threat: Clinical and Theoretical Studies*. ed. H.B. Levine, D. Jacobs, & L. Rubin. Hillsdale, NJ: The Analytic Press, pp. 111–150.

# Author Index

# Subject Index